Praise for *The Valley*

'*The Valley* is an oral record of the 20th century from the mouths of those at the bottom of the pile . . . The inhabitants of Dearne Valley have never been commemorated in literature before, and the likes of Winnie and [illegible] be seen again *****' *Daily Telegraph*

[illegible] well-crafted story of the human side of mining, there won't be anything better than *The Valley*' *Independent*

'How many social reports have you read that combine the epic sweep of *Gone With the Wind* with the microscopic intensity of Tolstoy . . . Extraordinary' *Sunday Express*

'A sprawling masterpiece . . . Social history as it is meant to be. Neither novel nor documentary, it is a compelling hybrid of both' *Yorkshire Post*

'Benson recreates the valley over a century through a kaleidoscope of lives . . . He transforms the long littleness of life into an epic, and a masterpiece' *Intelligent Life*

'*The Valley* is a landmark history, not because we know for sure that all these things happened just as Benson says they did, but because things like that did happen all the time' *Literary Review*

'The moving history of four generations of one Yorkshire mining family. Through them emerges the story of 20th century working-class England' *Woman & Home*

'The fascinating story of four generations from the same mining family whose way of life has now disappeared' *Daily Express*

'An intensely enjoyable account of four generations of a mining family' *Sunday Times*

'Four generations of a Yorkshire mining family as a way of telling the story of 20th century working-class England: meticulous, vivid, engrossing' *Evening Standard* Summer Reading

A NOTE ON THE AUTHOR

RICHARD BENSON is the author of the number one bestseller *The Farm*, which was shortlisted for the Guardian First Book Award in 2005, and was a 2006 Richard and Judy Book Club choice. He lives in London.

BY THE SAME AUTHOR

The Farm

THE VALLEY

A HUNDRED YEARS IN THE LIFE
OF A YORKSHIRE FAMILY

RICHARD BENSON

BLOOMSBURY
LONDON • NEW DELHI • NEW YORK • SYDNEY

First published in Great Britain 2014
This paperback edition published 2015

Photograph p. xviii is from the author's personal collection

Bloomsbury Publishing Plc
50 Bedford Square
London
WC1B 3DP

www.bloomsbury.com

Bloomsbury Publishing, London, New Delhi, New York and Sydney
A CIP catalogue record for this book is available from the British Library

ISBN 978 1 4088 3163 2

10 9 8 7 6 5 4 3 2 1

Typeset by Hewer Text UK Ltd, Edinburgh
Printed and bound by CPI Group (UK) Ltd, Croydon CR0 4YY

For my family

Contents

PART THREE

PART FOUR

PART FIVE

PART SIX

PART SEVEN

PART EIGHT

PART NINE

Author's Note

This is a book about real people, places and events. Its stories are taken from my own memory, from my family's memories, from interviews with relatives and other people who were involved with the family, and from historical research. The national and international events that bear on the experiences of people in these stories are written about from the points of view of those people. I have tried to show how politics and economics touched individuals' lives, but I do not present the book as a comprehensive or objective history.

When I started my research I wanted to write about a place changing through time. However, as I gathered memories and information, I realised that I was, inevitably, collecting individual stories rather than assembling a single narrative that encapsulated the history of the place – the Dearne Valley in South Yorkshire – in which most of the action takes place. This made me wonder if I should turn the stories into a novel. A novel would certainly have been neater, because a novelist orders significant events whereas in actual life they occur in inconvenient clumps. In a novel characters behave more or less as you expect them to, while actual people can be surprising and inconsistent and so more difficult for both writer and reader to assimilate. And the novelist need not spend time trying, as I tried, to stand up family anecdotes about spirits and ghosts that are, at least by the conventional standards of corroboration, unverifiable.

The problem was that too many of the things people did, and too many of the things that happened to them, would not be credible in fiction. In fiction, a character who is told their legs are permanently paralyzed but who learns to walk again through what seems to be sheer mental effort would seem unconvincing in the extreme. The same is true of a soldier whose life is saved from a bullet by a brass button on his uniform; a young mother who is visited by reassuring spirits when science and the church have failed her; or a middle-aged woman of puritan morals who has an extra-marital love affair with a man fourteen years her junior. Such people and experiences did occur in my family stories though, so non-fiction it had to be.

Details. On the few occasions I appear, I write about myself in the third person as 'Richard'. This was the least unsatisfactory of various unsatisfactory alternatives. To protect some people's privacy certain names have been changed, and the details of certain places left unspecified. The thoughts and feelings of characters who were dead at the time of writing are based on their accounts as told to surviving family members. Where possible, events have been checked against historical records, and I have used those records in the descriptions of some locations. In some cases prior to 1930, I have taken conversations recalled in passed-down family stories, and recreated them in made-up dialogue based on my knowledge of the speech and mannerisms of the people speaking. I list these passages, with the sources for the stories, online at richardbenson.com/thevalley.

It is true that some of the accounts of historical events that follow may test one's credulity. However, to doubt them would be to ignore a rule well known to people familiar with the history of South Yorkshire, mining villages and the Hollingworth family: namely, that the more improbable and absurd an event seems to be, the more likely it is to have actually happened.

THE VALLEY

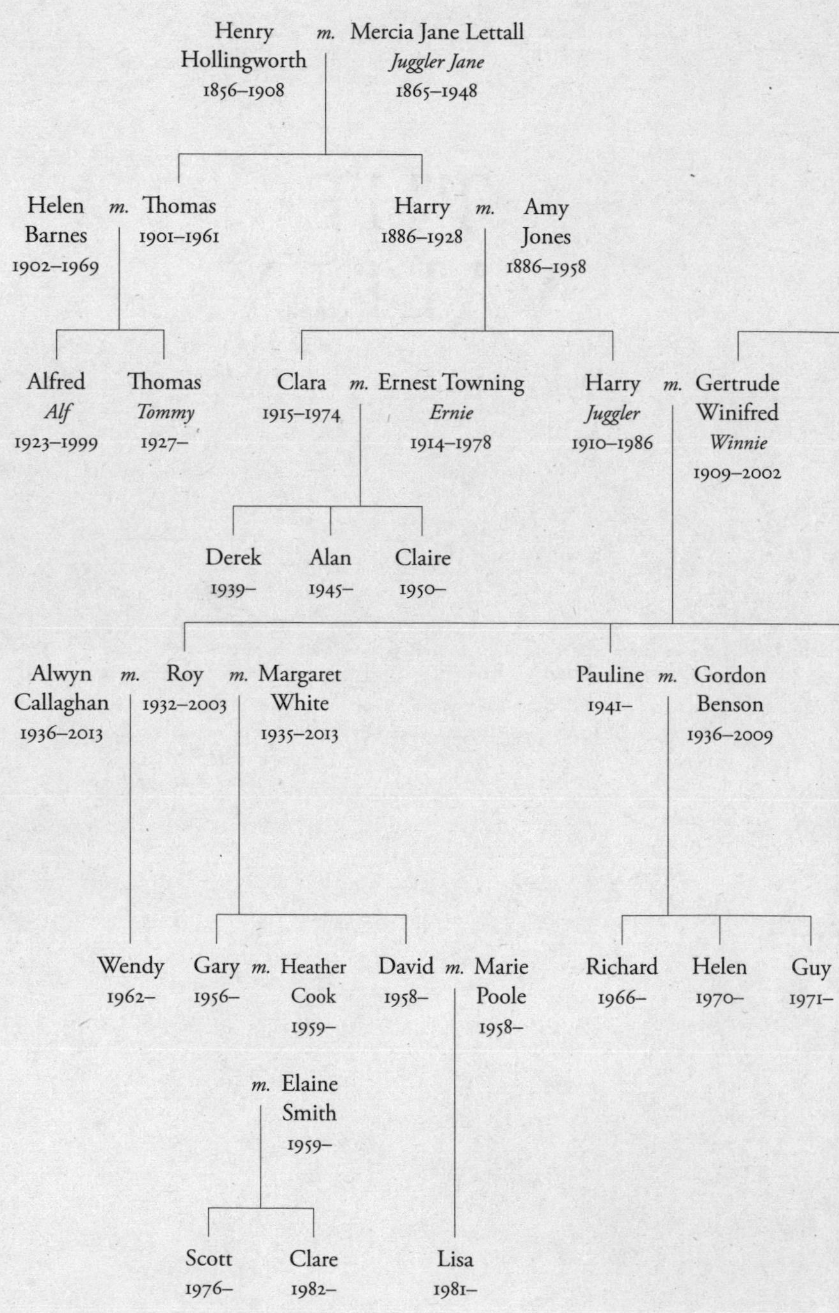
Henry Hollingworth 1856–1908
m.
Mercia Jane Lettall
Juggler Jane
1865–1948
Helen Barnes 1902–1969
m.
Thomas 1901–1961
Harry 1886–1928
m.
Amy Jones 1886–1958
Alfred
Alf
1923–1999
Thomas
Tommy
1927–
Clara 1915–1974
m.
Ernest Towning
Ernie
1914–1978
Harry
Juggler
1910–1986
m.
Gertrude Winifred
Winnie
1909–2002
Derek 1939–
Alan 1945–
Claire 1950–
Alwyn Callaghan 1936–2013
m.
Roy 1932–2003
m.
Margaret White 1935–2013
Pauline 1941–
m.
Gordon Benson 1936–2009
Wendy 1962–
Gary 1956–
m.
Heather Cook 1959–
David 1958–
m.
Marie Poole 1958–
Richard 1966–
Helen 1970–
Guy 1971–
m.
Elaine Smith 1959–
Scott 1976–
Clare 1982–
Lisa 1981–

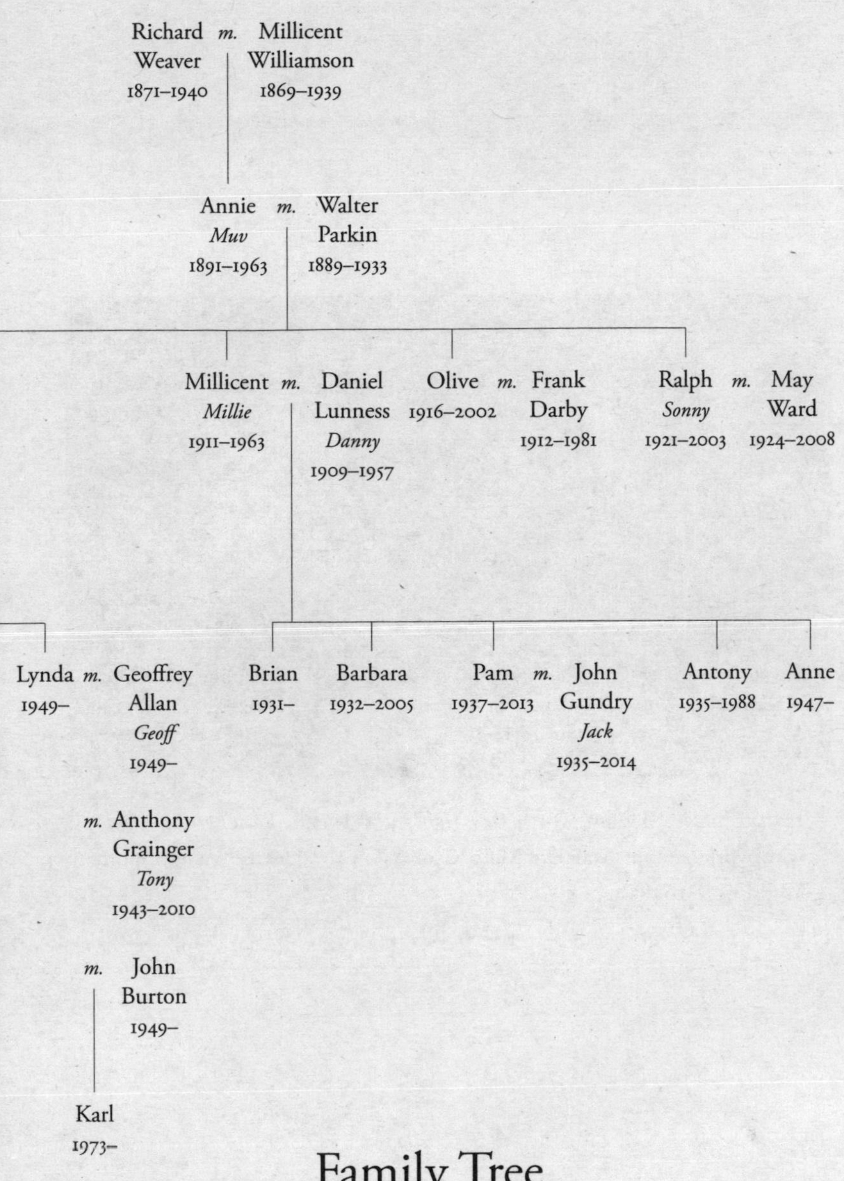

Family Tree

Simplified to show only people mentioned in the text.

Harry 'Juggler' Hollingworth (*far right*) and friend 'Lanc' (*third right*) with workmates at Manvers Main Colliery in the Dearne Valley, South Yorkshire, *c.*1948

'The Worst Village in England? I am sitting down to write this article in numb despair, for the mining community I have to describe is so repulsive that many who have never been near it will refuse to credit the story . . . Love of literature, love of the beautiful, seem almost entirely absent from the minds of the people. Women have not even self-respect enough to spend money on dress.'

The Christian Budget, 8 November 1899

'In a field of coal it is usual to put down a series of bore-holes for the following purposes: –

(a) To obtain a correct section of the strata passed through

(b) To find the depth of a seam or seams from the surface

(c) To find the thickness, quality and number of seams

(d) To ascertain the chemical qualities of the coal, and also the nature of the roof and pavement

(e) To ascertain the inclination of the strata and the number and size of "faults" in the field.'

George L. Kerr, *Practical Coal Mining: A Manual for Managers, Under Managers, Colliery Engineers and others*, 1900

'It's been said that in the Durham and Northumberland coalfield, when you're a kid in a pit village, you don't get "Goldilocks and the Three Bears" or "Little Red Riding Hood" as a bedtime story. You get Churchill and the '26 strike and the betrayal of Thomas and the railwaymen and things like that. And it's this I want to focus on, because it's this manner of carrying history, of awakening a deep curiosity in it, setting the starting-blocks of learning, which is truly the miners' history. It was, after all, the way we the miners carried our history in recent years before we could read or write.'

David Douglass, 'The Worms of the Earth: The Miners' Own Story', in Raphael Samuel (ed.), *People's History and Socialist Theory*, 1981

PART ONE

I

The Healer

Shirebrook, Derbyshire, 1907–09

The stone church is heated by a small coal-burning stove, and made shadowy by paraffin lamps turned down low. It has a faint smokey smell which mingles with those of furniture polish, damp clothes and soap-scrubbed skin. The congregation – housewives, shopkeepers, coal miners, farm labourers, domestic servants, shopgirls, the sick and the retired – are of mixed ages, dressed nicely, but many of them look thin and tired and poorly. They sit on mismatched wooden chairs, murmuring among themselves and looking forward at the four men and two women before them.

Each of the men and women stands behind a single chair and has on the floor beside them a towel and basin of water. They smile kindness and comfort at the crowd with the self-conscious spryness of athletes limbering up. They are making themselves receptive and putting out their magnetisms, Annie Weaver knows that, but the dead are hardly difficult to reach in here. In the audience, seated beside her mam, Annie feels them whispering and pressing in on her, nagging, insistent and irritable. You don't really get to choose when they come, and they turn up at all hours, many of them with good reason to be cross. Their messages and their history; sometimes she can barely breathe for them, all the shot soldiers, cholera victims, dead babies, the women lost in childbirth, the men lost in the pit. Three of them had gone down the shaft last month, Bill Limb, Bill Phillips and Arthur Burton, at half past five in the morning, when the cage broke, tilted and tipped them out to fall a hundred and fifty yards in the darkness. Their wives and mams might be in tonight.

When people die suddenly or unjustly, instead of passing into the spirit world they drift about trying to understand what has happened, getting angrier and sadder until they find someone to help them cross over. Annie tells the people at sittings and séances, 'Don't worry, those who have passed are forgiving and want us to be at peace.' But often it is a lie. The dead want to understand and be understood like the rest of us.

'Our healers channel energy from Spirit to wherever it is needed. And so I now invite you to pray as I call upon Spirit to send healing to those of us in need . . .' The prayer is led by Mrs Stone, the church president, who tells the people to settle themselves before coming forward. Then members of the congregation slowly, deferentially, move up to take their turns under the hands of the healers. Annie, here tonight as an ordinary member of the congregation, not as a medium, waits for the youngest of the four men, dark-haired, earnest and kind-looking. This is Walter Parkin, aged eighteen, two years older than Annie and a neighbour eight doors up in the row of cottages on Ashbourne Street. Tonight is the first time he has tried to heal in public; the women who organise the Shirebrook meetings are keen on young male healers, and want Walter to have a try-out, just to see. No judgement, they tell him. Healing depends on how the healer and the hurt get along, not the healer's powers alone.

Walter, like the others, talks to his subject, then, standing behind them, gently lays his hands on their shoulders and closes his eyes. Some fall asleep and then wake with a frightened and embarrassed start, but Walter is unperturbed. It helps people in different ways, he explains to Annie once she has come forward to sit in his chair. Her ailment, as Walter knows, is a dead thumb. Two months ago she pricked it on a rusty pin in the house where she is in service, and the pin poisoned the blood. Now the end is numb, swollen and black, like a ripened damson. Walter puts his hands to the curve of her neck and says, 'Close your eyes. Tha might feel faint, so tell me if tha suddenly feels hot or cold . . .'

He places his hands on her shoulders and holds them there to establish a connection. He closes his eyes and channels spirits who in the earthly sphere were doctors, surgeons, healers – spirits whose beneficence give them the power to heal. He moves his hands back up to her neck and she feels his rough thumbs and index fingers above the edge of her frilled collar. There is a tingle as the energy flows into her. And then they are silent in the darkened room with all the people whispering around them. Some of the onlookers fall asleep, but beneath Walter Parkin's hands in the shadows, Annie Weaver is wide awake.

*

After everyone has had their time and the service is over, Annie and her mam drink weak tea poured by the organising ladies, and talk to Walter. The chatting afterwards is part of the appeal – that and the chance to get touched up in the dark, according to the unbelievers. For Annie Weaver and her mam, who are sociable, it is a high point of their week, the only time they get to leave Annie's eight younger brothers and sisters at home with their father or a neighbour looking in. It is a chance to talk to people. Since the Weavers came to Shirebrook, Annie and Walter have had only a few short conversations on the street and in chapel, but she would like to talk to him more. 'You did very well, Walter,' she says.

'Thank you,' he replies, a little stiff and nervous.

'I'm sure my thumb feels better.'

He smiles. There is a lull, so her mam asks about his lodgings, and about how he finds the village. He has come from a village near Sheffield, twenty miles north, to seek his fortune in the pit. When Walter was twelve, his father, who laboured in the Sheffield collieries and on the land, abandoned his wife and seven children to sail to Australia. Walter's mother had taken up with a man from the village, a miner called George Shaw, moved him in and had three more children with him. Walter kept himself to himself and went to work on a farm. One day he came home to find his mother and George packing the few things they owned into boxes and bundles. 'We're going to Doncaster,' she said. 'You mun' look after thyself now, Walter, tha's old enough.' He was fourteen.

George Shaw went to work as a shaft-sinker, digging at one of the new, deep, modern coal mines being sunk near the boom town of Doncaster. Working in the shafts is wet and filthy work, with water pouring down on you, and the risk of collapsing walls and dismemberment by excavating machinery, but it pays better than farm work. Walter asked around, and when he heard the new pit at Shirebrook needed men, he set off walking. He was taken on by the Shirebrook Colliery Company to help maintain its 600-yard-deep shafts, which in practice meant standing on the roof of the cage that lowers the miners to the pit bottom, checking brickwork and water seepage. The shaft men are rough, but Walter reads books and doesn't care to drink away his wages. Having found decent lodgings in one of the miners' cottages beside the market place, he ignores the new public houses, hotels and shebeens, and seeks comfort and company in the chapel.

Many among the chapel congregation are also spiritualists, and for some people, these two go together with membership of the union and the Labour Party. For Walter Parkin these beliefs make sense of what he feels. They are assertions of his right to see the world how he sees it, and his right to be treated fairly. It seems to him that you can accept life's brutality and chaos, drinking your wages or abandoning your family, or you can try to make something of yourself.

'And that's what t' healing is, to me,' he says to Annie Weaver and her mam over half-drunk cups of tea in Shirebrook's spiritualist church this April evening. 'Bringing help from them who can provide it to them who need it.'

The Weavers came here last year, Annie's father having moved from another Derbyshire village to find work at Shirebrook's pit. Like Walter, Annie has found that having the sight helps her make friends, and now the two of them compare abilities. He says healing is a thing everyone can do, they just need to open themselves to a feeling in their hands and arms, not just to the thoughts in their minds. Annie is a clairvoyant medium, able to take information from the distant and the dead, though she doesn't show off like some. Mrs Andrews, who trained her when she was a girl back in the Weavers' old village, said everyone could contact Spirit if they tried, and communication was just a matter of being receptive.

Annie does not foresee the future; she dabbles with tea leaves for fun, but thinks it's a cheap gimmick. She has two spirit guides: a gypsy girl and a Red Indian chief. When the chief comes to her she shakes her head and shoulders as he settles the feathers in his headdress. Walter is guided by a passed friend, a lad who used to work on the farm with him and who died in his teens.

When her mam tells Annie she is leaving, Walter says he will come with them and they make their way down the muddy, gas-lit Main Street and King Edward Street. The town of Shirebrook, spreading out from the colliery that towers in its midst, sits in a five-hundred-acre building site known mockingly in neighbouring settlements as the Muckyard. Along its teeming, rutted, coal-scattered roads are new and half-built lines of miners' cottages, corrugated-iron shacks and grey tents pitched in rows as emergency accommodation for newcomers where the cottages peter out into fields. On higher ground above all this, good new houses built by the colliery company glow like beacons with the electricity generated at the pit. Everywhere in the lower streets there is the smell of soot, mortar and frying potatoes.

The women walking home discuss methods of removing soot from curtains and yard-hung washing, and gossip about the Main Street shops as they pass by. They discuss Popple's Drapers, Sam Brown the bootmaker and Mark Wilkinson's hairdressing shop, where Annie and all the fashion-conscious Shirebrook girls go. When Annie talks to Walter about subjects such as her hair, or her work as a maid, he listens, and then he tells her about his father in Australia, and the conversation runs easy between them. When they reach Ashbourne Street he says, after bidding the women goodnight, 'Well, perhaps I'll see thee at chapel, Annie?'

And Annie replies, 'Yes, Walter, I think you will.'

*

The Weavers are a lively and sociable family with a tidy house and a well-used upright piano in the sitting room. On sunny Saturdays, Mrs Weaver makes her husband wheel out the piano so she can give the street a sing-song. Annie, who loves a sing-song, soon discovers that she lacks Walter's rectitude; nevertheless, they are well suited in their spiritualism and their desire to improve themselves. She quietly adopts some of her employer's wife's clothes and manners, and enjoys the gratitude of people when she brings them messages from their passed friends and relatives. Annie and Walter's powers distinguish them in the village, which is populated by people who have come from far away to work in the pit and want to talk about the mothers and fathers and grandmothers and grandfathers they have left behind on the farms or the spent pit villages. With so many incomers bereaved and nostalgic for their old lives, Annie and Walter's gifts bring them modest status and admiration and give them hope of the better life. And so, at chapel and at the small stone spiritualist church, and on walks around the village with Annie's sisters, Annie and Walter become friends, and then begin courting in the autumn of the following year.

In the spring of 1909, a few days after Annie's eighteenth birthday, they go for a stroll into the fields and this time share more than ambition and a common interest in the supernatural. Several weeks later, as they start out on another walk, she tells him she is pregnant.

'Well,' he says, after the shock fades. 'We mun' get married, Annie.'

Many years from now, Walter and Annie's children will say he was an unusual father – strict, but exceptionally loving. They will remember their school friends envying them, and saying, 'Your father's lovely, I wish that he was mine.' Walter seems to crave a family and now, in the early summer of 1909, after Annie has accepted his proposal, he talks about the child and where they will live with a keenness and care that she adores.

They marry at Mansfield Register Office in September 1909 and move into three-room lodgings eight doors down from the Weavers. Mrs Weaver, who was taught midwifery, physicking and laying out of the dead by her mam, and treats villagers for what they can afford to pay, helps with the house, and cares for her daughter. After his shifts,

Walter trudges home, soaked in mud and water, hair plastered around his face, and warms himself against the banked-up fire, while Annie puts out his food. Later she boils water to fill the tin bath, and washes his back in the small, hot room.

One December Sunday, Annie goes into labour. Walter runs down the street to fetch her mam, and Mrs Weaver eventually delivers a baby girl. Annie has already decided the name: Gertrude, after one of Annie's sisters, with the second name of Winifred. Gertrude is a name the girl will grow up to loathe, calling herself Winnie and switching the order to conceal it, but on Sunday 12 December 1909, it is this name that Mrs Weaver gives to the baby as she lays her on Annie's breast. In reply, Gertrude Winifred gives a loud cry – a cry so loud, Mrs Weaver will later say, that she seems to be announcing her arrival not only to the fire-warmed room, but to the whole of Shirebrook, calling home her father, who has been sent out into the streets so that the women can have space inside the house.

2

Private Parkin No. 14171

Shirebrook; the Western Front; Oswestry, 1914–22

Four and a half years later, the young Parkin family is still living in the three rented rooms at 3, Ashbourne Street. Winnie Parkin, hazel-eyed and raven-haired like her mam, has started at Shirebrook school. Annie, twenty-three, has another daughter now, called Millie, after Annie's own mother. Walter still works at the pit and rules the home with pious discipline. Fearful of the Weavers' jollity, he hangs the walls with needlepoint mottoes: 'Bless This House', 'Cleanliness is Next To Godliness', 'Teach Me What Is Good' – the latter hung over the sitting-room table and silently indicated to command silence when the family is eating.

Shirebrook still has its bad reputation, but Walter and Annie see it improving. Two years ago British miners won a national strike for a minimum wage and since then there has been more money in the village, the shops, theatre and hotels full of men and women with payday pockets clinking. In June, the streets were cleaned and hung with flags for the visit of King George V and Queen Mary, and Winnie gathered with the town's children to cheer them as they walked through the market place. Some people said the King looked tired. Soon afterwards the adults will look back and wonder if this had anything to do with the political events in Europe they read about in the newspapers through the summer.

A few days after that royal visit, Bosnian-Serb assassins shoot dead Archduke Franz Ferdinand of Austria and his wife Sophie, Duchess of

Hohenberg in Sarajevo. On 4 August, Britain declares war on Germany. Thousands of miners make up some of the first new territorial units and in Leeds, the West Yorkshire Coalowners Association raises a miners' battalion for the King's Own Yorkshire Light Infantry. In Derbyshire, some colliery owners say they will give free rent and coal to the dependants of soldiers at the front; in some pits, colliers vote to have money stopped from their weekly wages so that it can be given to the families of miners who have left the pit to fight. In Shirebrook, miners and managers set up a recruiting station in the colliery offices. Underground, work slows because there is no imported timber for pit props. The local newspapers carry on their front pages Lord Kitchener's Appeal to England's Young Manhood – a letter to the youth of Shirebrook, Langwith and Warsop Dale, urging them to join up.

Walter, a strong believer in duty, enlists among crowds of young men on 2 September 1914. It is a hot day with a hot atmosphere in the market place outside the recruiting office at Mansfield Town Hall. There is a summer crowd smell of sweat, warmed stone and mud. Journalists interview officers and new recruits. There are already rumours of entire British battalions having been wiped out in the fighting and of a German spy arrested in the town. The crowds cheer as the men go in to sign up, and the new recruits – miners, clerks, farm labourers, young managers and tradesmen – turn to grin at the spectators.

This mood lasts through to the winter, the public resolve only hardened in mid-September by news of the first Shirebrook man to die in action: twenty-one-year-old Alf Whitehall, who worked at the pit and whose family live on Church Hill. Alf is killed near the Franco-Belgian border on day two of the first battle of the Aisne. No one feels his death should be in vain; a sound victory for the Allies here, it is said, will more or less end the war. From the town and the villages and the outlying cottages, young men keep coming to enlist.

Walter Parkin joins the Leicestershires and is then transferred to the Lincolnshire Regiment. He travels to Grimsby to train with the 3rd Reserve Battalion, and regularly writes home to Annie enclosing money: 'Don't worry lass, spirits high, it'll be done with soon.' He ends every letter the same: 'Kiss the children for me, and remember me to all at home, xxxxx.' As Private Parkin No. 14171, he sails for France in February 1915, part of a group sent to replace the depleted British Expeditionary Force. For the first few weeks he moves between reserve positions and holding trenches at Le Tilleloy, and then in March, his unit moves up to the front for the battle at the village of Neuve Chapelle. In the middle of the battle the Lincolnshires are ordered to charge, and Walter says a prayer, climbs out of his trench and advances with his comrades towards the German lines. Amid the bullets and shells he feels a hard blow to his chest and goes down. He ought to be hurt but – not really: studying his chest he sees a brass button of his uniform with a hole punched raggedly through it and there, lodged between it and the jacket, a bullet. Men pass him. Others are dead and dying around him.

A few days later two letters arrive at 3 Ashbourne Street, one from the War Office explaining Private 14171's injury, another sent from a hospital in France.

My Dearest Annie

I am writing to you from Rouen where I am knocking about in a hospital. I am alright except for a slight wound in the chest. I will be off back in about a fortnight's time, so don't worry, lass . . . Another mate of mine was left on the battlefield and we came off best in the end. I have got the bullet and button. I will send them on for you. I don't think we shall be long before we are back again, if we go on as we are doing now. They will soon have to give in.

Keep your spirits up. They have not broken mine, as heavy a fire as I have been under, and I don't think they will.

Kiss the children for me, and remember me to all at home.

Walter

Days later the bullet and the button arrive. Annie takes the trophies to Mr Wilkinson's hairdressing shop so that they can be displayed in the window, and then receives a visit from a journalist.

Mansfield Chronicle, 25 March 1915

SAVED BY HIS BUTTON

SHIREBROOK SOLDIER'S EXPERIENCES: SHOT IN THE CHEST

Knocking about in hospital at Rouen after having been shot in the chest, Pte. Walter Parkin of the 2nd Battalion Lincolnshire Regiment writes to his wife a most cheerful letter, and also sends as a memento the button that has saved his life. Accompanying the valuable metal, which has been pierced through, is the deadly bullet, with spiked lead, and the two will doubtless be kept by Mrs Parkin, who resides in Shirebrook Marketplace, and handed down to children's children as family heirlooms. The souvenirs are to be seen in Mr Mark Wilkinson's shop window in King Edward-street, Shirebrook.

Yesterday (Wednesday) morning Mrs Parkin received a second letter, in which her husband stated he was going on alright, and would keep writing, as he had little else to do. Referring to the encounter in which he was wounded he remarks: 'I suppose you will have read about the big charge that has been made. I was amongst the leaders in that, and we had a lively time of it, I can tell you, but it was a surprise packet for them.' Continuing, he spoke of the button, which he hoped had been received, as his friend, and added that the bullet came to stay with him after it had done the damage. A pal of his had said that if a bullet was for you it would go round corners to get at you, and it was no use trying to get out of the way. He hoped for better luck next time.

After returning to the lines, Walter is for some months settled in his unit's routine of holding the established trenches in the Neuve Chapelle area, four days at the front, four in reserve, four at rest. In February 1916 he is allowed home on a week's leave, but by early summer he is moving down with his battalion to the Somme, where there is to be a major new British offensive. Walter is among a group of men leading a charge. His role, for which he has been specially trained, is to throw himself down onto the barbed wire so that the rest of the infantry can run around and over him and breach the German defences. He gets through the first few weeks, but his battalion suffers so many casualties that for a while it has to withdraw to recover in order to assimilate new men and munitions.

Walter is promoted to lance corporal and learns in a letter from Annie that he is father to a baby girl named Olive. 'Kiss her for me and remember me to all at home,' he tells his wife. His mam writes to say that his father has died in Australia and that she has now married George Shaw; they will stay in Highfields, near Doncaster, and Walter must come to see them, she says. Indifferent to his father, and reasonably well disposed towards George Shaw, he seems untroubled by the news and his letters home remain cheerful. He is less confident of an early return though. His battalion, with men and officers who have survived with him, and replacements for the dead and injured, has moved north to Ypres in Flanders and are readying themselves for another offensive.

In Mansfield the newspapers carry lists of the dead, their tone sombre in contrast to the optimism of the sunny days of September 1914. An emergency legal dispensation allows women to labour in the pit yard so the government can call on more men from the mines to replace casualties at the front. Annie takes in some older children whose mothers now go out to work, and supplements Walter's wage by helping her mam with midwifery and laying out the dead. She makes a little from spiritualist sittings, but people tell her to be careful; the war has created an easy market for fraudulent mediums, and up and down the country police forces are raiding meetings. There are stories of mediums being taken away and charged with fraud – witchcraft even – and so gatherings are more often held covertly, in an obliging person's front room, or in public rooms that have officially been booked for non-spiritualist purposes.

Nevertheless, Annie uses some of her money to buy from another medium a small, green-tinged crystal ball and uses it to try to help the wives and mothers find their sons on the battlefields. Sometimes, when the children are asleep, she takes it from its black satin bag and looks through the crystal and across the sea and the mud for Lance Corporal Walter Parkin.

*

At dawn one autumn morning in 1917, on the front line at Passchendaele, a lieutenant with the 2nd Lincolnshire Regiment leads a contingent of men in a surprise attack through the wire and across a stewing bog of limbs and bones towards the German lines. Among the first up is Walter. The group reach the twisted loops of barbed wire protecting the opposing trenches before the Germans begin shooting. The men thud and splash over and around Walter as he braces his back and flattens down the coils. Once they are across, he gets to his feet, takes his rifle and moves towards the German lines. As he does so he sees in front of him his commanding officer, Lieutenant Smith, entangled with wire barbs sticking into his flesh and his uniform.

Crouching low to avoid fire, Walter moves to him and kneels, pulling and cutting. He tells the lieutenant to be still, pulls and cuts some more, and feels the splatter and percussion of grenades exploding nearby. Walter moves the last of the wire and Lieutenant Smith rolls free. Ahead, the British are going down under fire and retreating in disarray. Lieutenant Smith barks orders to retreat. Bullets are whizzing and phutting; arms, legs, hands and feet all over the place. Men hurry back but there is a blast, and Walter is caught. He will not remember much of what happens; he will recall only the struggling, his clothing in a mess, the barbs ripping his skin, his back cut and bleeding, and then the loss of consciousness.

Walter's cuts and wounds become infected and he is sent to England for treatment. 'Don't be downhearted, lass,' he writes to Annie from hospital, 'look after the children.' From his own hospital bed, Lieutenant Smith pens a recommendation to the regiment's commanding officer for Walter to receive recognition for his valour. Once the CO has had Lieutenant Smith's account verified, Lance Corporal Parkin is awarded the Military Medal, which is announced in the 28 January 1918 edition of the *London Gazette*. The medal, suspended on a red-white-and-blue ribbon, is a heavy silver disc bearing the King's head and on the reverse the words 'For Bravery in the Field'. It is almost as wide as Winnie's palm.

Returned to France once more, Walter joins a new unit, the 10th

(Service) Battalion of the Lincolnshire Regiment, the Grimsby Chums, who are on a period of rest and refit in Gomiecourt. In March 1918, he moves up with his unit to Arras. They are in forward positions when, one foggy night, the Germans launch the biggest barrage of the entire war. Mortars, smoke canisters, tear gas, mustard gas, chlorine gas; a million shells in five hours in an area of over a hundred and fifty square miles, and more than seven thousand Allied casualties before the German infantry go in. This time the bullets, or at least the shells, are meant for Walter Parkin. In the explosions Walter's body is torn up by shrapnel, his spine damaged, his skin scorched by mustard gas. He lies in the mud with the other injured, dead and dying men, vomiting blood as the mucous membrane of his lungs and bronchial tubes burns away. His skin goes a greenish-yellow, although he cannot see this because he has been blinded, his eyes glued shut by the gas. Between the retching, he feels his throat closing as if to choke and kill him.

Walter is turned onto a stretcher and sent back to Blighty blind and unable to walk. He is treated at Park Hall, a military hospital in the grounds of a timbered Jacobean mansion near Oswestry. It is here that eight-year-old Winnie Parkin sees her father for the first time since his injuries, when she, Annie, Millie and Olive come to visit. Winnie has pined for him while he has been away and now she gazes at him in his bed, his eyes bandaged, his voice abraded, speech hardly coherent. The nurses are kind but most of the soldiers seem to be dazed or dying. Annie, eyes brimming with tears, says encouraging things to her husband. Winnie rests her hands on the bed covers and gazes at him.

'Is our Winnie there?' he asks. 'And Millie and Olive?'

'Yes,' says Winnie. She does not cry, and does not look like crying. 'I'm here. I'll look after you.'

Walter is honourably discharged on 2 May 1918. He receives another medal, the Silver War Badge, and a pension, but crippled and partially blind he remains at Park Hall until long after the war has ended and the men have come home. He is moved to a convalescence home a few miles away, taught to walk again with the aid of wooden frames, and brought back to Shirebrook in the autumn of 1919.

Winnie, almost ten, is excited by the thought of her father coming home, but her excitement collapses into pity and horror when she sees him: bent, hoarse, and still half-blind, he is at thirty a frail old man. Stooping and shuffling, he barely speaks as he is helped into the house and up the stairs, and although he seems to be trying to force a pride and imperviousness, once he is laid down, he remains in bed for several weeks.

It is only on Armistice Day morning that, in the room downstairs, Winnie, Annie, Millie and Olive hear above their heads the sound of Walter forcing himself out of bed and dressing so as to be standing at eleven; he then marches up and down the room. It is an act he will repeat every Armistice Day for the last few years of his life. Often unable to move and racked with pain, he will make himself rise and dress, and put on his medals, and sometimes he will make it to the war memorial. 'I was lucky, Winnie,' he says. 'I saw you children, and your mam again. I'm a lucky one.'

Winnie, as the eldest girl, is kept off school by Annie so she can help nurse her father. Slowly she takes his arm and leads him around the village and some days he tells her about when he was a boy working the land, about spirits, and about saving Lieutenant Smith. On other days he is stern, rigid and critical. As he regains some strength he imposes an ever-stricter discipline: no talking at the table, barely any talking at all sometimes, this enforced with a banging of hands on the table and a threat of beating. Winnie simply obeys him and resents her mother and sisters when they disrespect his wishes. She knows it is the shrapnel and the gas, and she knows that her sadness will make him feel worse. So she learns to take it.

*

Walter and Annie have the bullet and button made into a brass handle for an ornamental dagger which they display on their sitting-room wall. The shell metal still embedded in his spine and legs burns him with pain, and he rubs coal dust into his wounds believing it might keep them from further infection. Whether or not the coal is to thank, he does, gradually, begin to recover. In the months following his return to Shirebrook he seems to will his limbs to action, walking a little more, helping men on their allotments for an hour or two, going under the hands of healers at the Spiritualist Church.

About eight months after his discharge from hospital he is back working at the pit, at first on the top, and then underground. This is dangerous work for the war wounded; not only is there the risk of falling rocks, but veterans' old injuries and mended bones often burst open or break again under the pressure of bending and lifting, and head wounds lead to dizziness and faints in the heat. When injuries have been caused by work the pit managers will usually pay compensation, but when the war wounded get hurt in the pits the managers say the responsibility lies with the Army. The War Office often counters that the injuries are the fault of the mine owner, meaning that the men who fought the war 'for Britain, the Empire and civilisation' are left unentitled to support and unable to work.

Compensation for injuries, though, is only one part of a fight between the men and the colliery owners that Walter walks into in the summer of 1920. Coal mining employs one in ten of all the working men in Britain and the war has left the industry in chaos. In 1917 the government had taken over the running of the mines, setting a higher, national level for wages, and guaranteeing profits for the colliery owners. Some safety laws were relaxed, with a consequent rise in deaths and injuries, and the government tried, on behalf of the mine owners, to lower the minimum age of boys employed in the pits and to suspend the eight-hour day. Men returned from the war to find that while food was scarce and rising prices were devaluing their wages, a high demand for coal was bringing money to the government and to mine companies.

In response, in February 1919, British miners voted to strike for a thirty per cent wage increase, a six-hour day, full pay for all miners demobbed but unemployed, and the nationalisation of the mines. The government, under Prime Minister David Lloyd George, headed off the vote by announcing a royal commission to investigate conditions in the industry. Reporting back in March, the commission called for the wage increase, the reduction in hours, a levy of a penny per ton of coal to improve housing and amenities in coal-mining areas and nationalisation. However, despite declaring his commitment to following the recommendations, Lloyd George dodged. Nationalisation was rejected, and all that came of the commission's enquiries was a reduction in working hours and the penny levy.

Walter and Annie, like most of the other families in Shirebrook, felt betrayed by the government's duplicity and confirmed in the belief that if you were not fighting to improve your pay and conditions then the coal owners would be degrading them. Years ago, in the village they lived in before Shirebrook, Annie's father, brother, grandfather and uncles had been among the miners striking against the colliery owner to force him to employ only members of the Derbyshire Miners' Association. Annie remembered the DMA medals worn on their caps as declarations of solidarity. Since then she, like Walter, has seen the cycle of booms, when the men strike for higher wages, and slumps, when employers lock out the men, and allow them back only when they accept reduced wages. They have heard the men talk about the union trying to stop the owners and managers taking risks underground to get more coal, and while they can be sceptical about the union leaders, both Walter and Annie believe that combining with their neighbours is the great hope for betterment. Nationalisation seems the logical next step of that combination, and if the government kept control of the mines – well, if it isn't a hope exactly, it is better than nothing.

A few months after Walter goes back to work – around the time that Annie tells him that she is pregnant for the fourth time – Lloyd George says he will pass control of the industry back to the owners next year, in 1921. Knowing the owners will cancel the agreements that gave them shorter hours and better pay, and fearful of having wages cut, the Miners' Federation of Great Britain draws up a list of demands. The miners, supported by the railwaymen and steelworkers, come out on strike in October 1920. For several weeks, Annie, Walter, Winnie, Millie and four-year-old Olive eat in the Shirebrook soup kitchens.

The miners go back to work in November and in March 1921, a few weeks before Annie gives birth to a baby boy – Ralph, but known from his birth as Sonny – the colliery owners take control of the pits and abolish the national wage agreement, effectively cutting wages. The miners threaten to strike and the owners impose a lockout. After three months the government offers a £10 million subsidy to fill the gap between the old wage levels and the owners' new deals, on condition that the miners accept the owners' terms and return to work. They accept. The colliery owners promise better wages but the agreements are broken, and within a few months unemployment and poverty are settling back across the mining towns and villages of Britain and the managers are sacking men deemed to have been militant in the strike. That year Walter receives two more military medals, sent as a pair to all eligible veterans: the British War Medal, issued to those who served in the British and Imperial Forces between 1914 and 1918, and in celebration, the Victory Medal.

Watching and taking this in is Winnie Parkin, who will remember the bitter stories her mother and father tell her for the rest of her life. She has acquired a companion. One day in 1920 she is standing out in the street on her own when she notices beside her a gypsy girl of her own age. None of the women walking past on their way to the shops can see her, but Winnie hears her saying she has come to watch over her and take care of her, whatever happens, for the rest of her life. Knowing what it means, Winnie walks into the house and tells her mam that she has met her guardian angel.

Annie, who of course has had one since she was a young girl, is pleased. 'She'll watch over you,' she says. 'All people have them you know, but they cannot always have the sight for them.'

Winnie likes this idea very much, and goes back out to the gypsy girl, who – along with Walter – immediately becomes her joint favourite person.

*

Even with Walter's military pension the Parkins are poor, and at times it seems to Winnie that the injustice and injuries might destroy her father. She has come to see him as a gentleman, a man of high taste and intelligence, like the heroes in the lending-library historical romances she reads, though sometimes he confuses her. In his gentle moods, he is benign and kind, but when he rages and shouts, she finds it hard to respond. To make this worse, there is the galling truth that he appears more indulgent to Sonny, Olive and Millie than he has ever been to her. There is a divide between the young women, formed by the harsh discipline of the pre-war days, and those whose memories all came after 1914; and in keeping with this, Olive and Millie have developed a cheekiness that Winnie envies. Unable to copy it, she instead tries to earn Walter's respect with her reserve and fortitude, sitting with her head bowed, looking down, and circling her thumbs around each other. It is the right thing to do, says the little gypsy girl: your father is poorly, and you must try to understand.

At other times, though, Walter takes her out to the fields, or to see the allotments, and then Winnie is at her happiest. He talks about the pit, the war, and about the strikes, and she is outraged with him.

One day in 1922 he tells her he has had enough of Shirebrook and that they will try their luck elsewhere. He has had a letter from his mother saying, why not come up to Doncaster? There are new powerful engines and winding equipment, new kinds of cement to seal the leaking shaft sides, new chemicals from Europe that freeze the earth so you can dig the shafts more easily, and the coal owners are using them to reach rich seams that were buried too deep before, thick bands of untold black treasure spoken of like a myth. With Walter's abilities, he will easily get work in the new shafts, and there'll be more hours and better wages than in Derbyshire.

He will give it a try. What's happened doesn't seem right to him, he says. What about the men that died? What about the men in the trenches and the men in the mines? They had laid down their lives and this is how their families are repaid: fear, poverty and homelessness. When it comes to it human beings can endure most things, he tells Winnie. Injustice, though, will destroy them.

3

The Buckle End of the Belt

Goldthorpe, West Riding of Yorkshire, 1925

In the Pennine Hills above Barnsley in the West Riding of Yorkshire, a thin clear spring breaks from a grass bank, trickles down a hillside and, at the bottom, becomes a runnel draining water from the hill. Over several miles the runnel widens into a stream, and then into a river that has carved a deep valley through the hills on which Barnsley is built. Leaving the town, the river turns south and slows, and opens up a broad, shallow valley of rich pastureland and water meadows. The river is called the Dearne, from the Old English word 'dearne' or 'dierne', meaning hidden, or secret, or dark. Its valley, five miles long, is properly called the Lower Dearne Valley, but the people who live there usually just call it the Dearne Valley, or more simply, the Dearne.

Until the early eighteenth century, the Dearne's meadow and pasture were sparsely populated, with stone farms and villages and cottage rows scattered like limestone stars in a green grass sky. Its people lived by farming, weaving and village crafts, and by digging coal in small bell pits or on outcrops on the valley shoulders. Then businessmen came with new machines and steam engines and used them to take coal from outcrops and shallow seams to the west and the south of the valley, and other businessmen built canals and navigations, and altered the course of the river to carry the coal to the cities. In the 1840s railway men were sent to lay iron tracks that crossed the valley first one way, then another, and then another, in deep cuttings and iron bridges that ran above the lanes and through the villages. The coal and canals and railways and mass of labour brought entrepreneurs, glassmakers, brickmakers, iron founders and textile weavers, and these men built new factories, foundries and mills. Day and night their steam trains sent out sparks that set fire to haystacks and crops in the fields, and hung the valley with trails of grey steam as they hauled coal trucks from the pits to the iron foundries and the glassworks and the mills and to the docks of Hull and Goole.

Britain and her empire fed on coal: coal for the houses and coal for the factories; coal to make the iron, and coal to make the glass; coal for the trains, and coal for the ships and coal to sell to the rest of the world. 'Coal has been put in the earth by God,' wrote an excited author in Charles Dickens's *Household Words*, so that humanity may live 'not merely a savage life, but one civilised and refined, with the sense of a soul within'. To feed these fires, engineers at the end of the nineteenth century built more powerful machines that could fetch coal from even deeper-lying seams, and financiers and businessmen bought the machines and leased land to build more mines. By 1910, in the five miles of the Dearne Valley there were fourteen of the vast, new deep mines, and dozens more beyond the valley sides. The landowners became rich on the mineral rights and built themselves grand homes, and became gentlemen.

The colliery owners constructed houses in the old villages in which to put the families who came to work in the mines, families from all over England, from Scotland, and Wales, and from Europe, all seeking work in the mines or customers for their trades: Irish builders, German pork butchers, Russian-Jewish tailors. The Dearne became a jumble of smoking hills and hollows, of haphazard sooted-brick villages and small towns, and of chimneys puthering dense black smoke. Up in the Pennine Hills, above smokey Barnsley, the spring now ran into a millpond dug out for a cotton mill, and the pond's overflow fed into the runnel. Down in the valley men altered the course of the river and poisoned its water so it became a slow and lifeless black sludge. But the new industry provided jobs, and for many people the work paid far better than the old work on the land.

*

It is to the Lower Dearne Valley that Walter Parkin brings Annie and their four children in the early years of the 1920s. They settle first near his mother and stepfather in the village of Adwick-le-Street, beyond the valley's western edge. Walter goes to work sinking new shafts at a colliery near Doncaster, but when that work is completed, he follows some other men five miles west, to the pit at Goldthorpe.

Goldthorpe, lying halfway between Doncaster and Barnsley, is one of four villages parted only by a few small fields in the heart of the valley: to the north, Thurnscoe, to the west, Highgate, to the south, Bolton-upon-Dearne. Twenty years earlier they were farming hamlets, but with six collieries sunk within walking distance of them all, they are now expanding frontier towns, their frontiers dark and underground. Goldthorpe is the biggest and busiest, with a market and the feel of the Wild West. Wherever you look, men are building new houses, shops and pubs; parts of the village have the look of a Wellsian science-fiction, with a clutter of chimneys, spoil heaps and pit headgears. The new church, built with money donated by Lord Halifax of Hickleton Hall, owner of mineral rights to Hickleton Main colliery at Thurnscoe, is designed in the Italianate style but made out of ferro-concrete slabs.

The Parkins move into a terraced house with steep stairs, thin walls and three bedrooms, built on a crossroads known as Gill's Corner, near the Wesleyan Methodist chapel. The family worships at the chapel, Walter stern and serious, Annie enjoying the socialising and the hymns. They are not well off, but they are at least in their own home. Walter travels to colliery sites where shaft-sinking is needed, although in the summers and autumn he will sometimes come out of the pit to work on farms, ploughing and handling the horses. Annie attends spiritualist meetings and continues her sittings, sometimes taking the children with her. She is respected for her powers. When a young girl goes missing, a local police inspector asks Annie to help find her, or at least her body; Annie sees in her crystal ball the girl's corpse lying in a well in a farm and her vision turns out to be true.

When Winnie reaches the age of fourteen, in December 1923, she goes into service as a housemaid. Service pays less well than the mills, but mill girls are brash, says Walter, and he won't have her working with them. He will have less luck with Olive, later, when work in service is less plentiful, he is ill and Olive is able to face him down. Winnie and most of the girls at school are fearful about life in service, telling each other stories they have heard about rooms with stinking mattresses, ambushes by red-faced sons, and the running of mistresses' fingers or handkerchiefs along furniture to look for missed dust. Feeling nervous, she finds work at the doctor's house in Goldthorpe, wages six shillings a week. She will get nothing for a month and then five-sixths of it; all but a shilling will be handed over to her mam. Not only that, on her days off Annie leaves the washing up for Winnie to do, and then asks her to black the grate, or beat a carpet ('I thought I'd leave them for you, seeing as you were coming'). It is typical of her mother's selfishness, thinks Winnie, but she cannot say no. Annie doesn't enjoy the housework, but Winnie, her father's daughter, cannot relax if there is a surface where dust has gathered.

She hears about better-paid work at the Broad Highway, a large modern travellers' inn on a junction of the Great North Road near Doncaster. Abutting a newly opened golf course and country club, it is the kind of place that has flourished with the popularity of the motor car. Staff can live in, so when Winnie obtains a position as a general chambermaid and cleaner there, she escapes her home and Walter's temper. Scrubbing floors and guest rooms, washing crockery and dusting bars, she feels freer: the Broad Highway is airy and light, and full of commercial travellers and coachloads on their way to the races at Doncaster. The work makes Winnie, boosted up on bread and dripping breakfasts, physically strong as she enters her late teens. Her sisters and friends note the stocky power building in her body.

Her boss, Mrs Bligh, the wife of the good-looking, get-ahead owner Thomas Bligh, is kind to her, and their daughter Marjorie ('Miss Marjorie' to Winnie) is friendly and protective. Miss Marjorie is three years older than Winnie, beautiful, radiant with glamour, and full of stories from the new, stylish arcades and dance halls of Doncaster. She has fashionable dresses made up in velvets, organdies and printed cottons from the town's market, and comes back from shopping trips in her father's car with silk stockings, cloche hats, make-up and perfumes with French names. 'Try some of this, Winnie,' she says, and applies deep red lipstick to the younger girl's tremulous, awestruck mouth. 'I've a new one of these' – holding up an almost empty bottle of Soir de Paris – 'would you like to take what's left?'

Miss Marjorie is the only woman Winnie knows whose parents do not labour for a living, and she tries to ape her manners and attitudes, as her mam had copied her mistress's before her. Winnie might not have her bone structure, and she could neither afford make-up nor risk it in her father's sight, but it costs nothing to mimic Miss Marjorie's elegant mannerisms which, she imagines, set her apart from the rougher girls in Goldthorpe. Miss Marjorie encourages her to share her feelings about Rudolph Valentino after she has been to see his films and in turn tells her about the new music, jazz and quicksteps, the comical dance moves to the Black Bottom and the Charleston that some of the girls do in the dance halls. 'If you go dancing you have to watch, because their legs go everywhere,' she says. 'They clip your ankles.'

Winnie says she hasn't been dancing yet.

'You want to be going soon,' says Miss Marjorie. 'Have some fun!'

At home, though, fun remains a vexed and dangerous area. Walter alternates between gentleness and rage, and despite Winnie being of working age, he still addresses and treats her as a child when she is there at weekends and on her half-day Wednesdays. His moods are erratic, possibly made worse by anxiety over money as the coal owners threaten to reduce the wages again. If Winnie complains she sometimes gets a sympathetic hearing, and sometimes a slap or the belt. The only difference her age makes is to increase Walter's aggressive protection of her against men, most of whom he regards as idlers, gamblers and ne'er-do-wells. Winnie does not go with boys, but this only makes Walter more suspicious. There is widespread moral outrage about the new style and mood among young women: the dance moves, the make-up, the music, the cheap fashions, the exposed arms and legs. Walter fears that such behaviour will lead Winnie into the arms of one of the new breed of young men whose politics are revolutionary and whose dress and demeanour imitate the heroes in films.

One night in 1925, when Winnie is fifteen, her father sees her talking to a young man at Goldthorpe's fish and chip shop. When she gets back to the house later, Walter instructs her to go to her bedroom and undress to her underwear.

If Walter's eldest had been a boy, the boy might have turned on him and stopped it, but Winnie is a girl, and this is how it works for girls. You get punished if the men decide you have erred, and if you complain you get punished again, only harder. Not bearing the discipline is a greater crime than the crime itself.

Dress, underskirt, corset fastened at front with bobble and hook. As she stands there and hears his steps on the narrow wooden stairs, she works out how this was her fault. He is a good man, fighting to cope with what has happened to him in the war. If he is a good man, and he has been so disgusted with her, then what is she? She stops thinking and just decides she will not cry. She won't let him see that the beating works and won't upset him by weeping tears that will induce the self-pity of a thwarted man. It is defiance, not only of his power, but also of what he is when he is like this.

'Tha can take that off.' Walter, face full of contempt, looks at her corset. She turns from him and unhooks it, exposing her bare back, mottled pale as pearls. She hears the pop and loose jingle of the belt buckle as he loosens it. The slither of the belt through the loops.

'Bend over.' The tone is the one he uses when dismissing a lie, or sending out a disgraced dog. 'Tha's acting like a whore, Winnie. Tha'll stay away from them lads.'

The gypsy girl is with her, beside her, and telling her she will be all right.

He uses the buckle end on her, which tells her he is at his angriest. The beating lasts until he is exhausted. She feels rising weals. She tells herself not to cry. She loves him, and because she loves him does not want him to see her weeping. She has learnt to hold it in.

'He could never make me cry,' she will tell her daughters, and then her granddaughter, many years from now. 'However hard he hit me, I wouldn't.'

4

The Worms of the Earth

Goldthorpe, 1926

A year later, in June 1926, Winnie Parkin is working with her father among the dry soil and thirsty vegetables of his allotment on the edge of the village. It is her half-day and she has come to help him and keep him company. He is always calmer out here – when he is well enough to come – moving in his own time, his sick back slowly rising and falling and rising again among the canes and the plant tops. Alone with him here, Winnie feels safe. She fetches water for him and pulls up knotgrass and nettles. She learns to plant out beetroot, beans and leeks, and she keeps tidy the tiny, dilapidated cabin he has assembled from old doors and salvaged planks. And when they stand to rest and sip water from Walter's pit bottle, she talks to him about his childhood on the farms, and about Shirebrook, and the miners whose struggle has come to seem to her as permanent a part of life as the weather.

This June, though, Walter is locked out with the rest of the British miners following the coal owners' reduction of their wages. The dispute had been building for years. The coal markets were down and the mine owners wished to retain their profits; the miners, however, were already on such reduced wages that they felt they might as well try to force the owners to back down. The government tried to head off the conflict in 1925 by commissioning another report and paying a nine-month subsidy to make up the wages. Throughout the months leading up to the report's publication and the end of the subsidy, Arthur 'A. J.' Cook, the miners' leader, had toured the coalfields with his rallying cry: 'Not a penny off the pay, not a minute on the day.' The local newspapers carried weekly reports about the situation, and the miners' newspapers were full of stories about the dispute. In the chapels, the preachers delivered solemn sermons likening the miners to the Children of Israel in bondage and the coal owners to the Babylonians and Egyptians.

The subsidy ran out at the end of April and the miners, refusing to accept pay cuts and longer hours, found themselves locked out by the owners. On May Day, the chief executives of all the TUC unions voted to strike in support of the miners, and to defend their own wages, starting at midnight on the third. The general strike lasted nine days but by June the miners had been left out on their own.

From the allotment, Winnie and Walter watch men searching Hickleton colliery's spoil heap for discarded coal while Walter tells Winnie stories about the lockout. The hero is always Arthur Cook, the villains Winston Churchill and Churchill's supposed friend, Nancy Astor. Churchill is Chancellor of the Exchequer in the Conservative government and keen to confront the miners. They have disliked him since 1910 when, as Home Secretary, he sent in troops to reinforce the police when miners went on strike in the Rhondda. There had been trouble and miners hurt, and the two sides had blamed each other ever since. 'You know what he said to Arthur Cook, Winnie?' says Walter. 'When Arthur said, "We'll let grass grow on those pulley wheels before we submit to tyranny"? He said: "And I'll make you eat it." Eat grass!'

Winnie looks at the grass and weeds around her and wonders what it would be like to eat, and how you would cook it. If the strike goes on, is this what they'll have for dinner?

'He reckons he'll drive t' miners back down their holes like rats. I'd give him rats! Like his fancy piece Lady Astor . . .'

'Her that called miners the worms of the earth?' says Winnie.

'That's what she said in't it! "The worms of the earth, toiling underground."'

Winnie shakes her head and trembles, the anger felt on her family's behalf more potent than any she would feel on her own. The stories are not in the national newspapers, but then they wouldn't be, would they? Officially recorded or not, they dramatise what the miners know to be true, and for Winnie they become History. It is the line about worms, the one supposedly uttered by a woman, that she will remember and pass down to her children and her grandchildren. Her father, who saved his commanding officer in the war, who was a healer, who did his best, though he could be cruel, dismissed as a scrap of blindness in the soil by a wealthy woman with a name like a perfume.

*

As they walk back through Goldthorpe, across King Street and Queen Street on to the High Street, men cluster on corners and police are in the side streets waiting to raid the slag heaps for scavengers. Some young men are in holiday spirit, idling and bantering, swimming in the brickworks ponds, playing football with their shirts and vests off, skins black from rubbed-in coal. There are men playing trumpets, and in a field on Barnburgh Lane, others organise pit-pony races, the animals having been brought up above ground while the pits stand idle.

It is the older men who worry most, dependent with their wives and families on the soup kitchens, the Distress Committee, and whatever they can steal or glean from the land. There are children with holes in their clothes, holes in their boots and, sometimes, with no boots at all, which makes Winnie glad the Parkins have only two little 'uns in Sonny and Olive. Their family is relatively comfortable with Winnie and Millie now both working and able to give their mam money. They have even managed to share some of their food with less-well-off neighbours.

Near the Parkins' house there is a working men's club known as the Union Jack Memorial Club, or less formally 'the Comrades'. It was founded in 1919 by ex-servicemen, and Walter will go there occasionally for the conversation. The steward has banned for life some members who have accepted the coal owners' new conditions, and the men have been ostracised and jeered at in the street. Walter doesn't know what to make of it: 'They should have talked to people, Winnie. People would have tried to help 'em, tha knows. If tha wants to get anywhere tha's to stick together.'

Winnie does know. You have to stick together because if you don't, they'll make you eat grass and be a worm of the earth. She loves these conversations with her father. Some men think their daughters unworthy of politics and history, but in this respect, and so long as she agrees with him, Walter sees her as nothing less than his equal.

'It'll never be right 'til they nationalise t' pits,' he says. 'T' mines for t' miners! Does tha remember when they used to say it in Shirebrook?'

She does.

'We shall live to see it, tha knows.'

'I know,' she says.

They will not see it this year, though, or the next. By the autumn, the miners' confidence is ebbing, and you can see people getting thinner from the scarcity of food. Clothes are looser, and gaps appear between waists and waistbands. More men go back to work and take the bans and the jeers. In Nottingham, where mine conditions are better and the coal is easier to extract, some miners form a breakaway group, the Spencer Union, and return to work. The coal owners and mineral rights owners stand fast, their leaders insisting that because Russian trades unions have contributed over a million pounds to the miners' welfare organisations, the fight is against communist sedition.

In November, the Miners' Federation agrees to go back to work on the owners' terms. Walter had guessed this would happen in the late summer, but he is furious almost to the point of weeping. 'All for nowt, Winnie. Again!' Those who have organised the strike or spoken out against the owners are put on blacklists and not employed. Many pits go on to short time, closing down for two or three days a week. Some who cannot find work travel south to London or to the new car factories in the Midlands, leaving the women alone with the children. Some end up begging on the streets of Leeds, Sheffield and Manchester. Those who stay and find work have their wages reduced, so that wives and daughters who still have jobs come under more pressure to provide for their families. Millie and Winnie's wages are now permanently eaten into by the household expenses, and so, in addition to the near breaking of her father's spirit, Winnie now adds to the list of Churchill and Lady Astor's crimes a lack of new clothes, a reduction in cinema visits, and the end of her hope of one day buying a gift for Miss Marjorie in return for all the inches and half-inches of exotic perfumes.

5

Dancing

The Welfare Hall, Goldthorpe, 1929

Three years later, on a warm summer evening, Winnie Parkin and her friend Mabel Stocks are walking down the hill towards the southern edge of the village, where the Miners' Welfare Hall – built in 1923 with money from the miners and colliery owners – proudly stands in wide green parkland and playing fields, near a working men's club that Dearne people call 'the Jungle'.

Both aged nineteen, they are going to their first public dance. Mabel, plainer and shyer than Winnie, wears a simple drop-waist dress she has made herself. Winnie's beaded frock has been handed down from Miss Marjorie, like her lipstick, rouge and scent. Tonight's dance, like Winnie's new wavy hairstyle, is Miss Marjorie's idea. For a year she has been urging Winnie to get her nose out of her historical romances and to stop bothering so much with 'spirits', and to get off dancing. Up until now she has put it off. Winnie prefers going to the pictures, attracted by the cinema's lush, warm, exotic interior, the way you don't have to worry too much about how you look, and the cheapness. Most of all she likes Rudolph, who seems to her the acme of modern manhood. All the women like him, Winnie, Miss Marjorie and the girls at work – and they have a song they sing, which feels a bit risqué.

In Blood and Sand
he's simply grand.

In the Sheik
he's simply great
He is a hero –
Rudolph Valentino!

Winnie has seen all of Rudolph's films. She even saw *The Son of the Sheik* during the lockout, when she was supposed to be giving all her spare money to her mother. His bashfulness and nobility set the tone for Winnie's thoughts about romance, and when he died unexpectedly in August 1926 she felt bereft, as if a world without Rudolph was one in which she could love no man at all.

The following year, however, her sister Millie announced her engagement to Danny Lunness, a miner and bantam-weight boxer from Goldthorpe. Millie is a year or so younger than Winnie, and Winnie knows that eldest daughters have to be careful because when the younger ones marry quickly, they end up stuck at home looking after their mams and dads. This is why the next time Miss Marjorie brought up the subject of dancing, Winnie said, 'Would you show me how to do that make-up again?'

*

Millie, who likes dances, suggested the one at the Miners' Welfare Hall because she was on the bill. She performs with a young amateur singer-comedian from Bolton-upon-Dearne known as the Juggler, and he had asked her to do a couple of songs with him and the band. 'You'll have to come and meet him!' she told Winnie. 'He's a good sport, but he's as daft as a brush.'

Winnie preferred thoughtful and intelligent men to ones who are daft as brushes, but perhaps you have to put up with that at dances, she thought. She had said she would go, and now here she is, walking with Mabel past the long rows of houses with their crimson bricks and grey net curtains and open doors where the women stand talking, to the hall. Even from a hundred yards away they can hear the bassy sounds of the music. Winnie shudders.

'It's loud in't it?' says Mabel.

'Isn't it just?'

'I'm not keen on that music.'

Winnie isn't sure herself. 'Come on,' she says. 'We might as well have a look now we're here.'

They walk up the path to the pillared front of the Welfare Hall and into the foyer where they pay a man at a booth. Winnie can already smell the sweat, candlewaxed floor and cigarette smoke from inside the hall. She suggests that they hang their coats in the cloakroom and go to the Ladies Room to put on more powder before they go in, and Mabel agrees. They both take their time.

When they push through the heavy swing doors into the hall, the music and the faintly sickly smell hit them like a wall. The men are wearing gangster suits and pointed shoes and some of the younger ones have an almost sinister look with centre-parted slicked-down hair and eyes emphasised by the deliberate leaving on of coal dust on the rims. The younger women have bobbed hair and deep red lips, low-waist dresses and bare legs. The band is playing jazz dance music and in the middle of the dancers some people are performing strange moves and waving their arms. Winnie once read a magazine article about Rudolph Valentino and his wife holding a Charleston contest at a party at their house in Hollywood; the article had shown you how to do it, and made it seem glamorous. This dancing does not look much like Rudolph Valentino's party though. It looks ridiculous.

Some people stand watching the dancers, while others do a sort of jog-cum-foxtrot around the edge of the dance floor. Winnie looks at the band, her eyes searching for Millie. When she sees her sister is not yet on stage, she and Mabel sit down at the side. The singer introduces a new song and the windmilling Charleston lot drift off the floor as new dancers partner up. When the foxtrot begins, a man comes over and asks Mabel to dance. Winnie sits alone, looking at the band and the other women in their frocks.

The man brings Mabel back, and a second man, his friend, takes Winnie off to dance. He feels hot and smells of shaving soap, and he holds her too tight and pushes himself against her. The girls at work talk about this sort of thing; it is exactly what she had worried about.

She smiles thinly and moves her body away, holding her partner at length by extending her arms until he takes her back to her seat. As she sits down Millie comes through the crowd with a friend in tow, a friend who is wearing full flapper get-up. Winnie can imagine what her father would have to say about *that*.

'This is my big sister,' Millie says to the flapper. 'She doesn't like dances much, do you, Win? But she's come to hear me and Juggler singing.'

'I don't *dislike* them,' says Winnie. She is anxious not to seem a stick-in-the-mud, but no one is listening. The band's handsome singer has announced the interval, and the flapper is squealing at Millie.

'You next. It's your big moment!'

'Aye, better go and get myself sorted out,' says Millie. 'Juggler says I have to swallow some VapoRub.'

'Vicks VapoRub?' asks Winnie, bewildered.

'Yes, he says it improves your voice. He's got some funny ideas, but most of them work. See you later anyway, I'm off backstage.'

A few songs into the second part of the evening, the singer steps up to the microphone and says, in a broad Barnsley accent that contrasts with the American one he sings with, 'Ladies and gentlemen, I'd now like to introduce a new double act who'll be singing a few numbers for you t'neet. Some of you may have heard them before – they're a young local pair, and I hope you'll gie 'em a right warm welcome. Ladies and gentlemen, Millie Parkin and Harry Hollingworth – also known as the Juggler!'

'Isn't *that* t' Juggler then?' says Mabel.

'It doesn't look like it,' says Winnie.

Both had assumed Millie would be joining the singer from the first half, but hearing their confusion, a man beside Winnie laughs and says, 'Nay, love, *this* is t' Juggler,' and points to the stage where Millie is standing in the spotlight with another, younger man who is not like the first singer at all. This man has slicked-back, centre-parted hair and is dressed in a wide-legged gangster suit. He is tall and broad-shouldered but his facial features look as if they could belong to various comic cartoon characters. His pale brown eyes are heavily lidded and topped by heavy, dark eyebrows that make him appear sleepy. Sticking out like giant handles, his ears seem too large for his head. His forehead is high, accentuating his height. When he opens his mouth to smile, he reveals a wide gap where his upper front teeth are missing ('Kicked out by a pit pony,' Millie tells Winnie later on).

Stepping downstage, he winks at someone in the audience and spins off three quick gags. Millie makes a joke about his looks and he frowns theatrically; more laughs. Then she says, 'For God's sake, Juggler, sing!' and the band starts 'Home in Pasadena', and Juggler steps forward. He presses his arms flat against his sides to make himself taller and straighter, half closes his eyes, and then opens his near-toothless mouth.

The voice that comes out of the strange face is a tenor as sweet, rich and strong as the sponge at the bottom of a sherry trifle. Winnie is amazed at its tunefulness, and senses the amazement of the others in the hall. When Millie's voice comes in, mixing with his, she thinks they sound wonderful, like singers you might hear on the radio. And as she watches she finds that although she feels thrilled and impressed by her younger sister, she cannot keep her eyes from drifting back to the gaping grin and heavy-lidded eyes of the Juggler.

Afterwards Millie brings him over to meet Winnie and Mabel, and a crowd gathers around them cracking jokes and catching at the Juggler's elbow. Winnie tells Millie she was marvellous and Millie squeezes her hand and thanks her, and Winnie feels more confident and comfortable in the crowd. Soon though, Millie is tugged away by some girls, and when Winnie looks for Mabel she isn't there. For a moment she is alone among all the loud, chattering people, but then, suddenly, somehow, the Juggler is there looking directly at her, and she feels paralysed and unable to speak.

'Now then, love,' he says.

Many years from now, when Winnie and Juggler are married and have had their many wars and sieges in their home, when there is no more dancing in the Welfare Hall and Millie has died a premature death of a broken heart, Winnie's daughters will say to each other and to their children at parties and on Sunday afternoon visits: 'I don't know why she ever married him. They were as unlike as you could possibly get.' And yet, years after that, Winnie's daughters will pass into her old lady's liver-spotted hands a cracked, faded and freckled photograph of her late husband performing on stage, and she will write on the back, 'Harry – how I miss him!' And through rheumy yellow eyes she will look into space, far away, and remember, perhaps, this moment in Goldthorpe Welfare Hall in 1929, when the band was playing and Juggler first appeared out of the hot, smoking crowd and spoke to her.

'Are they not talking to you?' he asks. Cocky so-and-so, she thinks.

She laughs self-consciously. 'I thought you'd be talking to our Millie about your singing.'

'I've talked to Millie,' he says. 'Or she's talked to me anyroad.' He affects weariness, and indulges what will be one of his great passions in life, the aphorism. 'Your Millie's a lass of few words, but she doesn't stint in using 'em.'

Winnie laughs.

'Tha's a right dancer, though,' he says. 'I've been watching thee.'

'You never have.'

She notices how pink and clean he looks.

He winks. 'Tha's got to have four pair of eyes up there. Tha don't know what tha'll find in here.'

'I enjoyed it,' she half lies. 'I thought our Millie was super didn't you?'

Winnie thinks 'super' is a classy and up-to-date word.

'That's cos she's had a right trainer.'

'Has she? Who?'

'Me.'

Winnie makes a show of stifling a laugh.

'I'm opera-trained, you know.'

'Are you?'

Harry tells her about his career as a tenor in the operas of Milan and Paris, and Winnie doesn't know what to say, dare not say, 'Get on with you.' And then Millie comes back and he says, 'Why didn't you tell them about my operas?' and Millie digs him in the ribs and says you daft 'apeth and Winnie realises it was all a joke, and the Juggler winks. He asks if he can walk her home. Winnie accepts on the proviso that

Mabel comes too. The three of them go half way together, and then Mabel breaks off for her street. The Juggler looks less handsome outside and he has whisky on his breath, but he is funny. He cracks jokes all the way home. He mentions working as a miner, and says that he knows Walter Parkin. He tells her he is learning how to play the drums by practising on his mother's sideboard, kicking the cupboard for the bass drum. When Winnie laughs he says it isn't a joke. He is playing in Mexborough the next night, he says, but why doesn't she come out with him the night after, to the pictures? She says yes. At the end of the street they pause. Her dad will be up waiting inside and she daren't let him see her with a lad.

'Right,' says Juggler. 'I'll sithee.'

He leans in to kiss her, but she pulls back. 'Awww, come on,' he says. 'Gie' us a right kiss.'

'I've to go home,' she says, and walks away, her heart beating hard and fast down in her whalebone and elastic.

'I'll see thee outside t' Picture Palace, half past seven!' he calls. And then the ring of his segs on the pavement and the sound of him singing to himself fade away into the darkness behind her.

Outside her mam and dad's house, in the gas-lit street, she is left with her spirit guide. The little gypsy girl will watch over Winnie when she is with lads – which, thinks Win, is fortunate. She has a feeling that if she is going to go out with Juggler Hollingworth, she will probably need some watching over.

6

Courting

Goldthorpe and Bolton-upon-Dearne, 1929–30

Juggler Hollingworth of Bolton-upon-Dearne was sent by the Devil to test Walter Parkin and his eldest daughter; that, at least, is how Walter will come to see things, finding in this young man not only an annoyance, but also a challenge to his own fixed view of life. Throughout his childhood, through his working life and through the war, Walter Parkin had maintained one simple belief about human conduct. As he saw it, a person could either give in to baseness and chaos or they could work at making themselves decent. This principle held because, in his experience, the chaotic were not ambitious; pleasure-seeking brought neither income nor respect, and therefore there was a clear choice to make between pleasurable pandemonium and success. A question that had never occurred to him, though, was what if there was a middle way? What if you accepted the pandemonium and tried to make something decent out of it? This was the question that Juggler Hollingworth was asking. And, unfortunately for Walter, Millie and Winnie Parkin were rather interested in some of his answers.

The day after the dance, Millie tells the Parkins Juggler's story. He is nineteen, from a family that has for generations beyond memory lived in Bolton-upon-Dearne, an old village of stone cottages and new brick terraces which lies on the river in the valley bottom. The eldest sons are always known as 'Juggler', the nickname going back to Harry's great-great-great-great-grandfather, a smallholder who performed juggling and trapeze acts in a circus. The trapeze work died with him, but the eldest sons and grandsons had all supplemented their farm-labouring and coal-mining incomes with juggling, singing, telling jokes and playing the concertina in music halls and pubs.

The current Juggler's father, who died last year, had been a concertina player, a comedian, a promoter of music-hall concerts, the founder of the amateur Bolton-upon-Dearne Athletic Football Club and a hewer at Wath Main colliery. He had given his son his love of music by teaching him the concertina and taking him to see his friends play in their works' brass bands. Juggler's mam, Amy, is head pastry cook in the kitchens of Hickleton Hall. His sister, Clara, two years his junior, works in the bar of one of the new golf clubs in Manchester. Since he was fourteen, Juggler has worked as a miner, first at Goldthorpe colliery, now at Manvers Main, a vast complex of mines, coal preparation plants, coke ovens, chemical works, brickyards, offices and railway sidings to the south of Bolton-upon-Dearne. As the wages do not meet his cravings for motorcycles, gramophones and gangster suits, he has pursued a sideline career in music. Aged sixteen, he climbed on stage at the Collingwood Arms in Bolton-upon-Dearne, warmed up with a set of jokes, and sang 'Because'. The audience began by shouting that he was frightening the dogs, and then ended up applauding. He tried Bolton-on-Dearne's other pubs, and then pubs in other villages. He bought a recording of 'Tiger Rag' and had it played as his introduction when he walked onto the stage. Step by step, audience by audience across the valley, singing, joking, showing off, he charmed people.

At public dances he studied the new jazz tunes so that he could later pick out the melodies and rhythms. Drumming was the thing: his body responded to the beats, and anyway, drummers made money because they were in demand and with his father gone, his family were hard up. To the bewildered frustration of his mother, he taught himself drumming first by tapping on the crockery at the tea table and then, as he had told Winnie, by going to work on the sideboard. He designated parts of it as drums, and played them: a lower cupboard for the kick drum, an extended drawer for the snare. With his singing, he earned enough to put a deposit on a small set of real drums and began practising in the front room.

One night after a dance, he went to a party where everyone was singing around the piano, and here he met Millie Parkin. He knew Danny who was courting her, and knew that her dad Walter was one of them that was still poorly from the war. Millie stood out: she had a true, constant pitch, and understood the nuances of a vocal line. 'Come and sing a couple of numbers with me,' he said, and they went from there.

*

'You want to go, Winnie! It's only a bit of fun!'

It is a Saturday teatime, a few weeks after the dance at the Welfare Hall. In the sitting room of Walter and Annie's house, Millie, not for the first time, is urging her elder sister to go out with the Juggler, who has again asked her to go with him to the pictures.

The three girls, and Sonny and their mam, are eating a meat and potato pie which has a good deal more potato than meat. Walter is in bed; it is one of his bad days and he is unable to walk or stand beyond a stoop. Now infected by tuberculosis, his body is slowly wasting. He periodically lapses into episodes of weakness, pain and fever as abscesses form around his spinal cord. He now works as a dataller, one of the men employed on a day-by-day basis to do whatever job is assigned to them, usually maintenance of the tunnel roofs. When he grows poorly he has to stay in bed. The only relief comes when the abscesses burst through the skin, leaving open, running sores.

The uncomfortable truth is that their father's sickness allows the three girls freedoms they wouldn't otherwise have had. With him distracted and ineffectual, Winnie has been able to get out to the dances, Millie to court Danny, and Olive will soon be off to become one of the mill girls, with all their brashness and good wages.

'Get yourself off, Win,' Olive says. 'Enjoy yourself for once!'

'I don't know . . .' Winnie feels her father's wishes pressing on her even when he is not with her.

'So long as you're back in for nine,' her mam says. 'You know what your dad's like.'

'I'll be with them anyway!' says Millie.

'That's what worries me,' says Winnie.

She knows what her mam really means: mind your dad's well and in a good mood when you tell him who you're going out with. Walter has recently been appalled by Millie's account of the Juggler dressing in a white swallow-tail coat and hiding in stone chest tombs at night so that he can climb out and scare passers-by by pretending to be a risen corpse. 'Ever so funny,' she said, 'because everyone thinks Bolton graveyard floods, and t' water brings up bodies and skeletons from t' graves. Juggler calls it the Bog Hotel.'

In the end Winnie agrees to go to the pictures with Juggler, and a few days later they go up to the cinema with Millie, who sits next to them and spends more time cracking gags with Juggler than Winnie does talking to him. He says he knows 150 jokes at any one time; he updates them with new ones he hears, and drops the ones that have gone out of favour. Millie says they've all heard each one 150 times, and Juggler laughs, and Winnie can't keep up.

She could be jealous, but instead of competing with other girls in wit, sauce and sexiness, Winnie takes a superior role of wise, soft matronliness. It certainly works on Juggler, who cajoles her and Millie to the pub afterwards, Winnie tugging at her sister's coat sleeve, Millie shushing her while Juggler tells stories and smokes cigarettes. Winnie sips at a half-pint of stout, and he keeps looking at her: her dark bobbed hair as black as her drink, the down-angled eyes, the smartness. She enjoys his interest. If she had imagined the man she would marry it would surely not have been a man like this – a comic and a livewire so different to herself – and yet, she likes him. She likes being with someone who is well dressed, and who knows all the other men in the pub, and she likes the daftness that is in such contrast to her disciplined home.

He is keen, too keen she thinks, and she breaks it off. Harry (he has told her to call him that) says he doesn't care, but her sudden withdrawal piques his interest. In the meantime, he keeps up his singing, comedy and drumming with bands, arriving home at midnight then rising at four for his shift. A range of abilities keeps you in work, he says. He works three or four nights a week, carrying his drums on the buses. Travelling home late at night, he sits among the tired, blackened miners and mill lasses, backchatting when someone recognises him, ignoring conductors who chuckle at his baggage, and otherwise shutting his eyes, clinging to the drum cases, and rehearsing his lyrics and gags.

His only enemy is a Bolton-upon-Dearne policeman known as Dog Uller. Policemen, regarded with suspicious hostility by some people in the Dearne since the 1926 lockout, either redeem themselves with blind eyes and words to the wise, or they persecute. Dog Uller, in his late twenties, fat and officious, persecutes. He tells anyone who will listen that his beat is so safe, his public so cowed, that he can leave his gold watch on the wall outside the Collingwood Arms and no one will take it. He drinks in the Collingwood and it is in the pub's tap room that Harry, also a regular, commits a misdemeanour against the policeman that reaches the ears of Walter.

'Now then, Dog,' says Harry one evening not long after Winnie breaks off from him, his hand locked on a straight glass of Barnsley Bitter. 'Anybody pinched thy watch?'

'Shut it, Hollingworth.'

Dog Uller is not a man to banter in the bar. Everyone is laughing. Everyone knows the gold watch brag, and thinks it absurd. Harry makes a show of looking at his wristwatch.

'I tell you this, Hollingworth,' says Uller, putting down his drink and turning to stand square on to Harry. 'You're a peril with them damned drums. If I see you on t' bus wi' em, I shall do you, and no mistaking.'

'Tha couldn't catch me.'

Laughter.

'Give over. I don't know what you think you're on with. Drums?' – Uller says 'drums' as if no such things exist – 'You can't play tiddlywinks, you, never mind *drums*.'

Harry winks at some of the men in the bar.

'Mind you your father were t' same, wi' that accardigan. He couldn't play that to save his life. The *Juggler* –' He says this as if 'Juggler' was the most shameful name a man could have.

Harry blinks, and glances down.

'Don't you do comedy and all?' Uller feels himself climbing now, coming back, dominating as he likes to. 'Come on. Tell us a bloody joke.'

'I'll give thee some comedy,' says Harry. 'Does tha know t' "Laughing Policeman"?'

He sticks his pint on the bartop, swings back his right arm, and punches Dog Uller in the nose. The police officer staggers sideways and says, 'You bloody swine.'

Uller lunges and grabs Harry's arms, but Harry dodges. Men around him eddy and regroup, make to hold him, but his fist smacks into Uller's face again. Uller steps backwards, stumbles, and is down in a clatter with Harry on top, knees pinning Uller down. The men try to haul Harry off. One pulls out Uller's whistle and blows it, another grabs Harry and gets him out of the pub, which now empties as if it were burning.

Dog Uller does not press charges, in order, public opinion assumes, to avoid embarrassment. Harry never talks about the incident. When Millie brings the story to the Parkin sitting room, Walter shakes his head and tells Winnie that now she has parted from him, she should make sure she stays away.

Meanwhile, a young man from the chapel, Ernest Sutcliffe, who works at Highgate pit, asks if Winnie would like to go out for a walk and she accepts. They visit the cinema. They go for more walks. Millie says that Harry is asking why she doesn't come out, and that Ernest is a wet blanket. She says Winnie should enjoy herself more, but Winnie feels Ernest is safe. She tells Millie not to tell Harry anything about her, although she knows she will.

Secretly, Winnie wants to marry. Most of the girls she knows are already wed and have got out of their in-laws' homes and into houses with their husbands. The house at Gill's Corner is too small for them all and their father's illness makes it seem even smaller, and she is afraid of being held back at home if her sisters leave. Ernest could be a safe bet. Harry, as Walter says, could not.

7

The Knuckleduster and the Wedding Ring

Goldthorpe, 1930

Around this time, Annie takes Winnie with her to a séance for the first time. It is held in the front room of the house of an old lady called Mrs Harris on a late summer's evening. Word has been passed around about it in the shops. A dozen women, from their mid-twenties to their seventies, gather in the sitting room and at about eight o'clock file through to the front room where Mrs Harris yanks the curtains across the grimed windows and the women sit down in a rough semi-circle. Annie, who is to be the medium, ushers Winnie to sit with them, and stands back, watching. When everyone is settled, Mrs Harris turns down the gas lamp and lights a candle with a red shade around it, and the room is hushed. Winnie feels very proud of her mam.

Annie says she is seeing some children, a boy and a girl. 'Has anybody lost any children?'

A lady has, but she had just lost a little girl, not a boy as well.

'No, I have a boy and girl,' says Annie. 'They've been away. They might have known someone here when you were a girl yourself.'

Although Annie finds no one trying to contact her, Winnie is enraptured by the séance. Later on, walking home with her mam, she says she would like to do it again. Two weeks later Annie takes her to a meeting place known as 'The Rooms' in a side street leading off the main shopping street, down past the concrete Italianate church and the

Sacred Heart Convent, under the black lour of the Hickleton colliery spoil heap.

The Rooms are in a narrow, windowless, brick building with a peeling green-painted door. There are two other mediums that night, and one – a fat, older woman in a shawl – sees the gypsy girl and says Winnie is lucky to have her. To Winnie, the spirit world seems more real and more meaningful than the world in which she lives. In the séances you don't have to be frightened of anything, and people think about what they can do for you, not what you can do for them.

*

A spring night in 1930. Winnie is preparing herself for a visit to the Empire cinema with Ernest. Millie, patting down the rouge on her pale cheeks in the sitting-room mirror, has argued with her, saying Ernest is a bore and that Winnie should come out with her that night. She is going to a dance at the Welfare with Danny Lunness. They are booked in to be married on 28 December and Millie is full of it; Danny not only has a well-paid job at the pit at Barnburgh, a village just east of Goldthorpe, but is also becoming sufficiently good at boxing for his manager at the gym in Bolton-upon-Dearne to plot a professional career for him. A local champion with cups and shields lining his mam's sideboard, he has already had his first professional fight, against a boxer called Billy 'Boy' Yates, in front of a thousand people at the Plant Hotel, Mexborough. 'Young Lunness' lost, but he was paid, and the match had a decent write-up in the boxing press. 'Making a name for himself,' says Millie. 'You don't know where it could lead.'

Winnie knows where this leads, though. It leads to Millie dismissing Ernest as a wet blanket and championing the Juggler. 'I don't know why you don't get on with him, instead of trailing after Ernie. Juggler's a good feller, and he always asks after you.'

Winnie flinches. There is a part of her that likes the idea of being the girl that Juggler Hollingworth asks after.

She and Millie go down the street towards the cinema together and wait by the bridge. Outside the Empire, in the gaslight and blue cigarette smoke, Ernest meets Winnie, and Millie meets up with two girls and goes on to the dance. After the picture Ernest buys Winnie a bag of chips which they eat from the newspaper while walking towards the Parkins' home. They talk about Ernest's mother and father, and Winnie tells Ernest about the book she is reading, a romance set in the days of Henry VIII. The ladies-in-waiting were right gossips, she says, things don't change do they?

Suddenly, as they step from under a railway bridge, a man jumps from the bank beside them, stumbles on the path, and lunges at Ernest. Winnie squeals. Ernest pushes the man away and the figure reels back before gathering himself and coming at Ernest again.

'Harry?' says Winnie. 'Harry? What are you doing?'

'I've come to teach him to leave thee alone.'

Winnie notices something in his right hand.

'Get on with you, Juggler,' laughs Ernest.

'What's that thing in your hand?' says Winnie.

'That's a knuckleduster!' says Ernest.

'You can't use a knuckleduster, can you?'

'Yes, I can,' says Harry, but Ernest looks unconvinced. Harry's hand drops to his side. 'Shut thy cakehole.'

Ernest shakes his head.

'Aw, what do you want to go with *him* for?' says Harry. 'He's nowt. *I* love you.'

'It looks like it, hiding under bridges with that thing on your hand,' says Winnie.

But she is not put off. All her life Winnie will crave romantic love and toughness; she will try to fill herself with the sentiment of romances and greetings cards, but what she loves is open declarations. Possibly now, even accompanied by a knuckleduster under a railway bridge, she falls for it.

'You lying swine, Hollingworth,' says Ernest, and pushes Juggler in the chest. Harry inexpertly swings the arm with the knuckleduster up into Ernest's jaw. It cuts the skin and blood runs down into his white muffler.

'Oh hell, sorry cock,' says Harry.

Winnie tells them to stop. Ernest comes back and swings at him. Juggler sidesteps and swings again, connecting clumsily with the side of Ernest's neck, and the fight peters out.

'Just leave me alone, you maniac,' says Ernest, holding his bleeding face and retreating.

'He's not a man,' Harry informs Winnie. 'You do as you like, but I love you,' and turns and walks down the street.

'Get away with you,' Win shouts after him. 'You're a bad 'un.'

*

The fight means Winnie is late coming in, and Walter bawls at her, but his back is bad, and in the end it all comes to no more than complaints.

She stays away from Harry for a while but he pursues her, asking her out, sending messages via Millie, and she comes round. Within months Winnie is visiting the cinema with him and going off to the dances with Harry, Millie and Danny.

One night Harry comes back to the Parkin home with Winnie and Millie, who is pregnant with Danny's baby, and tells his jokes and charms them. 'Sonny,' he says, 'I'm learning to play t' drums so I can be in dance bands, does tha want a job helping me carry t' kit on buses? . . . Olive, what sort of spirits does tha like, Winnie's kind or my kind?'

Olive thinks he is a hoot, and Annie thinks him marvellous, especially when he calls her 'Nance' instead of Annie. They sing songs and after a few with Millie, Harry sings a close harmony with Nance, sealing the relationship.

Perhaps Winnie is caught up in this convenient foursome. Perhaps she is scared of being left behind by her younger sister. Perhaps she is jealous, or disappointed in Ernest, or desperate to marry to get away from her father. Maybe she is impressed by Harry's rough declaration of love under the railway bridge. Whatever the reason, they are soon courting properly, and one evening Harry suggests they go for a walk (walk being code for sex). When Winnie tells this story to her daughters, and then her granddaughter, many years after, she does not go into detail, saying only that, 'he did something he shouldn't'.

Later, Harry says that as she could now be pregnant they should get married. She seems to have been so unsure of the likelihood or otherwise of actually becoming pregnant, and so deprived of the vocabulary and language to talk about the situation, that she is agrees. She tells

Annie, and then her father, that she is pregnant, and Harry comes to the house to discuss his and Winnie's marriage. Walter rages, but his initial anger subsides into a desire to protect his daughter. However much she forgives her father, Winnie needs to be free of the house. On the other hand, she is fearful that Harry's pleasure-seeking and carousing will overwhelm her. She likes to be the matronly carer and nurturer; it is the role life has allotted her and she is used to it, but she isn't that with Harry.

But still, a woman gets only a certain number of chances to escape. When she insists that she will undertake the marriage, Walter shakes his head. He knows men like Harry, he says; they represent the mud from which decent people like the Parkins have dragged themselves. He pleads with her. 'Nay, Winnie. Not him, lass,' he says. 'I've seen it before. You think you know, but –'

Winnie defies him. Quietly, but insistently she says, 'I love him.'

'I'm telling you,' says Walter, 'you do as you like, but you'll never be happy if you marry that man.'

PART TWO

8

Love and Marriage

Goldthorpe, 1931

Winnie Parkin and Harry Hollingworth marry at Doncaster Register Office on Saturday 14 February, 1931 – Valentine's Day – chosen by Winnie for its portent of romance and accepted by her future husband with a good-natured shrug. Winnie wears a smart cream two-piece which she has made with jersey fabric bought from Barnsley market, and their betrothal is sealed with a wedding ring bought from the pawn shop in Goldthorpe for six shillings and eleven pence.

Annie guides and helps her daughter with the wedding plans, but Walter is distant and aloof. He rues the marriage and his disappointment stews with worries about money and a resentment of his own painful, failing body. The winter cold aggravates his wounds and spinal injuries, so much so that on some mornings he can hardly move and has to stay all day in his bed. Even when he can walk there is scant chance of finding paid work, with the Dearne pits on three-day weeks and employing fewer men because of the trade slump. Often Walter will set off to Goldthorpe colliery and even before he gets there hear the buzzer sounding to tell the village that the pit will not open that day. At other times the only remaining jobs are too strenuous, but he takes them anyway and returns home exhausted, his scars stretched and sore and feeling as if they might burst. On those evenings he will try to go outside to walk off his discomfort, but after sitting he is unsteady on his feet, and will stand at the door swaying, and fumbling at the handle. If

Winnie is there, she will get up and take him out, steering and supporting him, as she did in Shirebrook.

The night before the wedding, she takes her father outside for a short walk. As they pause by the chapel before heading back, he opens his mouth to speak, but cannot think what to say. In the darkness he lays a hand on her forearm.

'Are you sure about this, love?' he says.

'I think so.'

'Do you only think so? Because you can still not marry him and stay with us, you know.'

'No,' she says, looking at him, 'I'm sure.'

Walter nods without speaking, his breathing is uneven. 'He'll be a trial for you. He might be a good lad underneath, Winnie, but he'll be a trial for you. Tha'll have to be strong tha knows. Tha'll have to master him.'

She says nothing and, feeling tears welling up in her, looks down. She senses that he is right, but she does not know how to be strong with a man, let alone master one.

*

The wedding party is small, just the Hollingworth and Parkin families, Winnie's friend Mabel and a mate of Harry's called Lanc. After the signing and the rice-throwing at Doncaster, they cram themselves into two cars and ride back to the Parkins' where Annie and her daughters have prepared a wedding breakfast of cold roast chicken, a boiled ham, salad and hard-boiled eggs. Lanc, a tall, gangly miner from Lancashire, is instructed by Millie, eight months pregnant but organising everyone nevertheless, to fetch a crate of beer. As they eat and drink, Harry takes two spoons and taps out jazz beats on the crockery, occasionally crooning lines from songs, and Millie joins in.

After an hour of awkward knee-plate eating, the two of them stand up before the range and begin singing whole songs. The younger guests sing along and Harry cajoles Annie ('Come on, Nance, gi'e us a tune as t' mother of t' bride!') into a duet of 'You Made Me Love You'.

At the end of the afternoon Millie, flushed and enormous, tops everyone with a solo performance of 'Till We Meet Again', and then Winnie and Harry kiss and shake hands with their guests, and walk together to the house where they have taken lodgings. Their rooms are in a dark, damp three-bedroom terraced house in Goldthorpe owned by Mr and Mrs Skelling, a couple in their fifties. Short of money, the Skellings have let out their front room and a spare bedroom, leaving themselves with three rooms to live in. Embarrassed by her poverty, Mrs Skelling speaks to Winnie and Harry with a spite that reminds them of their inferior status. When the newly-weds arrive, she gives them no congratulations, speaking only to remind them of some house rules, and to warn Winnie not to make a row when they go upstairs.

Even on her wedding night Winnie is losing out to music. Harry has bought, by mail order, a self-assembly crystal set so they can hear some tunes. He sits on the lumpy horsehair sofa with the circuit diagram laid out on the thin rug, trying to connect wires and junctions, and keeps telling his new bride that he'll soon be done. At nine o'clock he goes to get help from Lanc, who lives in the next street down and has made crystal sets before. An hour and a half later, Winnie climbs into the iron bed on her own and listens as her husband brings into the gas-lit sitting room downstairs strange electronic noises, snatches of American music, and foreign voices from far, far away in the night.

*

Marriage is uneven, a change for the women who leave work, but for some men little more than the swapping of housekeepers. The unevenness is clear to Winnie on the first Monday of their married life. Harry usually works early or day shifts (six in the morning to two in the afternoon), avoiding 'afters' (two until 10 p.m.) and nights (ten until 6 a.m.) so that he is free in the evenings to perform in the clubs or go to the pub. He and Winnie are woken for the day shift by the knocker-upper, a man crippled in a mining accident who makes his living scratching the morning windows with wires bound to the end of a long wooden pole. It is half-past four, and the house is cold. Rolling over and out of bed, Winnie puts her feet down on the damp lino and pulls on the cardigan and woollen coat that she has left on a chair. Along the landing and down the stairs, treading quietly for fear of waking Mrs Skelling; in the kitchen she lights a taper from a gas flame, then returns to the bedroom to light a candle for her husband.

Back down she goes to the Skellings' living room, where the range is, and takes a poker to rattle the fire that has been left banked and smouldering to warm the house. White ash falls to the hearth and Winnie feels the warmth of the glowing tangerine-coloured coals on her face as she shovels the ashes into a zinc pail. She takes the bucket outside. It is a dark February morning. Along the street there are lights on in some kitchens and smoke from chimneys joining with the hearthsmoke clouding the low belly of the valley as the men who have work rise for early starts at shops and glassworks. Standing there in the darkness, she will say later, Winnie Hollingworth feels for the first time like a married woman with wifely duties.

In the kitchen the flames of the fire lick at the bottom of the kettle. From a caddy decorated with Indian coolies, she spoons tea into a teapot, and fries creamy-fatted bacon and brown eggs in Mrs Skelling's beaten black frying pan. She can hear Harry padding about upstairs, pulling on his clothes. As the bacon cooks she makes food for work, or snap: black tea to cut through the dust in his throat, bread slathered with pork dripping for bulk and energy. She seeks out the brown salty jelly in the dripping bowl and layers it evenly over the plain grey fat before topping it with a second slice of bread, so that he will have some moistness and salt to savour against the grime and dirt. Then she puts it into the snap tin, a metal canister shaped like a sandwich which will be fastened to Harry's belt, snapped shut to protect the contents against the dust and the wet.

As she mashes the breakfast tea, Harry passes her on his way to the kitchen, wearing his vest and trousers, carrying his shirt, pullover and jacket. At the sink he splashes his face with cold water and pats it dry on a rag hanging on a hook near the tap.

'Here you are, love,' says Winnie, setting down on the sitting-room table tea, bacon and eggs and thick slices of bread, curved and uneven because she cannot cut the loaf straight. She will have her breakfast later, bread and margarine, the protein being reserved for the man.

'Thank you, my sweet,' he says, and takes from his jacket pocket a bottle of whisky.

With the salty steam of breakfast rising in his face, Harry pours a tot into the cap and then into his tea. A few men take a medicinal whisky like this at the start and end of the day, though Winnie's father never has. She stares as he slips the bottle back in his pocket, smells the hot alcohol across the room, and sits down and tries to ignore it. Harry begins cutting and forking the food into his mouth, and then as he chews, taps out a rhythm on Mrs Skelling's cruet set with his teaspoon. He doesn't seem to stop drumming except to drink or dance. After a week, Win will ask him to stop. After two, she will beg, and after three they will fight.

From outside come the sounds of slamming doors and men's voices and hobnail boots in the road. The early shift is going to work. Harry swallows the last of his tea, takes his snap and steps out of the back door, immediately cheery as he greets another miner in the street. They join a march of men walking down the road in the dark towards the pits at Goldthorpe, Highgate and Manvers Main. Winnie turns back inside and climbs the stairs to bed for two hours more sleep, for her and the baby. She will rise again at half past seven for breakfast and then to start cleaning the house.

*

A fortnight after they move into their lodgings, Winnie finds out that she is not pregnant. She feels a sense of mild anticlimax, her main thought being that now they might be able to have a child when they've saved enough money for a deposit on a rented house of their own. Harry has already had a rise, with the married man's rate set at thirty-two shillings and sixpence a week. If he earns money from his singing or drumming he spends it, or adds it to the savings for the house deposit. As the winter passes into spring and then summer, it is this thought of their own home that sustains Winnie against Mrs Skelling's contempt.

In the evenings Harry listens to dance tunes on the radio, and then goes out to a pub or a club to see a turn. On some Saturday evenings,

Winnie goes with him and they might meet up with Millie and Danny, if Annie is able to look after Brian, their baby boy. She no longer sees Mabel or any of her other friends, unless she bumps into them in the street, her day-to-day life consisting chiefly of servicing her husband and the home. To her sisters she seems more at ease working than sitting, eager to be cleaning or cooking even when she is resting. When there is no cleaning and cooking to be done, she crochets, knits, or makes rag rugs in such volumes and with such speed that she has soon covered the floors of half the houses in the street. The finer, more imaginative part of Winnie's life is lived elsewhere, in the historical romances she gets from the library and in the spirit world.

Seeing Harry tend to himself in private, watching him fussing and preparing to go out, is a shock to Winnie, more than the tots of whisky at breakfast. In public Harry seems casual about everything, but he makes it a cardinal point to always enter his home clean. Some of the men come and go in the old suits that they wear in the mines, but Harry always changes and washes at work. When he needs a bath, he doesn't use the tin one in front of the fire, but goes to Manvers Main which, unlike Goldthorpe and Highgate, has modern baths and showers. He spends hours at the kitchen sink, scrubbing his hands with a nailbrush, intricately working at the fingernails: nail plates, beds, folds, cuticles, lunulae, all scrubbed, scraped and wiped as if the hands were a second face to be presented to the world. For Winnie, who likes Harry's smooth cleanness, witnessing the scrubbing and preening spoils her pleasure in him. Her father, himself a clean man and fond of the adage about cleanliness and godliness, had not troubled to that extent; Harry's self-regard feels like vanity and seems to carry him away from her.

9

The Boy Who Came Back from the Dead

Highgate, 1932

One morning in the early winter months of 1932, Winnie Hollingworth is walking up the hill to a big, bay-windowed house, home to the Goldthorpe doctor. In her bag she carries a small bottle of urine, and money scrimped from the last fortnight's housekeeping to pay for a pregnancy test. When she goes back for the results the following day the doctor says, yes, she is pregnant, due mid-September, and she feels a mixture of relief – because she has taken longer to get pregnant than a lot of other lasses – and worry about where she and Harry and the baby will live. Mrs Skelling is not a woman to welcome babies.

Harry, who likes children, is pleased, although no more wordy in his pleasure than most other men in South Yorkshire. 'We shall have to be having a bigger house then,' he says, and goes to look at the rental advertisements in the *South Yorkshire Times*.

They work out that by taking in a lodger they can afford to rent a three-bedroom house in Highgate, the small pit village that almost abuts, and rather looks down upon, the Barnsley end of Goldthorpe. The house they look at, 34 Highgate Lane, is in a long and haphazard turn-of-the-century brick terrace that runs down the valley side towards Bolton-upon-Dearne. At the front it looks over a tussocky grass cowfield, a farmyard and a concrete mission church; behind the houses are large shared yards with privies, and, behind the privies, the backings

– a set of narrow alleys along the house backs on a grid of brief, treeless streets. At the top of Highgate Lane the terrace ends at a crossroads where the lane crosses the main Doncaster to Barnsley road, and here a group of buildings form the village hub: an old, high-windowed junior school, a fish and chip shop with pink and white stucco walls, a grand Edwardian pub called the Halfway Hotel and, alongside that, a bitumen-painted wooden hut that houses the working men's club.

Number 34, up eight brick steps through a little front garden, is dry, warm and solid, and Harry tells the landlord, Mr Meanly, who is waiting as they look around, that they will take it. On the walk home they laugh about his name. 'I hope it's not Meanly by name, meanly by nature,' says Winnie who, perhaps as a consequence of concealing the name Gertrude for two decades, thinks often about the power of words to shape people's destinies.

'T' rent he's charging for two walls, I should say meanly i'n't half of it. Twelve flaming shilling a week!'

'What about finding a lodger, then?'

'Don't worry about that,' says Harry. 'I've got an idea.'

They move in in the spring, helped by Millie, Danny, Olive and Sonny. A young man called Horace Hemsworth, himself newly moved in around the corner, brings them some pork pie and cake as house-warming gifts. Over the following months they gradually add to their furniture pieces from relatives, and items bought from the pawn shop and the Co-op, Harry dutifully lifting and placing them, and Winnie ordaining the layout, arranging the geography of the home.

The front door opens into a hallway or, as everyone calls it, the passage – a prestigious thing to have because most of the neighbours' front doors open directly into their front rooms, and a garden and a passage put distance between you and the street. The first door off the passage leads into the front room, to be used only on special occasions, and it is here that Winnie puts her best furniture. At the end of the passage is a flight of steep, narrow stairs rising up to the landing and bedrooms, and a door that leads into the sitting room. The kitchen is reached through the sitting room, both of these rooms having windows that look out from the back of the house. The kitchen and sitting room belong to the life of the backings and the communal yard, the passage and front room to the street and the wider world.

The heart of the home is the sitting room, dominated by the range and an upright piano. Its furnishings are minimal, the only glamour being Harry's picture of Dorothy Lamour and Winnie's of Rudolph Valentino tacked to the wall. The range, with its rag rug in front marked with black spots where spitting slatey coal has sent out sparks, is open to anyone equally, including animals, and is a place of liberation. Women stand in front of the fire with their backs to the flames and hitch up their skirts to warm themselves, an action they would consider outrageous if performed elsewhere. The fire itself is a conversation piece: good fires are admired, though one that is allowed to get too big will be criticised by guests after they have visited ('What's she want to be chucking coal on t' fire every verse end? I thought she were trying to cook us!'). In the valley there is a detailed knowledge of the various coals from the different pits and people discuss them in the way that winemakers discuss grapes, cursing the rubbishy slack of fragments mixed with dust that won't light, and exclaiming over the pure bituminous cobbles that give you a clean burning light with no ashes.

Beside the fire and within reach of the glossy wood-encased radio is Harry's chair, which will always have an ashtray on its arm. By tacit agreement this chair, the man's chair, is given up to him when he enters the room while Winnie's chair, facing the fire, can be used by visitors and children alike. Against one wall is a square wooden dining table with chairs tucked underneath. Opposite that is the piano, and against another wall is a sideboard. Above the sideboard is a wide, wooden-framed mirror in which Harry arranges his hair and adjusts his clothes before going out. Soon after they have moved in – to please Winnie, he thinks – he cuts out paintings of pink roses from a magazine and glues them round the mirror's edges.

Sideboards are important to Winnie, as to many of her neighbours, because, besides a piano, they are usually the most decorative large item in the sitting room. With their shiny wooden veneers and inlaid sections and mirrored cabinets, the valley's sacred sideboards display special-occasion goods such as fancy sherry glasses, spirits and jars of sweets, store mundane items, such as knives and forks (usually top drawer) and tea towels, and have the important household documents (rent book, insurance papers, driving licence) filed in the drawers. On the top, framed family photographs are displayed among the candlesticks and vases. Harry is assigned one drawer in which he keeps his cufflinks, tie clip, money, comb and brush, but apart from that he is discouraged from using it. To Winnie the sideboard is a sort of family sacristy-cum-altar, and she defends it like a warrior queen defending a castle against the besieging armies of untidiness. If Harry wants to leave anything on the surface he must have permission, and he must leave it in precisely the right place. She takes ignorance of its rules personally; her sense of self takes in items of furniture so intimately that it is as if they were other bodies she inhabited.

*

Most people on Highgate Lane work at one of the valley's pits. Often, during the day, women try to keep their home quiet for their husbands who will be on nights, and in the evening and early mornings the air fills with the sound of men coughing up black dust from their lungs. The Hollingworths share their yard with three other families. Winnie and Harry's house is in one corner, and next door are Nelly and Reg Spencer and their sons, Cyril and Terry. Reg works in the pit offices at Manvers, and is secretary of the working men's club; Nelly, a short and densely built woman who smells of green Palmolive soap, likes a bargain and has social aspirations. Next door to her live Comfort Eades, her husband Agger and son Donald. Agger is a hewer, like Harry, one of the men who digs the coal from the face. Comfort is a pale, quietly spoken woman known for her canniness. She and Nelly are lifelong friends, though often not on speaking terms because Comfort has heard that Nelly has been gossiping about her in the backings. Win discovers after a few weeks that people on Highgate Lane are frequently not speaking to one another. It doesn't mean much; you just ask the children to take messages for you, and wait until you or they come round.

In the last house on the yard live a retired couple called Arthur and Elsie ('Granny') Illingworth, who are loved by everyone by virtue of being old and not cantankerous. It is thanks to Granny Illingworth that Winnie finds favour in the yard two weeks after she and Harry move in. The old lady needs her washing-line stringing, as she is not strong enough to pull and tie it as she'd like. Seeing Winnie tying hers, she asks for help, and Winnie, with her strong arms, yanks it with a vicious snarl and makes it taut as cheesewire. Taut lines are coveted, a source of pleasure and status among the women, so when Nelly notices Granny Illingworth's line she asks about it, and comes straight to Winnie's door. Comfort, not to be outdone, follows minutes later. Soon half of Highgate is calling for her, wanting slack lines tightening, and in this way Winnie Hollingworth, her who's married to t' Juggler, becomes known and respected on the street for her sheer physical strength.

The women tell her about Mr Meanly, and she learns that she and Harry guessed right about his name. He owns dozens of houses on Highgate Lane and all his tenants say the same; his rent collectors want their money the minute it's due, but whatever he does with it, he doesn't spend much of it on the houses. Their windows are badly made and let in the wind, laden with soot and coal dust; when his tenants show him the sills he says that it can't *all* have come through windows, implying that it is you that is dirty. When the walls are damp, he says stop drying so many clothes on your fires. When something breaks he promises repairs but his men never come. When you ask for maintenance his rent man puts you off: 'Mr Meanly's not got time to be mending gutters' – as if his boss were the Mayor of Barnsley – or 'Mr Meanly's got more to bother about than thy fence.' Some people repair and improve their houses themselves, hanging new front doors, or repainting their windowsills. Others seem to absorb Mr Meanly's attitudes and not only ignore their own houses but mock anyone who does his work for him. It is Nelly who ringleads the opposition to the landlord, dispensing tips and ruses for getting repairs done, driven by an inventive frugality that is as impressive as Winnie's strength. She is famous in the yard for cutting all her buns in half before serving them because, she says, all the pleasure in food lies in the first two mouthfuls.

*

Winnie and Harry have been at Number 34 for two months before Harry reveals to her the lodger who will help them pay Mr Meanly's rent. It is his paternal grandmother Juggler Jane, so-called because she shares some of the eccentricities of the Hollingworth men.

Said to be descended from gypsies, Juggler Jane is old and wears long black dresses in the Victorian style. She carries at her waistband a fifteen-decade rosary, carved from Whitby jet and threaded on silk, which she uses in old healing rituals. Jane treats the rosary with a religious reverence, though she is not a practising Catholic. She says prayers with the beads, but also uses them to talk to her ancestors.

Like Annie Parkin, Jane helps with births and the laying out of the dead. She also brews potions from wild plants and herbs that she picks from the roadside and fields, her skirts often wet and muddied at the hem. She makes wine from nettles and dandelions, and cooks hedgehogs in clay. The Hollingworth family story that Winnie recalls best is the one about Jane pushing a pram through the village and the local bobby stopping her to pass the time of day and remark that he didn't know she'd had another baby. She hadn't; she had slit a sheep's throat in the fields, wrapped it in a baby's blanket, and was using the pram to get it home.

Juggler Jane now cares for four young grandchildren abandoned by one of her sons, who, after his wife died, left Bolton-upon-Dearne to seek his fortune. She moves between whatever accommodation she can find. The children – John, Joan, Tommy and Alf – are sometimes together, sometimes dispersed among relatives.

The day she arrives at Number 34, Jane brings with her the youngest of the grandsons, five-year-old Tommy. Her belongings are in a trunk, brought by one of Harry's friends in his car. 'Ayup young Juggler lad. Ayup Winnie,' she says as she walks straight past them into the passage, rosary and crucifix swinging with her skirts. She instructs young Tommy to take the trunk, and when he complains about its weight tells him to hold his tongue, and 'Pull, sirree, or else I'll be after you wi' my rhubarb again.' Jane uses rhubarb to whack naughty children's legs, and when men displease her she threatens to whack them with it too.

She moves into an upstairs room with Tommy, unpacks her cooking equipment (pestle and mortar, a small cauldron, and some metal implements Winnie does not recognise) into the kitchen cupboards and sits down with a bottle of pale ale and a clay pipe. The next day she shows Winnie how to cook hedgehogs, first rolling them in clay then baking them in the oven bottom. They taste less bad than Winnie is expecting, but their cooking smell is terrible.

In the late summer, Millie and Danny move into a house halfway down Highgate Lane with Brian and a newborn baby daughter, Barbara. Soon afterwards Annie, Walter, Olive and Sonny take one of Mr Meanly's houses at the bottom of the hill, which means Annie can help Winnie through her pregnancy and Winnie can look in on Walter. At the same time Harry's sister Clara moves into Number 34 for a few weeks when she comes home from Manchester.

'God almighty, what's she cooking?' says Clara, when on her first day of living there she finds Juggler Jane hunched at the range amid a vapour of unusual, offalish smells. Clara, having lived in a well-off part of Manchester, is up to date and fashion conscious, with bobbed hair and dinky hats. 'I'm not eating hedgehog, Jane. It's 1932!'

Winnie goes through her pregnancy relying on her mam's advice and half a pint of Mackeson's stout every night. When she goes into labour early in the evening of Sunday 24 September, Annie comes to the house and sits with her and tells Jane to go off to bed, and Harry to get himself out to the club. Winnie remains in labour all night. Harry comes home, sleeps in his chair, and goes to work. Annie wipes her daughter's face with a cloth dipped in cool water, and soothes her. The gypsy girl stands in the corner of the bedroom, telling them both that it's going to be all right, but by mid-morning Annie realises there is a problem that is beyond her abilities as a midwife, and sends Comfort to fetch a doctor.

By the time the doctor arrives, Winnie is bucking and grimacing in agony. Under her father's blows she has learned to cope with pain by stopping herself from feeling, but this does not work now. The doctor looks disdainfully around the small room and shouts at her to stay still. He examines her belly and she starts to cry. She feels as if her insides are a sink, the plates being not only washed up but also dropped in and broken.

There is a problem with the labour, the doctor says, and he will need to use the instruments. Everyone calls whatever the doctor uses 'the instruments', as if you could not hope to understand the differences in what they might do to you or your baby. He extricates from his leather bag a pair of steel obstetrical forceps, and Winnie reaches for her mam's hand. That metal on a baby's head! She winces and tries to breathe steadily.

The doctor barks, 'Will you please try to be *still*,' as if he hates her.

Slowly the forceps tug, and draw out, and tug again. Winnie gasps, and squeezes her eyes shut. She feels more tugging, and the baby comes out. There is no crying. She looks up to see the doctor holding up a baby with a buckled head and a face mauve-blue beneath its caul.

'A boy,' says the doctor, 'but it's dead.'

The room is silent. The doctor tosses the body to the foot of the bed. He examines her, and her mam wipes her face. Annie looks hurt and angry, but Winnie knows that she fears the doctor, and will say nothing.

And then, as the doctor methodically tidies away his instruments, there is a small, half-choked, wrenched cry at bed end, then a movement. Annie is the first to respond, whipping up the baby and massaging his back. Another cry, a millisecond longer; the doctor snatches him back and Winnie sees a limp, slow movement in the legs. There is urgent movement, and more massaging and then more crying, and finally, after what feels to Winnie like several hours, the baby is in her weary arms, he looking up at her and her looking back at him, the little boy brought back from the dead.

*

The boy looks like his father, Winnie later notes with some disappointment. Later she will say she thought he was ugly, although by then he will have turned out to be handsome and tall. Immediately she and Harry begin negotiations over the name. Before the birth Harry said that he would like a boy to be called Harry, because the name had been given to eldest sons in the Hollingworth family for generations. Winnie replied that she didn't like Harry, but had no other ideas. Her father's name was the obvious alternative, but she didn't like Walter either. Daft to argue, they agreed, because it might be a girl.

Now a boy has made an argument inevitable.

'I don't know what we shall call him,' says Winnie, drinking a cup of tea as the baby sleeps in a basket near the fire.

'I've said,' says her husband, 'we'll call him Harry.'

'I'm not keen,' says Winnie. 'It's not very modern.'

Harry freezes theatrically, mid-puff, and looks as he might if she had complained that the name Harry was not French. 'Of course it isn't modern. It's a proper English name.'

'Well. You *like* being modern.'

'I don't.'

'Yes you do. With your dancing and your . . . carry on.'

'I can do old-time and modern dancing.'

This is a bad angle for Winnie. Harry frequently likes to point out that he is a serious dancer and not restricted to crazes or old styles.

'We're not calling him Harry anyroad,' says Winnie.

'We are.'

'We're not.'

Harry walks over to the basket and addresses the slumbering infant. 'We are, aren't we, kiddo? I'll be the master in my own house, won't I?'

'It's our house,' she says. 'And we're not calling him Harry. Or "kiddo".'

At this point the argument is joined by Clara, who has come in from fetching more stout. Clara says she likes the name Harry as well, and she thinks they should carry on the tradition. Winnie tells her they are not carrying on the tradition, and the arguing wakes the baby, and Harry, exasperated, goes to the club for a drink.

They are still disputing the baby's name on the day of the christening as they get ready to leave the house. Amid the clatter and gathering and the sound of Roy Fox and His Orchestra on the radio, Clara points out that, given the indecision, Winnie will have to choose 'Harry'. Winnie remains silent, thinking, thinking, thinking.

In the chapel, before the service, the minister asks delicately if they have a name. Clara smiles with a look of triumph, and Winnie says, 'Roy.'

'Roy,' says the minister. 'And any second name?'

A second name! She hadn't thought of that. Clara will say Harry, and then just use that all the time.

'Fox,' says Win.

'Roy . . . Fox?' says the minister.

Clara's mouth opens, and does not close.

'Yes.'

'Roy Fox . . . Hollingworth. Very well.'

Harry sighs. He does quite like Roy Fox's band.

10

They Only Spend It on Beer

Highgate, 1932–33

While Winnie has been nursing her baby, her father's health has been deteriorating. The tuberculosis that makes the abscesses around his spine has spread to his lungs, causing him to cough blood, and his shrapnel wounds have opened and become re-infected, suppurating yellow pus under the bandages and poultices. On his left hip and right leg there are abscesses the size of his palm. Between them, Annie, Juggler Jane and the doctor have stopped the sores widening, but now the wounds grow deep, and are too painful for him to sleep.

The only Parkin child at home now is Sonny, Olive having married and moved with her blacksmith husband to mill country near Halifax. In the autumn of 1932, it is Sonny who helps his mam to carry Walter's bed down so that he can lie in the quiet of the sitting room, and not have to climb the stairs. When Winnie calls to see him in his new room in November, his skin is a bloodless grey, his face cold but covered in perspiration; he looks like something that has been dug from the cold winter soil.

She stays with him for the afternoon, baby Roy in the pram, while her mam goes out to give a sitting. Waking from a doze, Walter recounts stories about when he was a boy working on farms, and about his horses, and about his long walk to Shirebrook to find work. He talks about healing and Spirit and meeting Annie, and then he is quiet again, drifting between alertness and a sort of waking-sleep state in which his eyes are open but he seems not to see or hear. When he brightens he talks to his daughter about the strike and the coal owners. 'He said, "I'd like to see them eating grass." *Eating grass.*' Walter flinches as the pain bites at his insides. 'T' pits should be for t' people, you know. There's no need for all this . . .'

By 'all this' he means unemployment and poverty. In the winter of 1932–33, the South Yorkshire coalfield is at the lowest point of the slump; in some villages in the Dearne half the men are unemployed and many of those that have jobs are on short time, or drawing wages that will not support a family. They pawn their goods and borrow, and some have to go to the Public Assistance Committee, where committee officials ask questions betraying the belief that miners only drink away any money they get. In the areas where coal is easier to extract and there is less competition between districts, a man can live fairly comfortably on pit wages, but in others, fathers cannot afford shoes for their children, and whole families cram themselves into two or three rooms. Walter, like many miners, believes the answer lies in a minimum wage and the nationalisation of the pits; the mines for the miners. Some of the men had been saying this in Shirebrook when he first arrived there in 1903.

The young mother listens to Walter reminiscing until he drifts out again, and then she just sits, with her father and her son sleeping near her in the dwindling light. Dusty net curtains twitch like anxious ghosts in the window draughts. Outside she can see the empty lane and fields tufted with dead brown grass; in the room the firelight catches the brass handle of the ornamental dagger on the wall. She puts coal on the fire and watches the landscape outside grow dark until her mam comes home from her communion with the dead.

In December, as the diseased abscesses deepen and night sweats grow worse, a doctor comes to examine Walter and finds that the tuberculosis has spread beyond his lungs to his other organs. The healer has passed beyond the help of doctors and Spirit now; an old man, Annie she says to Winnie, just forty-three but a bleeding old bag of bones.

By the end of January, he is alternating between half-mad feverish gabbling and tired, sunken-cheeked stupefaction. Annie sits up with him through the nights, sleeping in the day when Sonny or Winnie can relieve her. In the late, lamplit hours of 6 February 1933 she is alone with him when he falls into a deep unconsciousness, and she listens to his breathing grow erratic and watches the skin of his fingers and scalp lose its colour. Finally she feels his spirit move and pull away from his body.

Annie closes her husband's mouth and draws down his eyelids, sends Sonny to tell Millie and Winnie the news, and then lays out the corpse of the young man who, twenty-five years ago in a stone church, had laid his hands upon her for healing. First she undresses him and washes him head to toe, wiping the old scars and badly mended bones, and then she pulls some cotton wool from its package and shapes it into stoppers that she inserts into each nostril and, shoving her hand beneath his body, his anus. There is more lifting and shoving as she cuts, folds and puts on a cotton-cloth nappy, and then slips over that a pair of clean long johns and a nightshirt. Almost done now, Walter. She binds his chin, enfolds his arms over his chest, and puts his prayer book under his right arm. Finally she takes from her purse two dark pennies which she rubs on her cuffs and places on his eyes. Then she kisses him and goes upstairs to sleep.

In the morning she will withdraw the money they had saved and order for him an oak casket with polished brass handles. Later, friends and sons-in-law will bear him past the houses with curtains drawn, down the hill to the Bolton-upon-Dearne graveyard at the bottom of the valley.

It is almost eighteen years to the month since he sent the letter about the bullet. *Keep your spirits up. They have not broken mine, as heavy a fire as I have been under, and I don't think they will. Kiss the children for me, and remember me to all at home.*

11

The Magic Half-Pint

Highgate and Skegness, 1936–38

'Right. Are you ready?'

It is an autumn night in 1937. In the sitting room at Number 34, Highgate Lane, an expectant crowd has gathered: Winnie, Juggler Jane, Danny, Millie and their new baby daughter Pamela, the children, Roy, Tommy, Brian and Barbara. In the passage Harry is calling to them as he waits to make his entrance.

'I said "Are you ready?"'

'Yes!' they all shout, they are ready. Get on with it!

The door opens, and Harry walks in wearing a curly ginger wig, a long satin skirt like Jane's, a shawl, and a hat with ribbons tying under the chin. Below the hem of the skirt his audience see the frills of a pair of bloomers. He is carrying a bottle of whisky and his gait is deliberate and slow.

Winnie sighs in mock embarrassment. Millie, Roy and Tommy laugh, and Jane, sucking at a clay pipe, looks nonplussed. The clothes are not old-fashioned to her, though she is puzzled as to why her grandson is wearing them.

'Mother Riley!' says Millie, and Harry smiles.

'Aye,' he says, 'but watch this.'

He walks across the room, pauses, and licks his lips, then he brushes back the ginger curls of his wig, puts his right hand under his long black skirt and produces from somewhere near his thighs a full half-pint of bitter, which he drinks off in one.

His audience is speechless. Roy breaks the horrified silence. 'How did you do that, Dad?'

'Do it again, Uncle Harry!' says Tommy.

'You're not really going to do that in front of people,' says Winnie. 'Are you?'

Harry repeats the trick, and then explains that it is part of a new act based on Arthur Lucan's Old Mother Riley character. In the last few years Harry has become popular as a drummer, comic and singer, well known in the valley for his ad-libbed version of 'All of Me', but he has been trying to think of ways to increase his bookings and his fees. Seeing his first Old Mother Riley film has given him an idea: a ribald South Yorkshire take on Lucan's act, but with the beer gimmick. If that works, he will add his version of the Sand Dance, which has become popular on the back of a craze for Egyptiana following the discovery of Tutankhamun's tomb, and for which he has bought fezzes, fake moustaches, long white nightshirts and sandals. To the two copy acts he adds a third one of his own. For this nameless character, Harry tapes pitmen's metal Dudleys to his body, and wears women's stockings with dripping tins pushed inside them. Over this he wears a floral-print dress and finishes off the look with the application of foundation, lipstick, eye make-up and rouge, and sometimes the ginger wig. The effect is more frightening than anything else, but when he takes his drumsticks and plays the Dudleys and dripping tins as if his whole body is a drum, the audiences will go wild.

Roy and Tommy want to see it all now. Winnie says he's barmy and she won't be able to show her face again in Highgate, but privately she thinks his ideas are good, and a part of her likes the idea of a husband who is popular and acclaimed.

Harry will never tell anyone how he carries the half pint under his skirt, but the trick and the Mother Riley take-off appeal to promoters. With Millie often performing with him, he is booked for bigger clubs around Doncaster and Barnsley and moves up the bill, adding the Sand Dance and the Dudley drumming as he goes. Winnie welcomes the extra money because pit wages are low and the chances of being made unemployed high; that autumn the Jarrow Marchers pass through

Barnsley, and King Edward VIII goes to mining villages in South Wales and says that something must be done to get the people work. For Millie the fees make up for the loss of earnings after Danny retires from professional boxing and shifts to training lads in the Bolton-upon-Dearne gymnasium. It is she who will be doing the travelling now, says Harry, and she had better get ready because this act is going places.

*

'Skegness?' says Winnie one Sunday morning in June 1938, as a hungover, late-rising Harry eats a breakfast of bacon and eggs, the radio humming fuzzily in the background.

'There's nowt wrong with Skegness,' says Harry. 'You like it.'

Skegness is busy and booming, with a Butlin's holiday camp just opened and new gardens, baths and a boating lake on its foreshore pulling in East Midlands families with money to spend.

'I do like it,' she says, 'but I don't disappear off to it on a Saturday night, though.'

'More's t' pity.'

'Shut up, Harry. Who's booked you?'

He tells her the name of the pub. 'Twenty-five bob.'

Winnie catches herself. Twenty-five shillings is a lot, even after it's been shared out with Millie.

'How are you going to get there?'

Feeling optimistic that the Skegness booking will be a success, Harry has already purchased a secondhand tandem from a couple in Goldthorpe. Millie, though doubtful at first, has decided she is game.

'Our Millie's as daft as you are,' Winnie says when Harry confesses.

'It's ambition,' he replies. 'Tha's got to start somewhere.'

After lunch on the Saturday, Harry and Millie pack their costumes and props into bags, tie them to the tandem's frame, and set off at a wobbling pace along the road that leads to Doncaster and then to the open flat country and the sea. It is a fine, warm day and they reach the town in five hours, stopping off at a pub on the way for a pint of bitter and a half of stout. The act goes down well and they are offered a repeat booking. As they cycle home through the warm, dark countryside, they sing their songs and make plans, and the next morning Harry tells Winnie that he was right: Skegness will be only the beginning of the venture.

Harry talks to some acts he knows and pitches them to promoters as a music-hall troupe called the Mother Riley Roadshow, with him as compère and Millie as vocalist. After a few weeks of rehearsing and plugging they get a foot-of-the-bill booking at a theatre in Rotherham, and Harry paints posters, drills the acts, and grows anxious and irritable with Winnie until the afternoon comes when he can get on the tandem and set off towards the bright lights of the city to the south.

Later that night, when Roy, Tommy and Juggler Jane have all been long asleep, and Winnie is reading a romance in the sitting room, she hears muffled sounds outside: laughter, singing and a fumbled scratching of keys on the door. In a burst of air and banter, Harry, Millie and Danny tumble in with a gang of comics and musicians, all of a-snigger and a-roar with booze. 'T' performance has gone down wonderful, my love,' says Harry, 'and t' manager wants us back. Bring my champagne and cigars!'

He turns on the radio and sends one of the gang up to the beer-off near the crossroads at the top of the lane to have an enamel bucket filled with ale. Annie laughs, Harry turns up the radio. Winnie goes to the kitchen to slice bread and slather on dripping and bacon. Coats off, cigs lit. A musician called Ronnie takes his guitar from his case and plays tunes as singers take it in turns to stand before the range, which makes a sort of backdrop hung with wreaths of cigarette smoke. Their mate comes back from the beer-off with the bucket slopping full of beer.

'We thought tha'd drunk thi' sen lad!' calls Harry. 'Get some glasses, Win.'

Performers and hangers-on dip their glasses into the bucket and sing harmonies, one after the other – novelty songs, ballads, old-style music hall and modern dance numbers. Winnie sits quietly, with the gypsy girl watching her, until Harry tells her to get some more sandwiches made. In the kitchen, as she cuts the loaf, she hears him cajoling Millie back to sing 'Play a Simple Melody', in which two singers argue over the merits of old-style music versus modern rag. In the middle, they break off into a mock argument:

Millie: 'This is a lovely old song, and not rubbish. This kind of song will outlive all your raggy nonsense.'

Harry: 'You're fifty years behind the times: we want something with a kick in it! I'll sing you a chorus that'll make 'em sway!'

The party goes on until two o'clock in the morning. Down the road there are other gatherings. In the backings, carousing, screams and blazing rows that some of them listen to and laugh at outside the back door. Winnie wonders about bed; should she go, saving her energy but annoying Harry by deserting him at what is the high point of his week, or should she stay up, when he doesn't really seem to notice her anyway, and make herself tired? In the end it doesn't matter because he isn't looking out for her. She just slips out as they take it in turns to sing in front of the range, and walks up the dark stairs, hearing behind her laughter and Harry and Danny singing 'Life Is Just a Bowl of Cherries'.

12

Swinging Down the Lane

Highgate, 1938

The financial arrangement between Harry and Winnie is that he tips up his whole wage packet for her, Roy and the house, and keeps the earnings from his acts for himself. Women think themselves fortunate to have a husband who tips up, so she lets him spend his showbiz money how he likes. From the cash he gives her she first takes the rent, keeping it in a tin on the sideboard until Mr Meanly's man collects it on Thursdays. She then places a pound spending money in Harry's drawer in the sideboard, and puts more aside to buy him his cigarettes (sixty Park Drive, sixty Gold Flake). Every once in a while Harry falls short in the week and borrows from the rent tin, and this makes Winnie curse him because it means her having to borrow from Millie, or a neighbour, just as they will have borrowed from her. The women are sympathetic and sanguine about this mutual lending from sideboard tins and drawers, but Winnie hates having to ask. In Highgate everybody knows everybody's business, and she dislikes people knowing her husband lets her down.

To save herself the humiliation she learns how to balance her home accounts using the Monday-morning method. On Sunday nights Harry comes home from the club drunk enough to have little idea of how much money he has left. In the morning, once he has gone to work, Winnie goes into the passage where the coats hang and picks from the pockets his remaining notes and coins, taking what she needs for the house, with a little bit extra to keep in reserve. The secret is to guess how much he thinks he could have spent. Winnie is a good guesser, and in more than fifty years of marriage Harry Hollingworth will never know – or wonder – how his wife coped with the unexpected fluctuations he caused in her budget.

On a Friday evening in 1938, Harry announces one such fluctuation when, having returned from a solo tandem ride to Manvers Main to collect his wages, he places the envelope on the sideboard and informs her that this week it contains a few bob less than usual.

'It'd better not do,' she shouts from the kitchen, where she is frying fish for the family's tea. She thinks he is joking.

'I've just had to take ten shilling out.'

She looks at him sharply and takes the fish off the heat. Ten shillings will leave them short on the rent. 'What for?'

He lays bravado on his embarrassment. 'Never mind what for.'

'I do mind what for. How will we pay t' rent?'

'Have a guess.'

'Damn you, Harry!'

In his thoughts this scene has been played out with Winnie enjoying the excitement and anticipation. He had not thought about the rent. He'd wanted to tease his wife, not start an argument with her.

'It's on t' road outside,' he says, trying again. 'Go and have a look.'

Parked on the lane is a large, highly polished BSA motorcycle. Not yet over the purchase of the tandem, Winnie is already wondering how much she will get from his pockets on Monday morning, and who she will have to ask to lend her the rest.

'What do you want a motorbike for?'

'To get about to do turns,' he says. 'We'll go a lot further on that than on t' tandem, and we can carry all t' kit in it.'

'How?'

'I'm going to make a sidecar.'

'You're going to make *what*?'

'A sidecar.' He shakes his head, despairing at her lack of vision. 'It'll not be much of a job. I'll put t' drums or t' costumes in it, and Millie can go on t' back.'

'Millie! Why should our Millie go on t' back?'

'She can go in t' sidecar if she likes! It doesn't matter, does it?'

'And how will you fasten a sidecar on?'

'With wood. I know somebody who's got some railway sleepers I can cut up.'

Is it reasonable to build a sidecar and fasten it to a motorcycle with part of a railway sleeper? Winnie has no idea.

'Where did t' motorbike come from?'

'Clarry's.'

'Clarry Basinger? I should have flaming known!'

This casts a new light on the purchase. Clarry Basinger is a short, thickset man who dresses in expensive, double-breasted suits, smokes cigars and owns a secondhand car business opposite the junior school. He arrived in Highgate with motor cars, petrol pumps and garages some time in the late 1920s, and sells the popular British cars and some flashier models bought from colliery managers and businessmen. Many people think he is a flattering, overly persuasive salesman of whom it is best to be wary. Harry, however, thinks he is terrific.

'It'll not go if he's sold it you.'

This riles Harry. 'Course it goes! Once I've got t' sidecar on, tha'll see it does. And I'll get my drums and your Millie in it, and we can get to some right places and earn some brass.'

'Millie won't fit in there with a drum kit.'

He looks from the motorcycle to his wife, and from his wife to the motorcycle. 'I am trying,' he says, 'to get on in life. Nowt comes from nowt, tha knows.'

*

The payments on the motorcycle are less of a drain than Winnie expects. Once he has built and attached a vast sidecar to the motorcycle Harry does get more work as a turn, with bookings in Wakefield, Leeds and Sheffield, where some venues pay top rates. As well as that, there is more overtime to be had at the pit. The collieries are increasing production and taking on more men to meet the growing demand from the steel mills. Everyone says it is because there is going to be another war with Germany. Lord Halifax has taken over as Foreign Secretary and had talks with Hitler, but no one thinks he'll do any good. The government plays down the chance of war, but in the Dearne everyone sees more coal trains on the lines, and more steel coming back, and they know the steel is for new tanks and guns. Terrible job, they say, but at least it means work and money.

Harry studies and passes the exams to become a colliery shot-firer, a job that requires intricate calculations of charges, fuses and air pressure, and that pays better and is less tiring than working as a hewer. He likes it because, while it is a promotion, it doesn't mean he has to tell a lot of men what to do; positions of authority do not appeal to him, and anyway, he thinks, they could be difficult to maintain when you appear on stage producing half-pints of beer from under a dress.

His chief interest remains the Mother Riley Roadshow. They perform most Fridays and Saturdays, and sometimes Harry asks Winnie to come with them to watch. 'Let Danny or your mam look after Roy,' he says, 'come wi' us and enjoy yoursen.' But Winnie won't go, or at least not more than once or twice a year; she likes to see her husband on stage, but the crowd's rowdiness and the drinking put her off. She feels awkward among the musicians and singers and boozers, and doesn't know how to act in their company. Some nights she feels a sort of jealousy towards them, and regards them, even Millie, as show-offs.

One night, when the troupe has been playing in Sheffield, Harry does not return home. Winnie does not sleep and then worries all the next day; when Roy asks where his dad is she says he's had to go away somewhere. He turns up in the late afternoon, dark-eyed and grumpy. There was a problem with the bike, he says, and the venue manager let them stay at his house. Then he changes the subject by telling her with some excitement that one of his distant cousins, who did a couple of turns with the troupe and left for London, is now working as a stand-in for a theatre actor in London.

Winnie does not care about his cousin. She is suspicious, but she also worries that she is overreacting, so she doesn't argue. She doesn't argue when he stays out the following week either, but then it becomes two nights, or all day and night on Friday when he is due home with his pay. They argue about his absences. He gets angry, and she asks her mam to come to stay, which makes him behave for a few days. When Annie leaves he lapses into the unfaithful spouse's random, inappropriate nastiness in the home and nothing is too minor or insignificant to decry. He complains about Juggler Jane cooking in the house, or about the food Winnie makes, or, one Saturday tea time when she brings fish and chips, the bluntness of the knives and forks. 'What's the matter with you, Harry?' she says, bewildered and fed up.

'You,' he snaps. 'You, going on wi' your damn . . . *questions*.'

*

A Monday morning in April: a washday. Winnie rises at six after seeing Harry off to work. In the kitchen she lights a fire in the small fireplace in the corner, fills a large steel cauldron with water and puts it over the fire to boil. As the water warms, she brings into the small kitchen dolly tubs, a washboard and a peggy-leg, and then cooks eggs and bacon for breakfast. She hustles Roy and Tommy and, once the children are out of the house, she brings downstairs big armfuls of soiled laundry, then strips the bedding and brings that down too. Having already laid Harry's pit clothes – the old black clothes and underwear he uses for work – in a separate pile, she begins sorting the whites from the rest: her bloomers, handkerchiefs, Harry's underpants, Roy's other school shirt, all with their individual imprints, ruts and blooms of dirt. She is sorting and dropping them to the floor like the skins of dead days and nights when she notices a mark on the front of one of Harry's shirts. It is dark red lipstick, smears rather than lip prints, near to where the collar would fit. She feels her heart quicken and her fingers tingle. She finds and works through the others. No, no . . . hang about. Here, the same lipstick.

Pursing her lips, she renews the washing with clenched vigour, bunches up a mound of whites in her arms and dumps them in the boiling cauldron with a cup of soap powder. The air fills with the fatty, raw chlorine odours of Rinso and Dolly Blue whitener and an underlying faintly acrid smell of dirty laundry. In the yard, Nelly is briskly pegging sheets to her line. Damn Harry! It is so typical. Sometimes these days it seems people are quite willing to accept this sort of thing. People feel everyone should be allowed to have a bit of fun, but pinching husbands – it might be one woman's fun, but to a wife it was the loss of her livelihood.

Using washing tongs, she fishes out the clothes and sheets from the cauldron and drops them into the dolly tub. She peggy-leg pounds them in the tub's convex, grey, corrugated torso, and then scrubs them on the washboard. A rinse in the second tub, and then she wrings everything through the mangle – quick quick quick because it all needs to be done by three. As she is viciously pegging the sheet corners to her line she wonders what to do. The sheets and clothing can be cleaned; if only there were cauldrons and chemicals that might wipe clean her husband's soul and boil away these women! She enjoys putting Harry's shirts through the mangle.

More sheets go out to dry, mangle-smooth and blue-white, like sails billowing in the harbourish yard; as there is no wind or cloud they are not yet flecked with soot or black dust. Next she is kneeling and scrubbing the kitchen, efflorescent with its wet washday scents and miasmas. By the time she has finished and has begun to fold the early drying parts of the laundry for ironing, she has had an idea.

The boys arrive home for lunch and she feels a renewed surge of love for Roy: the innocent among the guilty! She wipes her hands and takes from the cupboard three willow-pattern plates, three chipped mugs and some flaking cutlery, and lays the table. She removes from the pan the reheated hash made from Sunday's leftover meat and vegetables, and spoons it onto the plates, making sure Roy and Tommy get the meat. Her own helping she pads out with plain bread, and eats it standing up, sitting the plate on the ledge.

Roy is almost six now. Tall, and with his dad's droll, heavy-lidded eyes, he sits kicking his white, goaty legs in their grey flannel shorts, and flipping pages of the *Dandy* as Tommy tries to read it across the table. He is a cute kid and has become his mother's great love. Sometimes he just puts his thin little arms around the tops of her thighs and says, 'I love you Mam,' and these are Winnie's happiest moments. Years later she will remember these, rather than Harry's declarations, as being the first time anyone said they loved her.

*

The following Friday, at Winnie's request and knowing something must be up, her mam – Muv, as she is known by Roy and her other grandchildren – comes to stay for the night. At eight o'clock, after Harry has gone to the club, Annie babysits while Winnie brushes her bobbed hair, puts on her make-up and her overcoat and slips out of the house, through the yard door and into the backings.

The backings have a different code of behaviour to the street at the front: children play here, women stand talking, and you can wear the clothes you wear in the house, slippers, pinnies or hair turbans. Friends and neighbours use the backings to get to each other's homes, always entering by the back door; front doors are for strangers and official people, a useful distinction since it means that if your visitors are unwelcome, you can escape out of the back. Seeing you in the backings, neighbours assume you are going nowhere unusual, which is why this evening Winnie takes the long route through them to reach Barnsley Road. Unnoticed, she walks to the bus stop near the club, which is close enough to allow her to see the club doors. And then, in the cooling spring air, she waits. Gangs of men, a few women, walk from pub to club; motor buses and a couple of cars go by; in the field opposite, by the small chapel, cows lay cow-quiet in the grass as the light fades; children walk to a still-lit shop and clang the door.

Soon all life is in the club, its windows lit yellow in the dark. She has been watching the building for two hours when she sees Harry coming back from a circuit with Danny, Lanc and Sonny. Her brother has now left school and is working at Barnburgh colliery. Does he know? Surely not, she thinks; surely your brother would tell you?

She stands and waits again, an hour or more, until the time for last orders comes and loud, cheerful men begin to leave: single men, big groups. There goes Sonny, that's Nancy's husband, there's Harold and – Harry.

Harry with a woman.

The woman with her arm linked with Harry's is Mavis Stocks from Goldthorpe, one of a Scots family that has come to the Dearne looking for work. Winnie knows her by sight: she is short and dark, like Winnie, and unmarried. Taken by a strong, calm self-possession, Winnie watches them sway along the pavement. Mavis laughs at a Juggler joke, and then reaches to kiss him and misses. More lipstick on his shirt. It seems worse than if she had succeeded.

They cross the road to Winnie's side; she turns round and begins walking away from them, as slow as she can while keeping a good distance. She comes to the railway bridge. She hears slurring laughing behind her, and then the slaps of their drunken feet on the pavement cease and there is the sound of branches and grass. They have gone down to the railway embankment. Winnie stops and turns, walks back and follows on the path.

They are down on the embankment, lying on the ground. Harry is on his back and Mavis is sprawled on top of him. Harry doesn't see Winnie until she is standing over them. Winnie summons the strength in her packed shoulders and short, thick forearms. Saying nothing, she reaches down to Mavis's coat, takes hold of it with both hands, lifts her off Harry and chucks her headlong into some long grass.

She ignores Harry, who is frantically adjusting his clothes, and stands over Mavis.

'Right, lady,' she says. 'Get off my husband, and stay off him. Don't ever come near him, or me, or any of my family again. If you do, you won't know what's bloody well hit you.'

'Gi'o'er Win,' says Harry. 'It was just – '

'Shut it, Harry. YOU,' she says, turning back to the woman, 'keep out of my sight, or I'll let everybody know what you are.'

And then she bends down, looks intently at Mavis and slaps her hard across the face.

'That's to help you remember.'

She leaves them both there and strides up the banking towards home, the gypsy girl stumbling alongside her, trying to keep up.

13

On the Beach

Bridlington, 1939

The confrontation on the railway embankment is an important victory for Winnie and she underscores it by making Harry sleep in the front room and refusing to speak to him for days on end. If he needs to ask her a question or tell her something, he must do it through Roy, Tommy or Juggler Jane. Winnie does not enjoy the arrangement but she learns that by imposing awkwardness on the home she gains power; once she feels him to be broken by it she begins to talk to him and the house is calm and respectful again. Harry comes home each night, and Winnie goes out with him to the club more often.

She has come to loathe his drinking though, and his slurred indelicacies, stale-beer odour and phlegmy snores remind her of her father's warnings. She thinks to pass those warnings on to Roy to ensure he doesn't follow his father, and when she and he have eaten Sunday lunch, and she has left Harry's plate to warm because he is still at the club drinking, she takes him into the front room to teach him a lesson. Roy plays with toy soldiers or reads his comics, while Winnie listens to the radio news about Hitler and Germany. When she sees Harry coming back from the club, perhaps with Danny beside him, both weaving a little, feet falling a little clumsily, Winnie says, 'Come here, Roy, just look at this,' and takes him to her side and points to Harry and Danny, and Roy laughs, which is not the response she seeks. She puts her arm around him and guides his thoughts. 'The daft 'apeth,' she says. 'Look at him, he can hardly stand up!'

'Is he drunk, Mam?'

'Yes he is. He should be ashamed of himself.'

'He's funny though, in't he?'

Win says nothing. Roy slips her grasp, and runs out of the room and down the street to his dad.

*

Through the long hot summer of 1939 the radio news carries stories of Hitler's armies threatening Poland. Men come to paste up posters about evacuees and to cut down the iron railings outside Number 34; in the club and in the backings men and women say, Rubbish, it'll turn out to be a lot of fuss about nowt, you watch. Winnie and Harry agree, even when the council begins recruiting air-raid wardens and more men come to build a brick air-raid shelter in the yard. If anything, the feeling of unreality draws them and the people around them together and brings a mood of, if not quite fun, then at least casual abandon. On the last day of August, as German forces gather to attack Poland, and Britain mobilises its armies, Harry drives Winnie and Roy in the motorcycle and sidecar for a long weekend at Bridlington's South Shore caravan park with his sister Clara and her new husband, a Bolton-upon-Dearne man called Ernie Towning.

Bridlington is heaving. The 1938 Holidays with Pay Act has allowed millions of people to take a week's holiday with pay for the first time, and rearmament has put money back into their pockets to spend on such things as caravan holidays, amusements, fried food, cheap sweets, novelty clothing, music and beer. The TUC conference is being held here and there are suited union men in the pubs and on the streets. You've hardly been able to shift all summer, the people in the caravan next door say; the pleasure boats have been that busy the captains have been fined for overcrowding.

On Saturday, as Winnie, Harry, Roy, Clara and Ernie queue for ice-creams and sit on the packed beach, Bridlington buzzes with war talk. Hitler has invaded Poland, Britain has told him to withdraw. He hasn't replied but he will, he'll pull out, you just watch. At night they have to black out the caravan windows, but still no one thinks anything will really happen; on Sunday, the day of the deadline Britain has given to Germany, the Hollingworths get up early and take the steps that run from the low, grassy clifftop down to the beach. Winnie, in her swimsuit and cap, skin reddened by yesterday's sun, wades out to the sea and Harry sits watching her, wearing an old loose jacket and trousers and a tam-o'-shanter he has bought from one of the shops. Roy makes sandcastles and does handstands with Ernie and Clara. Around them there are men in old suits and black woollen bathing costumes, and women in flowery cotton dresses. The air is filled with the smell of salt, sand and sweet frying fat, and the sounds of children and seagulls and the North Sea waves splashing onto the sand.

At about quarter past eleven, the skies fill with the sound of sirens. 'Chamberlain's been on t' radio,' a stranger on the beach tells Harry. 'Germany's not withdrawn, so it looks as if that's it!'

Winnie, Harry, Roy, Ernie and Clara sit looking at each other.

'What have we to do?' says Ernie.

'I think we should go home,' says Winnie.

So does everyone else. All around them people are packing bags and leaving, as if sitting on the beach has come to feel frivolous and distasteful.

'Come on,' says Harry, and he, Winnie and Roy gather up their things, climb up the cliff and head off in the motorcycle and sidecar, inland from the sunlit shore.

PART THREE

14

Bombshells

Highgate and Sheffield, 1940–45

At first everything changes and nothing happens. Soldiers install anti-aircraft guns on the crossroads in Highgate and RAF men bring white barrage balloons to float high in the blue skies over the village. Harry volunteers to be an ARP warden and goes with men from the council to test air-raid sirens, and one night German bombers fly over, but they drop no bombs.

Many of the young men in the valley rush to join the armed forces. Lads have been signing up to escape unemployment for several years but now recruiting officers turn thousands of them away; foreseeing war and a shortage of men to dig coal for Britain's home fires and industry, the government has made mining a reserved occupation. Some talk their way in, others don't. Winnie's brother Sonny tries to join the Merchant Navy, but when he tells his recruiting officer that he is a miner the officer tells him to get back down the pit and not to come back or there'll be trouble.

Meanwhile for Harry a new opportunity presents itself. He stays at Manvers but signs up the troupe with the Entertainments National Service Association. ENSA – Every Night Something Awful, the troops call it – pays entertainers handsome rates to perform in shows for armed forces personnel. Reliable turns are in short supply, and as the Mother Riley Roadshow can provide a full evening's entertainment, the organisers like it. They pay up to £10 a night, and for this money Harry,

Millie – who now has a fourth child, Tony, born in the summer of 1939 – and the rest get on buses, borrowed cars and the motorcycle and sidecar to take the Sand Dance, Old Mother Riley and the snap-tins-and-Dudleys drag-drumming act to the troops and workers in the messes and NAAFI huts of Yorkshire's West Riding.

In these jumpy, undecided days at the start of the war, much of Winnie and Harry's young-marrieds' rancour dissipates. They become friendlier and by the autumn of 1940 Winnie is pregnant again, due in May. With Juggler Jane and Tommy, the arrival of another baby will take the number of people in the house to six. This does not seem too many to Jane, but Winnie would like some extra room for the second child, and anyway, with the ENSA money they can manage without Jane's rent. Winnie frets about telling her, but the old lady just says, 'Nay lass, when it's time to go, it's time,' and a few days later disappears in a swish of black satin and a rattle of the spirit rosary. The next time they hear from her she has taken Tommy to live with one of her nieces in a small stone cottage in Bolton-upon-Dearne. Harry buys the family a mixed-breed dog called Bonzo, and Winnie redecorates Jane's old room ready for the new baby.

*

One evening in December 1940, a few weeks after Win's pregnancy is confirmed, Harry leads the troupe to an ENSA booking near Sheffield. The concert is at No.16 Balloon Centre, an RAF barrage balloon base on the southerly edges of the city, which, because of the expected air raids on the steel mills, is heavily defended. Riding the motorcycle there with Millie, props trunk crammed in the sidecar, he sees ack-ack guns in farmyards and, tethered to moorings at road junctions, barrage balloons which look almost toy-like. As they draw closer to Sheffield they pass more and more army lorries and armoured cars, yet it all seems unreal; Coventry and Birmingham have already been attacked because of their heavy industry, but it seems impossible to think of the bombs being dropped on somewhere they know.

The concert hall sits among vast brick balloon hangars, accommodation huts and a rifle range. An entertainments secretary greets the troupe and guides them to a screened-off dressing room beside a makeshift stage in the Naafi where wooden chairs have been laid out. 'Look out for the nits,' he says, 'we're infested with 'em.'

Millie shudders and says, 'Flaming Sheffield lice, they'd better keep out of my hair.'

'Never mind thy hair,' says Harry, 'watch them wigs.'

They are putting on their make-up in the dressing room when they hear the air-raid sirens start up, and the scraping of chairs in the Naafi as men get up and file out. Half dressed, half made-up, the troupe follow some of the soldiers into the bomb shelters. Inside it is hot, overcrowded; the air smells of bodies. Joking gives way to listening as aeroplane engines become audible, and then the first distant crump of an explosion, then another, then another, until the individual explosions merge into one long rumble.

The heavy bombing lasts for hours. There are lulls, but the thumping and cracking goes on till four in the morning. When Harry comes out among the cold, dark buildings, there is a smell of burning on the wind and a red haze of firelight over the city. Sheffield's centre is in ruins, although the bombers have missed their real targets, the steel mills and forges lying to the north and east being mostly unharmed. Shaken, and with traces of make-up still on his face, Harry climbs on the motorbike with Millie in the sidecar and Barney, the guitarist from the troupe, riding pillion and heads north on the roads circling the city, back towards the Dearne. Many routes are blocked and some houses have been damaged by stray bombs. No lights, no signposts. Harry backs up, swings around, tries other roads, until he finds one that leads up past steel mills, collieries, coking works and factories and back to the moonlit ink of the valley.

Ahead of him is Winnie, standing at a window in her nightdress and dressing gown, staring at the red fires on the horizon. The window frames have been vibrating with the heavier bombing, and two doors down the Atkins have had their glass blown out. Roy has watched and listened to it all with her, but is now asleep again. She rests her hands on her tummy, and allows her mind to contemplate the calming bottle of stout in the larder downstairs.

The planes come back again three nights later and in those two evenings almost 700 people are killed, more than 1,500 injured and

40,000 left homeless. On the night of the second raid, Winnie and Harry stand side by side at the window watching the fires in the distance, drawn together in a sort of sadness and fear. Winnie will remember that moment, although it will be many years before she fully realises its significance. In one of those uncanny coincidences common in wartime, the fires they watch that evening set off a chain of events that will lead to an unexpected love affair, and to perhaps the most difficult decision of Winnie Hollingworth's life.

*

After Sonny Parkin was rejected by the Merchant Navy in 1940, the paperwork recording his failed application was stored, with all the other recruitment papers of men from South Yorkshire, in a local government building in Sheffield's city centre. In the December raids, that building was hit and the papers destroyed. News of this reached the Dearne Valley at Christmas, and Sonny decided to try again. This time he went with a friend – sixteen-year-old Alf Hollingworth, brother of Tommy and cousin to Harry.

Plotting their applications together, Sonny and Alf become good pals. Both are good-looking, well dressed and eager for adventure away from home. Together they take a train to Bristol and, claiming different occupations, sign on for a voyage on a merchant vessel carrying food and supplies to Freetown, Sierra Leone. After brief training on an old ship moored in the River Severn, they set sail in the early spring. Sonny sends the occasional letter to Annie and Winnie telling them not to worry about the German U-boats, but other than that nobody hears from or sees him, or Alf, for two years.

More planes fly over Sheffield and food grows scarcer, but gradually the war moves back abroad and life on Highgate Lane damps down. Harry attaches wires to his radio and threads them through windows, along the walls and into Nelly and Reg's sitting room so they can listen to the nine o'clock news through a speaker. The wives exchange and barter food to avoid waste, and Winnie makes and repairs the family's clothes so she can swap her clothing coupons for Nelly's food rations – Nelly likes new clothes and can live on her two-bite meals. At night children playing out late hear screams as men cut the throats of pigs illegally fattened on allotments. At Number 34, Harry supplements his shares in the secret pigs with an egg and chicken business. Every few months he takes the motorbike and sidecar to Doncaster market to buy boxes of yellow, peeping, day-old chicks which he brings home and places beside the range in the sitting room for warmth. After a day or so some are strong enough to climb out of the box and pick their way across the lino and carpet squares covering the floor, and soon flocks of tiny birds are occupying the room, living there until Harry decides they are strong enough to be moved to a shed on the allotment. Winnie despairs. 'I sometimes think your dad thinks t' war's an excuse for being daft,' she says to Roy.

On 4 May 1941, Winnie gives birth to a baby girl whom she and Harry agree to call Pauline. A few days after the baby's christening in the chapel, Juggler Jane comes to see her and stands gazing down into the pram, muttering a sort of prayer as she passes the spirit rosary between her fingers. 'The first great-granddaughter,' she says.

She shows the little girl the rosary, and lets her take it in her hands.

'You know what it is, don't you?' she says. '*She knows what it is, Winnie*.' Winnie looks at Jane and smiles.

But having commanded all his mam's attention for nine years, Roy resents the baby and is jealous when Winnie tends to her. He refuses to run errands to the shop, smashes ornaments, and runs off to see the soldiers in the nearby camps. The soldiers talk to him about the war, the Americans, and what Yorkshire girls do and don't do if you take them out. They have army ration chocolate, real chocolate, not the kind found in sweet shops that tastes like dry, crumbling vegetable fat. Sometimes they give him whole bars which he takes back to show the other kids, and these gifts console and fortify Roy in a home that has been ruined by the baby. The soldiers are living heroes to him, and he seems to feel personally allied with them in their fight against Hitler.

In the backings, where gossip burns like a flame on a fuse, Roy has by the time he is ten acquired an exaggerated reputation for naughtiness. There are accusations of theft and ringleading. One evening some mothers tell a bobby they've seen Roy encouraging a gang to knock on back doors and run off, when in fact he has been inside, listening to the radio with his mam. Winnie is furious. She knows all the ringleader stories for lies because Roy is not interested in gangs; he is most content on his own, building cranes and imagined machines from Meccano in the sitting room, or dismantling and reassembling parts of the motorcycle and sidecar with Harry in the yard.

One day in the summer holidays, an argument in the backings turns into a fight, and he runs home with a bleeding nose. Winnie soothes his face with handkerchiefs soaked in cold water, and sends him back out. Winnie is tidying the sitting room and Pauline playing on the rug when the door bursts open a second time and Roy runs back inside, weeping, with more blood on his nose, mouth and chin. Once again she patches him up, but this time she tells him to stay in.

As the afternoon reaches its hot midpoint Millie's son Brian appears, peering around the privy at the back before he warily enters the yard. Brian has been taught to fight by his dad, who spars with him in the front room, and he is tough. ('You have to fight because it's the only way you'll get influence,' Danny tells him; Winnie wishes her husband would give Roy such advice, but Harry won't even discipline the kids.)

The children in the backings stop playing and stare at Brian.

'Where is he then?'

'He's in t' house!' shouts another kid in the yard.

Brian steps nearer so he can see the back door, 'Roy . . .'

Roy is in the sitting room, watching Brian from behind the net curtains.

'What does he want?' says Winnie.

'Nowt.'

'Nothing.' Even at tense moments such as this Winnie attempts to improve her children's diction and manners.

'Nothing. He wants to get me.'

'Right!' She snatches Roy's upper right arm in her strong, stubby grip, yanks him out from the room and pulls open the door. Brian freezes long enough for Win to thrust Roy into the space between the door and the yard wall; she grabs Brian's arm and shoves him next to

Roy, and stands back, barring the escape. Behind her the children stand, watch and shout.

'Now, hit him!' she says to Roy.

Roy doesn't move. Brian looks angry.

'I said hit him!'

Roy swipes the side of Brian's face. Brian, ignoring Winnie, lunges back at him. 'Hit him harder!' she says. 'Harder!'

Roy hits Brian's nose, making it bleed, but Brian lays into him again. Roy, backed against the wall, fights back, but Brian, though smaller, has a boxer's technique and threatens to overwhelm his cousin. Winnie steps between them and drags Brian off. He stands looking at her and Roy, then turns and runs out of the yard, down the backings to his mam and dad's house.

'Well done,' Winnie says to Roy.

He looks up at his mam, triumphant.

She is pleased. Millie might come up soon, but she doesn't care; this is all for Roy, as she will tell Harry later on.

*

Sonny Parkin comes back home from the Merchant Navy in November 1942, intending to stay for a couple of months. After visiting his mam, he and Alf walk up to Winnie's house one Saturday afternoon, bringing stories of sea battles, U-boats, and the people and towns they have seen in Africa. Sonny, who models himself on Bing Crosby, has an easy elegance about him, fine facial features and a relaxed version of his father's principled courtesy. Alf is quieter, thoughtful and more tousled-looking, with chestnut-coloured eyes and thick dark hair that flops in a boyish kink near the parting. They are bronzed and confident, both seeming far older than their years. Roy gazes up at them in awe, and when Alf extracts a map from his jacket pocket and shows him where they've been, he takes the map in his hands as if it has been blessed, and carries it across the room to show his mam. Winnie looks to where he is pointing, and then she looks up, across the oceans and battlefields, at Alf. They catch eyes. Winnie has always felt sorry for Alf because of his having grown up without a mam or dad, and now her gratitude for this kindness to Roy, and for his politeness, sweetens her sympathy. Typical of her brother to pal up with a decent lad, she thinks.

Sonny says they are planning to sign on for another voyage but don't have anywhere to stay in the meantime. Winnie says they can stay in the front room for a few weeks if they like, and so they unpack their kitbags and bed down there. Within days, though, Sonny meets up with a girl he used to know, May Ward. May lives in Lancashire, but comes to the valley every now and then to visit her father in Thurnscoe. She and Sonny got along well when they last met in the summer of 1939, and now, taken by the strange, impulsive mood of wartime, they fall in love. Sonny decides not to rejoin the Merchant Navy and proposes to May, and within twelve weeks they are married, and living with May's father, leaving Alf the bed in the front room to himself.

Alf does not want to go back to the Merchant Navy without Sonny, and so he too stays and takes a job at Highgate pit. He works different shifts to Harry, which means that Winnie often has another man in the house when she is tidying up, or doing the washing. At first she thinks this could be a burden, but Alf is polite and amenable. He helps her to fold the sheets and clean out the grates, and he chats to her about the books she is reading. She talks to him about his travels in the war, and about his sad childhood with his dad taking off and Juggler Jane bringing him up. They laugh together about backings gossip, and tell each other funny stories about Harry and his acts, and Alf mends the broken things in the house. And this, in the hungry and unreal days of the Second World War, is how Winnie and Alf Hollingworth start to become something more than friends.

15

I Always Cry at a Brass Band

Barnsley, 1947

The newspaper stories and radio news bulletins say that Britain is winning the war, but in the backings on Highgate Lane the women say that if this is winning, God knows what it's like to lose. With no food in the shops, they feed their families on potatoes and on rabbits caught in the fields. In the pits the men are working all hours because the country is running out of coal; too many miners have left the industry since the 1930s, and by the winter of 1943 stockpiles have run so low that Ernest Bevin, the Minister for Labour and National Service, begins sending military conscripts to the coalfields to work in the pits.

In the Houses of Parliament, MPs discuss nationalisation of the mines. In January 1945 the miners replace the Miners' Federation of Great Britain, which coordinated the affairs of dozens of small, regional unions, with the National Union of Mineworkers, a national organisation to represent all of them. In July 1945, two and a half months after VE Day, the Labour Party, with nationalisation of the coal industry in its manifesto, wins the general election. In Highgate, where the Labour leader Clement Attlee is generally thought of as a good and decent man, there is a mood of happy relief. At Number 34, Winnie Hollingworth thinks of her dad and tells Harry and Alf that Walter will be looking down and smiling.

On New Year's Day 1947, the day when the ownership of the coal industry passes to the state, Harry rides down to Manvers Main, passing other miners marching to their pits. He watches the raising of the blue and white National Coal Board flag over the colliery and the uncovering of a plaque bearing the words, 'This Colliery is Now Managed by the National Coal Board on Behalf of the People.' Most of the Manvers men are there, and for the rest of that week they celebrate nationalisation, and its promise of justice, safety, security and better pay. But in the following months, the optimism is lost in the heavy snow, fog and floods of the harshest winter for half a century. Bitter Pennine winds whip snowdrifts over telegraph poles and street lights, and freeze the stockpiles of coal in the colliery yards. Fog mingles with smoke from the pits, factories and coal fires in foul yellow clouds that linger on the valley floor and squat poisonously among the spoil heaps and enter the children's lungs to make them cough along with their fathers. Because of the demand for heat, the country's coal supplies run out. In February the government cuts off the electricity for five hours a day, closing factories and putting people out of work. The newspapers, flimsy-thin because of newsprint rationing, announce the coldest days for fifty years and declare a national crisis. Nothing but corned beef and cheap green soap in the dingy shops, unemployment rising, and women so short of money that they set alight their clothes drying by the fire for the insurance. Press and public blame the coal shortages on Manny Shinwell, the Labour Minister of Fuel and Power who oversaw nationalisation. Shinwell demands that the miners produce more coal; the miners and their managers say they need more men, and Harry Hollingworth grumbles that the country is in a worse bloody mess now than it was in 1939.

By spring the government is able to lift restrictions on electricity use, but coal stocks remain low. Shinwell meets the leaders of the new miners' union to ask for more coal in return for his reduction of their working week from six to five days in 1946; production increases, but the country's factories and mills and workshops still struggle to find enough supplies.

In June, Shinwell and Attlee come to speak to the Yorkshire miners at their demonstration in Barnsley. The demonstrations are vast gatherings where mining families march with their union branches and colliery bands and listen to speeches, then enjoy themselves at a gala afterwards. This year's will be the first demonstration since the start of the war, and Winnie and Harry Hollingworth go to celebrate nationalisation and to respect the dead, nine men having died in an explosion at Barnsley Main colliery in May and five others at Manvers Main two years before that.

Roy, now in his final year at Bolton-upon-Dearne secondary modern and determined to escape the pit, refuses to go with them, but Pauline, a schoolgirl with small liberty bodices and tight brown pigtails, is excited, and squeezes between her mam and dad as they ride on the crowded bus into Barnsley. The day is bright; Pauline looks out at the countryside, with its scattered farms and villages, and at the roads crammed with buses and cars full of men, women and children. They, like the Hollingworths, are wearing their good new clothes from Whitsuntide. The women have freshly waved hair and the men hold their caps on their knees.

In Barnsley the streets are packed with families, men carrying banners, men fixing banners to frames, colliery bands in clean, colourful uniforms with polished silver buttons, warming up on trumpets and horns and drums. Pauline hears the different accents in the conversations around her – Scots, Welsh, Geordie, Lancashire – and looking at the banners she recognises some of the colliery names and images of historical scenes and past miners' leaders. The banner from Manvers Main carries the words 'Six Hour Day: Superannuation – Security – Stability' and a picture of a well-dressed man paying in money at the pensions allowances counter at the post office while a girl buys stamps. It reminds her of when her dad takes her with him to the pit to collect his pay on Fridays, and sits her on the counter while he waits.

Harry goes to join the men from Manvers, and Pauline and her mam watch the procession from a spot on the pavement near Market Hill. Soon all Pauline can see, up and down the street, is a river of people, men's caps bobbing up and down, the beautiful red and gold banners bellying out like the sails of ships: Highgate, Goldthorpe, Manvers Main, Barnburgh, Hickleton, Wath, Dearne Valley, *Peace, Love and Unity, Unity is Strength, All for Each and Each for All.* When her dad goes past, she calls out and waves to him, but at first he cannot hear her over the boom of the bands' drums. Then he sees them, and waves back. They follow the procession through the hilly streets of swarthy houses, factories and scrub patches to Locke Park, which has fountains, statues, and an ornate observation tower. They find Harry waiting for them by the Manvers banner, and the three of them approach the bandstand, where Manny Shinwell and Clem Attlee will give their speeches.

Manny, talking into a heavy microphone, his voice amplified through speakers around the park, flatters the miners, criticises the Conservative Party, and says he needs all people gathered there to help produce more coal for all the people of Britain. Then Clem moves to the microphone and begins laying into communism and the Soviet Union. He repeats what Manny has said about the miners, and says the nation's economy is built on coal, and Britain needs the miners' help. 'No one of us can carry on without depending on the work of other members of the community,' he tells them. 'It is the duty of every one of us, in whatever sphere of activity we may work, to give our best if we expect that others should do their fair share . . . You in the great mining industry are now working not for private profit but for the nation. You have the incentive of your earnings, but you have besides another powerful motive. You are at the forefront of the new society which we are building. What you will do now will be a great example to others.'

Harry, Winnie and Pauline join the long, loud applause.

In the future, Pauline's parents will reminisce about this day and the speeches in Locke Park. They will recall being moved by Clem's appeal, and by the feeling of connection with the other Yorkshire miners, and by a sense of atonement for the 1920s and '30s. Winnie's will be the purer and more straightforward recollection because even in 1947, Harry is sceptical about nationalisation. His wages have gone up, he says, but it's the same old gaffers in charge, and some of them are awkward devils. 'It's your pit now,' they say if he asks them a question, 'so why don't *you* tell *me*?'

Pauline will remember another moment from that Saturday, one belonging just to her and her dad. It is four o'clock and the park is washed in the soft, mellow sunlight of late afternoon. They are walking across the green on their way to catch the bus back to Highgate and her mam is a few yards ahead of them. They come to where a brass band is playing and they pause to listen. The tune is slow and dignified. When Pauline looks up at her dad she sees tears running down his cheeks.

'Why are you crying, Dad?' she asks.

He laughs a half-laugh. 'I always cry at a brass band, love,' he says. And then he puts an arm around her shoulder and they turn to go, the music lingering in Pauline's mind until they board the bus to go home.

16

When God's Not Looking

Highgate, 1948

Despite the bleakness and hardship of the post-war years, the Mother Riley Roadshow thrives. Audiences in the small theatres and clubs may be pinched, but besides food they are hungry for laughs, knees-ups and the cheap romance of American pop songs. Harry adds new acts and buys fresh props and costumes and a new enormous leather suitcase to keep them in. On weekdays after school, Pauline pulls the suitcase from the cupboard at the top of the stairs and in the grainy landing light extracts gaudy fabrics and exotic paraphernalia: maracas, two ruby fezzes; a *camisa de flamenco* in emerald green satin with black cuffs, and a pair of black satin trousers; heavy Hawaiian grass skirts that are worn by a man and woman with pan lids over their chests in a song routine with Barney on guitar. Propped against the wall beside the suitcase are silver-topped walking canes, a shepherd's crook, and a washboard that Harry plays with thimbled fingertips, accompanying himself as he sings his own adaptations of jazz and music hall standards.

The washboard act is one of several that he also performs solo, and with these turns as well as the troupe, the singing, comedy and drumming, Harry is out entertaining three or four nights a week, sometimes a couple of times on the same evening. Millie, despite having had her fifth child, a daughter named Anne, in 1947, still sings with him. The fees mean that he is among the most well-off men in Highgate, and this is not something he seeks to hide. One weekend in the spring of 1948,

Winnie, Pauline, Roy, Millie and Danny, Clara and Ernie are summoned to view Harry's latest acquisition from Clarry Basinger; a black, highly polished, nine-seater Daimler limousine, complete with running boards, dicky seat and glass partition with a speaking tube between driver and passengers. Second-hand, and possibly once owned by one of the old coal owners or industrialists, it symbolises to Juggler not only his own success, but also the modern pleasures of comfort and mobility that, he believes, can be had by anyone with hard work and verve. He celebrates by putting everyone in it – Pauline in the dicky seat – and driving them to Bridlington, talking to them through the chauffeur's speaking pipe all the way there.

The Daimler replaces the motorcycle and sidecar as the Roadshow's and the family's main form of transport. On a roll, he begins bringing home other new things, clothes, animals and musical instruments, as if determined to fill the house. On Fridays he calls at Goldthorpe police station to ask if they have stray pets that need looking after over the weekend, and he comes home with a carful of creatures and a different instrument borrowed from musician friends. This means that on most Fridays, Winnie struggles into the house with her shopping to find Harry in the sitting room playing a stilted version of a popular song on, say, a trombone, or a piano-accordion, before an audience of cats, Bonzo the dog, sundry mongrels and terriers, and a box of chicks beside the Yorkshire range. He greets Winnie with a long hoot on the trombone, which makes her even more cross, because it is a trick he always has over her – diffusing tension with a joke so he seems the easy-going one and she the trouble-causer. The dafter, the more successful, he becomes, the more she comes across as the stick-in-the-mud. 'Give it a rest, Harry!' she says.

'Take no notice of her!' he says to the animals, and kisses Bonzo, or perhaps a stray Yorkshire terrier, on the lips.

*

One Saturday a few weeks after the purchase of the Daimler, Harry is out drinking at the club and Winnie is in the sitting room. She has visitors. Her mam has come up to spend the evening with her, and Sonny's wife May has joined them while the men are at the club. May, twenty-three, is demure and keen to be recognised as a woman of good taste. She doesn't say as much, but she feels like an outsider in the Dearne Valley. To her it seems a crude and frightening place, full of men who walk around in their vests and women who speak to each other harshly. The backings, with their untidiness, slanging matches and gossip, are like a little vision of hell, though of course Sonny is separate from that, his sobriety and mildness all the more striking for their rough setting. When she is with him, she feels protected and able to enjoy the one Dearne quality she admires: its sense of fun. Without Sonny she feels vulnerable and it is this vulnerability she feels now, as the sudden cries and shouts of people walking in the backings make her wince, and she notices Winnie watching her. ('I sometimes think our May does it for effect,' Winnie tells Annie later. '*I* don't think it's noisy.') It is half past ten at night, the hour of coughing men, banging privy doors, barking dogs, buckets of beer, cheerful insults, laughter in the yards and drunks singing 'Bread of Heaven'. '*Guide me,/O Thou Great Redeemer,/Pilgrim through this barren land . . .*'

Sonny comes in, beery but still quite sober, and sits on a chair at the sitting-room table and tells them who he has seen at the club and what the men's gossip is. Winnie jumps up and hides *Psychic News* under a cushion because when Harry catches her reading it, he laughs, and when he's had a drink or two he never stops. She puts on a pinny over her brown, crêpe-de-Chine dress and goes to the kitchen to prepare the bread and dripping, and listens to Sonny telling May that he hasn't seen Alf, because Alf went off to watch Juggler do a couple of songs at a pub in Bolton. 'I saw our Millie though,' he calls to Winnie. 'She said she'd come round with Danny a bit later.'

'A bit later?' says May. 'It's a quarter to eleven!'

Minutes later there is an eruption in the kitchen and the sound of two men, wheezing with laughter, falling through the door and collapsing on the floor. The yellow bone-handled knife from the dripping clatters onto the lino beside them. It is Barney and Eric Roe, one of the singers.

'Ayup Winnie,' says Barney. And Eric says, 'Sorry about that knife.'

And then Danny is coming in, stepping over Barney and Eric with a drinker's over-carefulness, and starting to sing 'The Whiffenpoof Song'. '*We're poor little lambs who have lost our way . . .*' Barney and Eric, still on the floor, harmonise. Then Barney grabs his guitar and begins to accompany him. '*We're little black sheep who have gone astray –*'

Winnie tenses slightly. Sonny, her brother, the gentleman, recognises this in her and comes into the kitchen and puts a hand on her shoulder, while joining in the singing.

'Lovely voices,' May says to Annie, thinking these men, they talk so roughly, they are so proud of their hard and filthy work, and yet when they sing it is as if their sweet, soft voices transform them; as if the brass bands, the harmonic male voice choirs and the musicians are part of a kind of spell.

In the silences between lines, through the open door comes more shouting in the backings as the men make their way home: *'Gentlemen songsters off on a spree! Damned from here to eternity!'* The sweet tenor of Juggler Hollingworth, oiled with Vicks VapoRub and pumped loud and clear with adrenaline, cuts through the sour, smokey air of the yard, and elicits cheers from the men on the floor, and from Millie who comes in behind him.

'Hello, Millie,' says May.

'Ayup, May love,' says Millie, entering the sitting room. 'You should've come wi' us tonight, we've been wi' a right crowd.'

'Give us a kiss, my love,' calls Danny, as Millie is called back to the kitchen.

'Get off me you drunken swine,' says Millie.

'Ladies and gentlemen, my lovely wife!' says Danny.

The sitting room is full: the troupe, friends, family, neighbours, a couple of turns they've met, and Roy who has crept downstairs from his bedroom. Every now and again someone mentions the troupe's new chauffeur-driven '*lim-o-zeen*', and Harry, standing in front of the range in his new, bespoke suit and pointed shoes, promises to take people out for rides in it. He shouts into the kitchen to ask where the flaming beer's got to, and then as someone begins to play the piano, he invites Annie to stand up and give them a song.

In the kitchen, Winnie is furiously sawing at the loaf and spreading the thick, uneven slices with dripping, while Millie takes platefuls of food into the sitting room. Alf comes in carrying a bucket of beer from the beer-off and sets it on the sitting-room table so that everyone can dip in glasses grabbed from Winnie's kitchen or sideboard. Through the doorway, Winnie watches Alf, and notices that he scoops up only half a glassful.

May asks Sonny to come outside to get some air with her. As they go out, two men May does not know, carrying brown glass bottles of beer, are waiting to be let in. 'We've come for t' sing-song,' says one of them.

In the yard May and Sonny lean against a wall. Voices from the backings, silver stars. A toilet flushes and Reg Spencer from next door comes out, weaving slightly. Sonny affectionately tells him to get to bed.

'Crikey, Sonny,' says May. 'Hellzapoppin!' *Hellzapoppin* is the name of a film they saw just after Sonny came back from the Merchant Navy.

'Mighty fine party,' he says.

Sonny says 'mighty fine' a lot, it being a favourite phrase of his hero Bing Crosby.

Suddenly they hear shouting from a house in the next yard down. A man curses, a woman cries out, and there is the sound of something scraping on the floor. Sonny tells a startled May that it will be Arthur Copper laying into his wife, Peggy. He always gives her a good hiding on Saturday nights.

'Somebody should stop him.'

Sonny sighs. 'Whoever does, she'll go tomorrow morning and tell them to keep their noses out.'

Another cry, scraping, a bump.

May's eyes fill up. 'Wait here,' Sonny says, and he opens the door and calls into the sitting room. 'Juggler!' Stiltingly, clumsily the singing peters out. 'Come and sort Arthur out. He's giving Peg some right hammer.'

'What have I got to do wi' it?'

Harry is not known as a fighter, but he is sometimes asked to help out because he is tall.

'She'll gi'e me hell in t' morning,' he says, but he is going now, with Alf following, steam rising from the heat of their bodies as they step into the night air. Some of the guests come out and peer over the wall as Harry goes into the next-door's yard and slaps on Arthur's door.

'Gi'o'er Arthur! Leave her!'

A guilty pause: quiet in the yards, quiet in the backings, everything still beneath the stars.

'Bugger off Juggler.'

Harry, followed by Alf and backed up by Sonny, pushes open the door. In the yellow-gold rectangle of the kitchen light, May can see a woman holding her face. She hears the rush and clatter of fighting as Harry seizes Arthur and Alf throws a saucepan of water over Arthur's head. The scuffling subsides and soon all anyone can hear is Harry telling Peggy to get to bed and leave her husband where he is.

Harry and Alf adjust their collars and ties as they go back to the party, and Harry complains that he has a wet patch on one of his best shirts. 'Come on, Nance,' he shouts to Annie, 'leave thy crystal ball alone and let's have a song!' and everyone follows in behind them, and says what a bad 'un Arthur can be when he's drunk. Harry and Annie sing 'Beautiful Green', and then he and Millie sing 'Till We Meet Again'. Winnie sits on the sofa, somehow apart, watching. She always feels awkward at parties, unless she is making the sandwiches, or tidying up. She cannot banter; she likes to talk about things, but the men and women in the room don't really talk in the way that she likes, and so she just smiles, and tries to look content, as a lady in a novel might do. As Harry, Danny, Barney, Millie and her mam sing and lark about in the centre with everyone watching them, she looks on from the margins, moving her thumbs in circles around each other.

Alf comes back in from using the privy and sits beside her on the arm of the chair, and says what a daft lot they are, and what a wonder she is, making sandwiches for them all. And when she talks to him about the parties, and the tidying up there'll be to do tomorrow, Alf looks at her and listens. These brief conversations they have are her only ones that are not about the house and family, or making food, or ironing the costumes from the flaming trunk. They are as much an indulgence to her as the beer and the singing are to Harry, who is now in the middle of the room scolding Danny and Sonny for talking about work.

'When tha's at t' pit tha talks about boozing, and when tha's boozing tha talks about t' pit! Can't tha talk about summat else for a change?'

'Can't tha get thy dress on and pull us half a pint of beer from up it?' says Danny.

Sonny drains his glass and he and May say goodbye to everyone and move towards the door, to cheers and jeers from the room. As they leave, Winnie is talking to Alf again, while Harry and Danny, centre stage in front of the range, have recommenced 'The Whiffenpoof Song'. When May turns back to shut the door she sees Alf moving closer to Winnie, so close that their knees are touching, as Harry sings the last words in his ugly but beautiful gap-toothed tenor: *'God have mercy on such as we! Baa baa baa.'*

The party ends at three. The next morning, Peggy Copper comes round and tells Juggler to mind his own flaming business.

17

The Likes of Us

Highgate and Thurnscoe, 1948

One day not long after the party, another, older visitor comes to 34 Highgate Lane.

It is a Saturday morning. Harry is out on the allotment and Winnie has gone on the bus to Doncaster with Comfort Eades, chasing stories of meat in the shops. In the sitting room, Roy is listening to the radio and seven-year-old Pauline is trying to get him to play with her. Pauline has a compendium of games that her mam gave her for Christmas. In the heavy, green cardboard box are enough boards and counters to allow for a hundred different games (there were also playing cards but these have been thrown away by Harry because of their association with gambling, which he will not allow in the house). She loves the boards: they are thick, glossy and elegantly bound at the edges, and she wishes the family could all sit round together and play, but no one ever has the time. She has devised many ways of playing snakes and ladders, Ludo and draughts, on her own, but now she tries Roy again.

'Gi'o'er, our nip,' he says, 'I'm reading.' He always calls her 'our nip', because she is younger than him. She hates it because 'nip' is what people who were in the war call the Japanese, and the Japanese were cruel.

'*Please.*'

'Gi'o'er whinin'.'

'I only asked you to play with me.'

Looking annoyed, he gets up and comes over. As they work their way through the box, he cheats, surreptitiously moving counters and dice. Eventually Pauline notices and complains, and Roy, affecting to be hurt, goes back to sit beside the radio. She puts all the pieces back into their box and sits on her own at the table, staring at the distemper on the walls.

She is still staring when she hears the back door open, and a rustling noise, and then her great-grandmother Juggler Jane comes in the room. Jane says it is just a social call and she will stay and have a warm while she waits for Winnie to come home. Moving to stand in front of the remains of the fire, which Roy was supposed to keep going but hasn't, she looks into the embers and absently fingers the beads of the rosary at her waist. The beads make a tiny clicking sound, and as she works through them the crucifix jerks about against her skirts. Pauline watches, transfixed.

'What are you doing with them beads, Granny Jane?' she asks.

'I'm getting ready, love,' says Jane. 'I'm just getting ready.'

Roy, making a show of irritation at their talking, gets up and goes out, and Jane turns to look at Pauline. She smiles down on her, and notices the little girl's eyes on the beads.

'Do you like my rosary, love?' she asks.

'Ooh yes.'

'It's for talking to t' spirits. Would you like to see it?'

Pauline's mouth stays open, and she nods.

The old lady unfastens it from her waist, loops up the long black length, and puts it carefully and deliberately into Pauline's hands.

'Take care of it, won't you?'

Pauline silently takes the rosary and touches the beads one by one, saving the crucifix until last. Jane watches her again, and puts a hand on her great-granddaughter's head.

'I love it,' says Pauline.

The front door opens. Winnie is back, bags empty. 'There was only horsemeat,' she says. 'We thought we'd rather not bother.'

'Look, Mam,' says Pauline, and shows her the rosary.

'I was just showing it to her,' says Jane.

'Right,' says Winnie, with suspicion in her voice. 'It's beautiful.'

*

A few weeks later, in the middle of a rainy night, there is a knock at the door of Juggler Jane's cottage. She rises from her bed and on the doorstep finds a girl of about fifteen clutching a thin coat around her and shivering. Jane knows her as the granddaughter of an old friend who has moved up the valley to Thurnscoe. She asks her in.

'My nan's sent me,' she tells Jane. 'It's my mam, she's having a baby and my nan dun't think she's right.'

Jane tells her to go back home, and says that she will follow. She puts herbs and bandages into a bag and walks through the rain in to the woman's house, where she delivers the baby, and walks home again. Not long after this Jane falls ill. When Winnie takes Pauline to visit her in the cottage they find Jane lying quiet and pale in an iron bedstead in a cold room dimmed by drawn primrose-yellow curtains.

The following week, Jane dies peacefully at the Montagu Hospital in Mexborough. She leaves behind a brown paper parcel with a note in her will saying it is to be given to Pauline. Inside the paper is a smooth leather pouch, and inside that, the spirit rosary. Pauline tips it out and runs it through her fingers; it feels cool and old and important. This is the only thing she has ever been given by someone who was not her immediate family, the first object besides a toy that she has owned in her life. She thinks of a prayer for Juggler Jane and then pretends she knows enough people to have a separate prayer for each of the lovely, black beads.

*

One Sunday about a month later, Pauline is outside with the other kids from Highgate Lane. They are playing at the top of the lane, on a wide apron of concrete and asphalt in front of the beer-off, the chip shop and Sal Brown's sweet shop. Some of the children are eating toffee, because on Saturday Sal had somehow acquired a full slab to sell. It tastes like margarine, but everyone eats it anyway and imagines it tastes pleasant.

Pauline has a small waxed bagful and is fending off her friend Alma Taylor. 'I'm not giving you any, Alma. Your mam got all them bananas at Mrs Wilde's shop, so don't come cadging off me.' She walks away a little and looks at the cows in Benny Slater's field. You were only allowed to have two bananas but Mrs Taylor had somehow got four, to the irritation of the other women in the street. Alma says Pauline is a misery, and then chalks out a hopscotch cross.

'I love them cows,' says Pauline.

'Chewing like you,' says Alma. She is pleased with this observation, but Pauline ignores it.

'I'd love to live on a farm.'

'*Tchaw!*' said Alma, as if living on a farm was like living on the moon. 'It'd smell.'

'I wouldn't be bothered about smells,' said Pauline.

'But *you'd* smell.'

'I could have a bath.'

'Not every flipping night you couldn't. Come and play hopscotch.'

Pauline spins on her heel slowly and walks over to join the game. As she waits for her go, a young woman pushing a big blue pram comes down the street and leaves the pram outside the beer-off while she goes inside. Pauline thinks the pram is beautiful and walks over to admire it. She looks in at the baby, a girl of about six months old in a soft woollen suit, and watches the rise and fall of her body as she sleeps.

The bell clangs. The woman steps out of the shop, adjusting her shopping bag.

'Get away from that pram!' she shouts.

It takes a moment for Pauline to understand that the woman is shouting at her. 'I'm sorry,' says Pauline, not knowing what else to say.

'I don't want the likes of you round my baby,' says the woman.

Some people in Highgate have very clear ideas about their status in relation to other people, particularly with reference to where they live. They can distinguish not only between individual streets and the top and bottom ends of villages, but also the ends and sides of each street. The streets have their own complicated and subtle social geography. Barnsley Road has higher status because it is a main road, and its residents include shopkeepers and Mr Legget, who sets broken bones at the Montagu Hospital. Highgate Lane considers itself respectable, its people believe that the common residents, if there can be said to be any, live only at the other end of the street to themselves.

So 'the likes of you' comes as a shock to Pauline, because via books, radio and comics, the phrase connects her to miscreants and criminals. And when someone like this woman, who you assume has a sort of authority by virtue of living on Barnsley Road, makes that sort of comment, the feelings you have are complicated. You ask yourself, if you appear like that, does it mean the unpleasantness is in you, somehow? This is one reason that your appearance and cleanliness is important; it makes you feel less vulnerable.

She looks up the road to see if she can see her dad coming back, but there is no sign of him. 'I'm off in,' she tells Alma, and says 'ta-ra' under her breath to the cow.

*

In the sitting room Winnie and Alf, who has come back early from the pub, are talking about Juggler Jane. 'T' closest I ever had to a real mam or dad,' Alf is saying. 'I feel strange without her, Winnie.' He seems close to crying and Winnie looks almost as though she could cry for him. Since Jane died, they have been spending a lot more time together. Alf is bereft; Winnie, full of pity, seems to enjoy trying to help him.

The radio burbles in the background and there is a faint, bitter tang of coffee. Last week Marian Lawson had got some two-ounce tins of Nescafé instant coffee, looking modern and luxurious in their maroon and primrose tins. Nescafé (which everyone pronounces Nescaff, or Nescaffy) is far nicer and more exotic than Camp coffee, which is what Winnie has always bought. Winnie treats the Nescafé as a great luxury, using as little as possible, carefully measuring it out in a teaspoon, and shaking the tin after so none sticks to the sides. She and Alf are both sipping at their cups when Pauline comes in.

'What you been doing, flower?' says Alf.

'Playing,' says Pauline. 'Hopscotch. And watching t' cows in Benny Slater's field.' She is hoping someone wants to talk about the cows, but neither Alf nor Win seems interested. 'Can I have some coffee?' she asks.

'Aye go on then,' says Winnie. 'While I do it, fetch your rosary and show it to our Alf.'

Pauline runs upstairs to her room, finds the rosary in its pouch, and tips it out. It slithers heavily then tumbles all at once into her palm. She imagines Granny Jane and says some quick words to the Virgin Mary on the beads, unsure if they are right or not, but liking the saying of them.

Winnie shouts upstairs to hurry her. Downstairs a small cup of Nescafé is sitting on the table.

'Let's have a look at it,' says Winnie. The two adults pore over the rosary as Pauline drinks her coffee. When she has finished, Winnie tells her to go out and play. This always means the grown-ups want to talk privately, and she has no choice but to go outside again. This time she walks through the backings, past the allotments, and out onto a footpath through the fields on the west side of the village. She stops to watch rabbits running on the path ahead of her, and picks a little bunch of buttercups to take home, and then sits for a while thinking about the woman with the baby in the pram.

When she gets back to the house, Alf has gone. There is a little pile of plates and cutlery in the sink and the smell of coffee has been replaced by the trace of beer, meaning that her dad is home. He'll be upstairs having a lie down on the bed. Winnie is sitting on the settee, staring into space. She looks at Pauline, but says nothing.

Pauline senses the absence in the room before she even asks.

'Where's my rosary, Mam?'

'I've given it to our Alf.'

She is trying to sound aloof, but her daughter can hear the guilty embarrassment in her voice. 'Jane was like a mother to him, and *you* don't want it.'

'I do want it.' Pauline is not supposed to argue with adults, but this time she doesn't care.

Winnie scoffs. 'What you want that for?'

'So has our Alf got it?'

'Yes, I told you he has.'

'Can I have it back?'

'Don't you dare ask him for it back. You'll feel the back of my hand if you do.'

A feeling of unreality comes over Pauline, heightened by the jolly music on the radio. She nods and feels her lip wobble.

'Don't start that,' says Winnie.

Pauline sits down and drops the flowers on the table. She knows the emotion she is feeling: it is hatred. Some people remember the first time they feel hatred as well as they remember the first feeling of love, and Pauline will remember this moment all her life. Relating the story to her own, grown-up children fifty years later, she will feel the same keenness as she does now, although it will be hardened off, and her lip will not wobble. By then, she will know that this is the point from which her relationship with her mother began to deteriorate. At the time it is the selfishness she loathes the most; she knows that her mother has taken the rosary because she wants to give a gift to Alf, and that she had to take from Pauline because she had nothing of her own to give him, and no one else she could take from. It is not Winnie's abuse of power that Pauline dislikes so much as the weakness that gave her the idea in the first place.

Pauline is so disgusted and furious that she barely speaks to her mam for a month. When she awakes early one morning, when her dad is on earlies at the pit, and comes downstairs to see her nightgowned mother slipping into the front room – the room that contains Alf's bed – she thinks nothing of it beyond being reminded that her mam has taken the most beautiful object she has ever seen.

*

Pauline does not give up the idea of finding the spirit rosary and one afternoon, when her mam has gone out to the shops and the house is empty, she pads carefully into the front room to look for it. She is nervous. Alf's man's clothes and possessions seem so big and smell so unpleasantly of hair oil and feet that she is soon put off, and decides to search her mam and dad's room instead. She hunts on the dressing table and lifts layers of clothing folded on a chair. She opens up the wardrobe and looks onto the top shelf, timidly because this is one of the domestic frontiers of adulthood, like the *News of the World* and the club. Nothing.

Checking the net-curtained window every few minutes for her mam coming down the street, she looks under the bed and in the bedside cabinet, and then turns and crouches before the chest of drawers in which Winnie keeps her clothes and underclothes. With her heart beating hard she eases out the middle drawer and parts the blouses with her hand. There is a postcard of Bridlington in one corner, but that is all. In the top drawer just stockings and underwear, and in the bottom sweaters, a couple of scarves, and – wait, there in the back corner, what is it? A brown paper bag, which can't have the rosary in, can it? Whatever it is seems the wrong shape. Pauline takes out the bag, gently and quietly, and looks inside. Loosely coiled at the bottom, like a small, short snake, is a dark red rubber syringe. She does not know what it is, but thinks it must be secret. Is it to use on Winnie, or on one of the family? Is it a secret from her dad as well? She feels that she should not have seen it; she places the bag as she found it, worrying that she has not remembered exactly how it was, closes the drawer and slips out of the room. She is halfway down the stairs when she hears her mam coming in the back door.

*

Weeks later, Pauline is playing on her own in the sitting room on a dull Saturday afternoon. Winnie tells her to go out to play in the yard, while, unusually, she brings the tin bath inside and begins heating the water. Pauline has a child's sense of wariness in the disruption of routine and does not ask why her mam is having a bath on a Saturday afternoon. She sits and reads a book beneath the kitchen window, and then goes out to play in the yard. After what seems a long time for a bath, she hears Winnie stirring inside, and then the sound of water coming through the pipes, and then sees some light steam coming from the angled lead pipe that draws the kitchen sink into the yard grate. The water must have been very hot, and Winnie must be tipping the water down the sink in jugfuls, which is unusual.

When it comes out of the pipe, the steaming water is a light, cloudy pink. The kids crowd around it.

'It's blood!' shouts one of the girls. 'It is! It's blood!'

Pauline also thinks it looks like blood but, mortified by the attention and embarrassment, she says no, no it isn't, her mam's dyeing some curtains inside. This works. The children disperse, and she goes in.

Pauline notices her mam seems dazed, and her face and arms are a pale grey colour. Winnie sits down in her chair and stares into the fireplace, without saying a word.

18

Get It Out of My Face

Manvers Main Colliery, 1948

One morning in June 1948, Harry is out in one of the underground districts of the Silkstone seam at Manvers Main, wiring up explosive shots to blast away rock for the advancing roadway. Labouring in dim, shadowy electric light, and stripped topless because of the heat, he and his small group of men can hear as they work the dense, crumpling sounds of explosions and rock falls from other shot-firing in different parts of the mine. The first time Harry heard the noise he was a teenager, and thought it meant the pit was collapsing and he was about to be buried alive.

Talking about the women in the clubs, who is on the fiddle, the glass-backed devils on this shift, Harry waits for his mate to bore holes into the wet rock with a heavy, shoulder-mounted drill.

'Did tha do Mother Riley a' Sat'd'y then, Juggler?'

'Aye.' Juggler is serious and shy sometimes when asked directly about his act.

'Did tha drink that half-pint of beer?'

'I'm not telling thee how I do it, so don't bother asking.' This is how everyone begins trying to get it out of him.

'We shall be finding out one of these days. We allus find out, don't we lads?'

'I'll find thee out if tha don't get yon holes cleaned out. Shut thy rattle and get some work done.'

Harry checks for gas with his safety lamp, then takes greenish-brown sticks of explosive from a box and pushes them into one of the holes. Then he adds a detonator with a long lead and uses a rod to push that and the explosive to the bottom of the hole, leaving the lead hanging out. When he has filled all the holes like this, he connects the leads in a circuit and, with the nonchalant attention to detail of someone dealing with danger that they can control, connects that circuit to a roll of electric cable. He takes the men down the roadway to set them as sentries, checks again for gas, and connects the electrical cable to an exploder. From somewhere in the pit comes the muffled crump of other shot-firing, and the roof and floor shake around him.

'Firing!'

Harry crouches down in a hollow in the tunnel wall, winds the exploder's handle until its green light illuminates, and pushes down the plunger.

*

While Harry is waiting for electricity to pass through the cable to the explosives, Winnie is at home, perhaps at that moment serving Alf Hollingworth his breakfast at the table in the sitting room. She has not begun her affair with Alf flippantly. She has been married almost twenty years, but feels haunted by her father's prediction that she would struggle to find happiness with Harry. She had wanted not only to love her husband but also to nurture him, and even if he couldn't love her the same way she would have liked to feel that she was helping him. At this time, however, she feels ignored and taken for granted. And then into her home, via the brother she so loves, had come a man who talked to her and flattered her. Though he is so much younger than her – thirteen years – the attraction is founded less on lust than on a sort of romantic compassion. The gypsy girl understands and says she is right to feel as she does. This is a romance such as you might find in the cinema, or in books.

*

'Misfire,' says Harry. '*Damn* it.' He winds the detonator and pulls up the handle for a second try. Nothing. Must be a wire broken somewhere.

As he calls 'misfire' the sentries' bodies relax. Harry delicately uncouples the wires from the detonator so that the explosives cannot go off. He walks through the darkness, his helmet light dancing a white dot on the tunnel sides, feeling the cable for damage as he goes. Sweat with its fine suspension of dust drips into his eyes. From somewhere in the pit come more muffled booms and the noise of machinery. He reaches the blast face, and begins checking the leads in the circuit.

There is a bright white light, then nothing. He awakes to feel a hard surface behind his head. It is the floor, rattling with men's boots running, getting louder. Dust swirls. Raising his hand to his head he feels hot wetness.

'Juggler!'

The explosives have detonated. The men's voices sound distant behind the high-pitched hum in his ears. His skin burns, his torso, head and arms hurt and, worse than anything else, his face feels as if it has thousands of hot needles sticking into it. The men gather around him, frightened, their lamps shining on him.

'Clean my face,' he tells his mate. 'Get it out of my face, whatever you can.'

The blast has driven stars of rock and coal into his pale face and body. The men clean him with water from their Dudleys, carry him on a stretcher to the pit bottom and take him to the surface in the cage. Bright sunlight on the scurry from shaft side to first-aid room; a black police car and an ambulance waiting. All around and above are gigantic, smoking pipes, headgears, elevated cableways carrying muck to the muckstacks, and piles of timber and steel girders. There are coal preparation plants, coke ovens, railway sidings, science labs and office blocks, and, amid all this, run the small, insignificant black figures carrying Harry Hollingworth on a stretcher. The pit doctor calmly tidies him up, and then he is loaded into an ambulance and sped away to the Montagu Hospital for treatment.

There is an inquiry into every serious accident at a colliery, but the management at Manvers will never establish what detonated Harry's explosives. Perhaps he had not pulled the wires far enough from the detonator and they had sprung back and touched. More likely, Harry will think, someone didn't realise he had gone to check the circuit and reconnected the wires, but would not admit it to the investigators. With no conclusive proof discovered, Harry Hollingworth's injuries enter history as a mystery, a riddle or, in official language, 'Cause Unknown'.

*

Winnie knows there has been an accident as soon as she sees the policeman talking to Alf at the front door. You don't consciously expect your husband to be hurt in the pit, but as soon as it happens you realise how often you've imagined it. Her actions feel automatic. Once the policeman has explained what's happened, and that Mr Hollingworth is satisfactory but in hospital, she takes off her pinny and combs her hair, and Alf takes the keys from the sideboard drawer and drives her to the hospital in the Daimler.

Some miners take pride in their blue coal scars, but not Juggler Hollingworth. In several sessions over two days and nights, nurses, many of them the daughters of miners themselves, work at his face with a scrubbing brush and use long steel tweezers to pick out coal from his bloody face, arms and torso. He clamps shut his remaining teeth and screws up his eyes, and between the pickings and the brushings, nurses re-bandage and patch him, and take him out to smoke cigarettes. At the end, when they have taken all but the smallest blue grains from his face, his upper body is pocked with small raw, bloody holes and cuts, and his face is scabby, bruised and pitted. In the soft white skin of his inner arms there are small blue and black constellations where the presence of blood vessels has made it impossible to tweeze out the coal. Years from now these arms will be playthings to his grandchildren who will clamour for a look ('Show us t' coal in your arms, Grandad!') when they visit. Now, though, when his own children come to see him they look afraid. Roy is discomfited and quiet, and Pauline cries.

The nurses clear Harry's face so that it heals intact. There are just a few scattered, pinprick pieces left and one small midnight-blue smudge in his hairline. At the end, as the last nurse leans over to bandage him, she pauses and says, 'I have to ask you this, Mr Hollingworth.'

He looks up.

'Are you the one who does that trick with that half-pint of beer?'

'Yes, I am,' he says. 'But I'm not telling thee how I do it.'

19

The Broken Thumb

Highgate, 1948

Winnie is filling a bucket with coal at the Hollingworths' brick bunker one evening later that summer when she sees Alf come into the yard from the backings. He has been on earlies and his skin is lightly tanned from being out on the allotment in the sun. He smiles at her. 'Let me carry that for thee, Win.'

She tips a final shovelful of black cobbles into the bucket, closes the bunker, and smiles back. 'Thank you, love. What've you done to your hand?'

His right hand and wrist are heavily bandaged.

'I broke me thumb at t' pit, trapped it in some belting. It's nowt.'

Win takes the hand in hers. 'It doesn't look like nowt.'

'It's alright. They strapped it up for me.' He reaches for the bucket handle and they stand for a moment. 'You'd better come in for a cup of tea,' she says.

The house is empty: Harry at the club, Roy out cycling, Pauline playing in the backings. Alf places the coal by the hearth and goes over to her as she fills the kettle in the kitchen. He does not touch her, and she does not speak.

'Is tha alright, Winnie?'

She stares into the sink. He seems to know before she says it.

After she tells him they are quiet, silent as the knives in the sideboard.

'Is tha sure it's . . .'

'No. I think so, but I don't know.'

She doesn't know, and she never will. The child she is carrying could be Harry's. But she wants it to be Alf's.

'Well, that's good enough for me.'

'What do you mean?'

'I love you, Winnie. I want us to go away and get married.'

She does not cry. Her experience and her nature have made her almost vain about her endurance in the way that some women can be vain about beauty. She had borne her father's belt across her bare back, and she would bear this.

'Come away with me, Win.' He seems almost excited.

'How could I do that?'

'We could, couldn't we? We could go to t' coast, or go and get a little house in Nottingham. Our Harry doesn't deserve thee, so why should tha have to stay?'

'What about our Roy and Pauline?'

'You'd still see them. We could come back.'

There it is: just leave your kids, and we'll come back to visit them. He is, she thinks, a young man, twenty-six to her thirty-nine years. He has a childishness that she both pities and covets.

'I can't leave my kids. It doesn't matter what Harry's like. You can't ask me to do that, love.' She says she loves him; she says she would like to go with him, but not now. 'One day, when they're grown up. Come back and fetch me.'

'I will.'

'Will you?'

'Yes,' he says. 'I will. I promise.'

They reach the end of the conversation sooner than either would have guessed. Moving away from the window they embrace. It is ending so quickly, far more quickly than it would in one of Winnie's novels.

'I shall go and tell Harry now,' he says. 'And then I shall go away until I come to get you.'

Harry: she had wondered how to tell him. But now, right at the end, Alf is looking after her again. She feels grateful, and afraid.

*

Alf pushes through the club doors into roaring noise, heat and smoke. Men call greetings to him as he passes them, but he barely acknowledges them. He finds Harry at the bar, performing to a small, laughing crowd. His face still has fading bruises and red marks from the explosion, and there is the blue scar in his hairline. He delivers a punchline, and then looks up. 'Ayup, it's our Alf! Does tha want a drink, sirree?'

'Aye, alright –'

'That's a pity, cos if tha'd been here five minutes since, I were buying a round.'

The men laugh. The steward asks Alf what he's having, but Alf ignores him.

'Can I have a word with thee, Harry?'

'Is tha cadging money again?' The men listen for the punchline, but Alf leans in and then says, 'I need a word, Harry, serious.'

'Bloody hell,' says Harry. 'Wait here, lads, I'm just going to consult my stockbroker.'

They move away from the bar to a less crowded area near the billiard table. Harry looks bemused. Alf lowers his voice and says, 'Harry. Winnie's pregnant, and it's mine.'

Harry places his pint glass on a table and wipes his mouth. He says nothing. It is Alf who cracks first. 'What's tha got to say then?'

'I think tha's got a bloody cheek coming in here to tell me that, that's what,' he says. 'But never mind what I've got to say. I'd say it's thee that's got t' explaining to do.'

Alf confesses: the attraction, the conversations, the mornings when Harry was at work and the kids were at school. He tries to bring the exchange to a climax. 'Look, I've a broken thumb. If tha wants to go outside, I'll fight thee with one hand behind my back. That's fair because it's what I deserve.'

Harry studies his young cousin as someone might study a small child threatening to fight an adult.

'I don't want to go outside, Alf. What I want is for thee to get out my sight.'

'Well, I will then. But I'll tell thee one more thing: I've asked her to come away with me, but she won't come because of t' kids. So I'll go away from her, and you won't see me again, and I shan't tell anyone about any of it.'

'That's right big of you, cousin . . .'

'But there's one more thing, Harry. If you lay one finger on her, or them kids, I shall find out and I shall come back and I shall kill thee. I mean it.'

'Get out.'

'I mean it, Harry.'

'Out!'

*

Later that night, muffled bangs and shouting downstairs at Number 34 wake Pauline and Roy Hollingworth in their beds. Their dad accuses, their mam counter-accuses. A glass smashes against a wall, there is a lull, then the shouting begins again. Pauline gingerly comes downstairs and eases open the door. Her mam is shouting at her dad, something about his other women.

'Please stop it, Mam.'

Win glares at her. 'I should have known you'd take his side.'

'I'm not on anybody's side. I just don't want you to fall out.'

Harry stands by the fireplace, swaying. He stares at Pauline. Winnie effortlessly retakes control, sends Pauline back to bed, and then goes upstairs herself. For the next two weeks she and Harry do not speak to each other, addressing the other through either Roy or Pauline.

Alf leaves the Dearne Valley, taking the spirit rosary with him. Knowing the baby may be his, Harry accepts it as his own. Winnie believes Alf will come back; his vow is a promise of salvation, the child an embodiment of that promise. She tells this to no one until 1958, when she confesses to a new friend that, whatever Harry thinks, she has for ten years been thinking of the day in the far-off future when Alf will return to rescue her.

20

In Blood and Sand

Highgate, 1949; Suez Canal Zone, Egypt, 1952–53

Lynda Clare Hollingworth, Winnie's baby, is born at 34 Highgate Lane on 10 January 1949. Millie, Olive, Annie and Pauline say she looks just like her mam: her mother fingers the lay of the little girl's hair at the temple and thinks of Alf. Harry remains cool towards his wife, but treats the baby as his own, dancing her in the air to the radio and taking her out into the garden to look across at the fields, just as he had done Pauline and Roy.

In the months that follow, the Hollingworths and Parkins move into new work and change routines as the pinched, post-war pessimism gradually lifts, and food and fuel shortages become less frequent. Annie, sixty-two and with unevenly dyed greying hair, moves to Elland near Halifax, where she lives near her third daughter, Olive, in a one-room cellar flat, and supplements her pension with sittings, sock-knitting and occasional wins on the horses. To the envy of their friends and relatives, Millie and Danny and their children move from Highgate Lane into a new prefab in Bolton-upon-Dearne, while their eldest Brian moves to Newmarket to train as a jockey.

Harry, taking his accident as a kind of warning, resigns from the pit and works first as a builder on new coke ovens at Manvers Main, then as a driver on the penny-a-ride pit bus, and finally as a lorry driver for the glassworks in Swinton, a small town to the south of Bolton-upon-Dearne, delivering empty bottles and jars to pop factories, breweries, whisky distilleries and pickle plants. He enjoys the work, and soon he will say that as far as he is concerned the government should fill in every pit in the country and close them all for good. With his accident compensation money he buys a fur coat for Winnie, a Sobell radio and, at £98 (the bulk of the money), a fourteen-inch television set. The television occupies the space once taken by the piano, which they sell. It is the second television set on Highgate Lane, the first having been bought a few months previously by Johnny Keane, a comedian with the Mother Riley Roadshow. Roy, Pauline and the other children from the street have been standing outside Johnny's house in the early evening, trying to see the rumoured black-and-white figures glowing through the net curtains like ghostly apparitions.

The Hollingworth television is a novelty and a big draw for the family and neighbours, who treat it as a domestic version of a cinema, something to be watched together and to dress up for. When Annie comes to stay she watches the TV in much the same way as she experiences Spirit at a sitting; she knows the presenters can't see her, but she feels she has a relationship with them. Like Granny Illingworth, Comfort and Nelly, she feels compelled to put on her best clothes and pat her hair into shape, and lower her voice in the presenters' presence because they speak with such refinement and wear evening dress. The ladies always sit up nicely when the television comes on.

'They can't see thee, Nelly!' says Harry.

'I know, Juggler!' she replies, but still sounds unsure.

Nelly wouldn't defer to bosses or gentry, but the television screen makes her awed and gullible.

*

Roy, now in his late teens, is fanatical about the television set and the radio, and to Pauline and Winnie at least, he embodies a new public mood that comes with television, better-stocked shops and plentiful money. He is tall like his father, a fast talker and wide and lean in the chest from weightlifting and cycling. Dark hair, thick moustache, blue eyes: girls like him and he is courting the best catch in Highgate, June Lancaster, an auburn Bette Davis beauty from a well-off and well-respected family. If Winnie had hoped that he would settle down at Bolton-upon-Dearne senior school, a tall-windowed 1930s building where Roy's year was the first intake after it became a secondary modern, she was disappointed. Indifferent to lessons other than woodwork, metalwork and history, Roy, it seemed to his mother, liked to withdraw into a private world of books, comics and motorcycles. He befriended a boy known as Humpy Gascoigne, so called because he had a mild curvature of the spine. Humpy's father ran a scrap business near Highgate's marshalling yards, and the pair taught themselves to dismantle and repair old Vincents, BSAs and Royal Enfields given to them by Mr Gascoigne. Harry thought the Gascoignes were mucky and idle, and banned Roy from associating with 'the hump-backed little bugger', but Roy took no notice. He lied about where he was going, and spent most of his spare time in the Gascoigne's yard, or at home reading stories from military history.

When he talked to other boys from school or Highgate Lane, Roy told them he had grand ambitions which would materialise with or without the help of teachers at school. He was going to travel and get a good job that would take him away from Highgate. He wasn't going down the pit, nor living in a pit village: he wanted to be where people didn't crowd together and find comfort in being like everyone else. When *The Secret Life of Walter Mitty* came to the Dearne's cinema screens the boys, particularly the ones from the grammar school, started calling him Mitty Hollingworth, but Roy couldn't care less. One day, he said, he would just get on a motorbike and take off to travel the world, never to return. Either that or he would join the Army.

*

After leaving school at fifteen, Roy did go to work at Highgate pit, but he left after four months to work at another scrap-metal yard in Highgate. The scrap business was prospering because of the replacement of old plant in the pit yards. Roy learnt to operate a crane and was paid a good wage of £3 17 shillings a week. With the money he had left after paying board to Winnie he set about a course of self-improvement involving Charles Atlas magazine subscriptions, membership of the

Clarion Club and an acquired appreciation of jazz. Harry taught him to drive the family Daimler. In his late teens, he sees himself as a free spirit. His desire to get out of the nosey, backward Dearne Valley and see the world is, he thinks, a feeling that links him to other progressive people such as he hears on the radio or sees on the TV. At six o'clock every Saturday, after the family has shared fish and chips for tea, and Harry is smoking a cigarette and thinking about going to get a wash, Roy sits beside the radio, eyes closed, listening to *Jazz Club* and imagining himself far away and in better company. Pauline complains about the din and his dad grumbles about some of the modern tunes, but Roy ignores them and plans his adventures. All he needs is an opportunity.

The Army is his easiest escape route, and when his mam tells her stories about Walter in the Great War, he tells her he might join up before he's due for National Service. Merely considering this, he feels, sets him apart from the valley drudges, so he enjoys discussing it. Winnie is unsure and tells him to take care. However much she wishes otherwise, she knows Roy is not like her father, and worries that he has too much Hollingworth in him. Walter had an instinct for discipline and self-sacrifice but Roy is a seeker of experience and pleasure. She is not certain that discipline and self-sacrifice can be learned. 'They say the Army makes or breaks them,' she warns. 'Be careful.' Roy nods, but privately puts her comments down to a lack of imagination.

*

In the summer of 1951, the Army comes to Roy Hollingworth in the form of his National Service call-up. On arriving at Catterick, he holds back his jazz attitude and he and the Army get along well. 'Good build, fairly intelligent, and generally a moderate scholar,' the officer assessing him notes; 'healthy interests. Sensible, cooperative manner.' After eighteen weeks of training he is assigned to the Royal Tank Regiment at Tidworth, on the eastern edge of Salisbury Plain, and shortly after that is sent to the Suez Canal Zone in Egypt.

Soldiers who Roy talks to say the Canal Zone is the worst posting in the Army, worse even than Korea. It is a long hot strip of RAF bases, small towns and Army camps running alongside the canal and its tributaries in the Egyptian desert. After the end of the Second World War, Britain had kept its forces in the Canal Zone and retained control of the canal and its approaches, but in October 1951 the Egyptian government revoked its treaty allowing Britain to maintain its bases. There has been fighting between British and Egyptian forces, and between British soldiers and Egyptian civilians: local people are hostile because of the British government's support for the creation of the State of Israel, while the British and the Americans are concerned that the Soviet Union is gaining power in the region by supporting Egypt. And all the politicians want access to Middle Eastern oil because it is a cheaper fuel than coal.

Brimful of bluster, Private Roy Hollingworth, Army No. 22494282, 4th Royal Tank Regiment, leaves on a troopship from Liverpool, the first member of the family to travel abroad since Walter Parkin went to the Western Front. He is stationed at Shandur Camp, a mass of tents on the western bank of the Suez Canal, near a small town called Fayed. From inside the camp he can see across to the Egyptian territory in the Sinai Desert bank, where soldiers, cars and the occasional tank come and go in the shimmering daytime heat, and at night people randomly fire off rounds across the water. This is active service and discipline is strict; the days under the limp regimental and Union flags are spent on drills, training, guard patrols, parades, and scrimming up vehicles with yellow camouflage net. The canal stinks. The drinking water, brought in by escorted tanker because the filtration plant has been blown up, tastes of chlorine. There are no dances and no women. There are only risky trips into Fayed, drinking your weekly pay in the form of the thin, gassy Egyptian beer, and telling each other stories about the murdered soldiers' bodies dragged from the fetid canals.

Roy studies the tanks, learns to build bridges, and trains to get his gunner's trade certificate. In the evenings he takes his chances in Fayed with his best mate, a Northamptonshire lad called John McNeill, and enjoys himself. Some of the men at the base say the bloody wogs'll slit your throat as soon as look at you, but Roy and John banter with the street traders, and bargain for lighters, watches, dirty postcards, duty-free cameras and drinks in exchange for British postal orders. The traders smile at Roy and dub him Gary Cooper. He ventures into areas that are supposed to be too dangerous for British soldiers to walk around in, and encounters no trouble. The life is hard, but for all the rough living, sandstorms, dysentery and danger, in the first few months of his service in Egypt, Roy feels as fulfilled as he ever will in his life.

Then one morning a long column of Egyptian tanks, field guns and troop carriers comes down the road on the Sinai side of the canal and lines up opposite Shandur, guns pointing across the water. Shandur camp mobilises; officers shout orders, and young soldiers scurry between machines, the sun-ripened smell of the canal now overlaid by the smell of oil and diesel. The men move the tanks and guns to their canal bank, pointing back. Just a show, a sergeant tells Roy, they're always doing it, but the younger soldiers are afraid, and so is Roy. The Egyptian tanks are Soviet-made and, as Roy will tell people when he goes home, he feels as if a world war could be started by someone accidentally leaving off a rifle's safety catch.

After two days the British bring in more armour and the outnumbered Egyptians move off in a long, dusty column. The danger seems to have passed, but now at night, when the temperature drops, the roadways seem full of shadows and any movement feels threatening. Roy's patrol is shot at. Armoured vehicles with their hatches open have grenades tossed in, and someone inside has to calmly pick them up and sling them out again. At the end of patrols, Roy is twitching from the adrenaline and cannot sleep until he has killed it with gassy beer and stories.

There is another story, one that he tells no one until thirty years after his return from Egypt. In this one, he and another soldier are patrolling on foot somewhere outside the camp in the cold desert night when they hear gunshots. The man beside him cries out, and falls to the ground. Roy carries him back to the camp, but the man later dies. To deaden the shock Roy drinks beer until he is blind drunk. When Roy tells his daughter this story in the 1980s, he will be an alcoholic capable of drinking a bottle of vodka before 11 a.m., and the story will be offered as explanation. He will say he learned to drink to forget when he was in Egypt, and that he still drinks to make himself forget the things he saw there. Most of his family will be sceptical about this claim, and certainly if he wrote home about such experiences then Winnie and Harry did not receive the letters. The little mail that does arrive from him is upbeat and bullish. The story they will remember best is about a black-robed young woman who, one night in Fayed, thrust a baby at Roy and asked for half a crown. 'He says he went into a town,' they tell people who ask how their son is getting on in the Army, 'and an Arab woman tried to sell him her baby! For 2/6!'

When Roy returns to the Dearne Valley on terminal leave in the early summer of 1953, he comes as the conquering hero, greeting the family with a *Salaam!* around the back door, and introducing John McNeill, whom he has brought back because it's John's birthday that week and Roy thinks that they should give him a party. He distributes gifts of watches and jewellery to the family, and claims to have been mistaken for Max Bygraves on the train. He tells jokes and stories about tanks lined up along the Suez Canal, and of men getting their throats slit. He takes John out drinking, and he organises the party with Winnie. And then after three days he leaves again, taking John with him, and telling no one when he will be back, or where he is going. The family will not hear from him for several months, this being the beginning of a pattern of unpredictable departures and absences that will continue for much of his life. When Winnie is older she will feel that she knows what to blame for it. 'I told him,' she will say, 'I said the Army makes them or it breaks them. And when it came to our Roy, it broke him.'

21

Stars

Highgate, 1953

As soon as the date of Queen Elizabeth's coronation is announced after the death of her father, King George VI, in February 1952, the women of Highgate form a committee to raise money to celebrate with a party. Through the winter and spring Winnie and Granny Illingworth go from house to house and shop to shop, cadging sixpences, shillings and promises of prizes for the raffle, always on Fridays, because Friday is pay day, when everyone pays off their tick, buys treats for the kids, and chucks their change into the collection tins. With the other women who are collecting, they plan and schedule the day. The event is to be held in Benny Slater's field, and the food served in the club; there will be stalls and games, a tea, children's fancy dress, and on the Saturday a dance at the Welfare Hall with an exhibition by a ballroom formation team from Doncaster. At night there will be a spectacular finale of fireworks on the field organised, at his own insistence, by Juggler Hollingworth.

Harry's enjoyment and connoisseurship of fires and explosions expresses itself in a particular passion for fireworks and bonfires. He is one of several fathers in Highgate who every autumn persuades friends at the pit to save big, railway-sleeper-size lumps of coal to put on the Guy Fawkes Night bonfires in the yards, and every October he drives to the Standard factory in Huddersfield to buy a four-by-two-foot crate of mixed fireworks, some of which he sells to other people, and most of which he lets off himself in timed displays.

Harry had begun his planning for the coronation firework display immediately, urging the women to allocate as much of the budget as they could to it, and then topping up the kitty with his own money. 'It sounds like a lot to me,' says Winnie, when he tells the family his plans one teatime that spring. 'Are you sure you can manage that many crackers?'

'Manage?' he says. 'I'm a qualified shot-firer.'

'You *were*. But crackers'll be different to what you had in t' pit.'

He holds his knife and fork between his plate and mouth, pausing for effect. 'Is tha trying to tell me about explosives now?' he says with mock indignation. 'I'll get some scaffolding up,' and – turning to Pauline – 'we'll have a right do. It'll be like Buckingham Palace.'

'Lovely,' says Pauline.

'Scaffolding?' says Winnie.

Winnie, meanwhile, works on the costumes for the children's fancy dress competition. She makes a Little Bo Peep dress and bonnet for Lynda, and for Pauline she borrows a gypsy fortune-teller's outfit. Pauline however is shy, and tries to find reasons for not taking part.

'I'm *pale*, Mam. Gypsies have got brown skin.'

'We'll put gravy browning on you.'

'*Gravy?*'

'Gravy *browning*.'

She says this as if putting gravy browning on your skin is something people always do on royal occasions.

'And Our Muv says she's got summat for it as well,' says Winnie. 'She'll bring it when she comes.'

Annie's summat is socks: white ankle socks with red-white-and-blue tops, knitted for the occasion, and produced from her bag when she arrives at Win's at teatime the day before the celebrations.

'Do you think gypsies wear ankle socks, Muv?' asks Pauline, as she plays with Annie's swollen thumb. The poisoning has never fully gone away, and Pauline likes to knead the fat little cushion of flesh between her fingers.

'They do now, love,' says Annie. 'They're all t' fashion. I've got a gypsy girl comes to me, you know.'

'I know,' says Pauline, who has heard the story before.

'She watches over me. Have I to read your tea leaves?'

'Yes please.' Pauline knows what is coming, because Annie reads her leaves every time they meet. It is always the same: swirl the cup three times, tip it in the saucer, and, Ooh, one day you're going to meet a tall dark handsome man. Pauline prefers the crystal ball, whose scenarios are more varied.

After tea Annie and Winnie hang up bunting in the sitting room. Lynda plays among the trailing strings, and Pauline irons their fancy dress costumes. Soon the back door latch rattles and the door swings open, and there is a babble of voices as Sonny and May and their young daughters Carole, Amanda and Heather bundle through into the sitting room. 'Now then, are you all ready for tomorrow?' everyone says. 'What are you going in t' fancy dress as?'; 'Where did you get those socks, Pauline?' Sonny says he is singing in a concert with the Thurnscoe male voice choir tomorrow, and gives the room a few lines from the song programme. Winnie looks at the clock and wonders where Harry is. He is supposed to be setting up the scaffolding in Benny Slater's field, but he's been out there since dinnertime. There is another rattle of the latch, then a man crooning '*We're poor little lambs . . .*' and a woman saying, 'I'll give you poor little lambs!' and Danny, Millie and their children come through the door, laughing. They want to know what Juggler's playing at, because he was supposed to be ready and waiting to go up to the club.

'God knows,' says Winnie.

Everyone talks about the decorations in the village, and the fete, and the Queen, about how young she is, and how hard it has been for her losing her father like that. Annie says that Walter would have liked all the celebrations, because he always loved the King and the royal family. Danny tells Sonny to ask for a particular barrel of beer at the club, because that is the one the steward has added a bottle of whisky to for the royal occasion.

An hour later Harry comes in in his work clothes, grease smears on his hands and face. 'I've been working for Her Majesty,' he announces, and orders Millie out of the kitchen so he can have a stripwash at the sink.

'It's nowt I've not seen before, Juggler.'

'Humour him,' says Winnie. 'He takes more time getting ready than a woman.'

After he has washed and taken his time standing before the sitting-room mirror to comb his hair, knot his tie and apply a gold-plated tie-clip, the adults leave Muv with the children and clatter out of the door, down the steps and up the street towards the Halfway Hotel and the club. The sky is overcast, and to the west, towards the Pennines, banks of dense clouds are gathering. Across the road the cows lie in a fenced-off part of Benny Slater's field as if guarding the farmhouse. In the other part there rises from the ground a gigantic scaffolding structure, with a six-foot-high wooden platform and, at the back of that platform, a latticework of pipes, iron bars and wooden poles. The group stops to admire the size of Harry's construction. 'I just wanted everybody to be able to see,' he says.

*

The next morning the valley is hung with a veil of grey drizzling rain. With the radio news on, Winnie cooks and cleans while Harry shuttles between the yard door, where he looks up at the clouds, and the sitting-room table, where he draws little sketches on envelopes. At noon Win dresses Lynda as Little Bo Peep and then makes Pauline strip to her vest and knickers and stand on a newspaper while she rubs gravy browning into her daughter's arms, legs and face. Looking up, Harry says he thought they had an Arab in the house and performs a burst of the Sand Dance.

Once browned, Pauline dresses in her outfit: black blouse, long black skirt, bolero jacket, three-cornered scarf with brass coins hanging from its edges, and red-white-and-blue ankle socks. 'Lovely,' says Winnie, and if there is any danger in dressing someone as a copy of your own long-standing spirit guide, neither she nor Annie appears to be aware of it.

As the Hollingworths cross the road to the field in the faint drizzle, they can see everywhere Union Jacks and portraits of the Queen. Assembled for the fancy dress are Boudiccas, Queens of Hearts, princesses, cowboys, robots and clowns, and hundreds of children dressed up in red, white and blue, some in outfits fashioned from large flags with head and armholes cut in them. The scene ought to look joyful but, standing in a spitting Yorkshire rain, most of the children look uncomfortable and cold. As Pauline joins her age group she tastes something salty running onto her top lip and into her mouth; pink spots bloom on her arms, and by the time her line moves, a brown tide of gravy browning is soaking into the tops of her woollen ankle socks. She hopes that since the other costumes are so striking, and most of the girls are so pretty, the judge won't notice her. She is disappointed.

'And now, *The Gypsy*!' booms the judge – a man from the club committee – from under an umbrella. 'She's very good! But I don't think a gypsy would wear *ankle socks*!'

People in the crowd chuckle, and under the streaked browning, Pauline reddens.

'No, I've never seen a gypsy wearing jazzy ankle socks *like that*!'

'Sorry,' Pauline squeaks, but no one hears her because the crowd is still laughing.

The judge moves on to someone dressed as Britannia, and Pauline decides that in future she will refuse to wear any socks knitted by Muv, whatever the colour or occasion.

In the end, neither Pauline nor Lynda, who has been tottering along with the under-fives, receive a prize. Once the judge has handed out the firsts, seconds and thirds, and the rumours about it all being a fix have circulated, the mothers, fathers and children drift away to the stalls and games. The clouds and rain clear and the grass and roadways dry off. Winnie takes the girls home to change into sky-blue taffeta dresses that she has bought to wear in the evening, and Pauline begins pulling off her outfit as soon as she gets in the door. The gypsy girl's public incarnation has gone badly, but this will not be the day's only unfortunate ending.

*

At four o'clock they all go over to the club, where the ceilings are hung with bunting and Union flags, and a feast of quartered sandwiches, iced buns, and red jelly and custard awaits them on trestle tables for the coronation tea. Afterwards they walk back to Number 34 to watch the repeat of the coronation ceremony on television. Most families do the same, and for a few hours be-flagged Highgate falls quiet in the late-afternoon sunshine. In the field, in the dull, warmish early evening breezes tug at the tarpaulins hanging over deserted stalls and sideshows. In a corner away from the cows and pit ponies, a group of beery lads kick a football around. Benny Slater checks his fence and, up on the scaffolding, Juggler Hollingworth makes his last adjustments to the pipes, bars and poles, then climbs down and walks home to where the Hollingworths are drinking tea and watching the crowning of their young Queen.

When dusk falls the family put on their coats and shoes and step out into the night air. There is the sound of people laughing and shouting, and the smell of drying earth and bonfire smoke. In the field Harry goes to join a group of men clustered about the scaffolding, while Winnie, Annie and the girls take up a good position at the front. Harry selects a handful of fireworks from a metal box and then climbs up a ladder to the platform. He nails pinwheels to the wooden poles, inserts rockets into bottles, and sets individual fireworks on small plinths of bricks built to varying heights. Walking above the crowd in the twilight, checking a nail or straightening a brick, he looks like a compère of a ghostly mechanical theatre, though when friends in the crowd call out to him, he is too absorbed to answer. Finally, in the darkness, he leans down to confer with the organiser. Someone shouts out, 'Go on, Juggler, we're ready!' and he nimbly trots along the platform lighting the pinwheels until the field in front of the stage is illuminated by a bright, magnesium-coloured glow. The crowd oohs and coos. Hundreds of hands spatter applause. He lights a fuse linking several Roman candles which erupt in succession, casting colours and dancing shadows across the bodies in the crowd and over the concrete walls of the mission church behind. Danny, who is helping, passes up more tubes, wheels and rockets, as Harry dodges the still-lit crackers and lights new ones to keep the display going.

'I hope he'll be careful,' Winnie frets to Muv.

'Stop wittering, Winnie,' says her mother. 'He knows what he's doing.'

And then, as a shower of silver stars bursts in the sky high above the village, just as other stars are bursting above other villages in the valley, Harry lights three large crackers linked with a fuse, but they fizzle. Seeing something is not right he edges forward to look, but suddenly they all go off at once, with a mighty bang and a bright flash. As he steps back to avoid the sparks he feels part of the scaffolding give way, and he leaps clear. To Winnie, Annie, Pauline, Lynda and the others watching it is as if one of the crackers has blasted him off the stage and up into the air.

This, then, is how England's new Elizabethan age begins for the Hollingworths: with a little gypsy girl in gravy browning showing herself in patriotic socks, and the Juggler flying across the night sky over the valley, lit by the fiery-bright smoking lights of his own display, flailing about and falling. His body thuds hard into the earth and Winnie runs to where he is lying, face down and still in the damp grass.

PART FOUR

22

Victorian Underwear and Science-fiction Shoes

Highgate, 1952–55

'If I ever find out who was supposed to have tightened them bolts on t' scaffolding,' Pauline Hollingworth hears her dad saying, 'I'll stick a rocket up his backside that big that he'll go up and never come back down again. Take these plates away and turn t' radio up, will tha?'

It is a month after the great Coronation Day fireworks disaster and Pauline is on the stairs, listening to her mam and dad in the sitting room, and laughing to herself.

'Give me a chance wi' t' fetching and carrying, Harry. I'm not your flaming servant.'

'I'll gie thee flaming servant. Don't bother, I'll do it my sen. This damn thing won't let me move . . .'

The damn thing that will not let Harry move is a grey surgical corset, fitted at the Montagu Hospital, which he has to wear for three months. The corset holds his spine rigidly upright, and makes movement, and sleep, difficult. Occasionally Winnie says he is milking it, the accusations provoking a stream of complaints that end in imaginative threats against whichever idiots had reckoned to be tightening the bolts on the scaffolding.

Off work until October, Harry has still been spending odd mornings and afternoons down at Manvers Main, talking to his mates, and cadging materials for do-it-yourself projects. Goods from the nationalised pit yards are used in most home-improvement activities in the valley, one way or another: garden sheds are painted in colours from the pit stores, whole streets are wired with NCB electrical cable, and a generation of children is told that they had an ancestor so wealthy he had tools engraved with his initials: N.C.B. Hampered by the corset, Harry brings only small or light objects, transforming them with a little light work into items for the house and yard. A roll of rubber belt becomes a doormat, industrial brackets prop up radio speakers, a wooden crate turns into a new home for his chicks. Some of his curios are adapted for individual members of the family. When he brings home a six-foot-high, half-inch-thick sheet of white polystyrene foam, he tells Pauline it is for her.

'I'm going to show thee summat after tea. I've a right idea. For thy feet.'

'You can get it shifted, whatever it is,' says Winnie, who wonders how a man who needs his crockery carried can undertake such elaborate handicrafts. 'It's dropping bits all over t' carpet.'

After he has finished his tea and had a smoke, Harry tells Pauline to lay the polystyrene on the carpet, remove her shoes and stand on it. He then manoeuvres himself down to a kneeling position, marks a line around her feet with a knife, and cuts out the shapes. Finally he inserts the flat, white cut-out pieces of polystyrene into Pauline's shoes.

'There!' He looks triumphant. 'They'll keep thy feet right warm when it's cold.'

Pauline is always cold, and complains particularly of cold feet. In November, to save her from tonsillitis, Winnie bastes her in goose grease and makes vests from Thermogene wadding to wear under her liberty bodice.

'But it's not cold yet,' Pauline says to her dad.

'It will be in winter,' says Harry.

Winnie shakes her head. 'She can just wear them in t' winter then.'

'She wants to be wearing them in now.'

'They'll not wear in, Harry. They're plastic.'

'It's *polystyrene*. It's a material of t' future.'

Pauline intervenes by placing the insoles in her shoes and walking around the room. The shoes are tight and her feet feel uncomfortably hot.

'I love them,' she says, to dispel the tension. 'You want to try 'em, Mam.'

*

Pauline wears her new insulated shoes when she returns to Bolton-upon-Dearne secondary modern after the school holidays for her second year of senior school. Her futuristic footwear is in contrast to the pink, boned-cotton corset that her mam has made her wear since she started there. 'All t' other lasses'll also be wearing them. It's what you wear at that age,' she says when Pauline objects, but what she really means is, you're a woman now, and to be a woman you must tolerate discomfort. When Pauline asks other girls her age if they wear corsets, no one even knows what they are, so this becomes another thing to hide and worry about: underwear that feels Victorian, now offset by science-fiction shoes.

The contrast between the ideas of a restrictive past and a bright future based on novelty and innovation is experienced by Pauline not only in her own home, but also in the classrooms at school. For the girls of Bolton-upon-Dearne secondary modern in the mid-1950s, education is characterised by a struggle between two opposing factions of teachers. One is made up of approachable younger women who wear fashionably cut skirts and pastel tops, and who talk to you about topics that interest you, such as food and hobbies. To talk to these teachers is thrilling, if nerve-wracking, because, unlike other adults, they act as if your opinion is as valid as theirs. The other faction comprises older women who teach drier subjects such as science and geography. Some of them have taught your mam or your aunties in the old elementary schools, and are often said by your relatives to be right tartars. They wear thick, tweedy suits all year round and are greatly concerned with preventing contact with the boys who occupy half of the segregated school premises.

The leader of the tweedy Victorian group, and a strong influence on the atmosphere of the school, is Miss Grose, a short, squat woman who had briefly taught Winnie Parkin. Miss Grose teaches science in a room with wooden benches and stools, and concentrates almost exclusively on the topics of dinosaurs and the formation of coal from dead forests during the Carboniferous Period. The Bolton teachers often refer back to coal formation, presumably out of a sense of local relevance, though few children are interested, hearing quite enough about coal at home. What interests the girls most is the armadillo shell – curved so that the armadillo's tail is in its mouth – that Miss Grose displays behind her desk. At the end of each term she allows her pupils to stroke it, providing a treat that many of them consider to be among the high points of the year.

More than dinosaurs, coal or armadillos though, Miss Grose is interested in sex. She believes that all her charges' failings can be attributed to their interest in boys, and particularly to their desire to look at the boys studying gardening in the plots outside her classroom window.

'You're not listening!' she shouts at Pauline one day in her first term, after she has answered incorrectly a question about coal. '*I'm* not looking at the boys outside, and neither should you be!'

'I'm not, Miss Grose,' says Pauline. 'I wasn't even looking out of the window.'

'Yes you were. If I catch you looking again, I shall cane you.'

In fact, no one was looking out of the window. Even the bored, forward girls are uninterested in these boys, standing in a pimpled hairy line, pink monkey hands slackly gripping their spade handles. It is Miss Grose herself who is interested, though not in the boys themselves so much as the threat they represent.

The leader of the pastel faction is Miss Bryant, a brisk, forthright young Yorkshirewoman who teaches domestic science with great passion. She speaks with enthusiasm about modern technologies for the home, such as vacuum cleaners and electric irons, and makes the learning of brass-polishing techniques seem like an adventure in the acquisition of knowledge. Miss Bryant summons up images of dream houses and makes the new efficient ways of cooking and cleaning sound somehow invigorating. Food rationing is coming to an end, and *Woman's Weekly* runs stories about the attractive modern kitchens owned by housewives in America. One day, says Miss Bryant, we too will have such kitchens, and the skilful management of them will be a joy and fulfilment for which you will all be grateful.

Pauline is enthused by Miss Bryant's vision, but her favourite subject is English, particularly when taught by Miss Senior – one of the modern teachers – in Pauline's favourite room, the library. Overlooking the gardens, the library is dark and old-fashioned with floor-to-ceiling wooden bookshelves, long, waxed wooden tables and heavy chairs. Around the walls, the books' variously coloured spines, each with its own little number taped to its foot, look well against the polished oak, as pleasing to look at as the American kitchens in their way. Week by week Pauline works her way through those she has heard of – *Wuthering Heights*, *Jane Eyre*, *Sense and Sensibility* – and her comments impress her teacher. One afternoon in late 1953, Miss Senior is reviewing the class's essays about *Pride and Prejudice*. Outside there is slush, dirty snow, an unlifting wet, brown fog. The school gardens are dead and colourless. Here in the library the air is dozy with the heat from the big iron radiators, and the smell of camphor oil, soot and damp woollens condenses so thickly you could write your name in it. 'And now, Pauline Hollingworth,' says Miss Senior. 'Well this was *very* good. Keep studying like this, you don't know where it might take you.'

Pauline wants to ask what sort of places Miss Senior is thinking of, but instead she just says 'Thank you', and blushes from her scalp down to her polystyrene insoles.

She tells her mam that she likes school, but Winnie, always busy with the housework, has no time for it. It seems to Pauline that some of the women of her mam's age resent their daughters for not having to deal with the hardship that they endured in their childhoods. 'You girls don't know you're born,' they chide, making it sound like an insult. Even among her peers, Winnie seems particularly old-fashioned – often deliberately, wilfully so. When Pauline starts her periods she is so scared that she thinks she must be dying. She washes her underclothes herself, but not thoroughly enough for Winnie, who complains about the blood, explains nothing, and gives her daughter a crude cloth belt to tie around her waist with some pieces of rag, torn for the purpose, to attach to it with safety pins. Her mam's grumbling makes Pauline feel she herself is to blame. It isn't until Auntie Olive comes to visit and hears Pauline asking her mam for rags that anything changes. Olive reprimands her sister for never having been up to date, and buys Pauline some sanitary towels from the shop on the corner. No one ever explains what causes the bleeding though.

*

Gradually the new spirit of pastel cardies and American kitchens and labour-saving electrical appliances enters some of the homes on Highgate Lane. When Peggy Copper walks out on Arthur in 1954, she leaves behind her Singer treadle sewing machine, and Arthur, lost and depressed, allows Pauline to use it to make clothes with fabrics that Winnie brings back from Doncaster market. For herself, and for friends on Highgate Lane, she makes clothes like the ones she has seen in films and Pathé newsreels: gypsy skirts in pinstripes, full skirts with material printed with airline badges, tops to go with denim jeans and bumper shoes. On Fridays she sits in the living room with Winnie and Comfort and knits youthful cardigans in the firelight. These garments are the beginnings of what the newspapers will call 'teenage fashion', but Pauline doesn't know about that; she just thinks of them as pleasant, colourful things for young women who don't want to wear corsets.

Among the older women it is Nelly Spencer who is the first to embrace the domestic vision that has so enthused the likes of Miss Bryant. Nelly's parsimony might have been learned in the austerity of the twenties and thirties, but it means that in the 1950s she is able to buy the new household gadgets as soon as they arrive in Goldthorpe's shop windows. Her clothes are always current, and when the new kitchen units come to the shops of Doncaster and Barnsley, she is the first to have one. Electric irons have been in the stores only a few days before Winnie enviously beholds a smart, Morphy Richards model in Nelly's kitchen.

Most prized of the modern household items are the trim new fireplaces which replace the dirty black ranges in sitting rooms. Once you have one of the new gas cookers a range is no longer necessary, and with a fireplace sitting rooms look impossibly tidy and clean. Winnie thinks it wouldn't even be worth asking Mr Meanly for one, but Nelly says, with her chuntering up-beatness, 'You want to get one, Winnie. We love ours. We've just had one put in, you know.'

'Have you?' says Winnie.

'It looks grand. I brought Comfort round to have a look t' other day and she were lost for words.'

'I wish I knew how you did it, Nelly. I should love to not get so mucky cleaning that thing.'

'Do you want me to show you?'

Winnie feels suddenly naïve, a girl in the presence of a woman. 'How do you mean?'

'I mean I'll show you how to get a fireplace out of Meanly. Has Harry got a hammer?'

The following day, Nelly Spencer is on her knees before Winnie's range, its large grate pulled out, and a blanket spread over the oven bottom. Above her head she has Harry's ball-peen hammer tightly gripped in both hands.

'Look out,' she says, and brings the hammer down hard. It makes a muffled crack. She strikes again, again and again. 'Once more for luck.' And then like a conjuror she whisks away the cloth to reveal the range's shattered base.

Winnie's mouth is open, and her voice is small when it comes out. 'What have you done, Nelly?'

Nelly explains that landlords are bound to replace fixtures that are irreparably damaged, and no landlord is going to replace a range when he can have a modern fireplace cheaper. 'Tell him you dropped t' grate on it,' she says. 'Act helpless.'

23

Roy and Margaret

Thurnscoe, 1954

On a warm, light summer evening in 1954, a seventeen-year-old girl called Margaret White is wiping the counter in Thurnscoe's market café, and exchanging loaded glances with a young man seated at one of the tables. Margaret, slim, dark-haired and diffident, works at a sewing factory in Goldthorpe but is helping out at the café to cover for a friend who has gone to Blackpool for the week. Nervous of serving people when she started, she has after a couple of evenings come to enjoy taking their orders, slipping the correct plates before them and chatting as they settle their bills amid the steam, smoking fat and cigarette fumes. There are plenty of tips, food if you want it, and, after six o'clock when the young men and women replace the market traders and shoppers, the chance of a bit of fun. The man at the table, Sid, has just asked her if he can walk her home when she knocks off, and she has accepted. 'It's great for getting to know people,' her friend had said about the job, and she wasn't wrong.

Sid sits alone with a cup of tea near a table at which two loud young men are eating bacon and eggs and telling jokes. At quarter past eight, fifteen minutes before she finishes work, he pays her and tells her that he'll meet her outside. The two loud men watch him go, and as he leaves one of them gets up and comes to the counter. He is tall, lean and dark-haired, with heavy-lidded brown eyes and a cocky smile.

'That were smashing food, love,' he says. 'How much do I owe you?'

She tells him and he passes her a ten-shilling note.

'I bet you cooked it, didn't you? I thought as much. You want to be a chef or summat.'

'Give over,' she says, smiling.

'I'm not kidding, I'm serious. What's your name?'

'Margaret.'

'I appreciate a good cook, you see, Margaret. I need feeding up, because I've just come back from Army training. I'm off serving Queen and Country and I want looking after but I haven't got nobody, rotten i'n't it? Haven't you got a pal?' He winks at her.

'Sorry.' She hands back his change.

'Oh heck. I'm going to be all on my own again, and that's my reward for fighting in that horrible desert.'

'Oh dear,' she says. 'You'll find somebody.'

'What time they make you work till then?' He takes half a crown from his change and lays it flat on the counter. 'I'll leave you that.'

'I'm just knocking off now.'

'Have I to walk you home then?'

'No thank you! Somebody's walking me home already.'

'Well, tell me if you change your mind. I'll be outside.'

Margaret watches him go out into the twilit market place and light a cigarette. She turns to one of the girls behind the counter and they raise their eyebrows at each other. 'By gum, you're doing well tonight, Margaret,' says one.

'I am, aren't I? I think I'd better get off home before it gets out of hand!' Margaret slips off her apron and takes her cardie from a peg. 'I'll see you tomorrow then.'

'See you tomorrow. And watch that Sidney!'

Sid and the man from the Army are both standing near the door. When she steps out, the Army man darts in. 'Can I take you home then, love?'

Sid looks from the man to Margaret.

'No, I've told you. This man's taking me home.' Margaret looks at Sid. She notices the man's friend inside, still at the table, watching them through the glass door.

'You're never going with him!' he says, mock appalled. 'Come on, change your mind and come with me.'

Sid says, 'I'm taking her,' but he sounds unconvinced. Margaret looks at them both, not knowing what to do. The man from the Army unsettles her, but she feels attracted to him and impressed by his interest in her. Later she will say he seemed so keen and insistent that she just gave in.

'Come on pal,' he says to Sid, 'hop it. She's coming with me.'

'Who do you think you are?'

'Never mind who I think I am. I'm telling you to get lost. Now scram.'

Sid looks from Margaret to the stranger.

'Blow this,' he says. As he walks away, the click of Sid's shoes on the pavement is loud against the background café noise.

'Looks like I'll have to take you home then, Margaret love.'

'Sharp out of t' trap, aren't you?'

'For you I am. I'm serious, I just feel something for you. Can't explain it.'

Margaret's parents live on John Street, a tidy, narrow roadway lined with solid, brick terraced houses close to the market place. 'Let's have a walk round t' village,' says the stranger. They stroll away from the railway line and new pit houses, down through the old Victorian buildings, and past allotments, cemetery, cricket pitch and church. The night is warm and the conversation flows easily.

'I think Margaret's a lovely name,' he says. 'It really suits you.'

'Thank you,' she says. 'What do they call you, then?'

'Fox,' he says. 'No, don't laugh, I'm not kidding. I'm Roy Fox Hollingworth.'

*

Roy, now twenty-one, has been back in the Dearne Valley for a month. After leaving Highgate Lane the previous year he completed his National Service and enlisted as an Emergency Reserve soldier, which means that periodically he has to travel to camps for weeks of training. In between he wanders, turning up now and again to tell Winnie he has been working in the Midlands, say, or is living in sin with a girl in South Wales. He never stays for long. Harry cracks jokes about his son's obsession with the Army, and Roy, cocky, bulled up by the training and the travel, gets angry. Having been abroad and served the Empire he thinks he is due deference, not mockery; but then mockery's typical of this place, he says, storming out of the house and slamming the back door behind him.

This time Roy has settled back in his old room, and taken a job at Highgate pit to tide him over. Pit work is generally easy to come by and Roy is particularly valued because his knowledge of tanks and cranes makes him good with the new machines. The only drawback is his dad, chuntering at the tea table about his own pit accident, declaring the job too dangerous and a dead-end. Roy has to absorb this scolding respectfully because if he argues, Harry will find reasons not to lend him his car, and Roy needs a car to impress Margaret when he takes her out. He is tanned and confident, and speaks with the assurance of a TV show compère in an accent that is being smoothed by travel. The big car complements his style, and he likes to be seen in it.

*

At half past six on the Saturday following their first meeting, Margaret White is in the sitting room at home putting on her make-up as she waits to be collected by Roy. Her father, Horace White, is in the room preparing to go out with his wife Hilda. Mr White is a miner and union man at Hickleton colliery, veteran of the 1926 strike, and the treasurer of Thurnscoe's Coronation Club, a large working men's club in the village. He and Hilda are committed Methodists, and known for their pious decency and neighbourliness.

'You off to t' pictures, lass?'

'I am,' says Margaret. 'I think he's taking me up Goldthorpe.'

'Who's t' lucky fella?'

'You don't know this one. They call him Roy Hollingworth. He's from Highgate.'

Horace wrinkles his forehead. 'Hollingworth? Is his father called Harry?'

'I've no idea,' she says, 'I've only met him once.'

'Ask him.'

When she comes back that night her father is in the sitting room eating a supper of bread and gravy. Margaret tells him that yes, Roy's dad is called Harry, but they call him Juggler. He does turns, something to do with Old Mother Riley and half a pint of beer, she doesn't understand it exactly.

'T' Juggler,' he says, nodding. 'Be careful.'

'Do you know him?' She is interested in the warning, but not alarmed. Her father's ways are not everyone's, and he disapproves of a lot of people.

'Half of Thurnscoe knows him,' says Horace. 'If t' lad's owt like his father he'll be wide as wide. Just watch what you get into with him.'

24

The Man Who Came Second in the Bad Luck Competition

Bridlington, 1955

From the mid-1950s the higher pit wages and incipient, kitchen-transforming consumer boom began to alter the look of the Dearne Valley. There are new, modern estates of National Coal Board housing for the incomers from Scotland, Wales, the North East and Communist Hungary. There are brighter signs and windows on the shops, and new buildings in the pit yards. The pubs and clubs are renovated, modernised and expanded, and in Highgate the members of the working men's club raise money to have their wooden hut replaced by a low, modern brick building with a large function room and a detached house next door for the steward. It seems to be a time when money and power are being rebalanced, with the squires and the grand landowners slipping away. Lord Halifax has moved from Hickleton Hall to his estate in the East Riding and has let out the hall to a private school. To the Hollingworth children, Winnie and Harry's stories about people touching their caps when someone from the hall rode through Goldthorpe are like lessons from some disappeared dark world. This new generation's deference will be to the glamorous – to the bright-eyed and white-toothed pop stars, actors and presenters who enter their lives via the television screen.

As business remains brisk for Harry and his turns, the Hollingworths have ample money for home improvements. After admiring the new fireplace, Winnie and Harry wallpaper the house, and replace the solid internal doors with new ones with glass panels. They buy a larger television set, a record player with three speeds, and a kitchen cabinet that Winnie has seen in a TV programme about the Ideal Home Exhibition. She doesn't trust washing machines and won't have one in the house, but she does take possession of a two-tone Hoover Constellation vacuum cleaner for the green nylon carpet newly fitted in the sitting room. (In practice, she judges the Hoover to be less than adequate to the task of keeping the nylon in good order, and for the next two decades spends Friday afternoons on her hands and knees scrubbing the carpet with soap and water.) Harry, meanwhile, trades in the Daimler for a secondhand Hudson Terraplane, a sleek, American, tan-and-cream convertible with the steering wheel on the left. Parked on Highgate Lane it looks spectacular, or ridiculous, depending on your point of view. No one in Highgate knows how Clarry Basinger, who supplied it, got hold of an American model, but the Hollingworths and their friends agree it suits Harry. It is as if the car was meant for him, they say. As if it somehow found its own way from Hollywood to the Dearne Valley to find its true kindred spirit.

It is partly to celebrate the acquisition of this outlandish vehicle that in the summer of 1955, Harry takes the family away for the weekend. The destination, as usual, is Clara's caravan in Bridlington. He lowers the Terraplane's roof, packs in Winnie, Pauline and Lynda, Clara and Ernie and their daughter Clare, his mother Amy, and Bonzo the dog, and sets off in an ebullient mood.

'What's tha reckon to t' car then, Ernie?'

Ernie is wedged between Winnie and the maroon leather-trimmed door on the Terraplane's mono front seat.

'It's alright,' shouts Ernie above the noise of the wind whistling in everyone's ears.

'It's American. Fit for a king, or a millionaire.'

'I hope you've got a palace at t' other end,' yells Clara from the back. 'I don't know how we're all going to fit in t' caravan. There's seven of us, and it only sleeps four.'

'I can't hear thee.'

Winnie rolls her eyes at Clara, and Ernie begins to reply, but is cut short by Bonzo jumping across him and trying to leap out.

The next morning, after sleeping with varying degrees of success in the caravan, they are all eating bacon and eggs outside when a bleary Harry mentions that he has seen a poster advertising a talent competition at Bridlington's Spa Royal Hall. The winner will go on to some Yorkshire region heats, and the winner of those to the national final in London.

'We'll maybe go to watch 'em,' says Clara. 'There might be a star of the future.' Some of the family nod, others groan.

'It'd be nice,' agrees Winnie. 'Will it be dear to go in?'

'Never mind going to watch,' says Harry. 'I'm entering.'

*

The Bridlington Spa Royal Hall is a lavish, glass-domed Edwardian dance hall that, with the adjoining Spa Theatre, overlooks the beach at the southern end of the town. The competition involves about thirty performers, mostly singers, of ages eleven to over fifty. The judges, one of whom, according to the rough-papered programme, works in showbiz in London, are dressed in evening wear; the male contestants are mostly in dark woollen suits, some of them shabby and shiny at the knee, and the younger women have on sweaters and full skirts puffed out with nylon petticoats. A confident girl from Hull does a passable version of Dinah Shore's 'Sweet Violets'. Most of the men imitate Al Bowlly or Bing Crosby. There is a poor contortionist from Bridlington, and several ventriloquists.

The compère, a man called Peter, is dressed well and smarms on the girls: he asks one young brunette, who is about to tapdance, if she has a fella, which makes Winnie and the others sitting in the velveteen chairs down to the left of the stage tut. When Harry walks out under a wobbling spotlight at about a quarter past three that afternoon, he keeps his comedy mouth shut and plays it straight and as smooth as Nat King Cole. The lack of nerves throws Peter slightly, and Harry comes off looking good. He has brought his good suit, and he looks a cut above the other performers, and knows it.

'And what are you going to sing for us this afternoon . . . *Juggler*?'

Peter tells the audience about this name, which has been explained by Harry in a quick chat backstage.

'I'm going to sing a song which is a favourite of mine, Peter. It's a well-known song that's been sung by a lot of truly great singers, and it's called "Because".'

The clapping and the cheers from the Hollingworths down in the stalls subsides and Harry nods to the pianist. At the end of a fluent intro, Harry, voice smoked and sweetened with nicotine and VapoRub, places his arms by his side, and sings.

Because, you come to me with naught save love,
And hold my hand, and lift mine eyes above . . .

The audience applauds his big notes. By the time he approaches the end, most people are smiling in approval, and he finishes them off with a pleading stare into the white spotlight:

Because, God made thee mine, I'll cherish thee,
Through light and darkness, through all time to be,
And pray His love may make our love divine,
Because – God – made – thee – mine!

The applause is among the loudest of the afternoon. He smiles; the gap is safe to reveal now, the mouth's ugliness sanctified by its voice. Applause, applause – bow. 'Thank you.' Applause, bow quicker. Peter sidles on.

The handclapping fades. Peter's arm is around Harry's shoulders and he is asking the judges for their scores out of ten. No cards, they just say them: 8, 8, 9, 7. 'That's the best so far!' says Peter. 'Can anyone catch the Juggler from the Dearne Valley?'

Harry steps into the wings and watches a reedy tenor doing an Ink Spots number, an awful ventriloquist, and a lousy facsimile Rosemary Clooney. Victory seems to be in the bag for the Terraplane King, but then a light-brown haired, thin teenage girl from Pontefract steps up and, after being breathed over by Peter, announces she will sing 'Amazing Grace'.

She is very good. The audience knows it, Harry knows it, and when she finishes he claps from the wings.

'9, 9, 7, 7.'

'A tie!' says Peter. 'And just one more turn to go, can we bear the thrill?'

The last act is a soprano from Leeds, who sings flat. The judges award fives and fours. Peter comes back out. 'Thank you, ladies and gentlemen. And now please let's have a big round of applause for all our contestants out on stage!'

The contestants, except for Harry and the girl, who is called Wendy, are ushered off and Peter hams up the tension. They've never had this sort of thing before, ladies and gentlemen, and they'll try to settle it by getting the acts to sing again. 'First, singing for the second time and looking for that big money prize, the multi-talented *Juggler*!'

His performance is as good as the first. The audience claps loudly and cheers. Win says to Pauline, 'I wish your Auntie Millie was here, they'd walk away with it.' Harry wipes sweat from his forehead with a handkerchief.

Wendy, trembling, sings again and matches him. The judges huddle. Harry begins to look uncomfortable. He makes to say something to Peter, but Peter moves down to confer with the judges, and ladies and gentlemen this is extraordinary! The judges have come up with a tie again!

The audience oohs as Peter seems to want them to, but then Harry steps forward.

'Ayup – '

Peter, still babbling into the mike, doesn't hear him.

'Ayup, Tommy Trinder,' he says. Laughter from the audience. Compared with Barnsley on a Friday night, it is like making babies laugh. 'Come here – ' he takes Peter's arm. 'Gi'e it to Wendy.'

'Just a minute, Juggler,' says Peter.

'Just a minute thysen. She's a better singer than I am, and I've been doing it years. She's only a lass. Come here, love – '

In the spotlight, Wendy is wide-eyed and visibly shaking. Peter says something about it being the judges' decision, but Harry leans into

Peter's mike and says, 'I, The Juggler, officially concede to this worthy winner,' and pecks Wendy on the cheek. He leads the applause, and the audience joins.

Afterwards in the foyer Harry is with the family, Lynda clinging to his legs. Peter smarms over, 'Thank you, Juggler. I'm not sure what we'd have done without you.'

'They should give me thy job,' he says.

Peter laughs a smarmy laugh.

'He's not kidding. Tha wants to see what he can do wi' half a pint of bitter,' says Ernie.

Peter looks as if he is wishing they would go.

'Come on,' says Harry, swinging up Lynda into his arms, 'I'm due on at t' Palladium in half an hour.'

*

The Spa Royal Hall will have its own spotlight in the family's memory, remembered as a passed-on opportunity that could have led to greater fame and riches. 'Your dad and Auntie Millie could have gone a long way if things had been different,' Winnie would sometimes say to Pauline and Lynda years later, and the idea would become an article of faith among the children, grandchildren, nephews and nieces. Harry, however, is content with the part-time circuit in the North of England. Brought up in the age before television, he does not aspire to national audiences. The local one, within scope of a bike ride, feels enough; and anyway the North is where the ready money is.

His appearance in the Bridlington talent show comes at a time when popular entertainment is changing, though. Harry will continue drumming, singing and doing comedy on his own for decades, but in the mid-1950s he notices that the troupes and variety acts are falling from favour. The boom that has put new money in his pocket is also bringing new technology into homes, pubs and dance halls and, thanks to that technology, the old dance bands are beginning to lose out to pop groups, electric organs and performers who remind audiences of acts they have seen on TV.

One night around this time, Harry drives Millie, Barney and the rest of the gang to Skegness, suitcases packed with grass skirts and Sand Dance costumes. But when Harry walks out onto the stage to introduce the show, looking out from under the lights, he sees that the auditorium is less than half full. The promoter says he doesn't know where all the people are, but Harry does: they are at home watching the telly, or out at a modern dance where the music comes from a single organist. Driving home after performances he has seen the new dance halls turning out, and their crowds are larger and younger than those at the variety shows.

A few months later Harry disbands the troupe and decides to stick to his solo turns with comedy and singing, compèring, and drumming for singers. As an individual he can benefit from the changes because while the electric organs put some musicians out of work, they cannot always simulate drum rhythms that get people dancing in the way that a real drummer does, and the singers like to have a real kit behind them.

Harry's singing and jokes still go down well and he works almost every night that he isn't away with the glassworks lorry. Walking into pubs in the East Riding on the way to the coast he is accosted by men who have seen him doing the Hawaiian Hula act in the raffia skirt. Stopping off at a shop to buy cigs on the way home from Sheffield, he finds a shop assistant wondering if he hadn't seen him playing the washboard in a club in Rotherham. Despite this local fame, however, amid all the modernisation and increasing prosperity, his half-pint of beer trick remains a popular but unsolved Yorkshire mystery.

25

The Boy and the Dog

Beech Farm, Harlington, 1955

In her needlework class at school, Pauline befriends a girl who shares her love of clothes, patterns and fabric, and who has a talent for fitting sleeves that she particularly admires. Joan Benson, like Pauline, is shy. She lives on a farm in a village called Harlington, near Barnburgh. Some girls and boys from farms seem to think of themselves as better than other people, and certainly better than miners, but Joan is amicable and self-deprecating; some of her great-uncles had gone from the farm to work in the pits, and she and her brother and sisters had been taught humility and respect. Joan confides to Pauline that when she leaves school she would like to be a dressmaker. If Pauline would like to come to her house to have tea, she says, they could sew together and talk about patterns, and – this is a big draw to Pauline – go to see the family's cows.

Pauline visits one Sunday after dinner, taking the bus the two miles to Harlington. The Bensons' farm, which is rented from the Coal Board, stands between the edge of the village and a railway line on which wheezy colliery engines push and pull long trains of coal wagons between the collieries. The stone farmhouse adjoins the granary, cowshed and barn. As Pauline walks across the yard she hears the rustle of animals and a hammer ringing on an anvil in the dairy, where two men are patching hessian corn sacks, one her dad's age, the other taller and much younger with a cap pushed back to show a rag of curling black hair. When Joan lets her in to the house, Pauline notices how low the ceilings are and how dark and quiet the rooms. In some rooms she can hear the animals moving in the barn next door.

'Have you brought some wellies?' says Joan.

'My dad doesn't let me wear wellies because he thinks lasses shouldn't get mucky,' says Pauline. 'Was that your dad and brother in t' yard?'

'It will have been. Did they say hello?'

'No.'

'That'll have been them. They don't say much.'

'I quite like that.'

'You'll certainly like it here then,' says Joan. 'Come on, let's find you some boots.'

After they have looked at the cows, Joan shows Pauline some fabric her mam has bought at Doncaster market, and they talk about people at school. At five they go to help Joan's mam get the tea ready, setting out bread, a ham, tomatoes, fruit cake and cheese on a long white-cloth-covered table in the kitchen. With the Light Programme in the background and the kettle boiling on the range, Mrs Benson and Joan chat between themselves and Pauline listens. Outside the kitchen door there is a shuffling clump of boots, two low murmuring voices and a brushing of clothes to knock off straw. Mrs Benson turns off the wireless and Joan stiffens slightly. The door swings open and in come Mr Benson and Gordon, with the silent self-importance of men with their minds still on their work. Mr Benson washes his hands. Gordon waits, taking a pen from the sideboard and writing something on the calendar. Seeing Pauline he says, 'Ayup.'

'Ayup,' replies Pauline, thinking he might say something else to her, but feeling relieved when he doesn't. As the men sit down to eat, the kitchen reverts to a cowmuck-scented silence that is broken only when Gordon or his parents say something about the farm, using words that sound like parts of a foreign language. Pauline is quite glad of their indifference to her. Once she gets used to it their silence makes her comfortable, because no one expects her to say anything.

After tea Joan asks if she wants to look at film magazines for a while, but first comes what will prove the highlight of the visit.

Pauline asks if she can use the lav. 'Just down t' passage,' says Joan. Pauline thinks this means out of the door at the end of the passage, and she has to come back to be redirected. *It is inside:* the first inside lavatory that Pauline has ever seen. The little room, with its white pan and washbasin and hard black plastic seat, is so cosy and clean it feels like a facility in the house of a millionaire. The seat is warm against her thighs, and there are no cobwebs in the corners. When she tells Joan how smashing it is, Joan shows her the upstairs bathroom, which to Pauline is as glamorous as the homes of the stars featured in Joan's film magazines.

'T' farm's right peaceful, Mam. I loved it,' she tells Winnie later. 'And they've got inside lavs that are out of this world.'

*

Even more than cows, Pauline loves dogs. On her fourteenth birthday her Auntie Millie buys her a black-and-white collie-cross pup that immediately becomes her joint best friend. With Harry's help Pauline teaches the pup, which she calls Wendy, to fetch the *South Yorkshire Times* and the family's slippers from around the house. She takes her with the dogs belonging to her dad and neighbours for long lolloping hikes across the valley and surrounding hills. She walks along the railway embankments, and by the streams, and down on the low land where the Dearne flows slowly and floods in the spring; she walks through the old stone-cottage villages, and past the farmyards and new pit estates and allotments; in the sun and rain she walks by the railway bridges, the embankments and the mountainous spoil heaps that some people call the Yorkshire Alps. Miles and miles every day she walks, letting the dogs off the lead in the open, and gathering them up again at the roads. Sometimes she walks a route that brings her near to Beech Farm, and she will see Joan, or Joan's older sisters Eileen and Bernice paying a visit, or Joan's father and brother Gordon working in the fields, and they will ask her to stop and rest for a while, and give her a cup of tea, and the dogs some water. In this way the dogs and the countryside and the farm become part of the same pleasure for her, a small escape of green lanes, footpaths and open land that she prefers to the cinema and television. It would not be a great pleasure for everyone, but for her it is when she feels most like herself.

In the summer holidays Joan invites Pauline and Wendy to stay at the farm for a week. Everyone is busy with the harvest. During the hot, bright days Joan and Pauline go out into the stubble cornfields to stack sheaves, and in the fields all around them, reaching up to the horizons, men and women are cutting corn, stouking straw and forking the sheaves into trailers, and driving the tractors with their trailers full of ashy-golden grain and straw. In the middle of the day the roads quickly fill with men on foot, on bicycles and in cars, and with buses carrying more men who look out from the windows at the people working in the fields: these are the Barnburgh miners travelling to the pit for the afters shift, and soon afterwards, coming around the bends the other way, are more men, some with black faces, others washed and in suits, a returning army marching and riding in vehicles, coming off the early shift and going home or up to the Coach and Horses in Barnburgh village. They pass and the land falls quiet, the day bending again to the crops until darkness falls, when at the late shift-change time new columns of men come and go under the red, low-hanging harvest moons.

Gordon is often with Pauline and Joan, and Pauline comes to like how quietly self-absorbed he seems when he is chucking around the sheaves or when, in the yard, he is running his hands over the animals to greet them or to check their health. Sometimes he teases Joan, and early one evening at the end of the week, when he, Pauline and Joan are working in a barley field half a mile from the yard, he calls to Pauline as she stands up a sheaf in a stouk only to see the whole arrangement collapse.

'Tha didn't stand yon up very straight. I shall gi'e thee t' sack!' He stands grinning, smug because he is getting through his sheaves at twice her speed.

Pauline feels a wave of self-consciousness, but then something makes her shout back. 'It's you sticking your nose in and putting me off. Get on wi' your own.'

Gordon laughs and wipes his face. The warm air is cooling and they can feel the heat coming off the baked soil.

'You tell him, Pauline,' says Joan.

Pauline is privately irritated that the sheaves have fallen, but her self-consciousness has lifted from her. She likes doing the work outside, working as a team; it is hard, but she always feels good afterwards. It is very unlike housework.

She re-stacks the stouk, and moves up to where Joan is working on the next one.

At the end of the week Pauline goes home, but she continues to visit the farm over the summer and, when the new term begins, on afternoons after school. On wet days Mr Benson finds her and Joan boring catch-up jobs to do, sweeping the yard, greasing machinery, or weeding the farm's vegetable garden, but when it is dry and clear they are out in the fields with Gordon. The three of them become close friends, and Gordon's teasing intensifies.

'Tha's leant yon sheaf up all cock-eyed!' he says, striding towards her in the strain and swelter of the field one day in September 1955.

'Oh, not you!' she says. 'Sling your hook!'

'Tha wants to watch it, or I'll get thee.'

'I'd like to see you try!' she says.

26

By the Light of the Silvery Moon

Thurnscoe, 1955–56

The summer he meets Margaret White, Roy Hollingworth stays in the Dearne for four months, living at his mam and dad's, working at the pit and taking the lovestruck Margaret out in Harry's car. In the autumn he goes off to train with the Army – so he says – returning the following January when he calls for Margaret and takes up their courtship where he left off. There follows a period when he comes and goes with little warning, staying in Highgate for two or three weeks at a time and making a fuss over Margaret when he is there. They go dancing, they go to the pictures, they go drinking, and everywhere Roy seems popular and charming. He seems to know lots of people, and he makes everyone laugh with his stories and jokes. He may not call for her for weeks on end, and he may never say exactly where he's been, but she likes him very much, and because her questions often irritate him she doesn't like to ask why when he says he just can't be tied down to one place at the moment.

One night in the spring of 1955, when Roy is back after 'seeing a man about a good job down south', he and Margaret go out with another Highgate couple that he knows. The four of them go to the Halfway Hotel and stay until last orders. Harry has taken the car to drive to a pub he is performing at, so Roy and Margaret set off to walk back to Thurnscoe, past the school and the dog track and then into open fields.

Roy has a brooding silence on him.

'You're quiet,' says Margaret.

He snaps, like a man who has been waiting for the opportunity. 'I should think I am.'

'Why, what's up?' She takes his arm in hers, but he is unresponsive.

'What were you talking to Stanley for all t' time? You've hardly said a word to me all night!'

'What do you mean?'

'Don't bloody come that.' With sudden violence he shrugs her off, and she stumbles into the dew-wet grass beside the path.

'Come what?'

He says nothing.

'Roy?'

'Awww –' He slaps out and up with his right hand, and hits the side of her face. Margaret reels into the grass, stops, holds her burning cheek. 'What are you doing?'

'You made me look like a damn fool tonight.'

'I don't know what you mean . . .'

He hits her again, grabs her arm, and pulls her away from the road. As she falls he drags her up again.

She sees he is drunk. They are near to a gate in the hedge, and he pulls her through and into the field, right in so she cannot see the road. She pleads with him to let her go, but instead he starts hitting her, face, neck, ears, torso, arms. He swears and calls her a bitch. She hits the ground and covers her face. He bends over her and slaps at her head. Then, staggering, cursing and panting, he reels away back towards the gate. Across the earth, level with her ear, she hears his rough steps receding.

She stands up. Her body hurts, and her clothes are ripped and dirty. She finds her shoes and walks through the field barefoot. When she reaches the path he is gone.

Her dad and her two brothers want to try to find Roy straight away, but she begs them not to, and in the end they relent. In the morning she has a swollen, purple-yellow eye, but the beating feels like a terrible dream. When she thinks about it, she wonders what she said or did to provoke him.

On Monday morning at work the girls say, get shut, get rid, as soon as you can. Some of them say they know him and he has a bad reputation, but Margaret finds them tiresome. It has been only the once, she thinks, and the way people judge him only confirms what Roy says about how small-minded they are. She loves him and, just as important, she believes she can help him.

*

Roy stays away from the Whites until the following week when he finds Margaret as she walks home from work and begs her to listen to his explanation. He says he is sorry, and he seems to mean it. It's just because he loves her so much. It sounds crazy, but he just can't bear not having her all to himself, honest.

They begin going out together again and to Margaret it seems that Roy, in his good moods at least, is loving and committed. Her father tells her to keep away, but she ignores him; she is in love, she says, and they can't understand a person like Roy.

Soon, however, it is her turn not to understand. Saying he has to go back to the Army, he stops calling for her, but the following week one of the girls at work sees him in Goldthorpe. Margaret calls at his mam's house, but Winnie says he isn't there and no one knows where he's gone. Out the back door and down the backings most likely, thinks Margaret, but says nothing and catches the bus home.

In fact, after being seen in Goldthorpe, Roy does go away for two weeks' training with the Northamptonshire Yeomanry, but he stays away from his parents' house for weeks afterwards. One night while he is away, Harry arrives home from a late shift to find an unexpected visitor waiting at his gate. He sees that it is a young woman, standing pale and hunched in a thin coat. He recognises her as one of Roy's girlfriends.

'What's up, love?'

'I want your Roy,' she says, trying to appear angry, but sounding desperate. 'Have you seen him?'

'I've been at work.' He drops the end of the cigarette he has been smoking, and grinds it out with his toe. It is past eleven o'clock. He is getting fed up with Roy and his antics, coming home when he feels like it, borrowing money and never paying it back, but there isn't going to be a row outside the house at this time of night.

'I've not seen him.'

'Are you sure he isn't at your house?'

'Not as I know of. Me and his mam never know where he is.'

'When did you last see him?'

He looks at her: her mascara is streaked, her lips are swollen, and she is shivering. 'Tha's famished wi' cold,' he says. 'Look, sit on t' wall, and put this round thy shoulders.' He takes off his blue cotton jacket and hands it to her. 'Has tha asked his mam?'

'I came before and asked her, but she says she hasn't seen him.'

Next door, at an upstairs window, a face peeks through the curtains. 'Here she comes,' sighs Harry, and shouts up, 'Get yoursen' to bed, Nelly.' The curtain closes. When he looks back at the young woman she is crying.

'Has he said anything about me? I'm Margaret.'

'Nay, I don't know, love. Come on, don't cry over him, he in't any good for thee. Get thysen off home.'

'I really love Roy, you know.'

'Maybe tha does,' says Harry. 'But he's not here. Does tha want me to drive thee home in t' car?'

Margaret refuses the lift and in the end walks home alone, but she keeps coming back. When Roy returns they resume their courtship, and then, one Sunday in the late summer of 1955, she comes again, dressed in her best clothes, and bringing some news.

She had hoped to find Roy, but only Lynda and Winnie are at home. Winnie invites her in and sends Lynda out into the yard, and Margaret blurts it out: she is pregnant. She waits for Winnie to accuse her of trapping him but, after taking off her pinny to acknowledge the gravity of the situation, the older woman strokes Margaret's arm and offers her a cup of Nescafé. Winnie is terse, but not hostile. She even says Roy should have been more careful. 'You don't have to marry him, Margaret,' she says. 'I don't mind either road. But don't let people make you feel you have to get married if you don't want to.'

'I bet you just don't want him to marry me, though. I bet it's not what he wants.'

This might have been true, but to Margaret, Winnie seems sincere. 'I'm not saying it because I don't want you to marry him,' she says. 'But I will tell you, as woman to woman, I don't think you'll have a good marriage with him. I'm telling you because I've seen enough to know that women don't know their men. I didn't, and I had to get married, and it's been hard for me sometimes. Be careful.'

A double bluff to save her son? Margaret doesn't know. She doesn't want to be careful. She just wants to be Roy's wife.

*

They marry at St Helen's Church, Thurnscoe on a November morning in 1955. The gathering is thin, and Horace and Hilda White watch the ceremony in despair. Once he is wed, Roy goes to work driving earth-moving machines on the spoil heaps of Hatfield colliery near Doncaster, and he and Margaret move in with Mr and Mrs White.

After a few months, Margaret's sister Alice persuades the owner of the car garage where she works to rent the couple a flat above the repair shop. The garage occupies a former ballroom built in the 1920s. The flat is small, with a dark, narrow staircase leading down to the front door between the workshop and showroom. It is clean but there is a permanent smell of engine oil, and in the mornings Margaret can hear men beating car panels. When Roy is out working late or drinking she lies awake, frightened, listening to the building creak and wondering where her husband might be. Sometimes he doesn't come back until the morning, explaining away his absence with stories of breakdowns at work or promised lifts home that didn't show up.

Her due date is in April 1956 and the months leading up to it are gloomy. Roy seems to be on early or late shifts most days, so he is either out or asleep in the bedroom. He doesn't tell her what shifts he is working, so she never knows when he'll come or go. When he is at home he goes on and on about the Army, almost as if he is still serving. He rants about Nasser and Suez, and says people don't know what the Arabs are really like, or what it is like to live in Egypt. Sometimes he goes on about it when her mam comes to visit bringing bedding or bottles for the baby, and Margaret notices her mam observing Roy's broad, strong body and looking nervous of him.

She goes into labour in the morning of Sunday 22 April. Roy is there and he looks after her, but by noon, Harry, Danny and some other Highgate friends call to pick him up for the Sunday lunchtime drink at the club. 'I'll be back at two for my dinner,' he says as he clatters down the stairs. The contractions are not close together yet, so she tells herself not to worry, but Roy doesn't come back at two. Shortly before three, Margaret goes to the callbox down the street and phones her mam, who calls the midwife and then comes to the flat. With her mam and the midwife there, the baby, a boy, is born at four that afternoon. At six, as she lies in bed with the newborn, she hears the key in the lock at the bottom of the long staircase, and then the heavy, irregular steps of her husband coming up. As he enters Margaret can smell the drink, and she feels a tension in the room. She knows her mother would like to ask him where he's been, but both of them sense it might set him off.

'Ayup,' he says, leaning over Margaret and the tiny, pink baby. 'Look at this! Now then, little nip . . .'

He makes a fuss of the child, holding him in his arms and talking to him. Then he gives him back to Margaret so he can go to make himself something to eat. As he walks into the kitchen he weaves slightly, and Margaret sees her mam looking, and feels embarrassed. She thinks about her mam and dad pleading with her not to marry him. Even outside the church her father had said, 'I can turn this car around now if you'll change your mind, love.'

Later, Roy goes out for another drink to wet the baby's head. He doesn't come back until Wednesday.

27

How Do You Get Away? Who Do You Have To Ask?

Highgate; Harlington; Thurnscoe, 1956–58

If you stand on the doorstep of 34 Highgate Lane and look across the road and over the fields you can see the railway line that runs from Sheffield through Highgate on its way north. At night, the long freight trains move the coal and steel, their steam spreading out behind them grey against the black sky, sparks flying from their wheels, the orange glow of the firebox lighting up the drivers and the firemen in their cabs. Pauline Hollingworth often comes to stand on the doorstep in the evening so that she can watch the engines and trucks passing by; they make her feel both moved and calm at the same time. She likes it best when she can see the men in the cab; she admires their skill and concentration, and imagines them at ease in each other's company. She watches each train right until the last wagon disappears into the cutting, and then when it has gone she tries to sniff out its lingering smokey, greasy tang in the night air until it too fades away.

Pauline is in her last year at school and the arts and humanities teachers have put her at the top of the class in their reports. The school does not offer academic qualifications, but at Easter the headmistress, Miss Garbutt, asks her what she plans to do after leaving. Pauline says that she would like to work with animals. Miss Garbutt says she may be able to get Pauline a place on an agricultural course at Brampton

Ellis, the further education college a mile the other side of Manvers Main. She asks if Pauline would be interested and Pauline says she will have to ask her mam.

Her mam doesn't know if the course would be useful, and is wary of forgoing the money Pauline would bring in if she was out working. Having no one else to ask, Winnie walks across the road to seek the advice of Jane Seels, a young woman whose husband has that year bought the farm from Benny Slater. Jane is articulate and educated, so Winnie assumes she will know about further education courses, and believes her when she says Pauline should go. There could be no end of opportunities for a girl with qualifications, Jane says; she could work at a vet's, or in an office, maybe even as a secretary.

Winnie tells Pauline to tell Miss Garbutt to make her enquiries, and Pauline, having once thought the idea outlandish, feels excited. When Roy visits he says she does right to go to college, and he, Harry and Winnie make jokes about what she'll be like when she's in with the professors, and thinks herself too good to speak to them. Three days later, however, Miss Garbutt calls Pauline back at the end of a class to tell her the course is full. She says Pauline can always try again next year, but Pauline feels as if there is a brick wall collapsing inside her chest, and she knows the chance has passed. She looks bravely at Miss Garbutt, thanks her and says that she'll come for a reference before she finishes school.

Four weeks before the end of term Winnie is taken into hospital to be treated for what she will refer to only as 'ladies' problems'. Annie comes to look after the family for a fortnight, and she and Winnie agree that Pauline must help too. As she is due to finish school soon anyway, they decide there will be no point in her going back, and so in the end, Pauline will not even collect Miss Garbutt's reference.

This decision taken on her behalf is like a hard, dull blow against the senses. Pauline can see that although opportunities in school and college are real, her mam and Muv don't take them seriously. In some ways, she thinks, they are glad to have her done with education; they do not quite trust the teachers, or at least they do not trust their own ability to take from the teachers anything of lasting value. Not of lasting value to a girl, at any rate.

*

From the start of her mam's stay in hospital, Pauline realises that her grandmother needs the extra assistance not because of her frailty, but for reasons that are rather the opposite. To the family's surprise Muv has on recent visits been energetically courted by Mr Edwards, a retired widower from Darfield, the next village along the Barnsley Road. Mr Edwards is smart and modestly cultured, and Winnie has accepted him as her mam's 'friend', while knowing, as everyone knows, that there is a great deal more to the liaison than friendship. He and Annie, both young sixty-seven-year-olds, go on bus trips together, and he visits her at home in Elland and at Winnie's. The presence of Mr Edwards means that Annie's two weeks in Highgate become a romantic holiday for her. 'I'll just catch a bus up to see Mr Edwards, and then come back to help you wi' t' cleaning,' she says to Pauline and Lynda after breakfast, before slipping out and returning home at teatime after a day of walks, half-pints of stout, and leisurely visits to the Darfield bookies.

Pauline cannot complain because, school-leaver or not, she is still regarded as a child. She spends her last school days looking after her recuperating mother and covering for a courting grandparent. Her last communication from her teachers is via her final report, which arrives through the post in July: she has two A grades and the rest are Bs, but no one in the house besides her looks at it.

Pauline doesn't know what she wants to do, other than work with animals. Some of the girls at school had talked about jobs in the mills or a factory with their sisters or cousins, and how much money you could make there, but her dad scotches that the first and only time she mentions it. 'Tha needn't think tha's working in t' mills, cos tha's not.' Harry wants her to do something better, although he is unsure of what a better job might be, and even less sure of how you went about getting one.

He tells her to go to the Labour Exchange to ask for a job, so she puts on a red twinset and her best black skirt, slips her school report into her handbag and walks up to the Ministry of Labour building next door to the Comrades Club. The main entrance is through a panelled wooden door, and leading off the long, lino-laid corridor inside is another door marked 'School-leavers'. Pauline pushes it open gingerly. Down one side is a line of wooden counters, behind which stand men in suits: opposite some of the counters, young lads looking for work lean forward and speak in awkward voices. Pauline walks up to a man who has no one speaking to him. He is fiftyish with a tweed jacket, collar and tie, and sharp nose. He seems ancient.

'I've come to see about a job,' says Pauline.

The man writes down her name, age and address, and asks what kind of work she is interested in. Pauline says she would like to be a kennel maid; she has decided this at home, having read about kennel maids in *Our Dogs*.

'Righto,' says the man, and takes a box file down from a shelf. He nods slowly to himself as he leafs through the papers inside the file, and finds her a job as a kennel maid at Brandon Park House in Suffolk, accommodation provided, start next week. 'Just ask your dad to sign these forms to say you can go, and bring them back to me,' he says. 'Thank you, Miss Hollingworth, and the best of luck. Cheerio now.'

She smiles as she walks back through Goldthorpe and across the railway bridge, thinking how lovely it will be to be among dogs all day, and how her dad will think she has found a good job. If the unnerving prospect of living somewhere new comes into her mind, she pushes it down into her coat pockets with her fists, and rehearses the new-job speech she will give back at Number 34.

When she gets home her dad is in the sitting room, trying to get a tune out of a trumpet. 'I'm going as a kennel maid to Suffolk, Dad!' she says.

'No, you're not,' he replies. 'Suffolk's too far off. Anyroad, thy mam wants thee here to help her in t' house.'

Pauline has no idea where or what Suffolk is, but she would live at the North Pole rather than upset the Labour Exchange man. 'But I've told them I'll go, Dad.'

'Well then tha'll have to go back and tell 'em that tha can't.'

'Can't *you* tell them?'

He doesn't answer. When she goes back to the Labour Exchange, the man shouts at her. 'Young people,' he says. 'All these opportunities, and they don't want to know.'

The man does not mention any other jobs, and Pauline is too afraid to ask again. Unsure of what to do next, she spends most of August at Beech Farm with Joan and Gordon. She feels happy when she is there, but she knows that it is an avoidance, a means of putting off her adult life. What to do about a job? Would she be allowed to have another offer, having turned one down in the way she did? She likes the idea of Marks and Spencer's in Doncaster, working in a shop being the next best option and Marks and Spencer's the best shop. But how did you get a job there? People she has asked, people who know other people who work there, say you just go in and ask if they have any vacancies. Ask! They make it sound like something everyone does all the time, which persuades her that her shyness makes her an oddball – a square peg in a round Marks-and-Spencer's-shaped hole.

*

In early September, Winnie takes Lynda on a coach trip to see Blackpool illuminations, and sends a postcard home addressed to Pauline, who has stayed back to look after Harry and the dogs.

Dear Pauline,

Margaret Hanson's mother is on this trip, and Margaret works at Windell's in Thurnscoe and she is leaving on Friday. Go straight down and see if you can get the job.

Mam

Pauline knows no more of Windell's in Thurnscoe than she does of Suffolk, nor has she any clue how someone goes to see if they can get a job, but she is not going to disobey her mam. She puts the skirt and twinset on again, stuffs her school report back into her bag, and hurries off to the bus stop.

Windell's on Lidget Lane used to be the village pawn shop. Old Mr Windell had fought the Irish in the uprising during the Great War, and returned to Thurnscoe with haunted memories and a deep suspicion of Irish people. He had married, and set up the pawn operation with his wife in the late twenties, when many villagers relied on pawning to get through the week. The shop had prospered, but as wages grew in the 1950s pawning decreased until it was hardly worthwhile, and when Mr Windell handed the business down to his son Jack, Jack turned the shop into a haberdashery. It now sells clothes and fabrics for men and women: shorts, blouses, Wellington boots, wool trousers, pinnies, tea dresses, cotton, calico, wool and more. Piled to the ceiling with up-to-date clothes and pretty material, the shop likes to think of itself as a genteel outfitter and drapers, but its balance sheets also rely on a steady income from miners' work clothes and flat caps, sold out of cardboard boxes laid on the floor.

Jack Windell is in his early forties, tall, slim, and well dressed in navy blue blazer, collar and tie, and slacks. He nods slowly as he listens to Pauline's story about her mam's postcard and Margaret Hanson's mother, and asks to see her references.

'I haven't any references because I've never had a job before. Will this do?' She takes the brown envelope containing the school report, and offers it across the counter, arm trembling over the yarns and cotton.

'This looks first-rate!' he says. 'Can you start on Monday?'

Pauline's shifts are nine until six, Monday to Saturday, with a half-day Wednesdays. Jack pays her £2 1s a week and says he will put up the wage a little each April. Every Friday she hands over all her wage to her mam, and Winnie gives her back five shillings for herself, from which she has to pay the bus fare to and from work. Most girls that Pauline knows pay board, but she is at the highest end of the payers.

Jack Windell spends most of the day in his office at the back of the shop while Pauline and a girl of about her age called Marjorie Swift work at the front. Jack shows her how to serve people, and how to correct the broader parts of her accent and dialect, because a broad accent holds you back and makes people think you are thick. When she says, 'I aren't going,' or 'I waited while half past seven,' he says, 'Where's your grammar, Pauline?' and she says, 'She's dead!' and they laugh, but she remembers what Jack has taught her and gratefully corrects herself.

She likes some of the customers, especially the younger women who come in to buy fabric for dresses. With regular customers Pauline discusses new fashions, dress patterns and sewing techniques, and she begins to advise them on the shop's stock, and to make suggestions about new orders to Jack.

Selling the men's clothes is less pleasant. She is put in charge of pit pants, the blue trousers that miners wear for work, and has to keep the high piles of them neat and topped up with the weekly deliveries that arrive from the warehouses in boxes as big as her. Pit pants are manageable once she learns to judge the sizes, but her other menswear specialism, flat caps, can be an ordeal. Windell's trade in the caps is brisk. They sell about half a dozen a week, more in the winter, and for ease of access Jack keeps the various sizes and patterns in the cardboard boxes they arrive in, laid out on the flagstone floor. Like most other shops in Thurnscoe, Windell's is infested with cockroaches, and while the insects tend to avoid the pit pant towers, they do crawl into the flat cap boxes. Every time Pauline opens a box, or takes out a cap for someone to try on, several cockroaches scuttle out across her hands and up her lower arms.

'Oh dear!' Jack exclaims the first time he sees her leap back, wincing, from a cap box. He waits for the customer to leave before talking to her, and she anticipates sympathy. 'Remember not to let them see if the cockroaches come out, Pauline. Try to get yourself in between them and the box. If one runs up your arm, just flick it off without them seeing.'

*

Pauline tells Gordon Benson about the cockroaches, playing up the story because he wears flat caps. By now she and Gordon have become close friends, and she is relaxed in his company. Sometimes Pauline, Gordon and Joan meet on Sundays to go to church, or to walk along the criss-crossing paths in the countryside looking out for animals or with Gordon commenting on the progress of crops in the fields. In the evenings they go out into the fields to watch the rabbits and hares playing in the dusk.

One day the three of them are in the farmhouse kitchen after a family tea. They have cleared the table and are washing plates, putting away the willow-pattern crockery and sweeping the flagstones. Joan unlatches the back door and steps out into the yard to take food scraps to the cows. As Pauline wipes the tabletop she catches Gordon's eye. Both of them blush. She moves towards the door. 'I'm off to see what your Joan's doing,' she says, but Gordon darts across to the doorway and stands in front of her, blocking her path with his hand on the latch.

'What are you doing, you daft 'apeth?' says Pauline. 'Let me out.'

'Not unless tha gives me a kiss.'

'– you what?'

'– tha 'eard,' says Gordon. He looks as if he is about to laugh.

Pauline grins, bounces up onto the balls of her feet, pecks him on his stubbled cheek and then ducks down under his arm and slips out through the door.

'What've you been doing?' asks Joan.

'Me?' she replies. 'Nowt!'

No one mentions this again, but afterwards something changes between her and Gordon.

The three of them go out more, driving in Mr Benson's Wolseley to watch Westerns at the cinema in Goldthorpe. Gordon wears his charcoal suit and Brylcreems his hair, and buys Black Magic chocolates for them to share during the film. Pauline lets Joan sit in the middle seat, because it would feel strange to sit beside Gordon in the dark.

There are evenings when Gordon drops Pauline off at home and she walks in to hear Harry and Winnie, and sometimes Roy, shouting at each other in the sitting room. They argue about Roy staying at the house, about Roy being a good husband, and the arguments turn into personal rows between Harry and Winnie. No one ever talks to Pauline or Lynda about Roy though. Pauline was not even invited to his wedding, and no one had told her Margaret was pregnant; she only realised when Margaret turned up at their house looking a strange shape.

The arguments make her feel like an outsider trapped in her own home. She goes back to the front door and opens it, and stands on the doorstep to watch the trains travelling through the darkness. She imagines being the driver or the man shovelling the coal into the fire, engrossed in their work, joking with their companions, loving their train in the way men loved things like trains. She would like to get on one of the trains and go somewhere else, but she doesn't know how she would do that, or where she would go.

How did you get away?

Who did you have to ask to do that?

28

The Accident

Barnburgh, 1957

June 1957. Harold Macmillan newly Prime Minister, Elvis Presley newly King. The British military is testing nuclear bombs in the Pacific, and the Paymaster General has ended the petrol rationing introduced during the Suez Crisis. ERNIE is picking the first Premium Bond winners, and Diana Dors is divorcing her manager. The kids at the dances are wearing winged spectacles and A-line dresses, bobby socks, beetlecrushers and Tony Curtis hair.

There is a heatwave across England and in the sweltering, smokey Dearne Valley the mothers are stripped to their corsets to do the housework and waiting to slap the wet heads of sons who have been swimming illegally in the brickyard ponds. Under the cloudless mid-blue skies the girls tan in the parks, and the farmland toasts, the soil dusty and the grass so tindery that the firemen are stretched by the blazes lit by sparks from trains. Through the hot nights, men and women congregate in the yards of Highgate Club and the Halfway Hotel. In the backings the summer carousers shout and sing into the small, happy hours.

Half-past ten on a Saturday night and there is singing outside the back door of 34 Highgate Lane. The singing is always outside the back doors because the front doors have the steep steps that are troublesome to a man at half past ten on a Saturday night. '*Gentleman songsters off on a spree, damned from here to eternity . . .*'

Three men, drunk on beer, are serenading Winnie, and Lynda, who has woken up and come downstairs to have hot milk by the fire. Winnie is sighing and is about to get up from the fireside as Harry, Sonny Parkin and Danny Lunness stagger in through the door, laughing.

'My sweet!' says Harry to Winnie, who wrestles off his hug, pulls down the front of the kitchen cabinet and saws thick, irregular slices off a bread loaf to make dripping sandwiches. With clumsy grace he plants a kiss on Lynda's head, then goes back into the kitchen as Danny comes into the living room. Lynda is delighted to see her uncle, especially late at night with this secret pass to the shadow world of the grown-ups. Danny takes half a crown from his pocket and pushes it into her hand and makes a joke about drinking hot milk: that's what he's been having tonight as well, he says.

'And saying thy prayers,' calls Harry, 'in church.'

'Church,' mutters Winnie. 'I know your church. T' church where t' bibles have handles.'

Without the presence of Sonny, Danny and Lynda her remark could have flickered into a row. As it is, Winnie smiles and Harry just shakes his head. 'I'm off to get some holy water,' he says, and takes the white enamel bucket and slips out the back door.

'Is tha coming to t' wedding?' Danny asks Lynda.

The wedding is between Pam Lunness – Danny and Millie's middle daughter – and Jack Gundry, a placidly mannered teddy boy who works on the same coalface as Danny at Barnburgh Main. Millie has been in a bluster of organisation, annoying Winnie who has been trying to help only to find Millie disregarding her suggestions ('She thinks she knows it all!' says Winnie, feeling that Millie has never been the same since she joined the Buffs a few years ago). There is some anxiety over money because Danny recently damaged his thumb in a pit accident and has been off work for two weeks.

In the club that evening, Danny now tells Winnie, Jack has been worrying about beer for the wedding. Months ago Danny had agreed to buy a barrel for the reception, but if he doesn't get back to work soon he won't be able to afford one. 'I'm going on Monday if I can, but this – ' he holds up the still-bandaged hand – 'i'n't half giving me some hammer. I'm worried if I get working I'll do my hand altogether.' Danny's hands have been worked hard by boxing, but it is the ability to grip that he worries about. Without that you can't work, and can end up with a pit-top job.

'Tha manages to hold pint glasses all right,' says Harry, coming back into the room with the beer.

'I want to get back and get sorted out wi' em about t' ventilation,' says Danny, ignoring him. 'I had a right ding-dong wi' t' under-manager and I shall kick his backside before I've done. There's gas leaking through somewhere on our face. They reckon to have inspected t' ventilation but tha can smell it sometimes.'

This dispute has been running on and off for a year. Last summer inspectors detected explosive firedamp in a hole in the roof but then, after adjusting the doors that controlled the flow of air around the mine, they said it was no longer present. Together with the union man Danny, who is the lineman on his shift, requested another check by the miners' own panel of inspectors a few days before he hurt his thumb. They found no gas and said the ventilation was in order, and Danny, speaking on behalf of his men, had a row with both the inspectors and the undermanagers. He said the firedamp must be collecting in holes in the rock, it had to be. They said they couldn't find it and there was nowt else they could do.

'They need to shift t' doors to get air going round,' he says to Winnie. 'I *know* there's gas. I flaming know it.'

The heatwave lasts, and by the end of the month the River Dearne runs low in its bed and the firemen can no longer keep up. On the afternoon of Wednesday 26 June, as the valley swims in heat, Winnie retires to the cool of the sitting room to rest. The early part of Wednesday afternoons, before Lynda returns from school, is the time she takes for herself in the week to knit, sew or read. Today she gazes at a novel, but finds concentration difficult.

At just past three o'clock she hears voices in the yard that are louder and more numerous than usual, and when they persist she goes to the kitchen door. Through the gate she sees men and women hurrying up and down the backings. Comfort Eades is in the yard talking to two women from Barnsley Road. 'Summat's gone off at Barnburgh pit,' she says to Winnie. 'Accident or summat. They've just made an announcement at t' pictures, and asked 'em at Highgate pit if they can send some men down to help.'

She thinks about Millie and Danny, and Clara and Ernie. Ernie, who also works on Danny's face at Barnburgh, has just gone back to work after a stay in the caravan in Bridlington. Winnie asks Comfort to watch Lynda, then takes her bag and beetles down the hill to Bolton-upon-Dearne, the sun hot on her skin, the sound of a pit buzzer audible in the distance. As she nears Bolton, there are people on the street. Some are hastening along the footpaths towards Barnburgh Main colliery. Two police cars shoot past followed by a blue NCB ambulance with its bells ringing.

Clara has already left. Her neighbour, standing in the street, tells Winnie there has been an accident underground at Barnburgh. 'No one knows how many of them were in it,' she says, 'it's awful for them who've got somebody at work.'

Every miner's wife and mother lives with feelings of anxiety and foreboding that are quieted by routine. You know what time he usually gets back from his shift and you notice the first minute gap opened up by the long hand when he is late. Some women worry more than others, but they all wonder as they wait. There are always the little injuries to remind you: him coming home with a cut on his head; his vertebrae badly rubbed and scabbed; him having to go to hospital for a few stitches. When he is in an accident you are shocked, but the accident feels less like a random event than a buried fear breaking out from the earth. And you know people who have been killed or hurt, so it is nothing new, just your turn. Most mining families believe strongly in fate.

'It is frightening, love,' says Winnie. 'Let's hope Ernie's alright.'

'My husband's on earlies, thank God,' says the woman.

'My brother-in-law's been off for two weeks, and he was on about going back. He'll be glad he didn't now. I'll walk round to see them.'

At about the same time, Jack Gundry is sitting on a windowsill in the house in Bolton-upon-Dearne that will be his and Pam's new lodgings once they are married. He is decorating, seated with his legs inside the room and his body out, so he can paint the wooden frames white. The sun is drying the paint quickly, and warming his back and the pale skin of his neck. A transistor radio plays in the room, and over its chatter he hears the pit buzzer and wonders what's going off. As he is wondering here comes Reg Smith, a mate who works on the pit top, hurrying down the street, and calling up to Jack with an odd tone in his voice.

'Ayup Jack –'

'Ayup Reg.' On seeing Reg, Jack feels guilty because he has taken the day off pretending to be ill. 'I'm on t' painting and decorating today. I've got to get this done before we get married, like.'

Reg's expression changes as he realises Jack hasn't heard. 'Thy face has just gone up, tha knows –'

Jack drops the brush; it bounces off the pavement leaving a splatter of white on the dirt. Then he is rushing down the stairs and out onto the street towards Danny and Millie's house. Had Danny been at work today? He had said he would go back this week, but he hadn't been there yesterday, so probably not. Best to make sure though.

He runs past women clustered at front doors, their kids around their feet frightened and fascinated. Men pass by him heading the other way, towards the pit. A memory comes to him from a shift last week – him saying to his mate Derek Smith that the pit's ventilation engineers had the airflow wrong, that the way they had set their system of doors and curtains in the faces, gates and roadways could allow gas to accumulate. Derek had said Jack was fussing and Jack had left it at that, but now the face had gone up. If there had been an explosion, gas would almost certainly have been the cause.

*

Hall Broome Gardens, Number 7: Millie is at the garden gate with two neighbours. Jack's chest is rising and falling heavily.

'Ayup, Jack,' she says.

'Where is he?'

'He's at t' pit, love. He said he were going back to get that barrel.'

Jack stands silent and feels as if he could just float up into the air.

'I know there's been an accident,' she says, 'but we don't know what's going off yet, do you know what it is?'

'I'm not sure yet.'

'Has anybody said owt to you?'

'No,' he lies. He doesn't want to worry her.

More neighbours come out into the street to ask if anyone has any news and some of them set off for the pit, but Millie stays, not wanting to tempt fate. Jack stays with her. He has lost track of how long he has been there when he sees a policeman approaching, checking the house numbers as he walks up the street towards them.

The pit buzzer continues to wail across the valley and in the villages men rush into the clubs to alert the drinkers. Cinema managers order projectionists to halt the matinee reels and announce the accident to audiences, who then pile out into the sunshine to seek news, or head off to offer assistance. Along the roads and on the footpaths and in the summer-deep green lanes, hundreds of miners hurry towards Barnburgh pit top, and through the streets race clanging ambulances, roaring police cars, and tyre-squealing black cars of managers and officials, more and more and more of them and then gradually fewer and fewer until the ambulances begin to pass the other way. Soon the ambulances are shuttling back and forth between the pit and the hospitals at Doncaster, Mexborough and Rotherham, and all across the valley the people gathered on streets or in house doorways are sharing scraps of knowledge and rumour. *It's in t' Newhill seam. It were a big explosion, must've been gas . . . There's above two dozen men been hurt they reckon, and there's ambulances coming from all over. They've started bringing 'em out and they've took a lot to t' Montagu. A lot of 'em's been burned bad . . .*

At the gates of Barnburgh Main a crowd, mainly women and children, is looking for sons, husbands, boyfriends, brothers. They peer into the yard, asking each other what they know, watching black-faced miners in burned clothes carry men on stretchers from the shaft side to the ambulance room. One man, a fifty-one-year-old deputy with charred hands and face, busies himself ensuring that the worst hurt get seen first, and tends to the men as he passes among them. Others kneel over the injured to help them sip water from Dudleys, talking to them to keep them conscious. Doctors from Thurnscoe, Bolton and Goldthorpe arrive in their cars and go underground to treat the men who cannot be moved. The pit manager, colliery staff and NUM officials cross the yard and follow them down to inspect the accident scene. And one by one, the worst hurt are eased into ambulances and sped away. There are twenty of them in all, some so badly burned that friends who helped them on the pit top had not been able to recognise their faces.

*

'Mrs Lunness?' The policeman is one of several criss-crossing the village to find next of kin. In Millie's sitting room he explains to her and Jack that Danny was caught in the explosion, but has been brought out alive and taken to the Montagu. His condition is critical and no visitors are being admitted.

Millie appears calm but numb. When Winnie arrives and makes her a cup of tea, she talks only of the children: how to tell if Barbara and Pam have found out yet, how to contact Brian in Newmarket, and Tony, who is in the Army. Five times she will have to say it: your dad is critical, love, and you need to be ready to see him.

Pam comes, and is told. When she and Jack have steadied her, Winnie goes to Clara's house, where Clara is back preparing to go to Doncaster Royal Infirmary. Ernie has been caught in the accident and is ill, but not critical; their son Derek, who had been due to sail to Hong Kong as part of his National Service, is on his way home to see him. Clara tells Winnie the figures she has heard: four besides Ernie have been taken to Doncaster, four others are in a hospital in Rotherham, and eleven more at the Montagu. Some of them are very poorly. 'It's funny,' she says. 'You always know it could happen, and then when it does, you can't believe it.'

*

The following day the men in the Montagu are allowed visits from relatives and close friends, and Harry drives Jack, Millie and Winnie to the hospital. The injured miners occupy a single ward, and in the corridor outside a loose handful of forlorn children, barred from going in because of their age, crouch on heels, clutch dolls and run Dinky cars along the floor.

Winnie and Harry go in behind Jack and Millie. Before she is even inside the ward, the strong, nauseating odour of burned hair and putrefying flesh makes Millie retch. Many years later, when the visitors tell their children and grandchildren about the accident, it is the smell they remember; for many of them, the ward and the appearance of the burned men is hazy, as if the fouled air had made them drunk. Millie has a moment of dizziness, then takes in the sight of the ward. There are five beds lined along each wall. On each bed lies a block of ice the size of a single wardrobe. On each block of ice lies a man, naked but for a towel across his abdomen. Each man's skin is a black mass of scorched scabs, like the skin of a burned baked potato cooked in a bonfire, with a few small flashes of wet, red-raw flesh. Worst are the heads, swollen to twice their proper size, with most of their hair and facial features burned off, making it hard to distinguish one from the other.

There is silence, broken only by attempts at coughs from the older men. They cannot speak properly to call you, so all that is left is eye movement. As Jack, Harry, Winnie and Millie come into the middle of the ward, several pairs of eyes, bloodshot-white in the black heads, swivel to them. Some of the families sitting by the burned men, the Grattons and the Edwards who live close to Dan and Millie, murmur greetings. Millie gasps and reels. Winnie takes her arm. Jack thinks quickly and looks, trying not to appear obvious, at the record sheets clipped onto the iron bars at the bottom of the beds without visitors until he sees 'D. Lunness'.

Beside the beds the relatives sit, trying to think of what to say, and not breathing through their noses. Danny's lips are charred, and his mouth is a wet pink hole in the black crust of his face, like a hole in a burned pie. He can barely speak, but sometimes he looks yearningly at Millie and as he spasms with pain, he croaks, 'Get hold of me, Millie' – and she has to say, 'I can't,' because she knows if she holds him she will hurt him. For the hour they are allowed to remain in the ward the visitors have to take breaks outside because the smell makes them feel they will be sick.

After the visit a doctor takes Millie into a waiting room. The doctor, balding, eyes tired behind spectacles, is weary, hesitant, relying on a script in his head. 'It's difficult to say at this point, Mrs Lunness,' he begins. 'But – '

'Don't flannel me, doctor,' says Millie. 'I can see what state he's in. Just say it.'

The doctor nods. 'All right. Well, with those burns, your husband is lucky to be alive. We can't give you any guarantee, but if his body can build enough strength to begin recovering there is a good chance for him. If he stabilises here, we can move him to the Special Burns Unit at Wakefield, and then if he survives for a month, say thirty days from now, his chances of a full recovery will go up to ninety per cent.'

Danny does stabilise, and as he regains his strength he spends further visiting times telling the family what happened. Forty men on the two o'clock shift had been working on a coal face deep underground and half a mile from the pit bottom. They were making the face ready so that the next shift could cut coal from its seam. Some men repaired the tunnels, or gates, that led off at angles from the long, five-foot-high gallery with its wall of coal, while the wastemen moved the roof supports, allowing parts of the rock roof to collapse behind them. Danny was working as lineman for a team of eighteen wastemen. They were moving roof supports when Danny saw, many yards down one of the gates, a set of safety doors blow open.

There is a bright blue flash, and then a fireball of gas is rushing down the tunnel towards the men. Danny shouts, 'Get down!' and drops to his knees. The other men drop likewise, heads bowed tightly into their chests, hands protecting genitals. One, however, Jack's mate Derek Smith, stands up, spooked. Danny shouts to him, but Derek, panicking, gallops down the gate, trying to outrun the flames. Before anyone can stop him the flames engulf them all. As the fireball whooshes over him, Danny can feel it rip at his clothes and burn his body, and then there is a roaring, rattling hurricane of earth and coal dust being sucked into its wake.

For a second, time slows. Danny thinks about his skin, and about Derek, and about how bad everyone's burns will be. He has time to stand up in the thick, swirling dust, and make out the shapes of other men around him standing up and looking for the gates that lead off the face. He has time to search for the fireball, but when he spots it, it is rebounding off the brattice-cloth hurdles at the end of the face, and rushing back towards them. Derek is for a moment silhouetted prostrate on the ground. The men cannot get down again, and they take the full force front on. The blast scatters them like leaves in the wind. It blows off most of their remaining clothes, blasts their scalps from their skulls and burns lumps out of their ears and noses. As they regain consciousness their lungs feel as if the flames are in them, and because there is no oxygen in the air they are inhaling smoke, fire and coal dust. There is a strong smell of tar. The dust is so thick that you can see for only a yard or two.

Some men who are able to walk try the telephone near the face that links to the pit bottom and the surface, but it is out of order. It takes several minutes for the deputies to realise there has been an accident. Someone breaks open the boxes of morphine kept in the tunnels and dispenses it to the injured men. The colliery officials on the surface are alerted and SOS calls put out. The seam is evacuated and the remaining miners told to go home, but most stay to help find the men and get them above ground.

It takes more than an hour to take the most badly affected men off the face. Each one, burned, and dosed with morphine, has to be taken the half mile to the shaft, brought up and then carried to the ambulance room and readied for dispatch to the hospitals. The injured and dying men come up on stretchers, covered in blankets, but even the hot summer air feels cold on their burnt bodies, clumps of hair and scalp hanging down, skin and rags flapping. Some have their faces covered, but none are dead, yet.

'We told them, Jack, didn't we? I *told* him about that gas.'

Jack nods to Danny. He had thought the same.

'And people heard me. When I get out of here, I'm going to sue the bastards. There's kids could've lost their fathers.'

Everyone around the bed is quiet, taking in the story. Danny tries to smile. 'Never mind the kids,' he croaks to Jack. 'We'll still have that barrel.'

*

Danny survives to the end of the week. The doctors judge him fit enough to move, and order his transfer to the Specialist Burns Unit at Wakefield Pinderfields Hospital. The family, with his son Brian back at home now, begins daily trips to sit with him and as they tick off the thirty days, Danny keeps going. Three weeks after the accident he is growing stronger and is thinking about his options for suing the managers. He survives the first week in the new hospital, and then the one after that. Ernie, meanwhile, is slowly recovering in hospital in Doncaster.

The inspectors go in at Barnburgh Main, and the pubs and clubs are full of rumour. Jack and Pam decide to put off the wedding until Danny recovers, and Pam holds her dad's burned hand and tells him she won't get married until he comes out to give her away. Jack cannot stop himself feeling guilty for not having been at work and angry at the arbitrariness of it all. One night, he meets Derek Smith's mother in the street. Jack had been brought up with Derek on the same backings. When they were at school Jack had wanted to be a gardener and Derek had wanted to work on a farm; Derek had got a farm job, but then married and had children, and the pit paid so much better than working on the land.

'He's in t' hospital at Donny,' Mrs Smith tells Jack. 'He's been asking after you, love. He says he'd like to talk to you, will you go to see him and sit wi' him one night?'

Jack says of course he will, he'll go tomorrow night, but the next day, Thursday 4 July, a neighbour tells him that Derek has passed away in hospital. He is the first of the rescued men to die.

*

When the family goes to see Danny at the Burns Unit, the smell is still as bad but Danny can talk a little more easily. He has a healthy body, still fit from the gym, and he withstands the injuries well. He seems to grow neither weaker nor stronger, but the days pass and he is still alive at the start of the last of the four weeks. 'It's his strength,' Millie and his family tell each other as they gather in the kitchen before going to Wakefield, or coming home through the light, summery night. 'It's all t' training and boxing he's done.' 'Tha's going to be all right, Danny,' Jack says, and Danny cracks a white smile in his still-reddened face.

But the following week, twenty-two days after the accident, he grows weaker, feverish and tired. After tests, the doctors tell Millie he is recovering well from the burns, but there is a complication. The dust and gas have poisonous chemicals in them and when they came into contact with his raw wounds the toxins had entered his blood. Danny has leukaemia, and the doctors can do nothing to arrest it.

When Millie arrives on 24 July, the twenty-ninth of the doctor's thirty days, the curtains are drawn around Danny's bed. Millie assumes his dressings are being changed, but when she tries to slip through she sees doctors and nurses around the bed, and the doctors are peering at him. A senior nurse shuffles over, takes Millie's arm and leads her away.

There is fluid on his lungs, says the nurse, but the doctors are doing their best.

A few hours later, Danny Lunness dies.

*

Four more of the men besides Danny and Derek die from their injuries. Ernie Towning recovers in hospital, but suffers nightmares about the explosion, waking up confused to find himself on the ward. On the day he is discharged Clara and the kids go to collect him, and when young Clare sees his burned black and red face she thinks her father is a monster, and runs away from him, screaming. His flashbacks recur, and one afternoon, a week or so after returning home, he waits until Clara and the children go out, walks into the kitchen, turns on the gas oven, and puts his head inside. Clara comes back in time and wakes him, yanking him away from the oven by his belt. 'You silly bugger,' she yells. 'What the bloody hell are you playing at?'

He is ashamed and silent. She upbraids him, and afterwards tells people what he has done with words repeated so often they become a catchphrase: 'The silly bugger can't even get that right.' The words sound cruel, but they are only pitiless; Clara is of the old school and she knows that pity can weaken a person. Ernie slowly recovers stability, though he never goes underground again, taking a job above ground on the colliery trains. He suffers nightmares for the rest of his life.

In September the coroner records that Danny was 'by misadventure burned on 26 June 1957, underground in the North West 1 District of the Newhill seam in Barnburgh Main colliery, Barnburgh, in the West Riding of the County of York when involved in an explosion of fire-damp'. Danny's full name does not appear on the lists of British mining fatalities because someone at the NCB or the hospital mistakenly listed him as 'David'. Nor does his version of the accident appear in the official NCB report, which records that it was caused by a spark from an electrical cable with worn armour coating being carried for yards on air currents until it came to a pocket of gas.

The family bury Danny in Goldthorpe churchyard. At the funeral, the church and the cemetery are packed with men and women in mourning black, families of miners, boxers and neighbours. The women wipe their eyes with small flowered handkerchiefs and the men clasp their red, nicked, blue-scarred hands in front of themselves and look down. Union representatives carry the red and gold union banner.

Perhaps the younger Millie, the Millie who married her young boxer and who could match Harry Hollingworth for lip, would have made a fuss and had the name on the memorial corrected. But Danny's passing seems to reduce her to a pale, smokey ember. Within the year she uses her compensation payment to buy a sweet shop near the cinema in Goldthorpe to give herself an income, but it is as if something in her is broken. She finds she cannot sing any more and retires from public performances. Before the end of the decade the family will acknowledge that her incomplete recovery has become a permanent decline in her health.

*

Pam and Jack marry in a subdued ceremony at the end of August. Pam wears grey rather than white, and she walks down the aisle alone, refusing to be given away by anyone else. The men on the Newhill seam are given leave to stay off work for a day or two, but when Jack goes back to work, his undermanager makes him go to the scene of the accident to salvage the equipment. Jack asks if he could work somewhere else, since that was where his father-in-law and his best friend received their fatal injuries. 'No chance,' says the undermanager, 'and if you don't like it, you can get off down the road.'

At Highgate Lane, Danny is remembered alongside Walter as a hero and martyr to life's random unfairness; a smashing fella whose smashingness is somehow intensified in the memory by the unpleasantness of his death. The family being what it is, he doesn't fully leave them for a while anyway. One day, a few weeks after Danny's funeral, Winnie is alone in the house, cleaning, when she hears a man's voice in the room. She lays down her duster on the sideboard and turns to see Danny standing in front of the fireplace. 'Ayup, Danny love,' she says. 'How are you going on? Have you been to see your Millie?'

'Aye,' he tells her. 'I've just been down to see her, to see if she's all right.'

And then in the silent house he lingers, as he will linger for many years in the Hollingworth memory, looking bemused, as quick and flickery as flames in a fire, and as if he might at any moment burst joyfully into song.

29

I Said, 'Shut it!'

Thurnscoe, 1958

In the autumn of 1957 Margaret falls pregnant again. When she tells Roy he is sanguine and caring, saying it's a good job, they ought to be having a brother or sister for little Gary, their son. Roy does not stay out late for a while and the family has one of its periods of contented calm. Margaret has the flat how she likes it, Gary is walking and beginning to talk, and Roy is earning good money at Hatfield colliery. He still talks about himself as an Army man, even though he was discharged from the Emergency Reserve the previous December. The Army had recognised his qualities, he feels: in his discharge papers he had been described as 'a sober, honest and trustworthy man . . . who can be given a reasonable amount of responsibility, and who is prepared to work hard'.

And now, in his civilian career, he does work hard, clocking up the overtime on the earthmovers, and arguing with his dad about the strain when they go out drinking. Harry and his pals annoy Roy with their insistence that the young men complaining these days should have tried the pits under the old gaffers, on their bellies with picks and shovels. They'd not be able to stand it now, they say, they're different, a weaker kind of men. Roy is bored by this competitive suffering, and by the petty materialism that goes with it. His dad's expensive shirts and gold-plated tie-clips are ridiculous to him because, after all, 'they're only in bloody Thurnscoe'. Vexed by it all he goes home and tells

Margaret: No, he's not paying for new stuff, what did it matter if it was new or not? It's all show for the neighbours, and he hates it. 'I'm telling you,' he says, 'if there was a place where everyone had no possessions, and walked around naked, I'd go to live there.' Margaret tells him to stop talking daft.

*

Her labour begins on the evening of 3 July 1958. She is up all night, with Roy rubbing her back and encouraging her, but by the morning the contractions have faded away. Her mam takes Gary, Roy goes to work, and her dad drives her to the Montagu where she gives birth to another baby boy. Roy comes to see her after work in the evening, and he is gentle and kind, holding her hand, smiling down at the baby. He tells her not to worry and says he'll come tomorrow and bring her home.

The following morning, a Saturday, there is no sign of him, and no message. Margaret waits, and waits, and then a nurse says there is an ambulance going to Thurnscoe that can take her and her baby home if she likes. She gets back to the flat at half past twelve. Roy is sitting at the kitchen table.

With her senses and tolerance shot, her usual fear of confronting him falls away. 'Where've you been? I thought you were coming for me?'

'What's up with you? I was just going to come down!'

'Were you hell,' she says. 'I bet you've been out all night with them from Highgate.'

'Them from Highgate' means Roy's family.

'Aye, I went out for a drink. Then I came home, I got up and I was just coming down to fetch you.'

The baby cries in the basket. Roy and Margaret have a row. Roy storms out and doesn't come back for three days.

Margaret calls their new son David. He is a quiet baby, but nevertheless, with two children their one-bedroom flat now seems small. The boys' things fill all the spare space, and Margaret is up through the night feeding or soothing them. Roy recoils from her and the home, and soon he is staying away again, and irritable when he comes home. He takes off for days with no warning, and when he comes back he finds her upset and tired, but talks her round with stories about fantastic job offers that will make them rich. She lets herself believe him, but then a few weeks later he will disappear and she is alone with the boys again.

When she can, she takes Gary and David back to her mam and dad's house, but this makes Roy fume. Sometimes he leaves them all there and goes back to stay at Harry and Winnie's, until they run out of sympathy and tell him to look after his kids like a proper father. His moods darken. His attempts to be a kind, responsible husband never last the month and then he's off, staying out and blaming Margaret for her nagging when he returns. One night, when David is six months old and Gary is two, he turns violent again.

He comes back after being away for two days and enters the bedroom swaying. He holds a glass bottle of milk in his hand. Margaret gets out of bed and stands up to him.

'Where the hell have you been? I've been worried here on my own.'

'I've been working.'

'Working! Boozing more like.'

'Aw, give it a rest, love. I've been *working*.'

'Don't lie to me!' She pushes him. He pushes her back harder, against the bed.

'Shut it!' he says, and she sees him lift the hand holding the milk. Instead of hitting her with it, he removes the top, and pours the milk over her head, swearing at her as he does so. A few moments later he is gone.

Margaret sits on the bed, and looks over to the cots in the corner. David is awake and crying, and Gary is standing with his hands on the rail, watching the milk drip from his mother's body down onto the bedsheets.

30

Sexy Rexy

Barnburgh, Highgate and the Mecca Ballroom, Wakefield, 1959–61

Gradually, on trips to Scarborough and to the cinema, Pauline finds that she can talk to Gordon about things she cares about, things that other people find boring. He seems interested in her dog and in her story about Juggler Jane's rosary, and he laughs when she tells him about a pompous man trying on a flat cap at Windell's and finding a cockroach in it. She likes his stories about the farm, and the cows that come to the gate when you call their names, and some of the cranky people he delivers milk to, using his bike with a churn tied to the back. He is funny, but not a show-off. They get along and share their stories, and then one evening they go for a walk on their own, and just sit watching the rabbits in the fields for a while, and when she has cold feet afterwards she puts them on his knee and he warms them in his big hands. They go for more walks like that together, and go for a drive to Bridlington in the Wolseley. A few weeks later, on her eighteenth birthday, Gordon buys her a gold crucifix, which both of them know means they have moved from being friends to courting.

Because Gordon cannot dance and Pauline dislikes pubs, they spend their evenings walking, or going to the pictures, or – their favourite – watching the wrestling at the Doncaster Corn Exchange. One of the goodies is a wrestler from Doncaster called Rocky Wall, and Pauline and Gordon like to go to cheer him on, and to laugh at the old ladies who jump out of their seats to abuse the villains who, behind the referee's back, are twisting Rocky's fingers. Everybody, especially the old ladies, loves the wrestling for the release it gives you, and for the clear distinction between the goodies and the baddies. The ring is one of the few places where you can count on seeing a villain get his comeuppance, and people take a lot of pleasure from that.

*

It is a different sort of wrestling that leads to Gordon and Pauline's parting one Saturday night in March 1960, about a year after Gordon gave Pauline the crucifix. He suggests a ride in the car, which usually means driving somewhere, parking up and going for a walk, then going into Goldthorpe for fish and chips. In the past they have always driven along the main road running along the eastern lip of the valley, but tonight just outside Barnburgh Gordon turns off onto a narrow lane that goes up into trees along a rise called Melton Ridge. 'I've not been this way before,' says Pauline.

Gordon always knows where the little roads and tracks link up. 'It brings us out in Goldthorpe,' he says, 'eventually.'

He slows the car, eases it over into a flat part of the verge and switches off the engine. To their left is a gap in the woods, and through the gap Pauline can see the land falling away beneath them, trees making black patterns in the gloom. She sees the lights of a colliery, and street lights of villages and towns reaching into the distance. What has he stopped for? she wonders.

Suddenly, she feels Gordon's left hand come to rest on her right knee. Her body tenses, and in her mind she sees a series of scenes flash past: herself at home carrying an unplanned baby; women gossiping about her on the street; a shotgun wedding and a lonely and loveless marriage.

'Take your hand off my leg, Gordon,' she says.

'Come on,' he replies. 'What will you do if I don't?'

'I shall get out of the car and walk home.'

'Well . . . get out and walk then!'

She can tell he expects her to stay in the car. 'Right,' she says, and gets out, slams the door and sets off walking.

She is frightened because the road is very dark, and she doesn't know where she is. After a few minutes she hears the car starting up, and it occurs to her he might drive home and leave her, but in fact he draws up alongside her, the headlights throwing her shadow violently forward and then out to the side. She keeps walking.

'Come on,' he says. 'Get in.'

'No.'

'I'm sorry, love. Please get in.'

She would like to keep on walking but she has no idea how to find her way back.

'I'll get in if you take me home.'

'Alright.'

'And I mean *now*.'

She gets back into the car, and they drive in silence, down off the ridge and through the countryside, until they reach Highgate Lane. Pauline gets out without speaking and walks up the steps to Number 34. Gordon drives away, and that is that. No fall, no submission, knockout.

*

'Flaming lads!' says her friend Enid Morris when Pauline tells her about the Melton Ridge incident. 'Come out dancing with us instead!'

'Us' is Enid (brunette, serious, conservative) and Alma Winder (redhead, often described as bubbly). They live on Highgate Lane and go dancing together at weekends. When they take Pauline out she is surprised to see how much rock 'n' roll the band plays, and how wild the dancing is. The boys have narrow trousers, suede shoes and their hair combed up in greasy crests, and when they dance they throw the girls all over the place. This looks like good fun to Pauline but she has no idea how to do the steps, and so the next day she puts on loose clothes and walks down to Enid's house to learn.

Enid brings a Dansette into the front room and, to the sound of Adam Faith, teaches Pauline to rock 'n' roll. Hips, stockinged feet, heel and toe, lift the stylus back to the outside edge of the record and start again: by the time she goes home she is converted and euphoric, and her mam and dad's sitting room feels stupefyingly dull. *Sing Something Simple* is on the radio, confirming the imminent end of the weekend. Harry is having a wash in the kitchen before he goes up to the club, Winnie is making boiled eggs and toast for tea, and Lynda is watching a ballet on TV.

'Enid's been teaching me to dance rock 'n' roll,' she says.

'Rock 'n' roll's not dancing,' says Harry. 'It's not music either.'

'I like it.'

'Gi'e o'er,' he says. 'It's kidology.'

'Gi'e o'er yoursen, Harry,' says Winnie, in the stout voice she has begun using as she approaches middle age. While her husband sticks with the music of his youth, she has opted to keep up, and is all for rock 'n' roll. 'It's only t' same as when you used to do t' Black Bottom and t' Charleston, and wear bell bottoms.'

'Them were proper trousers, not hosepipes – '

'Drainpipes, Dad.'

'I'm not bothered what they call them, I'm talking about what they look like. Anyroad, you needn't think you're going up that Astoria, because you're not.'

The Astoria is the dance hall at the top end of Goldthorpe, and some of the bands there play almost exclusively rock 'n' roll music. Working on the village logic that suggests the further away people in a settlement live, the more vulgar and corrupt they are, Harry regards the Astoria as a seat of depravity.

'Who said I was going to t' Astoria?'

'There's lasses going in there wearing next to nowt, and half of them lads are thugs. If you think I'm having my daughter going with that lot on a Saturday night you've another think coming.'

'We're going to Highgate Club. There's a dance on.'

Highgate Club's large function room hosts dances, or 'so-called dances' as Harry calls them, where bands play a lot of rock 'n' roll.

'Well, just don't come crying to me when somebody drops you and breaks your neck,' he says.

*

The dance at Highgate Club gets off to a bad start when the man on the door laughs at Pauline and asks her if her dad knows she's here, and she has to ask Reg Spencer to sign her in. Inside, as soon as the quickstep is announced, a man in his mid-twenties asks Pauline to dance and holds her so tightly she can feel his hipbones. Afterwards Alma says, 'Don't be frightened to give 'em a slap if they get wandering hands, Pauline. Men today have got it on the brain,' which makes Pauline nervous. When the lead singer announces the rock 'n' roll section, she dances with Enid while Alma accepts a dance from a man in a blue suit who throws her up in the air then half-drops her.

When the girls regroup on the chairs down the side of the dance-floor, Alma says to Enid, 'I see they brought Sexy Rexy with them tonight.'

'Sexy Rexy?' says Pauline.

'She means him, there –' Enid indicates a man across the room, standing with a group of lads Alma had said hello to earlier. 'That lad with t' black hair, who came wi' 'em tonight. They call him Rex Jackson. He's from Wombwell.'

Rex Jackson from Wombwell is in his early twenties, with hair that tumbles in curls over his eyes, and a languid way of leaning against a wall. He is good-looking and well aware of it.

'What do they call him Sexy Rexy for?'

'Cos they all fancy him I suppose. Are you going to go and ask him for a dance?' says Alma, laughing.

'No, I'm flipping not,' says Pauline. 'I think he's horrible. I'm sticking with Enid for tonight.'

*

1960 turns into 1961. In the yard behind Number 34 the last air-raid shelter is knocked down and the ground is made into a garden. All the fellas are trying to buy *Lady Chatterley's Lover*, while all the girls are staying in to watch *Coronation Street*. Pauline passes her driving test, and because she finds the Terraplane too large to drive, Harry part-exchanges it at Clarry's for a meek little Austin 7. In the Austin, Pauline, Enid and Alma pursue the cause of rock 'n' roll around the Yorkshire coalfields: Thursdays at the Danum Hotel in Doncaster, Saturdays at the Mecca Ballroom in Wakefield, Sundays at Wath Pavilion, Friday night for a bath and putting your hair in rollers.

At the Mecca, Pauline meets her first date since Gordon Benson, a shy man called Albert who works at Waddington's games factory ('On t' Monopoly line, mostly,' as Winnie boasts to Nelly and Comfort). Pauline gets as far as going to Albert's house for tea, but is put off by his mother, who takes her down to the cellar to show her dozens of boxes of soap powder and tins of fruit that she is hoarding in case nuclear war breaks out.

After Albert comes Harvey, who talks about nothing but his new Ford car, and after Harvey comes Tom, who when given a lift by Pauline asks to be dropped off a couple of hundred yards from his house, which means he is married. For a while she gives up on courting, and limits herself to friendships with a group of local lads that she, Alma and Enid have palled up with. The lads are a jolly but tight-fisted Yorkshire lot who will never meet the girls before a dance for fear of having to pay for their admission.

'I know why you always meet us inside, you know,' Pauline tells one of them, a young miner called Roland, one night at the Danum. 'But you needn't worry about paying for me. I pay my own way.'

'Oh,' says Roland. 'One of them are you?'

It is through this group that she is introduced to Sexy Rexy, the fourth and final dalliance of her rock 'n' roll period. They are all out in the Mecca one night when Rex comes over to talk to one of the boys. As the band begins a version of The Shadows' 'Apache', he leans towards Pauline and touches her elbow.

'Can I have t' next dance, please my love?'

Smooth, she thinks.

'If you like.'

'I'm Rex,' he says. 'Pleased to meet you.'

He is a good mover, and they dance together through all the band's rock 'n' roll sections, even trying some jiving when the music gets fast enough. In between dances he buys Pauline a lemonade and himself a lager, and they discuss what Rex calls 'the scene'. He uses all the new words, such as smashing, chuffed and gogglebox, and loves music and the telly. He likes *Oh Boy!*, and much prefers it to that *Boy Meets Girls* rubbish that's on telly now, with Marty Wilde and the Vernons Girls. When Pauline tells him her dad hates rock 'n' roll, Rex says he sounds like a right square.

The last song at the Mecca is at midnight. When they leave, he asks Pauline if she wants to go on the back of his motorbike, just for a ride to the fish and chip shop. 'I don't know about that,' she says. 'Don't you need a helmet?'

'A skid lid?' says Rex, smiling. 'I don't bother, they take all t' enjoyment out of it. Just put your arms round me, nice and tight.'

She dislikes riding on the motorbike, and although she and Rex go out together for six months, his interests – among which the bike features highly – come to seem narrow and offputting to her. 'Don't you ever fancy going for a walk instead of dancing, Rex?' she asks.

'Nay,' he says, 'but we could go for a buzz round on t' bike if you like?'

'I'd like to go for a walk. I like sitting and watching t' rabbits coming out.'

'Rabbits! Gi'o'er with your rabbits. Come and get on t' bike.'

One night when she is on the back of the bike, Rex stops at a junction and Pauline looks at the back of his head and decides she has had enough. She moves her feet from the rests, places them on the ground and stands up. When he drives away, she is left standing alone, bow-legged, in the road.

'I don't want to go on your motorbike any more, Rex,' she says when he comes back for her.

'What's up with you? Other lasses go on it.'

'I'm not other lasses, am I?'

'You don't lean properly going round corners, that's your trouble. Everybody *knows* you have to lean on a bike.'

'Oh, shut up,' she says. 'Will you just take me home, or do I have to catch a bus?'

*

That autumn Gordon Benson goes for a haircut in the barber's shop next door to Windell's, waits until Pauline comes out on her break, and then steps into the street and invites her to a dance at Wath Pavilion. She accepts, but at the dance she feels nervous and spends most of the time avoiding him, and at the end of the evening she leaves without saying goodbye.

Later, as she sits drinking Ovaltine and listening to Fats Waller records with her dad, she hears a knock at the front door. It is Gordon. Harry shows him into the sitting room and then goes up to bed, leaving the two of them alone.

Gordon is clasping and rubbing his scrubbed hands. 'Will tha marry me, Pauline?' he asks. '*Please?*'

Pauline is so surprised that when she answers it is like hearing someone else.

'Oh go on then,' she says. 'Warm my feet and I'll think about it.'

31

The Fugitive

Thurnscoe, 1959–61

After the night when he pours milk over Margaret, Roy swings intemperately between tender husbandliness and a cross-grained resentment that grows and grows in him until, with no announcement, he stays away from the house for two or three weeks at a time. When he returns he will start out again as a patient and devoted dad who comes home every night and treats the family kindly. He takes Gary and David to the park, makes balsa-wood model aeroplanes with them, and reads stories to Gary at bedtime. At night he watches television with Margaret and says how much he likes being with her and the lads. He buys a car, an ex-police Ford Zephyr, and takes them all out for day trips. Margaret says he should sit his test and get a licence, but he insists that a qualified tank driver like him doesn't need to bother with things like that.

If Margaret complains, or questions him about where he has been, though, he becomes irate, and sometimes he hits her. People talk about Jekyll-and-Hyde characters, she thinks, but worse is the man with a side you don't know at all. It makes her feel she is going insane. Where does he go? Sometimes she has no idea; at other times she knows very well that he is at his mother's. When he is at Winnie's, Margaret feels she ought to go there to fetch him back, but it is impossible. If she calls at the house Winnie denies he is there. If she makes a fuss in the street it looks bad. If she waits outside, he goes down the backings.

In the end Winnie always sends him back to her anyway. The routine is unchanging. Roy turns up at Number 34, cursing Margaret, begging his mam for help, never mentioning the violence. Winnie feels sorry for him, blames Margaret for having pursued him so doggedly when they were courting, and tells him to stay. Pauline, watching the scene from the hallway, looks at Lynda and says, 'We'll see how long it lasts this time,' knowing that in about a week their mam will be sick of him coming in late and borrowing money. Then Winnie will tell him to face his responsibilities and go home, and Roy will return to Thurnscoe claiming renewed purpose and optimism.

In 1959 he quits Hatfield pit so that he can look for a job more in keeping with his ambitions, and begins spending time at the Gascoignes' scrapyard with Humpy, who is helping him to put word out. Margaret runs out of housekeeping money. She had given up her employment to take care of Gary and David, but now she takes a cleaning job at the sewing factory, leaving the boys with her mam or, if she has to, Winnie. Roy gets a job as a crane driver and banksman for a Doncaster plant hire company, whose machines are being used on the new sections of the A1 being built to the west of the town. Having placed its faith in the motor car the government is widening roads, building bypasses and laying down across Britain broad black belts of new motorway, with space-age service stations and complex, looping interchanges. Fashion-conscious young couples go to dinner at service station restaurants, and coachloads of tourists travel to see newly opened sections, photographing the smooth new tarmacadam channels to the future. Building these roads, bridges and elevations, manoeuvring their steel and concrete road sections into place, is skilled and precise work, and Roy is good at it. Harry, greatly impressed by bypasses and their benefits to lorry drivers, is for once openly admiring of his son's career choice. He is in demand, and the demand takes him further and further out onto the roads, further and further from home: Leeds, County Durham, Tyneside, then God knows where. Margaret doesn't see him for weeks at a time, and when he does come back, he needs a drink and doesn't return home until she's asleep.

*

Early summer, 1960. Roy has been away for four weeks and Margaret, having had to pay the rent at the end of the month, has no money for food. Has Roy been hurt? she wonders. Would anyone know to tell her if he had been killed?

She takes the day off work and goes to a callbox to ring the operator for the number of the firm Roy works for. Once she has the number she calls the office to ask for their address, takes the bus to Doncaster with Gary and David, and walks to the firm's yard on the outskirts of town.

A secretary in the office goes to find a manager and Margaret, Gary and David wait in the reception. Outside the yard is full of big yellow-painted machines and oil-stained men who stare at the family through the open office door. The manager comes and introduces himself and says Roy has been working in North Yorkshire and staying in a caravan, but there is no reason he should not have come home at weekends. He will make some enquiries; if she doesn't hear from Roy, she can call the office again.

That night Roy comes home in a rage.

'What the bloody hell did you go to t' office for?' His expression suggests he is expecting an apology.

'I didn't know where you were, Roy! We've heard nowt for a month, and I had no money to buy food for t' kids with!'

'Don't bring them into it. It's you that can't look after them, not me.'

'But I've no money!'

'Don't blame me! You're working, aren't you? You're just a bloody useless mother.'

'I'm not a bad mother! What sort of father are you then? You're not even a man!'

He pushes her against the wall and punches her. She covers her head and squeals, and he punches her again. Gary pushes in between them and tries to stop him, but he keeps thrashing at her over Gary's head before he tires and storms out of the flat.

He comes back later, drunk, and sleeps on the settee. In the morning he is sorry and regretful. He gives Gary some superhero comics and sends the two boys to play in the bedroom while he talks to Margaret. He apologises and says it will be the last time. She asks him why he does it: he doesn't answer, but promises that he will change. She says all she wants is a nice family life like the girls at the factory have, and she doesn't understand why she and Roy can't have a better time of it. 'I'll change,' he says again, almost crying. 'I really promise. I swear.'

Unconvinced, Margaret goes to Goldthorpe police station to ask if they can help to stop Roy from hitting her. She talks to Sergeant Bell, who is from Thurnscoe. Nothing they can do, says the sergeant, it's a private matter: 'The police can't get involved, you see, and half these women, if you do go in they tell you to stay away.'

'I wouldn't tell you to stay away,' says Margaret.

'I know, love,' he says. 'But . . . Let me know if it doesn't stop.'

Alan Bell had been in Margaret White's year at school. When he goes off duty that evening he finds Roy in the Halfway Hotel and warns him to leave Margaret alone. Roy tells her off for that, but he doesn't hit her, and for a time he behaves. Then she goes for a day out to Blackpool with the girls from the factory and he accuses her of going with other men while she was there. 'There were no men with us!' she says, but for that he shoves her against the wall and hits her in the face.

Her family and friends see the bruises, but her parents are afraid of Roy and she won't listen to the girls at work. They tell her to fight back, but how can she? Roy is a big man, and all the mouth in the world is useless when a man like that gets started.

He goes back to the motorways and stays away longer than he did before, and Margaret has to borrow money from her mam. Then one night in the spring of 1961, when Roy is at home, he answers a knock at the door and Margaret, listening at the top of the stairs, hears alarming words: station . . . report . . . questions . . . all spoken in an unfamiliar voice. Peering down to the foot of the stairs she sees a police officer. When Roy comes back up he says he has to go to Goldthorpe police station, but it's nothing serious and she needn't worry. He is away all night, and when he comes back the next morning he says he's had a right run-in with the head bloke there, Sergeant Grimes, but he's put him straight. It's nowt, he says, just a little knock that he's had in the car.

The next day more police turn up and take him back to the station, and this time when he comes home he confesses to having been in a car accident, and says he will have to appear in court. Margaret thinks there could be more to the story than he is telling her. She knows he has no licence or insurance, and it would hardly be a surprise if he had been drinking, but she daren't ask.

Roy goes to court in Doncaster on his own and does not come home. That evening another police officer calls to tell Margaret that Roy has been sent to prison for six months – the maximum sentence for driving drunk without a licence and causing an accident. The officer gives Margaret Roy's prison details and asks her to insert into her letters to him certain questions about his friends, and about his intentions on being released. She should take care of the letters he sends back, he says, and someone from the station will discreetly call to read them. This request, together with the long prison sentence and other subsequent events, will suggest to Margaret that the police suspected Roy of some more serious crimes, but lacked the evidence to convict him. She will never know if she is right or not.

The police officer hands her a handwritten list of questions, and then leaves. Margaret locks the front door and goes to comfort Gary and David, who are sitting on the settee in a state of confusion, wondering where their dad is, and when he will be coming home again.

32

Passing Over

Highgate and Storthes Hall Hospital, Huddersfield, 1962–64

In her seventies, hair coloured a piebald black and grey with a comb-through dye, a turned ankle necessitating heavy black support shoes, Annie Parkin finds the dead bothering her far less frequently than they used to. Walter comes now and again, to buck her up or give her advice when she needs it, and she can still get hold of the odd passed relative for people, but since meeting Mr Edwards she has felt their presence dwindling.

One night when she is giving a sitting in Elland, she looks out at the audience and feels a sort of tiredness go through her, from her toes to her head to her poisoned thumb. The people still come, young and old, and the interest remains the same – stronger, if anything, since everyone got televisions. But for reasons she cannot explain, she is losing interest. She is glad when the sitting ends, and as she puts on her coat and the organisers clear away the chairs in the hall, she feels inside that she has had enough. She takes no further bookings, drifts away from the people on the circuit and dedicates her time to Mr Edwards and the bookies. More and more the scents of flowers come to her, signs that someone she knows has died. On some days she smells them from the moment she wakes up until she falls asleep again at night.

When she wants to visit Mr Edwards she travels down the Pennine valleys by bus to stay at Winnie's, sleeping with Pauline in the big bed that used to be Roy's. The usual arrangement is that Annie will put on a smart skirt and jumper, Mr Edwards will call at Number 34 and they will sit together watching television, sipping at gills of beer that he has bought from the beer-off. Mr Edwards always asks after Annie's children and grandchildren, and chats to Winnie about Roy's children, Lynda's schooling, the plans for Pauline's wedding. Winnie notices, and remarks to Pauline, that Mr Edwards says very little about his own relations, but puts this down to a male aversion to discussing family. It becomes suspicious only when, one evening in the autumn of 1962, he visits Annie at her cellar room in Elland to tell her he is breaking off their friendship. Offering no explanation other than that he has 'been thinking about it' and doesn't 'reckon it's right', he says goodbye to her on the pavement, and walks down the street towards the bus stop without looking back.

'I think he's found another woman,' she tells Winnie, and Winnie wonders if he is not a widower at all, and if the other woman is a wife who has found a piebald hair on his suit collar.

The want of explanation and the abruptness of Mr Edwards's departure disorientate Annie, draining her of her wit and energy, and leaving her depressed. A broken heart is Winnie's diagnosis, but the doctors who see her that autumn, after Winnie and Olive decide their thin and insomniac mother needs medical help, choose dementia.

Seeing her in the hospital in Halifax, with Winnie and Olive present, a doctor identifies her illness by asking questions. What is today's date? Who is the Queen? Can you tell me the name of the Prime Minister? The doctor's manner is perfunctory, and he does not appear to consider the possibility that a sad, recently jilted seventy-one-year-old woman may have lost track of the date and Harold Macmillan's name. Annie had not had the right to vote until she was thirty-eight: thirty-three years later, ill and tired, she finds herself unable to name the leader of the country and is declared mad. The sisters and Sonny accept the judgement meekly. Muv is without doubt unwell, and doctors have an unequalled authority, the more so since the National Health Service revealed to their generation the number and complexity of their medical conditions. It is Mr Edwards who the family blames, his name cursed by Winnie in the Austin 7 all the way back to Highgate Lane.

On 27 November 1962, an ambulance conveys Annie Parkin from her room to Storthes Hall Hospital for the mentally ill, a rambling former Edwardian pauper asylum near Huddersfield. The hospital stands in woodland behind black iron gates, its forty-six ward buildings still overcrowded with patients moved there in the last war when other institutions were requisitioned for troops. Its reputation as a lunatic lock-up extends across the West Riding, and in the Dearne it is a backings insult: when someone acts strangely, or is thought to be stupid, people say that's where they'll end up. For Winnie, her mam's admission to one of its wards is, if not quite an embarrassment, certainly too painful to discuss with the neighbours. When she visits and finds her mam allowed to walk around freely, and talking easily with the nurses, it is little consolation – though had she asked a nurse, she might well have been told that her mam was like hundreds of elderly women sent to them by doctors: undeniably depressed, vague, and easily confused, but no more likely to be suffering from lunacy than from anaemia or despair at a bereavement. One way or another, love was always sending women doolally, but men would not tolerate it in the old. Those with visiting sons and daughters could hope to get well and be discharged. Others, through drugs and apathy, could sink into that torpor that was the nightgowned no-woman's-land between madness and real life.

*

While Annie is being settled into Storthes Hall, Winnie is being pulled up and down Highgate Lane by other family matters. First there is Millie, whose health is now declining rapidly. The sweet shop is comfortably profitable, being the shop that people call at to buy treats on their way to the cinema, but two years after taking it on Millie had fallen ill and the doctors had discovered cancer in her bowel. They had operated on her but now she has to spend most of her time in bed, Winnie nursing her while Anne, the youngest of Millie's children, runs the shop.

Besides tending to Millie, Winnie also has Pauline's marriage to arrange. Pauline did not accept Gordon's marriage proposal on that Saturday evening after the dance, but asked for time to think about it. Gordon came back the next day to ask Harry's permission (Harry requested livestock as a dowry: Gordon, naturally serious and literal, asked how many cows he had in mind), and on Monday night they had gone to the cinema and Pauline had said yes. The next week they joined the early Christmas shoppers in Doncaster to find a ring and a building society that would give them a mortgage on a house. So that she can save for her wedding Pauline asks her mam if she can pay board rather than handing over all her wages: Winnie says this is a bloody cheek, but then relents and compromises by increasing Pauline's spending money to ten shillings a week.

Amid all this Winnie is sustained by a new job, and a new friend. Jane Seels, the woman who had advised her about Pauline's studies, stops Winnie in a Highgate shop one morning and asks if she could help her clean the farmhouse: Jane is pregnant with her first child, and there is the farm to help with and soon there will be the baby, and she can't see how she is going to cope. Winnie collects her spare pinny and cleaning brushes from home, and goes directly to the house to begin work. This initiates an arrangement that will continue for the next thirty years, and a close friendship that will last for the rest of Winnie's life. It is to Jane, and only her, that Winnie discloses the affair with Alf, and her enduring belief that one day he will come back to take her away.

*

Dreading the idea of being on show, Gordon and Pauline say they would like a wedding ceremony early in the day, with as few guests as possible, but neither dare even tell their fathers, who both want a generously sized party. When the Cuban missile crisis escalates in the autumn, they think they may have to postpone it anyway, because there will be another war. For a while President Kennedy and the missiles are all anyone talks about; at the shops, the pits, the factories and coking plants and bus depots it is the same, the young worried about having to fight, and the old avowing the need for another war to sort out the Russians. Pauline and Gordon barely mention the wedding, even in their own homes, until the crisis is over and Kennedy appears to have won.

Annie is discharged from Storthes Hall in January 1963, during a blizzard that leaves the asylum sill-deep in snow, and well in time for the wedding which takes place at St Peter's Church in Barnburgh on a wet Easter Monday in 1963. For presents, Harry gives them the Austin 7 and Winnie gives Pauline a bottle of the French perfume that Miss Marjorie used to wear. On the day Winnie looks poised in a new moss-green outfit with a tan cloche hat, while Harry, in a new light suit, is more nervous than his daughter. Having organised a coach to take people from Highgate to the church, he spends the morning fretting that it and the wedding cars will be late. In the sitting room and kitchen he keeps taking off his suit jacket, checking himself in the mirror, then putting it back on.

'It's me that's supposed to be agitated!' says Pauline.

'I'm not flaming agitated! Does this jacket look better on or off?'

'Off. I can't believe after all you've done on t' stage you're bothered about giving me away in Barnburgh church, Dad.'

'I'm not bothered about it! Shut up,' he says, and stomps outside to the lav. This is the first time in her life that he has shouted at her. She looks in the mirror: veil down, armour on.

At the reception in the Green Lane Social Club, Barnburgh, the function room is divided down the middle between hushed and ponderous Bensons and chattering, roisterous Hollingworths. Pauline and Gordon move between both until half past four when they escape to catch the train to London, from where they will fly to Guernsey for their honeymoon. The taxi driver who picks them up at King's Cross drives recklessly and speaks in an accent they cannot understand. That's probably what London's like, they agree, fast and incomprehensible. Gordon says he'd like to have a proper look around. Pauline looks at him in surprise and says it's funny what you find out about people once you've married them.

*

Once Pauline has left home, Winnie brings Millie up from Bolton-upon-Dearne to live with them at Number 34. Harry collects her in his new car, a white Rover, and sets her up in a bed beside the window in the front room. From this position Millie can see all her old neighbours on the lane going back and forth to their shifts or the shops, and wave at them, or even converse through an opened window.

At times in the summer of 1963, she seems to be rallying, and begins threatening to get out of bed to dance around the front room with Harry. But this good news is offset by a letter from Olive saying that Muv has slipped back into her previous vagueness and kind of speech that has only a loose relation to anyone else's idea of reality. Her claims that Walter will soon be coming to fetch her are at least understandable, but not so her visions of her sisters and mother, or her old home in Shirebrook. 'I told them not to come any more, Mam,' she tells Olive. 'I told them. And they've not been near since!'

In July, Annie is re-admitted to Storthes Hall. Once a week Winnie, wishing Mr Edwards a long fall down a pitshaft, is driven to the hospital by Harry. On her second visit, towards the end of the month, the nurse who comes to escort her to the ward says that Annie is now well enough to be allowed out of the locked ward into the landings and corridors. The wards are two-storey stone buildings set in the hall's landscaped gardens. Inside, the wide corridors are tiled, and two-flight stone staircases connect the floors. As Winnie comes through the doors to her mam's ward, Annie is standing at the top of the staircase, two-tone hair brushed, smart skirt and jumper on, waiting.

'That's my daughter!' she tells a nurse when she hears Winnie's voice. 'It's our Winnie come to see me!' Beaming, she shuffles forward to the first step and misplaces her foot. Her ankle gives, and her body topples over and down the stone stairs, so that as Winnie ascends the lower flight, she sees her mother's body tumbling towards her like a dropped marionette. Winnie cries out and watches as the nurses arrange her limbs and take her pulse. She is unconscious. A nurse rushes off to bring two men who lift Annie onto a trolley and wheel her away. Winnie and Harry are led to a small room with wooden armchairs and a table, and they wait there sipping at unwanted tea until the nurse brings a doctor. He has not been able to save her mother, he says. Annie had not regained consciousness and died as a result of the brain haemorrhage sustained when she fell.

It is a death that, with a few modifications, could have come from one of Winnie's novels: a doting mother dying almost in the arms of her daughter on a grand stone staircase, tragedy yet again rushing upon and overtaking love. The experience is shocking to Winnie, though in the future she will find it easier to relate the details of her mother's death than those of her father's thirty years earlier. She never mentions her own feelings about the fall to anyone in the family either later or at the time, though she will say that the little gypsy girl came to comfort her.

At Storthes Hall, once she has taken in the news, Winnie swallows hard, sets her tearless face against misfortune, and tells Harry to drive to Olive's house where she will explain what has happened. Later, back at home, she sits down to tell Millie about their mother's death and begins organising the funeral. The family buries Annie's body in the cemetery in Bolton-upon-Dearne on 27 July 1963, lowering her into a wet, black grave beside the remains of Walter Parkin.

*

In a novel Winnie might now be given time to reflect and meditate on the loss of her mother but, to her occasional regret, she does not live in a novel and in real life her sister's health is seriously deteriorating. Through August and September, laid beside the front-room window and waving to the people outside, Millie shrinks down to six stone. It is as if she is dissolving into the air. The doctor prescribes more morphine and Winnie, May and Sonny administer it until Millie experiences painless lucidity only as rare moments between drowsiness, pain and sleep. Her speech is laboured.

'Shall we have a song, then, Juggler?'

'Aye, come on then.'

And Harry sings 'Simple Melody' as she slowly slips back into unconsciousness.

This is a lovely old song, and not rubbish. This kind of song will outlive all your raggy nonsense . . .

Millie sings and waves to the end of her life. She dies in the front room in October at the age of fifty-two, and for the second time in the year the family walks to the church and cemetery in Bolton-upon-Dearne to reunite a wife with her husband.

The following year, Sonny and May leave the valley to live in Newmarket, and with Annie, Millie and Sonny gone from the valley, and her son and eldest daughter gone from the house, Winnie and the gypsy girl adapt to a world that is rapidly changing. In her mid-fifties, Winnie begins wearing spectacles and dyeing her hair, and she uses facepacks made to her mother's recipe of witchhazel and oatmeal to keep her skin taut and clear. Her relationship with Harry, who is now losing his hair and becoming a little slower in his movements, becomes more equable. She keeps her mind open to the new music and programmes on the TV, and to the latest fashions and long Beatles haircuts on men. It is she, not Lynda, who decorates Lynda's bedroom walls with posters from *Jackie* magazine, and it is she more than anyone who, in the coming decades, will keep her home open to the new generation of Hollingworths as they make their way in a world that is both familiar and different.

PART FIVE

33

The Whistler at the Gate

Highgate, 1961–64

Lynda Hollingworth is different to how her older sister Pauline had been as a young girl: in some ways she is a practically minded tomboy, in others she is away with the fairies. She likes riding in the glassworks lorry with her dad; she wants hobnail boots so she can make sparks fly like the lads do; she has progressed from dancing on her dad's feet to watching ballet on television, and from there to dancing up and down the backings on her own pretending to be in *Swan Lake*. Dolls she considers dull, preferring to play at 'offices' using old office equipment that she keeps in a shoebox – used envelopes, stamps, rubber bands, pens, a stationery catalogue and a carbon copypaper receipt book that her dad once brought for her from work. In this game the shoe box becomes a desk, such dolls as she owns a queue of people with paper-work to process, and she the woman in charge of processing it: sign, tear, stamp! At other houses children dress up or play with toys, but at Lynda's you dance or pay money off your payment books, and devise new, efficient filing systems.

As she gets older, Lynda dreams of real offices, finding herself far more stimulated by the idea of office work than by the knitting and dressmaking that so interest her sister. One Friday evening in 1960, when she is eleven years old, she has a sitting-room epiphany when she comes downstairs to find Pauline, her mam and Comfort knitting in the firelight. Pauline has her hair in rollers, Comfort and her mam are gossiping, and their needles go clicketyclicketyclicketyclicketyclickety. Her dad is adjusting his tie in the mirror before going out.

'Look at Rudolph Valentino here,' says Winnie.

'Look at t' flamin' wool factory, click, click, clicking,' says Harry. 'It's May. Are you cold?'

'It's no good waiting until t' weather changes to start knitting you jumpers, is it? If I do you'll be moaning because I didn't get on with them sooner.'

Lynda sees him roll his eyes, and imagines him thinking of the fun he will soon be having in the club. Looking at the knitters and then back at her dad, she thinks he has the best of this set-up, and no mistake. If she could she would go out with him instead of staying here with the clicketyclicketyclicketying. She has an urge to snatch the needles from the women's hands and fling them out of the window.

'What's up, Lynda?' says Winnie, noticing that her daughter seems to have entered a trance.

'Nowt,' says Lynda.

'You mean nothing.'

'Nothing, then.'

Lynda has in the past sat down to sew with her mam and Comfort, but tonight she says she won't bother. She goes back upstairs in search of better things to do, and spends the evening reorganising the contents of her shoe-box desk, and thinking of the equipment she will buy when she earns money of her own.

*

When she is grown up, Lynda will look back on her childhood and say she felt part of a generation that seemed more impassioned and less parochial than their parents, and people younger than her will think she is talking about the politics, pop music and fashions of the 1960s. She is, partly, but she will think there was somehow both more and less to it than that. Her keynote memory is of all the mams and elder sisters taking their satisfaction from duty and decorousness while she and her friends just wanted to laugh and dance.

Winnie does not object to the young Lynda's interest in laughing and dancing and offices, but she is strict. She slaps Lynda's legs for a word out of place, and thumps her in the back if she complains about having her hair brushed. If anyone from outside the home criticises Lynda, though, her mam is onto them like a terrier on a rat. When a primary school teacher pulls a knicker leg over a cheek of Lynda's bottom and smacks her in front of her class, Winnie marches up to school and threatens the teacher so furiously that Lynda fears she might commit murder. This is how it works, she comes to realise, protection and control; in the home, your mam fights against you, out of it she is on your side.

By the time Lynda goes up to secondary modern school in the summer of 1960 she has watched dozens of ballets on the television, and is keen to try formal dance. In her first lesson at the new school her dance teacher, Mrs Buxton, instructs the girls to make pairs, think of a story together, and tell that story through their performance. Lynda and her friend Margaret make up a tale about a fairy bewitched by a tree, and Margaret, who isn't keen on dancing, lies down pretending to be a log. Lynda flits about to the music playing on a Dansette, but when Mrs Buxton lifts the stylus, Lynda carries on dancing. The bemused teacher tells her to stop because there is no music and Lynda replies, 'But I hear it in my mind, Mrs Buxton, I hear it in my mind!'

In Lynda's second year the school governors remove the walls and railings that keep the boys apart from the girls, and the school introduces mixed classes. During the day, Lynda and her friends are indifferent to the change, while the boys welcome it because it means they can look at the girls through the gym windows, and climb up drainpipes to watch them in the showers. It is to life outside of school that it makes the most difference. Previously, the only boys the girls knew were those they had been at primary school with. Now, having mixed lessons and mixed break times, boys and girls recognise one another when they meet in the street, and are generally less afraid to acknowledge each other's presence, or open a conversation. For the first time in Highgate, large groups of boys and girls from different villages can now play and pass the time together in the parks and outside shops.

On some evenings after school, a group of boys from Lynda's year walks down from Goldthorpe to the Highgate beer-off to buy bottles of Coca-Cola and lemonade. They stand on the steps outside, swigging from bottles, bantering with Highgate kids about pop music, football and bird-nesting, and coolly recounting their adventures in the wild country on the village edges. The Goldthorpe boys have chased the White Lady, a ghost that stalks the Hickleton colliery spoil heaps between Goldthorpe and Thurnscoe. They have sneaked into the old warehouses to jump across open lift shafts. They have slid down the spoil heaps on lengths of discarded belting, and even dived to the bottom of the forbidden brick ponds in Bolton-upon-Dearne. They are braver and cockier than the Highgate Lane kids, so the Highgate Lane kids congregate respectfully and listen to them, and the more daring ones ask to go with them on their next ghost hunt or spoil-heap slide. Lynda listens, and gets the same feeling she used to get from seeing boys making sparks with their hobnail boots. 'I'll come with you,' she would like to say. 'I'm not scared of ghosts. Some people in my family regard them as personal friends.'

One of the Goldthorpe boys, John Burton, a particularly witty and well-dressed youth known for never refusing a dare, likes to stand on the top step of the beer-off and sing Elvis Presley songs as if the step is a stage. He does 'Heartbreak Hotel', 'Hound Dog' and, to mellow the mood and tempo, 'Don't Be Cruel'. Elvis is the pinnacle, he says. Yes he was better before he went in the Army, but he's still way out in front, as a musician and as a man.

Lynda finds it exciting when John talks like this, and comes to the front to get a good look at him. One night as he's preaching she catches his eye. 'Our Pauline and her fiancé are taking me and my mam to see Cliff Richard at t' Doncaster Gaumont,' she says. 'She's been to see him before. She says t' lasses scream that loud, Cliff can't hear himself sing.'

John is unmoved. 'Cliff Richard's rubbish. He just copies Elvis.'

'A lot of people like him.'

'That means nowt. People like all sorts of rubbish, it doesn't make it good.'

She could just back away, but this idea is new and intriguing to her. 'What else do you think's good then?'

'Ah well,' he replies, standing down from the step. 'Let's have a think.'

That evening Lynda and John agree that the Beach Boys and Motown artists are good, and decide that they're not really sure about the Beatles. the next day they add other names to the list, and as they talk more at the gatherings on Highgate Lane they become friends.

At first they don't tell each other much about themselves, but this changes after an incident at school one day in 1964, when Lynda is in her third year. She and John are in the same class. The form has just come into its classroom for morning registration when the teacher, Mr Brown, notices John standing by the doorway, repeatedly opening and closing the door. Mr Brown asks him what's the matter. John stops moving for a moment and says, 'They've got my boots.' Mr Brown asks who has what boots, but John just repeats himself, and carries on opening and closing the door.

A boy shouts out, 'He's having a do, sir!'

'I didn't ask your opinion.'

'But he is, sir.' Others join in. 'He has dos. He goes in trances if somebody upsets him, and he's having a do now because somebody's pinched his football boots.'

Mr Brown tells John to calm himself and to look for the boots in the cloakrooms. When he comes back empty-handed he is wan and subdued, and for the rest of the lesson sits hunched over his desk, staring downwards in silence. At breaktime his friends rag him; some of them make jokes about Storthes Hall. John tries to shrug it off, but Lynda, watching, sees that he is slightly discomposed. She elbows in and tells the boys to shut up. They jeer back at her, but with the moment broken they drift away.

She finds John standing alone near the school gates. 'Ayup,' she says.

'Ayup.'

'Don't take any notice of them going on about you and your boots, you know,' she says. 'They're flipping idiots, most of 'em.'

'I won't. They're alright, they're only kidding. It's just my mam I'm bothered about. She'll be right upset because she just bought me t' boots.'

'Just tell her what's happened, she'll understand. I'm sure they'll turn up.'

He nods, and they stand silent for a moment, thinking. 'Thanks, Lynda,' he says.

*

Later that year, Rocky Wall, the wrestler from Doncaster, buys a small shop at the bottom of Pit Lane in Highgate and converts it into a coffee bar. For the young people of Goldthorpe, Highgate, Thurnscoe and Bolton-upon-Dearne this is a wondrous development, easily eclipsing the White Lady and the open lift shafts. Occasionally presided over by Rocky himself, and dominated by a huge jukebox and the smells of coffee and boiling milk, the café attracts them in garrulous, gaudy perfumed crowds, the girls in mini skirts, knee boots, bobs and beehives, and the boys in winklepickers, turtle necks and kiss curls. They listen to the music, dance, shoot pinball, spill frothy coffee over each other and ask Rocky about the bouts they've seen on the television, but mostly they just talk. Suddenly it seems there is such a lot for them to talk about – not least who's in the café, what you did the last time you came, and when you'll be coming again.

Lynda and John become closer. When Rocky Wall's café opens they go as part of a large group, but then John begins asking beforehand when she'll be arriving. By the time Lynda is fourteen, they are meeting there early every Friday evening to have hamburgers and chips for tea and to listen to the new singles that Rocky has put on the jukebox, so they can decide if they are good or rubbish. Sometimes they stay in the café until it closes at ten, sometimes they career round the new roller-skating rink in Goldthorpe, and on other, warmer, nights they just gather outside the beer-off. He tells her jokes and makes her laugh, and instigates mischief whenever they are with a group. On Bonfire Night it is John who works out that if you throw a Roman candle into a length of pipe closed at one end, it will shoot out like a rocket from a rocket launcher; when they go to Skegness Butlins with a group of mates, it is he who befriends the waiters and ends up jumping into the pool with them, fully clothed. It is as if life lived at the speed chosen by other people is too slow for him; he moves rapidly, like a finch, his speech quick as a whip. Bored by a slow conversation, he amuses himself by tickling your ear, tweaking your hair, tapping your shoulder and darting to the other side when you turn around.

John has the good sense, however, to behave himself in the vicinity of Winnie. He is wary of her, so the first few times he calls for Lynda at home he stands at the gate whistling rather than coming to the door, which Winnie likes ('Look sharp!' she calls. 'He's whistlin' you again!'). When he comes in and sits down, forcing himself not to fidget, she is impressed by his shock of black, quiffed hair and smart clothes, and decides he is a good prospect. 'Best-dressed lad to come to this house,' she tells Lynda one night after John has gone home, 'and a lovely straight pair of shoulders.' She even allows him to sleep over one night after they have been to a party, on the condition that he stays in the back bedroom, at the other end of the landing to the one in which Lynda, Margaret and their friend Jenny are sleeping.

But then Winnie hears a rumour about him, a spiteful and suspicious scrap of gossip passed between the bored and the malicious in the backings and shop queues. He has fits; there's summat up with him; he has to carry something called phenobarbitals. Warned 'to watch that lad your Lynda's on with', Winnie stops complimenting John and is terse when he comes to the house. She tells Comfort what she has heard, and Comfort soon reports that she has seen him hitting Lynda one night when the kids were all standing around near the beer-off. This becomes Winnie's excuse. Waiting until she and Lynda are alone in the sitting room, she says, 'If he hits you now, he'll hit you when you get older. I'm telling you to stay away, Lynda. Are you listening?'

'But he was playing about, Mam! He's always like that. He does this thing where he taps you on your shoulder and . . .'

'Stop covering up for him. Tell him not to come to this house again, and if I catch you seeing him again, there'll be trouble.'

Lynda senses there is something more to this, and she is right. John Burton has a mild form of epilepsy. He has had only a few seizures, but this is enough for the gossip, and the gossip is enough for Winnie, who has an almost superstitious fear of fits. She wants good lives for her daughters and, Lynda will come to realise, she is at times more protective of her youngest child than she had been of Pauline and Roy. Lynda suspects that her mam also fears the disrepute that John, as a boy who 'has dos', might bring to the family. Everyone including Winnie liked to say that they didn't care what other people thought of them, but in a village where you had to rely on your friends and neighbours, public opinion could have serious practical consequences for your day-to-day life.

Lynda dare not argue for too long, but she feels like someone wrongly convicted of a crime. It would be one thing for her mam to judge a boy unsuitable because of his character, but it is quite another for her to judge him on gossip that is next to a lie. She cries. 'Why would you believe Comfort and not me? I know him and I know he'd never hit me! We love each other.'

'Love!' says Winnie, bitterly. 'How could *you* know what love is?'

And with those words, spat out like poison across the sitting room, Winnie abruptly closes the conversation. It will be fourteen years before Lynda reopens it.

34

Gary and David

Bolton-upon-Dearne; Flamborough, East Riding of Yorkshire; Highgate, 1963–65

By the middle of the 1960s the new motorways and widened roads being built across South Yorkshire have brought the Dearne Valley within a half-hour car ride of Leeds, Wakefield and Sheffield, and a twenty-minute drive of Doncaster, Barnsley and Rotherham. These roads and increasing car ownership encourage an influx of commuters' families and property speculators, and in fields across the valley builders come to construct tracts of trim, modern bungalows and semi-detached houses in clean, warm orangeish brick. The new homes are coveted not only by city families seeking an affordable rural escape, but also by ambitious young local couples who imagine themselves relaxing in the wide back gardens, or showing off the fitted wooden units and serving hatch in the kitchen. These couples and families save for deposits and take out mortgages, and when their mams and dads come down to tea they tell their children how marvellous the house is, how superior to the poky holes that their generation had when they were first married. And after the mam and dad have been dropped back home in the husband's car, the couple feel contented and proud because, even if the stairs are still uncarpeted and the front lawn devoid of grass, they are bettering themselves and getting on.

To the astonishment of his family it is with one such home that, in 1963, Roy Hollingworth comes good on a promise of a fresh start. He tells Margaret he has secured a mortgage on a pristine new bungalow in Bolton-upon-Dearne. 'And you can stop working if you like, and stay at home and look after t' lads. I can afford it,' he says. 'My problems are over.'

Since the end of his sentence two years ago, Roy's problems have driven the family all the way across Yorkshire and back, and then left them briefly homeless.

He arrived home from prison one Friday evening, driven by a man in a Jaguar car. Gary had opened the door and hugged his dad as the driver took a holdall and two large paintings from the boot. 'This is your Uncle Mick, Gary,' said Roy, ushering him and the man with the paintings inside. Margaret brought a bottle of whisky and three glasses into the sitting room and Roy poured the drinks.

'Look at these, lads.' He took the paintings from Mick, and held them up for Gary and David to see. They were portraits of Indian chiefs with headdresses. 'Your Uncle Mick's painted these for you. There's one apiece. I'm going to put them up over your beds, and they'll watch over you and keep you safe.' The boys loved the idea of their dad arranging for them to be watched over and sat looking at the Indians while the adults talked. The next day Roy put up the paintings in the boys' new rooms, but they never saw Uncle Mick again.

Roy was relaxed and cheerful for two weeks, but then one evening he shouted at Margaret about the letters she sent when he was in prison, and said he had found out that she was working with the police. She admitted it, and tried to explain that she had not dared refuse them, but then he accused her of sleeping with a Goldthorpe policeman. Soon after that he came home with a knife wound across his face. He said he had been attacked at random in the street, but privately Margaret did not believe him.

They moved into a council house on the same street as Mr and Mrs White, and Roy found another job with a construction company. He was back to working away from home: when Gary was diagnosed with tuberculosis, it was a full week before his dad knew about it.

In the spring of 1963, the police turned up at the new house looking for Roy, but he was out. The next day Margaret came home from work to find Roy waiting for her. 'Get your bags packed and the lads ready,' he said with a forced cheerfulness. 'You're coming with me, up to Flamborough.'

'What for?' says Margaret.

'For a little break. I've got us a lovely little cottage.'

'For how long?'

'We'll see. However long we like.'

They put the boys in the car and drove through the night to a cottage in a remote, fishing village on high chalk cliffs to the north of Bridlington and stayed there for two months, spring into summer. Almost every day Roy took the boys walking along the sands between the white cliffs and the brown sea, and sometimes he sat with them in the cottage and watched films on a TV with a fuzzy reception. He took them to his pal's garage in Bridlington and his pal showed them a German soldier's helmet with a bullet hole in it. He and Margaret did not fight or argue even when Roy had been to the pub, and for a while it was like being in one of the normal, contented families on the television. Gary and David thought they would live there for ever.

Then one morning Roy told them to pack up their things because they were going back to the Dearne. By now someone else had moved into the council house, so Margaret and the boys moved in with her mam and dad, and Roy went to Winnie and Harry's. Margaret did not know what would happen to the family and she didn't dare to ask, but a month after they moved back Roy called round and told them about the bungalow. He and Gary began decorating it in the evenings and weekends, and a fortnight later they moved in.

Once they are established in the bungalow, Roy takes a job at Manvers for a short while so that the family qualifies for the miners' free coal allowance, and then he resumes working on the motorways. The work is local, he comes home, and they have money. He rents a television, and buys a new, walnut-veneered sideboard and an up-to-the-minute radiogram that he demonstrates to the family and friends by playing his new collection of stereo LPs. Margaret sees pals from the factory who live in Bolton-upon-Dearne and makes friends with women in the other new houses. They take their children out for walks together and sit in each other's kitchens drinking coffee.

Happiest to have Roy around again is Gary. Aged seven, he is sensible to what is and is not normal in families. At school there is another boy who doesn't have a dad, but his father was killed at the pit so the other children don't ask questions about him. They ask a lot of questions about Gary's dad though: Is it true that you a'nt got a dad? Why doesn't your dad live with your mam? Why does your grandma always pick you up from school? Gary learns to lie and to remember what he has said. 'Yes, but he works away from home'; 'He's rich, and we have to travel around'; 'He's in the Army.' Some boys who live on Highgate Lane, or near the Whites, stare at him doubtfully when he recites his stories, but he stares back at them until they look away. Now his dad is at home, Gary hopes he'll take him to real places that he can describe to the doubters at school.

'Do you want to come and give me a hand on site today?' Roy says one Saturday morning, standing in the kitchen in his overalls.

'Course!' says Gary, and they drive out of the valley, past canals, fields, woodland and long spoil heaps that Gary imagines to be volcanoes, to a mud wilderness of gouged earth, yellow bulldozers and cranes. Men are steering vast machines back and forth over the dark brown soil. Gary and his dad get out of the car and pick their way through the mud to a bulldozer.

'Are you drivin' or shall I?'

Gary grins, 'I'll drive!'

They share the seat. His dad starts the roaring, juddering diesel engine, then lets Gary rest his hands on the levers as he lowers them to set the blade. When the bulldozer advances the soil bulks up violently and wonderfully and then falls away to the side.

After a while they stop and go to have a sandwich at a caravan where other workers are eating, drinking tea and smoking. The men talk about the motorways and how they'll be a waste of money because no one will use them. 'You're wrong, everybody'll use them,' says Roy. 'In ten years' time everything'll travel on them, you watch.' He tells the men that he is proud of Gary's bulldozer-driving, and Gary moves closer to him, and blushes. His dad is always in a good mood in places like this, talking to other men. Gary thinks if his mam would stop picking at him, he would not go away so often. He thinks that if he could make his dad proud enough, he would stay with them all the time.

But after they have lived in the new bungalow for a few months, Roy and Margaret start arguing again, this time about money. One day at home he hands her a five-pound note for groceries and tells her to bring back some change.

'What do you mean?'

'I mean get up there and do your shopping, and bring me some bloody change back from yon fiver.'

'I only asked what you meant, Roy . . .'

'You're not only asking, you're trying it on. Get to those bloody shops, and bring some bloody change back, that's all.'

Angry, she spends the lot. When she gets back with her shopping bags, Roy is listening to an LP on the radiogram. 'Where's my change then?'

'There wasn't any.'

'What?'

'I needed it all. You want feeding, don't you?'

He leaps up from his chair, and snaps off the record.

'What are you going to do, Roy? Hit me again?'

He walks out of the room, and snatches a jacket from the hall. David cries and runs to his mam. Gary runs to the window to see his dad storming away down the path.

This becomes the routine every time Margaret asks for money.

Roy stays away more often, and when he does come home he drinks heavily and is belligerent. After a while he sells the radiogram and the LPs to Pauline, and when she and Gordon come to pick it up with their car and trailer he asks them to take the new walnut-veneered sideboard up to his mam and dad's. He's gone off it, he says; it doesn't suit the bungalow. As Gordon and Harry heave the sideboard down the passage at Number 34, Winnie exclaims over it as if it were a bowl of diamonds. 'Isn't it a lovely surprise, Pauline?' she says. 'He's a smashing lad sometimes, our Roy. He's good to me.'

*

Easter 1964: the school holidays, Roy away working. Gary and David are reading comics in the sitting room when they hear their mam arguing with someone at the front door. Gary goes to the hall to see four men in dark suits, one with a briefcase, standing outside. Behind them is a large van. The man with the briefcase is closest and he is talking to Margaret as a schoolteacher talks to a naughty pupil. Margaret is crying. 'It's mine,' she is saying. 'A lot of it's mine. I bought it from t' club at work.'

The man confers with the others, then turns back. 'You tell us what's in your name, and we'll leave that and take t' other.'

'Now?'

'I'm afraid so.' Gary scuttles back to the sitting room, followed by his mam and the suited men. The briefcase man asks Margaret what in the room is hers, and she points to the dining chairs, hearth rug and table. 'Right,' he says to the others. 'Take t' telly and t' suite.'

The items are carried out and put into the van, and the neighbours come out of their homes to watch. They take the boys' beds and the kitchen chairs, the clocks and the paintings of the Indian chiefs. When they have taken all they want, they close up the house, and Margaret, Gary and David walk away from the new bungalows and up the hill towards Thurnscoe, the repossessed bungalow shut up behind them. When she finds Roy at Winnie's, he says he's sorry, the bailiffs shouldn't have come because he had the money for the mortgage arrears payment.

'Roy says I've not to worry, because it's only bricks and mortar,' she tells her mam later. 'He says, "You can't get tied down by material things." And I said, "It'd be nice to have a choice."'

Margaret, Gary and David stay with Mr and Mrs White, and Roy avoids his wife and her parents for almost twelve months. It is during this time that Gary begins to form a strong attachment to Harry and Winnie and their home on Highgate Lane. He blames his mam for driving Roy away, but his Grandma and Grandad White and his mam's brothers and sister tell him off for accusing her, and he comes to feel that he is not wanted in the house. When he and David stay at their Grandma Hollingworth's, it feels like a comforting respite. He can talk about his dad without having to hear him called a bad 'un, and Winnie listens to him telling her about the cartoon characters on television, and then tells him stories about when she was a little girl. One night they have a little party in the sitting room with their friends and neighbours who can play some of the instruments. Gary and David get to stay up two hours past their bedtime, and their Grandad Hollingworth stands up in front of everyone and tells jokes. As he makes everyone laugh he winks at the boys, which makes Gary feel proud.

There are days when Roy comes to stay. He argues with Winnie and Harry and makes the boys promise not to tell Margaret that he is here. Sometimes he takes Gary to the motorway building sites, or to see Humpy Gascoigne at the scrapyard. The yard is strange and dark with dismembered cars all over, and in the main house there are always Christmas decorations on the walls and ceilings, whatever the time of year, so it is not long before Gary is asking to go back to Highgate Lane, where his grandma will give him bread and butter and Ovaltine to drink.

Gary tries to shelter David during these strange days spent with either their mam or dad at their grandparents' houses. They make an unspoken pact to accept what is happening, and to not concede that there is something wrong with their family. Sometimes he has to cut in over David if he starts to tell the Whites something the Hollingworths have said about them, or vice versa. If, back at the Whites' house, Gary lets slip that he has seen his dad, Margaret will bang her teacup down in its saucer, or poke at the hot coals as if she were stabbing the devil, and fire off questions about Roy: How long did he stay? Where does he live? Did he have anybody with him? The questions make Gary miserable, all the more so when his Grandma and Grandad White join in because once they have started on Roy, they start on the rest of the Hollingworths.

'Shut up!' says Gary. 'They *aren't* bad.'

'Nay cocker, I didn't mean . . .'

But he knows what they mean. He cries in a torment that they call 'one of his rages', and runs out of the house into the street, and David watches it all from the edge of the room, feeling afraid and wishing it would end.

35

Ask Your Mam

Highgate, 1966

Lynda is in one of the top classes at school, and her form teacher Mrs Buxton asks her if she would like to leave at Whitsuntide or stay on for another two years to study for O-level exams. Her mam says she should stay on, so she does. Most of her friends go to work in the sewing factory at Goldthorpe and most of the lads start at the pit. John is asked to attend trials at Bradford City Football Club, but it seems a long way to travel, and he doesn't fancy going on his own.

In the Dearne there are still lots of pit jobs, although the money isn't as good as it was. Harold Wilson, who wins the general election in 1964, says mining will be a special case for his Labour government, and that rather than buying more cheap oil from the Middle East he wants to increase British coal output. However, coal sales decline and oil sales increase, as had been the case since the late 1950s. Railway steam engines are being replaced by diesel models; power stations are being fitted with oil-fired boilers; and industrialists, business owners and families continue the shift from coal to oil that had been given an impetus by the Clean Air Act of 1956. The government begins to close mines, reduce the workforce and hold down wages. By 1965 in some coalfields the number of mining jobs is half what it had been in the nationalisation year of 1947. Some politicians warn that unless action is taken to attract new industries this could lead to mass unemployment in mining areas, but most of these warnings go unheeded by those with the power to act on them.

In Scotland, South Wales and the North East, where pits are closing, more families pack up and move south, some of them into new estates of National Coal Board houses in the Dearne Valley. The Dearne is in a coalfield that has fewer closures because the NCB believes it to have potential. Output is increasing. In 1961, Highgate and Goldthorpe – known in the local press as the 'family pits' – break production records, digging out double the national average of coal per man. There is upgrading and amalgamation: a new power station and a coalite plant in Grimethorpe, just north of the valley; new tunnels to join up Highgate, Goldthorpe and Hickleton collieries, and more to link Barnburgh, Wath, Kilnhurst and Manvers. In Highgate, parents tell incredulous children that if you go into the garden and dig down to a pit tunnel, you'll be able to walk nearly all the way to Sheffield. In the shops, yards and clubs people joke to each other that their villages are so undermined the whole place will one day just sink down into the earth and be buried.

Non-pit jobs are also plentiful in the West Riding, and the sense of prosperity and faith in the future is given solid form by the new buildings in town and city centres. Doncaster gets an Arndale Centre, much of Barnsley's town centre disappears under brutalist concrete and Goldthorpe acquires a boxy modern building with a broad rectangular awning for the Co-op. For the teenagers there is a new youth club in Bolton-upon-Dearne that makes an alternative to Rocky Wall's café. Lynda can talk to John there, but not for too long because she is afraid someone will tell her mam. Someone always tells her mam in the end, and her mam always listens, particularly if they're telling her about John Burton.

She sees him a few weeks after he has been taken on at Highgate pit. He tells her about being stone-dusted, a ritual in which new lads are stripped naked, covered in machine oil, and rolled in the stone dust from the machines. 'It's alright,' he says as she shudders. 'It's just getting t' oil off after.' John had started on the haulage, but after having a mild seizure he had been reassigned to the lamp room on the pit top, which he prefers. The job is sociable because you get to see all the men going on and off their shifts, and they say he has a knack for the work.

Lamp-room men prepare, or 'spot-up', each helmet lamp for a shift by placing it in a long box and tuning the beam to a set mark. It is an important job because the miners below ground get used to the focus and intensity of the light that they use to see with, so inconsistent spotting-up is irritating and hazardous. John's quick mind and agility make him precise and efficient, and some of the men ask specifically for his lamps.

Hearing about John's work makes Lynda feel young and inexperienced, a schoolgirl to his adult. She changes the subject to her admiration of his new high-collared white shirt and jeans, bought from a boutique in Doncaster, which is the sort of place he can afford to shop now. He goes to serious men's outfitters as well, he says. Mr Morris, one of the travelling Jewish tailors who make Harry's clothes, is making a three-piece suit for him. Other boys and girls in the youth club join in the conversation about shops and boutiques where they spend their wages, and Lynda suddenly feels conscious of her homemade dress. As the weeks pass, she thinks more about having less money than her friends, and when she is at the youth club or at Rocky Wall's, she feels more and more self-conscious. When she mentions her embarrassment to her mates, they tell her to come and get a job at their factory, earn some money. What is she going to do with O-levels anyway?

She isn't sure, really. Because when she tries to imagine the future she sees John Burton. Forbidden John Burton in his best mohair suit.

She gives a week's notice at school and begins work at the Co-operative sewing factory in Bolton-upon-Dearne.

*

In the spring of 1966, through friends she has made at the youth club, Lynda meets a lad called Kevin Gould. Kevin is the same age as her, well dressed, blond and handsome; the consensus in Highgate and Goldthorpe is that he looks a bit like Adam Faith. He is also mature for his age and capable of carrying off a conversation with her parents about his future plans that make him seem capable and ambitious without being a show-off. Winnie likes him very much. 'You and Kevin sit in t' front room, if you like,' she says when he comes to visit. 'Put some of your records on, your dad'll not mind if you use his record player.' She even allows them to close the door.

He comes most Saturday afternoons. Winnie gives them fruit cake and bottles of fizzy fruit-flavoured green drink that Harry brings back from his delivery journeys, and they sit on Winnie's new, orange crushed-velvet settee listening to the Dave Clark Five, Manfred Mann and the Beach Boys.

One day they are halfway through a Dave Clark Five album when Kevin says, 'Your dad's not your real dad, is he?'

Lynda makes a what-are-you-talking-about face.

'Yes. Of course he is.'

'That's not what I've been told.'

'By who?'

'By Bruce Phillips.'

Lynda feels her certainty leave her with the sudden pop of a stylus lifting from an LP. Bruce Phillips's family live on Highgate Lane. Bruce works in a garage that has opened up on the corner of the lane and Barnsley Road. A few weeks ago Lynda had walked past the forecourt, and seen him and Kevin in conversation. Lynda had heard Bruce say, 'She's a bastard, her.' At the time she had not understood what he was talking about.

'What did Bruce say?'

'He just said to me, "Her dad's not her real dad."'

'Well,' she declares, 'he is so far as I know, so Bruce can mind his own business! Shall I put another record on?'

On Sunday, after she and her mam have had their roast dinner, Lynda is lying in front of the fire, Winnie sitting on the sofa crocheting a blanket. Harry's dinner is being kept warm in the kitchen until his return from the club. Lynda knows that if she is going to ask the question it will have to be now, when she and her mother are alone.

'Mam, is Dad my real dad?'

Winnie abruptly looks up from her crochet hooks. A moment passes.

'Yes he is,' she snaps. 'Why are you asking me?'

'Somebody said summat to me about him not being.'

'Who?'

'Somebody at school. They told Kev, and he told me.'

'Who at school?'

'Bruce Phillips.'

'Tell Bruce Phillips to keep his mouth shut then. And stop talking like that.'

Lynda hesitates. 'Are you sure?'

'Yes I am. Don't ask me again.'

The following evening, after Lynda arrives home from work, Winnie goes out with one of Muv's sisters visiting from Shirebrook. While she is gone Margaret Westerman, a neighbour and the wife of the Highgate club steward, comes round, knocking and then letting herself in at the back door. She enters the living room where Lynda is watching television, but does not take off her coat.

'I'm not stopping, Lynda. I've just come for a word with you.'

'Oh. All right.' She cannot think what Margaret might want to discuss, especially when *This Is Your Life* is on.

'You haven't half upset your mother saying what you said to her.'

Oh, right, she thinks. That.

'Why, what have I said?'

'What you asked her yesterday. When I came in this morning she was stood at t' ironing board crying her eyes out.'

Crying? Her mam? Something inside Lynda snaps. How is *she* the one being blamed? She fixes her visitor with a cool, even stare. 'Are you going to tell me what's going off, Margaret? Because I'm sad if I've upset my mam, I really am, but it's me that's been told my dad isn't my real dad and I want to know the truth. Are you going to tell me?'

Perhaps Margaret had forgotten how old Lynda is, or perhaps in her day girls hearing rumours about their father were made to be quiet. Whatever the reason, sympathy overwhelms her resolve.

'It's not for me to tell you. You'd better ask your mam.'

*

In the end, Winnie sits on the settee knitting her thumbs, and tells Lynda the story, from Alf first coming to the house with Sonny, to him begging her to go away with him. 'He was just always that kind to me, you see. He used to come up and ask me if I was all right and he'd rub my arm, or just put his arm around me, and it was nice. Then one day when he was staying in t' front room, I went in to see to something, and he was there, and we got talking and one thing led to another, and . . . that's when it happened.'

Later she will tell Lynda that she could equally well be Harry's daughter, but now she touches her daughter's temple and says softly, 'I know you're our Alf's. Your hair grows like his, the way it kinks at the side there. It's the same.' She is silent for a moment. 'Will you promise me never to tell your dad that you know?' Lynda knows she means Harry. 'He's been good about it, and he's always treated you like his own. He'd die if he thought you knew what happened.'

Lynda promises. It is an easy promise to make, because her feelings about her dad are unchanged. That night, lying awake in bed, she thinks she ought to be upset, but actually she doesn't feel any new emotions about herself or her family at all. Her mind is mainly occupied by the discovery that her feelings of love and loyalty are determined more by someone's actions than by their biology. That may not be true for everyone, but it is true for her, and the realisation is liberating: rather than weakening her love for Harry, it strengthens it.

Since she was a little girl, Lynda had listened for her dad walking past her bedroom door at night on his way to bed. If she is still awake when he comes in, she calls out to wish him goodnight and he calls back.

That night she lies awake, listening, until he comes, creaking the floorboards of the steep stairs and then the landing.

'Goodnight, Dad,' she shouts as he passes.

'Goodnight, love.'

Stronger, not weaker, she thinks. Not less, but more, somehow.

36

A Little Less Conversation

Goldthorpe, 1967

After her discovery Lynda breaks off with Kevin Gould and spends more time with John Burton at the youth club and the café. She tells her mother she is going out with other friends, and if Gary and David stay she takes them to the park as a pretext when she is meeting John there. But even when Winnie is tipped off by friends, her opposition to John is less fierce than it was. Her confession of the affair with Alf has subtly altered her relationship with Lynda, and working at the sewing factory has given Lynda more independence. With Winnie's power over her daughter diminished, her hope and fear are exposed. Her hope is of nurturing Lynda both for her own sake and, perhaps, as a proxy for Winnie's memory of Alf: her fear is of being publicly tainted by an association with John. She attempts to dissuade Lynda from seeing him, but Lynda steadily pays less attention. When they do split up in the summer of 1967, it is because of John's actions rather than the doom-laden hectorings of Lynda's mother.

It begins with a youth club trip to Malgrat de Mar on the Costa Brava. Excited by the prospects of travelling abroad and going on holiday with John, Lynda encourages him to come, but he refuses. He says he would need to borrow money from his mam, who cannot afford it, and anyway he is not interested in Spanish tourist resorts. Lynda knows these are excuses, but drops the subject and goes on the trip anyway. She sends John postcards so he can see where he would have been staying and then, thinking that he might regret not having gone and be in need of cheering up, she finds a record shop so she can buy him a Spanish-issue Elvis record that no one else in Goldthorpe will have. She finds an EP which is perfect: four songs including a 'Down by the Riverside' and 'When the Saints Go Marching In' medley, and a sleeve with a picture of Elvis looking cool in an orange shirt.

On the day she arrives home she puts on light-coloured clothes to show off her tan, and walks through Highgate, past Rocky Wall's café and up the main street to the Burtons'. John's mam shows her into the front room where he is sitting on the settee. He does not stand up when she comes in.

'*Buenas dias, amigo!*' says Lynda.

'Ayup.' He looks at her only briefly, and does not smile. His manner is that of a wronged man in an aggressive, unforgiving mood.

'I'm back.'

'Aye, I can see.'

'I've bought you this.' She holds out the Elvis EP in its pink-and-white striped paper. John takes it, slips it from the bag, looks at the sleeve and lays it on the settee beside him.

'Thanks.'

'You're welcome.'

Silence.

'What's the matter?' she says.

'Nowt.'

'Right,' she says. 'Shall I go then?'

She stands wondering what she has done wrong. One day John will explain that the fault was not hers: he loved Lynda above anything else but knew that her family disapproved of him. That and the idea of being in the discomforting setting of a foreign country with her had eaten away at his self-assurance. Confronted by her and her perfect gift, he just wanted the complicated emotions to go away. Aged eighteen, he can't tell her this, and, still sitting on the green vinyl settee, he shrugs and says, 'If you like.'

Silence again.

'I'll go now then, shall I?'

Lynda walks out, expecting him to follow. She closes the door and stands outside the house waiting; she walks down the street listening for his footsteps, but he doesn't come. All the way home she goes back and forth over the conversations they had before she left, the messages she sent on the postcards, and the choice of record, but she can think of no good reason for his rejection of her. After a few days she decides that he probably just wants some freedom to go out with the lads, but the mystery will play on her mind at intervals for the next ten years. One person, however, sees the good in it.

'You don't love him, you just think you do, love,' says Winnie as Lynda sobs in the sitting room. 'You want to get on with your life now, and not bother with him. He's not good enough for you.'

Winnie had preferred Kevin Gould all along. He was a nice, sensible, mature boy, and he didn't have fits.

37

The Two Wives of Roy Fox Hollingworth

Bradbury, County Durham; Redcar, North Riding of Yorkshire; Bridlington, 1965–66

In the summer of 1965, Roy calls to see Margaret and asks her if she and the lads will come with him to County Durham, where he is employed by a construction company with a contract to upgrade part of the A1 to a motorway. He has been working on the new roads, living in Flamborough, Bridlington and Redcar, keeping his head down and sorting himself out, he says. His wages are now more than enough to support her, Gary and David and, if she'll come, they can stay in his caravan while they look for a flat.

Lonely, poor, and, despite everything, still in love with her husband, Margaret agrees. Roy drives them to a village called Bradbury, just outside Sedgefield in County Durham, and they park in a steeply sloping field beside a farmyard overlooking the A1. Margaret had imagined a large mobile home on a campsite, but the solitary caravan in the field is small: when Roy shows them in, their suitcases take up half the floor space, and she sees they will have to rearrange the foam cushions on the settees to make beds. There is a chemical toilet and no running water. 'We'll not be here long,' says Roy, seeing the expression on her face. 'We can all just muck in for a bit.'

In the morning Roy goes to work on the road, leaving neither money nor information. Margaret goes to the farmhouse to ask where she can buy food, and the farmer's wife gives her bread, tea, milk and eggs so they can have breakfast. As they eat inside the cold caravan Margaret listens to the cars on the A1 contraflow, the earthmoving machines in the distance, and the occasional bellowing of livestock. It starts to rain, and the rain sounds loud on the roof, like stones falling. Margaret offers up a small prayer of thanks that the caravan does not leak.

The next day is rawer and dourer than the first, and a mood of embattlement seems to be spreading out from the roadworks. They are in the County Durham coalfield, and because the earth is sinking into the disused mine workings there are problems with the road construction. The motorway is behind schedule, and for the first few weeks Roy eats in a canteen on site and has to work a lot of nightshifts, sometimes around the clock. Margaret and the boys go days without even seeing him, though his road runs along the bottom of their field.

After a month he finds them a family-sized caravan on a park overlooking the beach at Coatham Bay. A few miles from the work site, Coatham Bay is on the edge of Redcar, and across the River Tees from Middlesbrough. The caravan park is exposed to the North Sea, and if its residents look northwards they see Teesside's steelworks looming, but there are shops close by and the caravans have running water. Roy says he will find a flat for them nearby, and Margaret asks people on the site about schools for the boys to go to in September, and begins to feel optimistic about their future.

And then one Saturday morning, Roy brings visitors. He has been away all night – working, he says – but he returns to the caravan with a dark-haired woman of roughly Margaret's age, and a little girl who looks a few years younger than David. Something about the way the woman stands in relation to Roy makes Margaret think she has a territorial stake on him.

'This is Alwyn,' he says. 'And this' – gesturing at the girl – 'is Wendy.'

'Hello,' says Alwyn.

'Who's she?' Margaret asks Roy while looking at the woman.

'A friend of mine,' says Roy, and Alwyn smiles.

'Why is she here with you now?' asks Margaret. 'Is something going on?'

'No! I just wanted to bring her and Wendy to meet you and t' lads.'

Alwyn smiles again.

'I don't . . .' Margaret addresses Alwyn directly. 'Will you go, please?'

Alwyn looks at Roy. Margaret feels a rush of adrenaline. 'I want you to go,' she orders. 'Get out. Go!'

Alwyn takes Wendy's hand and hurries out of the caravan and across the park. Margaret darts to the door to shout after her, slightly surprised at herself but enjoying the feeling. 'Don't come back or I'll flaming kill you.'

Roy is laughing.

'Is that your fancy woman?' asks Margaret.

'Of course it isn't,' says Roy. 'When would I have time to see a fancy woman? Come here.' He hugs her. 'She's just a friend, sometimes cooks for t' men in t' caravan. I just said I'd bring her to see you and t' lads, but I wouldn't have bothered if I'd known we were going to have that carry-on.'

'But . . .' Margaret is unsure. She does not trust the woman, but knows there is a caravan that serves as a canteen on the works site where women come to cook for the men, so that part could be true. 'Alright,' she says, and sits down. 'I just want to have a normal life, Roy. That's all.'

He stands and fills the kettle at the tap. 'I know, and we will. Come on, let's have a cup of tea.'

They do not have a normal life, and Roy does not find them a flat. He spends more nights away from the caravan, and gives Margaret little money for food and clothes. Once in a while he comes back drunk and threatens to hit her. Margaret feeds the boys on cheap tinned food and white bread, eating as little as she can so as to be able to fill their plates. Her weight goes down to six and a half stone.

One day when she has only a few coins left for food, and Roy has been absent for three days, Margaret goes to the council offices to ask the woman on reception if anyone there can help her. The woman eyes Margaret and the boys warily as if they might steal something, and directs them to some nearby offices where she says someone will talk to them about National Assistance. The offices are dingy, with unwashed windows and an unwelcoming atmosphere. One of the staff, an officious but personable man of about forty, takes down her details, and those of Roy, and listens when she says her husband doesn't give her any money. 'He says he can't afford it,' she says. 'But I need to feed my children, and I wondered if you could help me?'

The man fetches registers and files, checks some of their pages and then looks at Margaret with curiosity.

'You're Mr Roy Hollingworth's wife?'

'Yes, I'm Margaret Hollingworth. These are his two sons.'

The man glances at Gary and David. 'Could there be any confusion about that?'

'No! I'm his *wife*! And these are his two lads.'

'And where do you live?'

Margaret curtly gives the address of the caravan. He looks sceptical. 'It's temporary,' she says. 'He works building motorways.'

'I have no record of a Mr Hollingworth at that address. We have a Roy Fox Hollingworth in Middlesbrough. We have him down because his wife's in receipt of National Assistance.'

'But that can't be him because I don't get National Assistance! That's the problem!'

'Yes, but that's the only Roy Hollingworth we have. And your name . . .?'

'Margaret.'

'Yes, Margaret . . . but you see his wife is a Mrs Alwyn Hollingworth.'

'Alwyn? She's not his wife –'

The man looks at her with pity.

'I think you need to have a word with him, and come back to me,' says the man. He knows she is looking at the register and he lets her keep looking long enough to remember the address.

*

She and the boys catch a bus into Middlesbrough, and then find the address on foot, asking directions as they go. There is no reply at the house, so she stands and waits for a couple of hours until she sees Alwyn coming down the road with Wendy. Alwyn lets them all into the house. Margaret notices a pair of Roy's shoes near the door.

'What's going off, Alwyn?'

'What do you mean?' Cool as a cucumber. She says yes, Roy might come round sometimes, but they're just good friends. She says no, she has no idea what he's told the National Assistance.

Margaret thinks that Alwyn has a very good idea what he's told them, and the two women argue, the three children casting their eyes downwards and stealing looks at one another. Alwyn refuses to yield, and Margaret realises that Roy might have kept the details of the National Assistance money from her too. It is him that she needs to question. She takes the boys and walks back to the bus stop.

By the time he comes home her anger has subsided into despair. He says she's got the wrong idea and that there has been a mistake. The council people are idiots: Alwyn is a friend, he calls to see her now and again, but that's all. She was engaged to a soldier who died, you see, and talking to Roy helps because he understands, having been in the Army himself. Why does Margaret always have to be so jealous and mean-spirited about everything? Surely he can help somebody who's pining like that? 'Anyway let's not fall out,' he says. 'Let's have a fresh start and move out of this van and into somewhere proper.'

He keeps promising a flat, but moves them to a bed and breakfast in Redcar, to another caravan park along the coast, and then back to Coatham Bay. Margaret suspects that he is dodging rent. She cannot find out if there really is a flat for them because most of the time he isn't around to ask, and when he is, he is in no mood to discuss it. She believes that some of the time when he is away he is with Alwyn, though of course when she says so he shouts and says she's talking rubbish.

By October the park is emptying of families and fewer and fewer of the caravans are occupied. One night when Roy returns home from a night drinking, and the boys are in bed, Margaret demands to know when they will move into the flat. He tells her to stop nagging. She says she needs to know so she can send the boys to school. 'It's not the lads you care about,' he says, 'it's yourself.' He lurches at her with his hands raised. She staggers backwards and the table flips up and over, and he is shouting, and punching his fists into her. He is wilder than he has been before. She begs him to stop and tries to get away, but he is above her and in control. She expects him to reach down to yank her up, but no, he is kicking her in her back, up and down her spine, his shoe toe in her bones. She screams. Gary and David are peeping round their bedroom door. Roy kicks until he is tired, then stops and walks out into the night.

In the morning she feels sick and wobbles when she stands. There are bruises and welts all over her face and body. When Roy comes back she shows him what he has done, and he seems embarrassed and ashamed and then tells her she needs to go to see a doctor, almost as if it was someone else that had caused the injuries. She is worried. She wonders how thin and damaged you have to be before you die. 'Can you take me to t' station to get a train back to Thurnscoe, Roy?'

'Aye,' he says. 'Leave t' lads here, and you go and get sorted out. I'll get packed up here and we'll come down. We'll have a new start, I promise. Don't take notice of that Alwyn, it's nowt. It's you that I love.'

She travels back to the Dearne alone by train. It has been the worst beating he has ever given her, but at least seeing the damage he has done seems to have changed Roy, she thinks. Once he's back with her in the place they belong, things will be different.

*

Margaret moves back with her mam and dad, and goes to see a doctor in Thurnscoe. The doctor knows what has caused her injuries, and tries to advise her. 'There's no need for you to put up with it, Mrs Hollingworth,' he counsels, with the tone of a man who has found himself in this situation before. 'If he doesn't stop it, you must leave him.'

'I know,' she says. 'But he's coming back, and we're going to make a fresh start.'

At the end of two weeks, Roy is not there and has not contacted her. Margaret's mam and dad tell her to put in for a divorce. She applies for National Assistance and at some point in the course of telling the clerk that she is separated from her husband, and that her husband does not give her any money, she acknowledges the truth: her husband has another woman, and he isn't coming back. Worse, he has the boys.

At first, the realisation that Roy does not intend to bring Gary and David home makes her feel as if she is in a dream. Each morning she wakes and instinctively listens out for them, to see if they are up or not, and then she remembers they are with Roy, and lapses into numb listlessness. If she thinks of trying to retrieve them, she is seized by terror and nausea. As she recovers her strength she investigates ways in which she might get them back, but no one seems willing to help her: Social Services say they can't get involved, and the police in Goldthorpe say the same. Harry and Winnie deny knowledge of Roy's whereabouts, though Margaret thinks that they are covering for him because they prefer their grandsons to be with Roy.

*

Meanwhile, Gary and David adjust to life on the salt-wind whipped caravan park. David, now eight, feels anxious and frightened, and Gary tries to looks after him, even though he is scared himself.

Roy goes out in the mornings and sometimes he doesn't get home until eleven or twelve at night. Most days he leaves the boys locked in the caravan with a tin of beans for their lunch. On Saturdays, Alwyn and Wendy come, and Wendy plays with the boys while Alwyn bakes, and makes them platefuls of sausages and chips, and scolds Roy for neglecting his children. Alwyn washes their hair in paraffin to kill the nits, and then they go out together to the amusements, or to the beach. But then Alwyn has a row with Roy, and she and Wendy stop coming, without explanation. The boys are lonely and, as summer draws to an end, they spend much of their time just looking out of the window at the other caravans. One day Gary starts to get dinner for himself and David, and finds just a half tin of baked beans and a bag of flour, a vestige of Alwyn's baking visits. They eat the beans but two hours later David says, 'I'm starving, Gary.'

'Aye, I am an' all.' Gary sees his little brother's face and tries to think what he can do. 'Let's see if we can find something.'

But they can't. David looks mournful. Gary remembers Alwyn making pancakes on the stovetop; he can't remember all the ingredients, but he knows one of them was flour. He takes the flour bag from the cupboard, shakes the contents into a jug and mixes the flour with water. Then he pops on the gas. 'Just a minute, our kid,' he says. 'We'll have some pancakes.'

With shaky hands he pours some of the white liquid into the pan and attempts to scrape it into a pancake shape and flip it over, but it looks a mess. He scrapes the mess onto two plates and they try to eat it, forcing down mouthfuls until they catch each other's eye.

'It's not right, is it?' says David.

'No,' says Gary, and takes both their plates to scrape them into the waste bin.

Another day they are looking out of the window when they see workmen gathered around one of the empty caravans on the far side of the field. The men back up a truck to it, attach the towbar, and drive it away. In the afternoon they come back for another. The next day, and every day after, more workmen come, moving the caravans one by one. The holiday season is over. Eventually there is only the boys' caravan and one other. To Gary and David it is as if everyone is being taken away and dropped into the sea.

On a Saturday morning, when there are just the two caravans left, Roy tells Gary and David to come with him to the gates of the caravan park because he has a surprise for them. They stand in the cold wind, shivering, until a bus comes to the gates, and Alwyn and Wendy get off. Alwyn runs to David and Gary, and puts her arms around them and cries into their thin little bodies. 'These two want something to eat, Roy.' She makes Roy take them all to a café where she tells the boys they are all going to live together.

The next day they pack up the caravan and move into a flat in Redcar. Soon after that, they move into another caravan park in Bridlington, and Alwyn sends Gary, David and Wendy to a school in the town. For a while the two brothers feel safe and part of a family again. There are teas eaten in cafés, balls booted about on beaches and comics featuring soldiers and superheroes, bought from newsagents. On evenings when he isn't at work, or in the pub with Alwyn, there is their dad, sitting on the caravan settee under the big window, telling them about what he did in the Army, and about Montgomery, and the Duke of Marlborough, and other great men who, like soldiers such as himself, had fought to make the country what it was, to create Great Britain and the Empire, to defend the race of heroes.

Outside the sea wind blows and the white lights on Bridlington promenade sway. 'Tell us another one, Dad,' says Gary. 'Go on, tell us another story about t' war.'

38

You're Never Telling Me You're Going to Do it on the Street?

Bridlington; Thurnscoe; Highgate, 1967

One night soon after Margaret has moved back in with her parents, she is watching *Crossroads* with her mam when two uniformed policemen and a man in a suit come to the door. They are looking for Roy. Has she seen him? 'Chance would be a fine thing,' she says. She assumes he's at the caravan at Coatham, though he's not replying to her letters. They leave, but the following morning the man in the suit comes back. He is Roy's probation officer, Mr Bullard, heavily set, dark-haired, worldly and sympathetic. He says the police want Roy in connection with a traffic offence. They are having trouble finding him because all the caravans in the park where he was staying have been cleared for the winter. He wonders if Margaret knows anywhere he might have gone.

Her immediate thought is the boys. If Roy is missing, where are they? She buckles and leans against the wall. Mr Bullard asks if she wants to sit down. Her mam comes to the door. 'Them Hollingworths,' she spits. 'I'll swing for that Roy . . .'

'How will I get them back?' Margaret asks her mam and the probation officer. 'I don't even know where they are!'

It is Mr Bullard, acting out of personal compassion, who helps her as various institutions bat her away. He tells her where and how to engage a solicitor, what the solicitor needs to find out and who they need to tell.

With money given to her by her dad from his savings she employs a solicitor. The solicitor contacts the police, who locate Roy, Alwyn, Gary and David in the caravan park in Bridlington. Margaret's elder brother Leonard sends a friend with a motorcycle out to the coast to check, then the solicitor drives to the caravan himself, returning to tell Margaret that taking the children back will be harder than they had expected because Alwyn and Roy are claiming that Gary and David are Alwyn's children. The next time, Margaret goes to see them herself, with the solicitor accompanying her. She finds Roy and Alwyn waiting for her in the caravan with a vicar. The vicar tells the solicitor that, as far as he knows, Alwyn is the mother of all three children.

'How can *you* know?' Margaret loses her temper, and screams. 'How can you possibly know? You're a liar! Get back to your church!'

'This is what it's like,' Roy says to the vicar. 'Do you see? Do you see what I've been trying to tell you?'

The children watch, David and Wendy cowering behind Gary. Margaret has no choice but to leave the boys behind. She hugs them tightly, trying not to cry, and the solicitor leads her back to his car, and takes her home.

*

Through November and December and into the New Year, Margaret visits her solicitor two or three times a week to sign papers or just to hear what has been done and what Roy has said. The social workers agree that Margaret should have custody, and decide that Gary and David should pass into her care in Bridlington on a set day that coming spring.

She travels up the night before with Leonard and his wife Shirley, and stays in a guest house. In bed Margaret lies awake listening to the distant sea, playing back memories: that first night at the market café, the boys as babies, Winnie trying to warn her about getting married. She falls asleep and dreams that she is separated from Gary and David by a door that she cannot open; she can hear the boys, but however hard she pulls or pushes, the door stays closed. She wakes, with the door still unopened, at 5 a.m.

The exchange is set for eleven that morning, a Saturday. The social workers, a well-spoken woman called Miss Shepherd and another young woman whose name Margaret never catches, meet them at the guest house after breakfast.

'Are you all right?' Miss Shepherd asks.

'Yes, we're all right,' says Shirley. 'You just concentrate on keeping this Alwyn out of our way. Because if you don't, I'm going to maim her.'

'I understand,' says Miss Shepherd, being careful about what she says. 'We'll keep her out of the way. Shall we go?'

It is a blue day, cold and dampish. They make their way through side roads to one of the main streets where a few early morning shoppers are out with their bags and trolleys.

'Here we are,' says Miss Shepherd. 'We'll just meet them here.'

'Here?' says Shirley. 'You're never telling me you're going to do it on the street, are you?'

Miss Shepherd looks hesitant, then guilty. Shirley is incensed. For her, though clearly not for Miss Shepherd, it is a breach of a basic code of decency: you don't conduct your private business in public.

'They're less likely to try something on if there are other people around,' Miss Shepherd offers limply, and there is just sufficient hint of expertise and specialist knowledge in her voice for her to get away with it.

They wait on a small square. At eleven o'clock another social worker comes through the crowds, Alwyn alongside her, ushering Gary and David. Their hair is unkempt and lousy-looking, and their ill-fitting clothes seem to hang off them. Roy is not there. Miss Shepherd had expected him, but as Shirley says, no one is surprised by his absence, and Alwyn offers no explanation. Margaret falls to her knees on the pavement and pulls her sons to her. Passers-by stare. Shirley glowers at Miss Shepherd, and Miss Shepherd tells Alwyn to leave.

Back at home in Thurnscoe, Hilda White gets down the tin bath and warms the water so the boys can wash. When they undress, Margaret sees their bodies are grimy, and her mam starts to cry.

'Never mind,' says Margaret. 'It's over now.'

'We hope,' says Hilda.

*

Margaret and the boys stay at her mam and dad's house again and she re-enrols them at school. On the solicitor's advice she files for divorce, and then she walks around the shops and factories in the villages until she finds jobs to get her off the dole – cleaning at the fish and chip shop, picking potatoes in the fields, and putting up wallpaper for people, with Hilda and Winnie taking it in turns to look after Gary and David. She has to steel the boys against taunts and gossip, but she knows it is hard because she feels the humiliation herself. The failure to be a family: a failure you feel not only on the street, but also in your own home every time you see a perfect, happy family on television or in a magazine.

Her embarrassment smarts most at an appointment at the housing office in Wath-upon-Dearne. The clerks at the housing office, like the clerks at the Labour Exchange and the doctors in the National Health Service, are like gods among the general public, the services set up to help the people seeming in practice like divine powers, their premises as intimidating as courtrooms. Margaret, with Gary and David at her side, is directed to a room occupied by a clerk called Mr Edritch. Mr Edritch has small round spectacles, a black, bristling moustache and heavy eyebrows, and he peers at them from behind piles of papers on his desk. His speech is that of a man wearied by having to explain incomprehensible rules to people whom he considers insufficiently grateful for his time. He over-pronounces every word, drags out the final syllables, and when he speaks he stares at his desktop until he reaches the end of the question, then looks up sharply, with his heavy eyebrows raised. He talks not as a god might, but as a middle-ranking courtier-cum-administrator to the gods, a man who believes that his job sets him apart from the common herd. Gary imagines him as a clerk to the Nazi officers in one of his war comics.

Mr Edritch works his way through a form, making very deliberate ticks. Gary watches the process closely. He feels angry with the man for not being kinder to his mother.

And how long have you resided at that address?

And how many children have you?

Where are you employed?

And your husband?

They always ask that. When Margaret explains her circumstances Mr Edritch tilts his head to look at Margaret, arches a thick wiry brow with its coarse greys in the black, and says contemptuously, 'Ah, no husband, have you? Hmm, hmmm . . .' He writes something down on the form, the noise of the pen pressing through the paper into the worn varnish of the desk seeming loud in the unkempt room.

Gary senses that he, David and his mam are meant to feel ashamed. He lifts his elbows onto the desk in defiance of Mr Edritch, but the clerk seems not to notice and goes out to find some papers. They sit quietly, talking in whispers, as if quietness might be rewarded with a house. He comes back: they will be kept informed if anything comes up. 'There is nothing suitable for you at present.'

Suitable *for you*, Gary remembers. Suitable *for the family without a dad.*

*

Margaret files for divorce on the grounds of persistent cruelty, wilful neglect to maintain a wife and child, desertion and adultery. At the first hearing, at Doncaster Magistrates' Court on 29 November 1967, Roy does not turn up. When they try again in March the following year, his solicitor denies the adultery. In the meantime the court grants Margaret an order preventing Roy from coming near her and the boys except at prearranged times of access. When he comes to collect them, he makes more fuss of Gary than of David, something he knows will anger and hurt Margaret.

Rebelling, Gary tells his mother that he's sick of her and wants his dad, and he runs off to Number 34, drawn by the welcome he'll get and by a sense of loyalty to his dad and his dad's family. He likes the plain predictability of the house, the smell of cooking, the grandmotherly cosiness of the settee fabric and the eiderdowns: Winnie in the sitting room, telly on in the corner, his tea ready and waiting, and

Lynda being like an older sister. Sometimes his mam lets him stay there the whole weekend and his grandad takes him out in the glass-works lorry and tells him stories about history and geography. He points out the pubs and clubs he has sung at, or the spoil heaps where the sponcom – spontaneous combustion – breaks out in red fires in the night. He recounts ghost stories from the pits, and teaches Gary the names of the different seams running through the earth below them, the Parkgate, the Melton Field and, most famous of all, the Barnsley bed. The Queen has Barnsley bed coal from Brodsworth pit, he explains, because Brodsworth coal burns so hot for so long. If they pass a pit where there was once an explosion that killed men he tells his grandson the story, and then shows him the blue scars in his arm and describes his own accident at Manvers Main, fifteen years ago now. 'Don't thee go down t' pit, Gary,' he says, 'no grandson of mine's going down that hole.'

When they come back and Gary tells his grandma what his grandad has said, she ticks Harry off. 'It's a living, Harry, and miners are as good as anybody else. Take no notice of him, love.'

She berates Harry again on Sundays, which are always the same. Winnie gets up early to cook the dinner, Harry has a lie-in, and Gary and Lynda watch the strange foreign programmes on Sunday morning television. Harry gets up and goes to the club, and later in the afternoon Winnie calls Gary into the front room with a loud whisper – 'Gary! Come in here.' Through the window they watch Harry coming home, swaying as he walks towards the house.

'Look at him,' she says. 'The drunken swine.' Gary looks and smiles.

Harry crosses the road, and comes in crooning. 'Ayup, love!' he says to Gary, with a gap-toothed smile.

'Ayup, Grandad.'

'Your dinner's ready, Harry. You want to have it and get yourself to bed, you drunken so-and-so.'

Winnie is displeased, but less vitriolic than she once was. All three of them know that a small part of her is playing up the conflict to amuse her grandson.

When Harry goes upstairs to lie down, Gary settles on the settee with Winnie to watch an old black-and-white film, and listen to her telling him about the old days when she was a girl. He loves hearing Harry and Winnie talk about the past, and delights in the grand dramas from which their stories hang like loops of film. Most of Winnie's stories are about the family, and all the ancestors who are looking down and whose good characters, she says, remind her very much of Gary. As his grandad sleeps she tells him about her father being hurt in the war, about the union, Churchill and Lady Astor, and about the miners being called the worms of the earth. He has heard much of it before from his Grandad White. 'Don't listen to thy father telling thee about Churchill,' he always says, 'I'll tell thee about Churchill', and tells him about 1926, and about Churchill sending troops to the Welsh valleys when the miners there went on strike in 1910.

Gary will remember these tales of cooperation, decency and organisation built from adversity; the struggling, the mothers working all hours, the sleeping four to a bed, the injuries to their fathers. To him it is a secret history, a kind of pedigree, an inheritance of sorts. When he thinks about his mam and dad he feels as if he is in deep water with an uneven bed, so that when he puts down a foot he never knows if there will be anything to meet it. Here, though, safe in the house with Winnie and Harry, he feels as if he has found the rockbed and, when he puts his feet down, there is solid ground beneath them.

39

The Beautiful, Beautiful Glowing Light

Harlington and Goldthorpe, 1968–70

After their marriage, Pauline and Gordon Benson grow into coupled lives that are attuned to the farm, and, at least to begin with, content. They buy a new, semi-detached house close to the farmyard, Gordon works with his father, and Pauline gets a job in the post office in Barnburgh. They buy a Staffordshire bull terrier puppy, and in the house, Pauline paints the kitchen cupboards in various pastel shades in the modern American style. In February 1966 she gives birth to their first child, a son, Richard. Gordon's parents fuss over him (he is their first grandson and therefore, they think, the future of the farm) and when Winnie and Harry come to see him, Winnie has an unusual, almost philosophical, mood. 'This,' she says, holding the baby in her arms, and looking wistful, 'is where your heartaches begin.' It seems to Pauline that her mam is saying this as much to herself as to her daughter, and she will later ponder whether the statement was simply about parents and their children, or also about feelings Winnie usually kept hidden.

The remark turns out to be in some ways strangely prescient, although what now begins for Pauline and Gordon are heartaches connected not to the birth, but to a series of deaths that will change the way Pauline thinks about the world, and lead ultimately to her and Gordon's departure from the Dearne Valley.

To start with, Gordon's mother, at the age of fifty-six, is diagnosed with throat cancer. When she becomes so ill that she needs nursing and there is no one to feed and clean up after her husband and the farm workers, Pauline steps in, helping to run the household while looking after a year-old son and a dying mother-in-law. She learns how to get the blood from the handkerchiefs and sheets; she learns what to cook, and how to clean quickly. This is not the home economics she had learned at school, the economics element in particular unlike anything she has previously known. Gordon's father is parsimonious and determined to put his money back into the farm, and when Pauline needs money for his housekeeping she has to request it. When he gives it to her he wants receipts in return, as if women cannot be trusted with finances. He is not unusual among farmers, says Gordon, but it is unusual for Pauline. On Highgate Lane it is generally the women, not the men, who control the money.

Mrs Benson dies at home in April 1968. The following summer, when Pauline is three months pregnant with their second child, Mr Benson is killed when his new tractor topples over the edge of a heap of silage, crushing his body. Gordon is working in the yard when it happens, and he finds the wreck with his father in it. Pauline is washing the crockery in the sink and is alerted by a neighbour at the kitchen window ('One of 'em's under t' tractor, Pauline!'). She thinks it is Gordon, and for a few panicked seconds stands frozen, believing herself a widow until another neighbour brings more news.

In the aftermath of the accident, Gordon assumes the landlord, the National Coal Board, will allow the tenancy to pass from his father to him, but three days later the NCB's land agent turns him off the farm. The Board representatives say it is because they have a consolidation plan, driving for efficiency. The farm fields are included in a larger, single parcel and rented out at a higher rate, the yard is sold for housing, and the NCB gives Gordon and Pauline twelve months' notice to quit Beech Farm.

*

In late January, Pauline gives birth at home to a second son, whom they name Jonathan. He is drowsy and always sleeping and his movements are slow; he takes an hour to drink a four-ounce bottle of milk. The doctor, from a nearby village, says he'll be fine. But they fret. Gordon, who had not nursed Richard because he was afraid of squashing him, looks mournful, and takes the baby in his thick hairy arms as if he was made of gossamer and nurses him and talks to him, and they convince themselves he will be alright. But then one evening four weeks after his birth, just after tea when Gordon is at work, Jonathan begins a shrill crying that Pauline cannot calm. His face turns a deep red. Pauline calls the doctor on the telephone, anxious. The doctor says don't worry, it's not important, it'll just be a bit of colic, that's all.

'But he's in pain, I know he is. Babies don't cry like that if there's nothing wrong.'

The tone of the doctor's voice betrays his impatience. 'It'll be *fine*, Mrs Benson. You young mothers think every little thing's a life or death matter. Just give him some of the medicine I left last time and trust me. He'll be all right.'

Pauline replaces the handset in the cradle and sits beside her baby son hoping Richard won't wake up. But he doesn't get better and she calls the doctor again. He is crosser this time.

Gordon comes in at nine and sits with them for a while as she strokes Jonathan's head. Pauline, trying to convince herself it is colic, tells her husband to sleep, and that she'll call him if she needs him. At midnight, after Gordon has turned off the light and she has walked up and down the room with Jonathan, he stops crying, and the house falls silent. His pumping chest calms, his eyes begin to close, and then she notices his mouth. There is a bluish tinge to the lips and the tongue, and as she looks it seems to spread and deepen; and then she is sure.

She shouts up to Gordon, who comes running downstairs pulling on his clothes, and she phones the doctor, who says he will come. Then Gordon is running to the next-door neighbour to ask if they will look after Richard, and the neighbour is coming round and Richard is on the stairs, and the doctor is at the door, and when he comes in and sees the baby he says, crossly, 'How long has he been like this?' and Pauline says, 'Since I last rang you!'

'He can't have been,' says the doctor.

'That's what made me ring,' says Pauline. 'If you remember, you wouldn't come before.'

The doctor calls the hospital, and the hospital says to bring Jonathan in, and they get into the car, Jonathan on Pauline's lap, and drive fast through the night to Mexborough.

At the hospital the doctors and nurses put Jonathan in a room and make him calm, and tell Pauline and Gordon to go home and to phone at seven in the morning. Pauline and Gordon try to sleep but cannot, and at 6 a.m. the phone rings. Gordon answers.

'Come straight away,' says the nurse. 'He's not very well. Can you tell us his name? Yes, I need his name, because we've got the chaplain here to christen him, just in case.'

When they get to the hospital, Jonathan is dead. Gordon has to identify the body; his son's little face is blue-purple. A nurse tells them she is very sorry, and as far as the hospital goes that's it.

*

Later on that day a uniformed policeman calls to tell them the results of the post-mortem. Jonathan had been born with only three heart valves and one of those had been defective, so his heart had been unable to pump sufficient blood around his body. 'He might have lived to be seven,' the policeman says, trying to sound comforting, 'but he would have been a cabbage. Ordinarily he would have been born a blue baby.'

'But he was pink when he was born,' says Pauline, 'that beautiful baby pink.'

The policeman, in his dark blue uniform, may or may not know what shade of pink she means, but he nods, and he listens and in the listening he seems not only dutiful, but also decent.

After the policeman come the man of science and the man of God with their explanations.

The doctor apologises without making eye contact.

The vicar says Pauline must understand that the child is now at rest with God. Having barely spoken to him since her wedding, and sitting alone with him in the sitting room six days after Jonathan's burial, she is hesitant and nervous in his collared presence, and feels confused by his consolation. At rest with God: it is a puzzle rather than a comfort. She has faith in a God, but this does not make sense to her. Why did God want her baby? Doesn't He have enough to look after?

She tells the vicar, 'I don't understand why, if God cares about us, he would take a child that would have been loved. Can you tell me why? Because I want to know.'

He says something about people not always being able to understand how God works, but this makes her angry, angry at the vicar and angry at herself because she cannot make the vicar understand. She had thought that she *did* understand God, more or less. 'What I mean is, if a child's happy in heaven, why not take children that are unhappy on earth? There are all those children in Biafra . . .'

There have been reports about the mass starvation in Biafra on the television news, and Pauline has watched in tears. 'There were some on television last night and their mothers were dead and they were starving to death. Why didn't God take them, and leave Jonathan where we can look after him?'

The vicar looks at her with an appalled expression. 'Now that,' he says, 'is a selfish thing to say, Mrs Benson! Those little children have as much right to life as yours, wherever they may happen to be from. Do you see?'

More than selfish, Pauline now feels thick. She feels she has made an awful mistake without knowing quite what that mistake is. 'I didn't mean to be selfish. I was trying to say I didn't understand why God took my little boy.'

Not long after the vicar leaves the house, her mam visits. Winnie says everything has been connected: that Jonathan's heart had been damaged by the shock Pauline had when she thought Gordon had been killed under the tractor. Winnie listens to Pauline, and says she will try to think of someone who can help her. Pauline does not know what her mam means exactly, but a few days later Winnie comes down to the house again to tell her that if Pauline would like it, she can take her to The Rooms in Goldthorpe.

Having grown up with her mam's spirit guide living in the house, and with Annie reading her tea leaves for her amusement, Pauline is open-minded about spiritualism. Gordon says she should go, and she accepts Winnie's offer. Gordon will never tell anyone but Pauline, but he has been visited himself. Close to midnight one night in the week of Mr Benson's funeral, Pauline had heard Gordon return home from harvesting barley alone in one of the fields; she had heard him come in but he had not come up to bed. Putting on her dressing gown and slippers, she had padded downstairs to see him seated at the table, head bowed, with tears making thin uneven trickles of clean skin through the dust on his face. He had felt his father come to him as he worked, he told her, he had felt his father's hand laid on his hand, and heard a voice saying, 'Tha's done enough for tonight, lad, go back home.' Panicking, he had stopped the combine harvester in the middle of a row and driven home at speed on the tractor.

'If tha wants to go to T' Rooms, love, then go,' he says to Pauline. Whatever happens, he adds, it will probably do her more good than the vicar or the doctor had done.

*

Pauline drives her and her mam up to The Rooms one clear night a few weeks after Jonathan's death. The building, near the Italianate church, is darker and more careworn than she remembers it. As she steps through the door she sees the venue is already packed full of solemn-looking women and a few scattered men. Emotion surges through her and she feels full of something. She begins weeping, not from grief, but from relief and gratitude, and the tears will not stop until she leaves.

There are wooden chairs set out in rows. Winnie speaks to a few acquaintances, and she and Pauline take their places in the middle. At a quarter to eight the medium, who had been sitting to the side of the room, stands up and comes forward to face the audience. She introduces herself, sits down at a small table and talks about the people who are coming through. 'I have someone who . . . had been alone a long time.' 'I have someone with a sign . . . like . . . a rose.'

As she talks, some members of the audience say, 'Well, my brother lived on his own,' or 'My mother loved roses', and the medium tells them what she can make out from the person coming to her. Pauline, with tears all over her face, feels a warmth and kindness in the gathering, but also some sceptical bemusement because of course anyone could say these things and someone would pick up on them eventually.

'You've just lost your father – '

The medium is speaking directly to her.

'No,' she says, 'I haven't –' but Winnie nudges her elbow and whispers, 'You have, in a way.'

'I'm sensing that you have, love,' says the medium.

'It –' Winnie looks at the woman. 'It was her father-in-law.'

'Oh. Oh, alright. It could be –'

Here we go, thinks Pauline. Trust my mam to fall for this.

'He's saying you've not to worry,' she says, and listens again. 'He says he's got your little boy with him.'

Pauline feels a moment of fear and clarity, an abrupt gathering of herself. Jonathan had been buried in the same grave as Mr and Mrs Benson.

'He says he's got your little boy there, and he's looking after him. He's all right. They're both all right. And he says not to worry. That's what he wants you to know, that you mustn't worry yourself.'

The medium comes closer, and speaks as if there were just the two of them in the room. 'Don't worry, my dear, and don't be afraid. Your little boy is with your husband's father. They are going to be all right, and you're going to be all right. You have a beautiful light around you, you know. You have a light that's been there all the time you've been in this room. A beautiful, beautiful glowing light.'

The people in The Rooms smile at her and it is as if she has a beautiful light that is bathing her as she sobs.

Afterwards, Winnie will swear that she had told no one about Pauline's bereavements. Pauline will never know for certain that the medium was not tipped off, but when she thinks about the evening later in her life this will hardly seem to matter. It will not be the belief or non-belief she remembers, but rather the calming feeling, the thought that someone she knew was taking care of her baby, and the being told, there in the darkness, that she had a beautiful light.

*

In the end, Pauline and Gordon look for a new farm to rent outside the Dearne Valley. It takes a year to find one, in which time Pauline gives birth to a baby daughter, Helen. The farm, which they buy at an auction, is a small one in a village on the Yorkshire Wolds, fifty miles from the Dearne. Rose Farm lies next to the village church and was built in the 1830s by John Rose, who was reputedly a faith healer. They move the agricultural equipment up there week by week during the spring of 1970, and one day that summer, Gordon and Pauline pile Richard, Helen, two dogs and the farm cat into their car, and drive out of the Dearne Valley for good. A year later, Beech Farm and its outbuildings are demolished, and the land covered with smart modern houses and bungalows.

40

The Duke of Highgate Lane

Thurnscoe; Redcar; Doncaster; Highgate, 1968–69

So that he can stay in contact with his dad without angering his mam, Gary Hollingworth secretly calls him from telephone boxes using loose change and a number that Roy has given him. They arrange meetings outside the scope of the court order, and although these encounters at Winnie and Harry's, or on days out in the car, thrill Gary, he will sometimes return to the Whites' with familiar accusations for his mam. It is her fault his dad isn't there; couldn't she give him another chance? He might come back and be a good dad if only she left him alone a little. David, quieter and closer in temperament to his mother, and confused by the twin claims on him, watches the arguments in bewilderment.

The secret-meetings arrangement goes awry when Roy moves back to the North East and begins to test the effectiveness of the court order. First David sees him watching the house, then he collects the boys from school and takes them home to Redcar, and the police have to bring them back. One day he collects Gary at the school gates but leaves David to go home. 'Gary went with Dad,' David tells his mam when he gets home. 'He came in t' car and picked him up at school.'

'Where did he take him?'

'I don't know.'

'What about you?'

'He said I had to come home to you.'

The police bring Gary home, but the abduction unsettles everyone. Roy keeps on breaking the access agreement, returning the children after the specified times. Gary quarrels with his mam more often; he becomes tense, apprehensive and prone to explosions of anger, and he suffers from constipation and incontinence. To get away from the arguments he hides at Winnie and Harry's, or in books. He visits the library beside the bowling green in Thurnscoe, walking down by himself on Saturday mornings to borrow science fiction, war stories and history books. One day he finds a hardback copy of *The Iliad* and reads that, impressed by its similarity to the superhero stories in the comics that his dad buys for him. His favourite character of all is Iron Man, alterego of Tony Stark, the American millionaire industrialist who, after a severe chest injury, builds a hi-tech suit of armour that enables him to do battle with his enemies. In tribute to him, Gary wears an Iron Man T-shirt, bought for him by his dad.

He is wearing the T-shirt on the wintry Saturday morning late in 1968 when he stuffs some clothes, comics and pocket money into a duffel bag and sneaks out of the house to catch the bus from Thurnscoe to Doncaster railway station, as arranged during calls to his dad. Alwyn meets him at the station and takes him on the train to Redcar, where Roy and Alwyn file a new custody claim. They acknowledge that David is happy with Margaret, but say that Gary wants to be with them, and Gary agrees. The claim, resisted by Margaret, goes into a legal process which will lead to a court hearing. In the meantime, Gary adapts to a new family life with Roy, Alwyn and Wendy.

Roy now works at the steelworks in Hartlepool. He has become a shop steward, and after tea, while the rest of the family reads or watches television, he studies books about employment law and trade union history. Most of the time, outside of working hours, he and Alwyn are around the house, but every few weeks Gary and Wendy come home from school to find the house empty, and they have to take care of themselves for a few days until Roy and Alwyn stagger back drunk, and fall asleep on the bed upstairs.

The custody hearing takes place at Doncaster Magistrates' Court in the spring of 1969. Gary puts on his Redcar school uniform and Roy drives him and Alwyn to Doncaster, urging Gary to speak up for himself and not to let Margaret browbeat him. He stops outside the court and, looking up and down the street, explains that he can't come inside because if he does he'll be arrested.

The courtroom is small, tatty and stale-smelling. Gary and Alwyn sit on one side, and his mam and the Whites on the other. Uncle Leonard, freshly shaven and looking big in his suit, glares at Alwyn. The judge questions the solicitors and social workers, and the solicitors question Margaret and then Alwyn. Gary tries to understand it, and waits for someone to ask him where he would like to live. He has come with an idea. Sick of all the fights and wrangling, and unable to keep both his mam and dad happy at once, he will just live with his Grandma and Grandad Hollingworth. It seems the perfect solution to him, but in the end no one even asks his opinion. The judge declares that custody will pass to Margaret, and tells Gary to go across to her.

He refuses to move, and Margaret flinches. Uncle Leonard rubs her arm.

'Gary, you must go,' says the judge. 'Come along.'

'I'm not going.' He cries as the court usher tries to guide him and Leonard steps in to take his arm. Gary drops to the ground, prostrate on the black tiles. 'Nobody listens to me! Why does nobody listen?' He feels like property. Men's hands close around his arms and drag him across the cold floor.

*

Margaret gets a council house at the peaceful, cemetery end of Thurnscoe and a new job as a cleaner at the Albion sewing factory. Her mam and the neighbours help with the boys, and she carefully budgets with her wages and the family allowance so she can afford the bills and occasional treats – nice cushions for her sitting room, a day out with the lads, a couple of Crimplene trouser suits for herself. Gary grudgingly accepts his new home and in return Margaret tolerates him spending many of his afternoons, evenings and weekends at Winnie and Harry's.

Number 34 has been bought by the council now, Mr Meanly having sold up when the government passed a law compelling landlords to install indoor toilets and washing facilities. He had offered the house to Harry for £200 but, against the urging of Winnie, Pauline and Lynda, Harry had indignantly declined. ('I'm not buying two walls at £100 apiece for anybody's money, and I'm not owning half a wall with Nelly and Reg Spencer.') The council carries out repairs more quickly than Mr Meanly and has installed the anticipated bath and toilet suite, which has not only brought a warmth and luxury to daily life, but also helped Winnie and Harry's marriage. Until its arrival, Harry had continued to use either the Manvers Main baths or the bath at his friend Wilf Mallion's, and in her wary moods Winnie had suspected him of using these trips to cover up visits to the pub or to other women. He had always denied this, but now the contention is shelved altogether, this vague resolution of old disputes becoming something of a trend during this period of their marriage.

Winnie, now almost sixty, still has her solid vigour and deftness, though nowadays she is depressed by Roy where once she might have rained fire and judgement on him. Her hair has turned the colour of white garden-fire smoke and her face is lightly lined under the pale freckles of late middle age. The power relationship between her and Harry has shifted in recent years, and she has begun the process, although she does not yet realise it, of acquiring the mastery over her husband that comes to most Highgate Lane wives in the end. As he subsides into bemused and grudging acceptances of words and actions to which he might once have objected, she finds she can risk gentle public mockery of him, and this becomes a new way of discharging old tensions. Harry and his flaming cars. Harry and his flipping clothes. Harry and the carry-on he has with his music. He always laughs now, and the way he laughs makes her like him more.

He even plays the funny man to her straight complaints and laments, and this sets a new tone for them both. Increasingly they resemble a domestic version of Morecambe and Wise: Harry the comic blunderer who ruins what would otherwise be a sophisticated life for Winnie, Winnie the long-suffering, respectable pillar of the community whose censoriousness and lack of humour leaves her talented husband under-appreciated. In the years to come it will be in this comic take on their earlier life that they find a matured version of the feelings they had for one another when they first began courting in the 1920s.

In their own ways, they both work hard at keeping up with contemporary tastes. Winnie takes an open-minded interest in her grandsons' ideas of fun, which comes naturally to her. Caring for them feels easier and less complicated than it had been with her own children, and she enjoys sharing this rich second flourishing of affection; if her grandchildren find solace and support in her home, they may also return it by becoming the simple objects of love that she had always wanted.

Harry, meanwhile, maintains his collection of 150 jokes, and still sings and drums for the organ players. When his old partners retire he searches out new ones and has started a partnership at the Collingwood with Albert Blessed, a lorry driver and organist in his twenties whose cousin Brian did panto at the Welfare Hall and is now in *Z Cars*. 'You have to move on with an act,' Harry tells Gary. 'It's no good playing what you want, it's what your audience wants. That's entertainment, *mon brave*.'

*

A Saturday in the autumn of 1969: all afternoon Gary has been out on the allotment with Harry. The allotments are at the rear of the houses across a potholed cinder track, filling the space between two streets and a small farmyard. They are a mess of different neatnesses: individual runs of fencing, narrow pathways, tumbledown greenhouses, tarpaper-roofed sheds, and gardens of green plants and canes. The smells of soil and onions mingle with pipe smoke, cow dung and the sound of men's murmuring conversations against the rumble of lorries heading west to the M1 motorway.

Harry is shaking soil from a scalp of potatoes so that he can take them in for Sunday's dinner. He has been telling Gary about looking after the pit ponies, how he would share his snap with his favourite and how the pony would steal sandwiches from your pocket. Gary has drifted off his job of cleaning tools and is imagining a sole brave English Tommy hiding out from the Germans in these allotments. Where would you hide? In one of the sheds? Would a hand grenade lobbed into a shed kill you?

'Would a hand grenade kill you, Grandad?'

Harry smiles and drops the potatoes into a carrier bag. 'It wouldn't do thee much good.'

'Did you nearly die when you were in t' explosion?'

'Nay, I've telled thee before. I could have done, but I was lucky.'

'What did you do?'

Harry gathers up the potatoes, straightens his back and he and Gary walk the thin paths through the allotments towards the backings and the snug houses, where the first lights are going on at the windows in the violet haze of late afternoon.

'T' first thing I did, Gary,' he says, as they step into the kitchen, catching the sound of Kent Walton's wrestling commentary from inside, 'I told them to clean my face. I didn't want my face being a mess. I wasn't bothered about t' rest of my body. But I didn't want coal and scars in my face.'

'He's vain, Gary, that's why,' says Winnie, coming into the kitchen to brew her two men some tea. She puts the pot on the table and pours it out. Harry takes his mug and adds whisky.

'It's not vanity,' says Harry, scrubbing his fingernails. 'It's pride in thy appearance. Nobody wants scars in their face.'

Under the electric light, if he looks closely, Gary can make out fine blue pinpricks in Harry's face, the smudge in his hairline. This blueness is the keel to his grandad's vanity, making it noble, giving him the valour of a soldier.

After watching the wrestling, and eating a tea of fish and chips, Harry lets Gary come upstairs to help him get ready to go out. In the bedroom, Gary leans back on the sweet-smelling eiderdown as his grandad, freshly bathed, dresses, and tells him about the tailor who makes his suits. He reaches into the wardrobe for shirts on hangers, taking them out as carefully as he might take delicate old books from a high shelf, and shows them to Gary: whites, creams, pale blues and candy stripes. 'Look at this one, cocker: that's a Rocola shirt, just feel t' cloth on it. Which have I to wear?' Gary reaches out and rubs the crisp, starchy cotton, and chooses a plain cream.

'Fetch us my gold cufflinks out of yon drawer.'

Gary brings the cufflinks from a small drawer at the top of the dressing table, and Harry holds out his cuffs. As he threads the little steel spikes through their slits, Gary can sense his grandad preparing to relax once the cufflinks are in. With the last push and the tiny flip of the spike to secure it, he stands back; his grandad slips his hand into a trouser pocket to fish out some coins, and gives them to his grandson for sweets.

Thinking they are ready to go downstairs Gary runs off down the landing, but Harry calls him back. He opens one of the small drawers and pulls something out.

'Here.' Harry puts into his hand a silver wristwatch with trillions of tiny abrasions on the glass and a creased, cracked leather strap, and a tie pin polished like the gold bars you see in films on television. 'These are for thee. My dad gave them to me a long time ago, when I was a lad. They called him Juggler and all, tha knows. Make sure tha takes care of 'em.'

'I will, thank you, Grandad.'

They both clatter down the stairs and turn right into the sitting room, where Winnie looks up at them from the television. As she smiles, the skin at the outer edges of her eyes folds into little crinkled wings. 'Here comes our Gary with t' Duke!' she says, the Duke her affectionate nickname for her preening husband. Gary feels the warmth of the reflected glory. He sits down beside his grandma on the settee-throne, prepares to inspect their domain of the TV schedules with her, and toasts his aristocratic heritage with a glass of green fruit-flavoured pop.

PART SIX

41

A Pork Pie and a Pint of Milk

Thurnscoe; Goldthorpe; Highgate, 1971–72

'Today you will be shown some of the opportunities that are now open to school-leavers like yourselves. Remember, this is a big employer. Those of you who'll be looking for work after Easter or in the summer, make sure to listen, and don't be afraid to ask questions. Does anybody have any questions for me before we get on the bus?'

Thurnscoe comprehensive school's fourth-year boys, gathered in the school hall for this briefing from their careers teacher, look down at the parquet floor, or out to the playground where two private-hire coaches are waiting for them in the bright, March morning sunshine. Several of them edge towards the exit in readiness for a race for the buses' back seats.

'Stay where you are, Crossley, McGregor, and the rest!' Mr Clark, the teacher, bangs his clipboard on the table for emphasis. 'I hope you'll bear in mind this is an educational visit, and not an excuse for a day's larking about. A lot of trouble's gone into organising this trip for you. Now, if there's nothing else before we go –'

A plump boy raises his hand. 'What about us dinner, sir?'

'Dinner? Is that all you've got to ask about?'

The boy blushes as the others jeer at him.

'It's all laid on for you, you'll no doubt be glad to know, Spence. They're being very generous. Make sure you repay their generosity with good manners. Right, off you go.'

The boys stampede out of the school, and scrabble aboard the two coaches. Among them is Gary Hollingworth, crop-haired, face framed by wispy, teenage-whisker sideburns the size of lamb chops. He sits with his friend Kenny near the back of one of the buses, and pitches in with the insults and banter about who will and won't get taken on.

'They'll not take Spence on 'cos he'll eat all t' food in t' canteen!'

'They'll not even gi'e thee a button job, Crossley, 'cos tha's scared o' t' dark!'

'They'll not take thee on, 'Olly, 'cos thy hair makes thee look like a psycho.'

'And they'll not take thee on, McGregor, because tha'd want to take thy mam to work wi' thee!'

Gary rubs his head, irritated by McGregor's suggestion. He and Kenny had recently persuaded Kenny's dad to shave their heads in the skinhead fashion because they thought it would look rebellious and nonconformist. On seeing them in school, Mr Taylor, the deputy head, made the two boys stand on chairs in assembly while he denounced them as the sort of thugs who mug elderly women. It was ridiculous; Gary is not at all violent, he just enjoys acting like an outsider. Almost fifteen, he believes that his dad's absence has taught him to be strong and independent of other people; when he looks in the mirror he sees a kind of wispy-sideburned skinhead Iron Man. Like most of the other boys he is impatient for adult life. His mam says she needs another wage coming in anyway, and his dad tells him to get to night school and make something of himself.

He turns away from the pillocking. 'Only a couple of months and we'll be free, Kenny.'

'Aye. Two months too long.'

Kenny's dad works at Houghton Main colliery, a mile to the west of Thurnscoe. He has told his son what to expect on the trip. 'We might get set on wi' a job today tha knows. We'll soon be earning, 'Olly lad.'

The coaches drive through the village and, ten minutes after leaving the school, turn into the car park of Hickleton Main colliery. Hickleton's training officers have arranged today's visit so the boys can be shown around and invited to apply for jobs, all as part of an NCB recruitment drive currently being promoted on television and in newspapers and boys' magazines. That month an advert in an issue of *Goal*, with a grinning Gordon Banks on the cover, urges readers to 'Get the Best Industrial Training in Britain and Nearly £10 a Week at 15'. Underneath this headline a comic strip shows a pretty blonde girl rejecting a grocery delivery boy named Paul. 'Get lost,' she tells him. 'I only go out with real men!' Paul's friend sees that he's upset and asks, 'Why don't you get a real man's job and join me and my mates in mining? You get a darn good training in basic engineering.' Paul heeds the advice and joins an NCB training scheme. In the final frame he is reunited with the now-adoring blonde. 'Honestly, mate,' his friend needlessly reminds him. 'You can't go wrong in mining . . .'

Hickleton pit yard sits in the lap of the spoil heap, like a hamlet at the foot of a black mountain. Concrete and iron girder headgears tower over the brick offices, sheds and piles of equipment like watch-towers, looking down on the boys in their black blazers as they follow the colliery training officer into the canteen. Here there are long rows of Formica-topped tables with room for hundreds of men. The training officer directs the boys and their teachers to a reserved row, introduces himself as Mr Eldon, and gives a lecture about prospects in the coal industry. Mr Eldon is youngish and friendly, and when he sits down to talk he takes off his suit jacket, and perches side-saddle on a table. It's a modernised industry with a big future in Yorkshire, he says, and the old stories they will have heard don't apply in today's mines. Hickleton is just about fully mechanised. Computers will be coming in, and there are all sorts of training courses and welfare benefits.

Before they go to look around the yard, the boys are sent up to the canteen counter where serving women give each of them a pint of milk, and a golden-brown NCB pork pie served on a white melamine plate. Then Mr Eldon gives them a tour of various buildings, and explains the work that is done in each. Some of the boys are dismayed to find that they're not being shown the real action, and ask if they can go underground.

'Er, not today, no.'

'But what's t' point of coming to look round a pit and not going down it?'

'We've some leaflets about working underground,' says Mr Clark, staring at the boy asking the question. 'Let's get finished out here, and then we'll go back to the canteen for a chat.'

Back inside the canteen a table has been piled with NCB pamphlets, and some lads are hoping there'll be more pork pies. At another table boys can sign up for a job for after they leave school at Whitsuntide. They form a queue. Gary joins it, and adds his name to the list.

*

When Gary turns up for his first day at Hickleton Main the recruitment officer rejects him because he has had tuberculosis.

The next day Gary cycles around asking for work at building sites, workshops and farms until he gets a job with a building company that is installing bathrooms in council houses. He gives most of his wages to his mam and the rest goes on clothes, records, sci-fi and history books and, occasionally, beer. Tall for his age, he finds it easy to get served in pubs, and he finds that he likes being among older men who will talk to him about the Army and the war, or the history of the Dearne villages. He wonders how old he will need to be before he can have a drink with his grandad.

On New Year's Eve 1971, Gary, Kenny and their friend Les go out to celebrate in the packed and roaring-hot pubs of Goldthorpe. In some, Slade, T-Rex and Rod Stewart are on the jukebox; in others, organists and singers perform standards against the din. By ten o'clock the crowds are dense and unyielding and lads not from Goldthorpe are likely to get themselves punched if they push too hard at the bar. When Gary knocks a stranger's arm, slopping the man's beer onto his clothes and the floor, the boys catch the man's malevolent stares, drain their glasses and escape, at Gary's suggestion, to the Unity Club.

The Unity is a squat, single-storey building on a tidy street on the edge of the village. It used to be the Catholic Club, but in the late sixties the committee dropped the religious membership requirement and adopted the new name, although no one dared to remove the large brass crucifix on the bar-room wall. The change brought in a different crowd and allowed for the employment on Friday, Saturday and Sunday nights of an electric organist and drummer: Jack Sharpe and his friend Juggler Hollingworth.

Tonight, standing in a corner at the back of the concert room with Les and Kenny, Gary peers through the cigarette smoke at his grandad and Jack seated on the low stage, playing standards and songs from musicals. Backed by swags of old Christmas decorations and faded mustard drapes pinned with tinsel, the two musicians look trim in their suits and striped shirts and ties, both of their faces flushed from the heat of the crowded bodies on the small dance floor and at the tables. Harry's suit jacket hangs on a peg at the side of the stage.

'That's my grandad playing t' drums,' says Gary. This was the reason he had suggested the Unity; he had wanted to see Harry playing, and he had wanted Kenny and Les to see him too.

'Is that t' Juggler then?' says Les. 'He could do with some new material. A bit of Black Sabbath!'

Les and Kenny talk about music, and the lasses dancing, but Gary listens to the drums: the thuds of the bass, the crisp snare rattles, the hissing hi-hat. Once, Harry had set up his kit in the front room and let Gary have a go, and it had been harder than it looked. 'No music written down for t' drummer, Gary,' he had said. 'Tha's to feel t' rhythm, and to lead.'

Feel the rhythm and lead: how do you learn to do that?

The club grows hotter, the crowd louder, and the cigarette smog barely moves. Harry and Jack break for a drink. Gary has lost sight of his grandad and has slipped into the conversation about lasses, when he feels a hand on his shoulder. 'Ayup, Grandad!' says Gary, trying to hide his beer glass.

'Never mind ayup,' says Harry. 'Finish them drinks now and get thysens off home.'

It isn't quite the welcome Gary had hoped for. 'Why?'

'I'm going to teach thee summat now. See yon bell up there?' he points behind the bar. 'When that rings for t' New Year, they'll all be kissing each other . . .'

'We're not bothered about that!'

'Aye, we might get a kiss!' says Kenny, and he and Les laugh and look to Harry to see if he's laughing too.

'It's after t' kissing tha's to watch. After t' kissing they'll all be fighting.'

'How do you know that?' says Les.

'Trust me,' he says. 'Now get home. I mean it, Gary. I want you out before midnight.'

He turns and pushes back to the bar. The boys drink their pints and at quarter to twelve ease their way through the crowd, stopping in the foyer to look back. The bell strikes and people cheer and throw streamers, and Harry and Jack kick into 'Auld Lang Syne'. The crowd folds in on itself, hugging and handshaking and shoulder-clasping; couples cuddle and hold lingering kisses. Suddenly there is a little surge and an eddy of bodies and then scuffling noises come towards the exit.

The three boys, tipsy and laughing, push through the doors into the cold night air and run down the road and back towards the busier streets. Stars shine above them and the pavement glitters with frost. On the main road solitary revellers stagger and reel, while some folk embrace and others argue. Flushed with beer and worldly wisdom, Gary runs with his friends through the sparkling darkness towards home and adulthood and 1972.

*

Around this time Margaret becomes close to a Goldthorpe man she meets when her workmates take her out for a drink in Thurnscoe. Nine years her junior, Colin Greengrass is an unassuming companion and wary of commitments after an antagonistic and financially ruinous divorce. He and Margaret establish their friendship in a low gear, testing themselves with each other before they risk confidences, and then begin a cautious courtship.

With David and Gary he is plain: none of them wants a substitute-father relationship, so he will be a friend and seek no authority. He fosters David's new interest in fishing, and shares with Gary local history and mining stories. Colin works underground at Highgate pit and his father, who had also worked there, was of the same generation as Walter Parkin. He had been in the 1926 strike, and the experience left him cynical and dispirited for the rest of his life. 'They thought they'd be supported,' he tells Gary, 'but they weren't. And tha knows what they got called . . .'

'Aye,' says Gary, 'I know.'

It is through Colin that, in the early weeks of 1972, Gary and David experience the first national miners' strike in Britain since 1926. The strike begins in early January, but the discontent that prompts it has been fermenting for at least five years. Through the 1960s, British coal has had increasing competition from cheap imported oil. To help it compete, the NCB has been keeping wages down, reducing employee numbers and closing pits. Believing the Labour government to be committed to the coal industry, the miners' union leaders have accepted the reductions in good faith. However, by 1967, when the government proposed the closure of seventy pits, the miners realised that jobs would go regardless of any pre-election promises. And there are other grievances. Mechanisation has improved conditions, but in many pits men still extract coal by hand, and where the new machines are introduced, their chains, blades and belts kill and injure hundreds, and their dust slows the rate of decline of pneumoconiosis. The rising cost of living diminishes wages still further: from being twenty-two per cent above the average manufacturing worker's wage in 1957, the average miner's pay is, by 1969, two per cent lower. Despite the claims of the NCB adverts, Yorkshire school-leavers now find they can earn more as bus conductors than as colliery surface workers.

Suspecting that government ministers are intent on running down their industry, men like Colin Greengrass, who had previously been wary of national strikes because of the experiences of their fathers' generation, come to believe that they might as well risk a stand. There are some unofficial disputes, but the miners' loyalty to the Labour government, and gratitude for nationalisation, makes many reluctant to strike. In June 1970, though, Edward Heath's Conservative Party is voted in and the following year the miners claim wage rises of up to forty-seven per cent, a rise that would contravene the government's incomes policy. When the claim is rejected and negotiations fail, they vote to strike.

The strike stops work at all of the 289 NCB collieries. Miners picket storage depots, power stations, steel works and docks to disrupt deliveries of coal and coke around the country, and the tactic works. On the last weekend of January 1972, a cold snap causes a surge in the demand for power which drains the national grid and rapidly reduces the remaining coal stocks. Twelve power stations close and steel works and cotton mills shut down because they have no coal. There are power cuts across the country, and some homes have electricity only on a three-hours-on/three-hours-off basis.

In Whitehall, traumatised civil servants discuss plans for governing a Britain without electricity. An episode of *Blue Peter* features Peter Purves and John Noakes telling children how to use newspapers to keep old people warm during power cuts. Police, pickets and strike-breakers clash on picket lines, and on Thursday 3 February, a lorry driver recruited by the Central Electricity Generating Board drives through a crowd of police and pickets at the power station in Keadby, near Scunthorpe, and hits and kills Fred Matthews, a thirty-seven-year-old miner from Hatfield. As the news of Matthews's death spreads, the mood on the picket lines and in mining areas darkens. Pickets are arrested, and in the House of Commons Tom Swain, an MP for a mining constituency in Derbyshire, warns that 'this could be the start of another Ulster in the Yorkshire coalfield'.

Colin Greengrass, who has been picketing power stations, comes home the night of Fred Matthews's death looking disconcerted. He has seen lorries driving into the crowds before, he says, and thought someone might get killed.

A week later Colin, Margaret, Gary and David are eating tea in the sitting room, with the TV on in the corner. Gary is in his work clothes, with paint on his hands and plaster dust in his hair, and Colin still has on the old jeans and sweater he wears on picket duty. When the newscaster for the teatime television news mentions the miners, Colin lays down his knife and fork beside his unfinished fish fingers and chips, and listens intently. The story is about a mass picket of the West

Midlands Gas Board coke depot in Saltley, a suburb of Birmingham. At the start of the miners' strike, the Gas Board, like all coal and coke suppliers, had been given instructions, agreed between the NUM and the government, to supply only customers with pressing needs, such as hospitals. The board directors have ignored the instructions and the plant has been selling hundreds of lorry loads every day, undermining the miners' efforts to choke off supplies. In the last few days news reporters have been covering the story as miners from different areas of the country travel to Saltley to picket the depot, and the police have brought in reinforcements. Arthur Scargill, a young union representative from Woolley colliery who is the spokesman for the Barnsley strike committee, has travelled down with 400 Yorkshire miners and is directing the surges of the pickets as they try to block the lorries' paths. Government ministers, aware that the closing of the depot would be portrayed in the press as a victory for the miners, have told the chairman of the West Midlands Gas Board to keep the plant open.

Tonight, the news shows thousands of people converging on the coke depot. Trade union members, the reporter explains, have held one-day strikes in support of the miners and up to 20,000 have marched to Saltley to join the picket. Seeing the size of the crowd, Birmingham's chief constable has instructed the Gas Board managers to close the depot; the television news pictures show the gates closing, Scargill making a speech, and a great mass of men and women, old and young, cheering him. When Gary looks away from the television and across the table, he sees that Colin is silently crying. Colin will later explain that the Saltley picket had made him think of his father, the public support seeming to show an understanding and vindication of his generation's struggle in 1926.

On 11 February, the day after the Saltley gates are closed, the government imposes more power cuts and a three-day week on British industry. More than a million and a half workers are to be laid off, but public support for the miners holds. In deadlock, the leaders of the Board and the NUM agree to hold an inquiry into working conditions in the modern mines, beginning on 15 February, to be chaired by the law lord, Richard Wilberforce – descendant of William Wilberforce the anti-slavery campaigner. Across Britain people buy candles, add newspapers to their beds, and wait.

*

Six o'clock on the Friday evening after the Saltley Gates news bulletin. A gloomy dusk hangs in the valley: yellow lights in the houses, a mist haze out on the fields, rooks settling in the bare trees. On the bridle path that cuts across the fields, a young man is walking from Thurnscoe towards Highgate. He has cropped hair and wears a long black leather coat, and as he nears Highgate, he breaks into a jog, which makes the coat flap about him so that he resembles a giant, blown-about crow. Past the greyhound track, past a scrapyard with a smouldering brazier, past the school, then down into the backings, across the yard and in through the back door of Number 34 Highgate Lane.

'Ayup, Gary love,' says Winnie. 'Have you come for your tea?' She stands at the cooker frying fish and wild mushrooms from the Seels's field. Yes, Gary says, he'd like tea, and his grandmother takes from the fridge another yellow fillet and lays it in the sizzling pan.

In the sitting room, Harry is roasting the backs of his legs against a big furious fire, the smell of heated Crimplene competing with the aromas of food from the kitchen. Lynda is at the table in dressing gown and towel turban, applying mascara.

'I've come to borrow my grandad's work boots,' Gary tells Winnie, 'if he'll lend them to me.'

The boots are Harry's highly polished oxblood Dr Marten's, a form of footwear that, to Harry's confusion, has become fashionable.

'Course he will. They'll look nice wi' what you're wearing.'

Winnie always encourages Gary's experiments with fashion. She had been the only one of his family to approve of the leather coat.

He goes into the sitting room and Harry looks him up and down and says something about the Gestapo, then curses the uselessness of the coal as a hot lump is spat out onto the floor. He scoops it up with the shovel from the companion set and looks up at the television. Arthur Scargill is on the local TV news. 'Has tha seen this one, Gary?' Harry says. 'He could brainwash his scn.'

'I saw it on t' telly last night.' Gary is about to mention Colin saying Arthur did a good job, but stops short because mentioning his other family always feels like some sort of betrayal.

'Pushing and shoving wi't' bobbies, look,' Harry says with a note of sadness in his voice. He adds, as he often does, that the government should fill in all the pits and close them down, and Gary replies that he thinks the pits are a bit different now to what they used to be.

Winnie brings in the food, and tells her husband to stop running down mining. 'T' miners have to stand up for their sens,' she says. 'Nobody else will.'

'Can I borrow your work boots to go out in, Grandad?'

Harry pretends to be amazed, as if such a breach of fashion etiquette is incomprehensible to him. 'Going out in work boots,' he says, and wearily shakes his head. 'I don't know. I think t' world's going mad.'

Winnie looks at Gary and rolls her eyes. 'Gi' o'er, Harry. You used to wear a swallowtail coat and hide in graves when you were his age.'

'*Tombs.*'

'In tombs then. Anyway, you don't know what's in fashion, you're too old. Our Olive says that in Halifax they all wear rubber gloves to go out in.'

After tea, shod in his grandad's boots, Gary walks back to Thurnscoe to meet Kenny and Les in the Fairway Hotel, a large pub with a concert room. The Fairway is favoured by people in their teens and twenties who like music, and on Fridays its concert room is usually given over to Sound Syndrome, a mobile disco with banks of multi-coloured lights and lamps that project psychedelic patterns onto the walls. Tonight, because of the power cuts, the disco is cancelled and the concert room closed. A transistor radio is playing at full volume in the candlelit tap-room bar, where the eccentric heavy-rock fans who usually come out for the disco have gathered among the regular drinkers. The heavy rockers express their sense of kinship with theatrical and unconventional rock bands like Black Sabbath, Led Zeppelin and Genesis. On one table there are four china cups and a teapot full of beer, and a young man a few years older than Gary pouring out cups of bitter for others seated around him, sipping at one himself, periodically asking the barman to pull fresh pints into the teapot. At another is a small group of young men and women dressed like the Marx Brothers. Elsewhere there are girls with glitter on their faces, boys with shoulder-length hair and long beards, and girls putting dabs of glitter on boys' cheeks for a laugh.

Gary, Kenny and Les, who know most of the people, buy pints of bitter and move from conversation to conversation in the shadows. There are mentions of the strike, of picketing and the lads who have been down to Birmingham. To general agreement a man with long hair and a beard says, 'It's our turn now.' He could be referring to fashion, music, work or politics, but to Gary at that moment they all feel like aspects of the same thing.

*

Lord Wilberforce's court of inquiry hears evidence on 14 and 15 February, and at the end of the week publishes a report which endorses the miners' arguments. Before them have been brought for testimony men working in different areas of the industry, including some who have been bypassed by the modernisation of the 1960s. Here, in 1972, is Jack Collins from Kent, who labours in a pit so hot the men work naked, and who in 1963 had earned the equivalent of £5.50 for a shift, but now earns £5. Here is James O'Connor, sixty-two, from Maltby, not far from the Dearne Valley, who is earning £5 a week less than he did in 1966. Here are men still creeping on their bellies, slopping through water, defecating in the best places they can find, trying to bring up families on £18 a week and whatever means-tested social security payments they can get. There is also testimony from Coal Board officials arguing against the wage claim. Derek Ezra, the NCB chairman, says the wages as discussed do not reflect the fact that miners receive benefits in kind, such as the free coal allowance worth £2.30. Lawrence Daly, the NUM president, points out that Ezra has not disclosed the benefits in kind that supplement his salary of approximately £20,000 per year.

Wilberforce's report says the miners had been asked to make unfair sacrifices when their pay was rationalised in the mid-1960s, and that the closures and job losses have caused great hardship. 'This rundown, which was brought about with the cooperation of the miners and their union, is without parallel in British industry in terms of social and economic costs it has inevitably entailed for the industry as a whole.' The national economy needs competitive and efficient coal mines, and they need a satisfied and capable workforce to run them. The miners, it concludes, have 'a just case for special treatment'. Lord Wilberforce and his colleagues duly propose pay increases averaging eighteen and a half per cent, enough to lift mineworkers twelve per cent above the wages of the average manufacturing worker.

The NUM, however, rejects Wilberforce's recommendations and holds out for the full pay claim. They don't get it, but in negotiations with the Heath government the leaders obtain fifteen further improvements in conditions. On Monday 28 February 1972, Colin Greengrass, Kenny and many of the boys from Gary's year at school return to work as some of the best-paid industrial workers in Britain.

Like the closure of the Saltley coke depot gates, the miners' victory in the strike has significances that vary according to perspective. For many miners it brings feelings of greater confidence and recognition, and of power. For certain government MPs, it has been a pay claim won by holding the country to ransom. For Gary, it means that his grandparents' memories are not just stories, and that for once, the television news has some connection to him and the Dearne Valley.

42

Wrong Decisions About Men

Highgate; Goldthorpe; Bolton-upon-Dearne, 1969–74

As these political conflicts play out in the valley, Lynda Hollingworth is experiencing personal struggles of her own. It begins with John sending her away, though for the first year of their separation she cheerfully assumes he will soon change his mind. While waiting for him to do so she works on her career prospects and prepares to apply for office jobs. She attends elocution classes run by an ex-actress in a room above the Co-op, leaves the sewing factory and enrols on a typing and shorthand course at a commercial school in a nearby village. Her friend Carol, who works in London as a nanny for Eamonn Andrews's family, writes to say she can arrange a nannying job for her if she comes down south when her course has finished.

Unfortunately when Lynda mentions this to her mam and dad, her dad tells her to get the idea out of her head, because he won't have her going to London. 'You're going nowhere,' he says, and this last sentence is truer than he intends it to be. Winnie had not questioned the commercial school's claim to improve employment prospects, and Lynda had not questioned her mam, but when she applies for secretarial jobs she realises the school is not accredited with examination boards. Its thin certificates are no more use than the picture cards in packets of tea. Feeling foolish and guilty, Lynda quits early to save her mam a few weeks of fees, and takes a job stitching flannelette pyjamas and nighties at the Silhouette sewing factory in Thurnscoe. It will do until something else turns up, she thinks. She is fast enough on the overlockers to earn bonuses, and she likes the shop floor's open amicability. Most of the women there are young and sociable like her, their chatter as quick and sharp as the sewing machine needles. On Friday afternoons the anticipation of the weekend makes the building feel like a big bottle of Babycham being shaken, the bell at 2.30 releasing energies that last the girls right through to Sunday evening.

One Saturday night out at a working men's club near Rotherham, Lynda meets a man called Geoff Allan. He is the same age as her, with fair, curly hair, boyish face, and the affable humour of a man who has grown up as part of a large family in a small house. They arrange to meet again and soon they are seeing each other almost every weekend, out in a club on Saturday nights, relaxing in Highgate on Sundays. They go to the Halfway Hotel and the club with Harry, and when they see Lynda's friends there, Geoff gets along with them, and everything is easy and jolly and comfortable. It is not a serious courtship, but it is pleasurable and convenient; Lynda thinks Geoff will be good, undemanding company until her reconciliation with John Burton.

Lynda is in the Halfway's tap room with Harry and Geoff one Sunday lunchtime in the autumn of 1968, when she sees her friend Maureen. After exchanging pleasantries, Maureen says, 'Have you heard from John, then?'

'No, not a skerrick. Have you?'

Maureen used to live near John's family in Goldthorpe. She frowns. 'No, but . . .'

'But what?'

'Nowt . . . It's just that I saw him a bit since, and he reckoned he was going to see you and sort it all out. I thought you must have told him you weren't interested.'

Lynda feels a smile rise up through her whole body and force her lips into a grin. 'It's news to me,' she says. 'He knows where I live, anyroad.'

'He's on with getting married now though, in't he?'

The smile sinks back down through her and she feels sick. 'Is he?'

'Aye, to Susan Swift. He's not been courting her five minutes.'

Lynda does not know who Susan Swift is. She asks Maureen as many questions as she can without seeming too concerned, and then goes back to sit with Geoff and Harry. When she picks up her glass, she sees the surface of the Martini and lemonade rippling from the shake in her hand.

'Come on. My mam'll have t' dinner ready – ' She puts her arms around him and squeezes him tightly, and Geoff says, 'Crikey. What's brought this on?'

Six months later, in April 1969, they are married at Goldthorpe church. Lynda wears Pauline's old wedding dress with a lace jacket made by a friend, Geoff a new slim-cut suit with a fat patterned tie. The mood is playful and giddy.

At the reception in the Dearne Miners' Welfare Club near the Welfare Hall, Harry sings a song for them. His response to the marriage has been inscrutable ('Do what tha likes,' he said when Geoff asked his permission to propose) but during the preparations he had insisted that he would sing: the song he chooses is 'Marta', an old favourite, but swapping the name 'Marta' for 'Lynda'.

Lynda, rambling rose of the wildwood
Lynda, with your fragrance divine,
Rosebud, of the days of my childhood,
Watched you bloom in the wild wood,
And I hoped you'd be mine.

The newlyweds honeymoon in Redcar, then move in with Harry and Winnie while they save for a home. All that summer the news is unsettling: trouble in Northern Ireland and Rhodesia, macabre mass murders in Los Angeles, the war in Vietnam, astronauts landing on the moon. People find it difficult to accept the reality of all the events and say the world's off barmy. In this fictional-feeling world Lynda feels she is acting out a game with Geoff, and she makes herself believe they are soulmates. What she actually feels is that if she cannot be married to John Burton then Geoff seems as good a bet as anyone else.

In the spring of 1970 they rent a one-bedroom flat, smart and clean with new Scandinavian-style furniture, above the dentist's in Goldthorpe. Lynda gets a job as the dentist's receptionist – her own desk at last. The dentist even allows her to reorganise the office. 'I couldn't ask for any more, really,' she tells her mam.

On Wednesday afternoons, her half-day off, she tidies and cleans the flat. A few months after they have moved in, she is cleaning the windows and watching the pit buses come up Doncaster Road for the change-over of the shifts. The lights change, and as the traffic slows to a stop the top deck of one of the buses is almost level with her window, blocking her view of the Co-op opposite. Through a thin white film of Windolene she looks without really seeing into the bus, and notices John.

He must still be working at Highgate pit then, she thinks. He appears to be looking at the flat, not into the window but just staring at the upper floors of the building. She feels a pang, and allows herself the guilty indulgence of imagining a conversation with him. She knows he is married and that Susan is pregnant, but it would still be funnier and more intimate than most of her conversations with Geoff, even now, after three years of not speaking to each other. Geoff isn't much interested in talking any more anyway. He goes out at night with his friends from home, and stopped asking her to come with him when they moved into the flat.

She stares at John, thinking he might not have seen her, willing him to smile or acknowledge her, but the bus pulls off, and he slides past her and away. She polishes the window hard.

The following Wednesday afternoon the bus goes by again. John is in the same seat. The bus doesn't pull up this time, but she sees his head turned towards the flat, looking, looking, looking, but not acknowledging her. She smiles, and gives him a small, modest wave. He does not wave back.

It is the same the next week and the one after, and on most weeks after that, John always in the same seat, always looking over but never waving, like a memory come to life in front of her.

*

Geoff goes out by himself three times a week. One night Lynda looks down from the bedroom window and watches him getting out of a car with a woman in the driving seat. 'She's nobody,' he says when Lynda asks who she was. 'Just a lass who gave me a lift home, I can't even remember what she's called. Why are you asking?'

'Because of the way you creep in after midnight and avoid talking about where you've been,' she would like to say, but instead she just shrugs and tries to believe in his hurt innocence. She keeps believing when he takes up karate classes in Mexborough, and when he comes home and doesn't make eye contact with her, but then one karate night in the autumn of 1971 she questions him and he admits he has been seeing his old girlfriend from home. There have been others. Lynda tells him to sort it out. He says he is going for a drink, and storms out of the house.

Alone in the flat Lynda realises that unless she decides she deserves better, no one else will decide it for her. She switches off the TV, and listens to the flat's ticking quietness and the night-time whooshes of the cars on the road outside, thinking.

Then she goes to the bedroom, puts a few clothes in a suitcase, and walks back to her mam's.

The following evening Geoff comes to beg her to come home. When she says no, he cries. She looks at him and feels nothing, as if she doesn't know him. On her next half-day, she goes to see a solicitor about getting a divorce.

*

Lynda moves back in to her old room at Number 34, with its Cliff Richard and Elvis posters, and concentrates on work. A career rewards you reliably and fairly, she thinks; better to study for qualifications than to entertain deceitful men buying you drinks and giving you easy compliments. She reorganises the dentist's office again and at lunchtimes scans the ads in the *Barnsley Chronicle* for secretarial courses.

Beryl Tasker, a friend from the sewing factory, is also looking for a course, and they meet up to talk about studying and career plans, and just to have a conversation without men butting in. She keeps her dealings with men to a minimum now, afraid that her bad judgement will lead to her being hurt again. Beryl tells her not to blame herself for John and Geoff's actions, but then, Beryl is happily married.

'You get a good marriage by making t' right decisions about men, Beryl,' says Lynda. 'And I make t' wrong ones.'

Beryl says it's just bad luck. 'Something'll come along,' she says. 'Sometimes things are mapped out for you, you know.'

Beryl's next-door neighbour is a young divorcee called Tony Grainger. He calls one evening when Lynda is visiting to borrow a cup of sugar, and while Beryl makes him coffee he talks to Lynda in the sitting room. He is in his early thirties, dark and thick set. His manner is a little hesitant but his conversation is sophisticated and interesting: politics, books that he is reading, his job on the railways, his time studying at Ruskin College, Oxford. One subject flows into another, and he listens to her opinions and makes her feel intelligent. As he leaves he asks if she'd like to go out for a drink to carry on their discussion. His shyness and his age put her at ease.

'Alright,' she says. 'Why not?'

In public Tony is more diffident. He and Lynda's dates are in quiet pubs in Bolton-upon-Dearne or at Tony's house, where they watch documentaries on TV. His main source of friends is the Fellowship of the Services, and at the local branch's social evenings in the saloon bars of quiet pubs he introduces Lynda to men he met while on National Service, and to other ex-servicemen and their wives. These evenings out are not exciting, but in private Tony is all romance. His gifts of flowers and boxes of chocolates flatter her, and his age and physical bulk make her feel safe. The onerousness of making decisions falls away from her, because she gives up and leaves it all to him. She forgets about secretarial courses, and takes Tony up to meet her mam and dad. He is awkward around them, and makes an ugly joke about men keeping women in check by threatening to smash their faces in.

'I'll smash your face in if you talk to our Lynda like that,' says Winnie. 'And that's not a threat, it's a promise.'

When he leaves, Winnie is pessimistic. 'I don't know about him, Lynda. When he walked in this house, I had a feeling like cold water running down my back.'

'Here she goes,' says Harry. 'Get t' bloody ouija board out and see if he's put a curse on us.'

'Don't joke about ouija boards. I'm just telling you what I felt.'

'He's fine, Mam,' says Lynda. 'We're just enjoying ourselves for t' time being. We're all right.'

*

They are all right until May, when Lynda realises she is pregnant. When she tells Tony he just stares at her.

'No,' he says, 'I am bloody well not happy. I think you should get yourself off and do summat about it.'

'I can't do that.'

'Why not?'

'Because I just can't. It's not as simple for me as it is for you.'

He bangs out of the house and returns fifteen minutes later with a bottle of gin. 'Here.' He holds it out to her. 'Now get upstairs and run a hot bath.'

'I'll do no such thing. We're having a baby, Tony. You'll have to get used to it.'

He lays on the settee in the sitting room and sulks. Lynda thinks he will be happy once he accepts the news.

She moves into his house, a shabby semi whose atmosphere now seems dismal. A few years ago his mother died in one of the bedrooms, and before that his father had gassed himself in the kitchen. Tony expresses little discernible emotion when he tells these stories.

In July 1972, without telling anyone, they drive to Doncaster and marry at the register office where Winnie and Harry were married. No cake, no flowers, no photographs; when they remember they need witnesses, they ask two strangers off the street. In the afternoon they drive up the A1 to the Thorp Arch trading estate, just for somewhere to go. They wander around shops that sell Dralon suites, self-assembly furniture and Japanese music centres, and then have sausage rolls and coffee in the small self-service café.

'Well!' says Lynda, looking at the pale pastries on their plates and smiling. 'Is this the wedding tea then, do you think?'

He meets her gaze, but does not reply.

Back at home, he complains about having to move furniture for the baby's things. He can't find his books, he says; his watch has been moved. Why can't she leave well alone? She's a stupid bag, buying the wrong food, watching rubbish on the television, putting too many blankets on their flaming bed. Every day he seems angrier. In the past, when he talked to her about politics, he had said that vulnerable people should fight for justice against their oppressors but, she notes, he doesn't extend the principle to home and his pregnant wife. He had told her before that his mother, to whom he, the eldest of four children, had deferred, hated the idea of women working, and believed that they had a moral duty to stay at home to look after their husbands and children. Lynda, however, had not understood until now that he also took this as a model for marriage. After all, for men he demanded equality and freedom; it made no sense until you understood, as she now began to, how radical men could be so conservative about their homes and families. His mam had made sacrifices in the 1930s, so Lynda should make them too. To enforce this he denies her housekeeping money and tries to stop her friends coming to the house.

An old school mate called Lucy McGrevy lives nearby, and is also pregnant. When she calls round to compare experiences with Lynda, Tony is cross. 'You want to tell her to keep away,' he advises, when Lucy leaves. 'That woman fills your head full of rubbish. She's evil.'

'But she's only telling me what's happened to women she knows. What's wrong with that?'

'It's all lies,' he says, and then recounts stories that his mother told him which contradict Lucy and expose her as a deceitful scaremonger.

The baby is due in February, so at Christmas, Lynda gives up work, which makes Tony happy. When she waddles in with her box of stationery, pens and dentist-surgery-scented mementoes, he says, 'I'm relieved you're out of that place. You should be at home.' At home looking after him, is what he means. Within a week he is demanding that his tea is served more punctually, and that she improves her cleaning of the house.

When she goes into labour in the early hours of 22 February, Tony stays in bed because he has work the following day, and Beryl sits up with her until Lynda calls an ambulance. Just after midnight she gives birth to a baby boy with a mop of blond hair and, says the midwife, the loudest cry in the hospital.

At visiting time Tony hardly speaks; he is even silent on the subject of names, leaving it to Winnie to propose Lynda's eventual choice, Karl. Back at home he is uninterested in caring for the baby, and as these milky, anxious and raw-eyed newborn days wear on, his sullenness curdles to disgruntled, unpredictable aggression towards his wife. He becomes petulant about the cold, slapdash meals and untidied shelves and the keys he cannot find in the sideboard. He wants to know why she needs to take Karl out so often. Why do her friends spend half their lives in their house, eating the food he pays for? What does she want to be going out with friends for, leaving Karl with him? A proper mother wouldn't even want to do that. If Beryl or Lucy visits, he picks an argument with Lynda afterwards, and when Lynda goes to visit anyone, he starts on her when she gets home. If she argues back he bangs on tables, or stalks out of the house slamming doors shut behind him. Soon he is knocking over chairs and punching ornaments from the mantelpiece.

*

A year passes. Karl learns to walk, and Lynda learns to avoid the subjects that inflame Tony. In October 1974, Clara, who had been an ally and a comfort to her in Bolton-upon-Dearne, dies after a short illness, leaving Lynda a little more isolated; Tony hardly acknowledges the death or his wife's upset. She hears that John Burton has left Highgate pit and moved his family to Coventry, where he works as a chef at a Forte hotel. She thinks of him often, but hopes he is happy with his wife and children.

Lucy McGrevy still inspires Tony's most violent loathing – simply, it appears, for being Lynda's friend. To reduce his rages Lynda stops seeing her, and for two months Tony is calmer. Thinking his antipathy has mellowed, Lynda invites Lucy to visit one Saturday afternoon and ushers her into the sitting room where Tony is reading *The Times* and

Karl is playing on the carpet. When he sees Lucy, Tony stands up and shouts, 'Don't you come in here! I don't want you here, causing alarm and despondency. She doesn't want to see you.'

'But I'm her friend, Tony,' says Lucy.

'She doesn't need friends,' he says. 'Go.'

Lucy glances at Lynda. Lynda looks at the door, and with guilty eyes says: best go, he might throw something.

She goes. Lynda watches her friend walk out of the house, and feels as if someone is squeezing the air and blood from her body. 'What did you do that for?'

'Because these so-called friends just make you anxious and unhappy.' He talks to her as if she is a naughty child.

'And can't you let me decide that for myself ?'

'No. Because you can't see it.'

She laughs out loud at this. 'Who taught you how to read women's minds then? Your mam?'

Suddenly she feels her head jerk sideways, and her cheek is smarting. He has slapped her, hard. He curses and pushes her into the kitchen, back against the cooker so that it rocks off the floor and bangs the wall. He pushes her again and walks out of the house.

A few weeks later, when Karl is asleep upstairs, they have another argument which Tony ends by punching Lynda to the floor. The next day he is remorseful. He blames the house, and goes out to look for other property to rent or buy. She thinks this is probably a good idea. Leaving plenty of time so that Tony will be well away from the house, she puts Karl in the pushchair and walks without thinking through the village, past the railway line and across the river bridge into the level countryside of the valley bottom. It is early autumn, the sun lowering behind the peaks of coal and spoil heaps at Manvers Main, tractors faintly growling in their fields, thistles going to seed in the lanes' verges. The world quietly handsome, busy and indifferent.

Soon it will be winter, and then Christmas. She wishes that she could just keep walking.

43

Long Hair? Take Care!

Thurnscoe and Houghton Main Colliery, 1970–75

While Gary can often be found among the more talkative and extrovert crowds in discos, David Hollingworth is more content to sit back and listen to the music and observe the people. More of a Parkin, says Winnie, thoughtful, and without the notorious Hollingworth gab. Because he used to be shielded by Gary, some people in the family believe him to be shy, which he thinks is wrong; it makes him sound as if he doesn't have friends, when in fact he has plenty. The girls at school like him because, they say, he has dreamy eyes and looks a bit like David Essex.

He is at his happiest fishing in rivers and lakes in the countryside. A few years ago when he was twelve, a cousin had taken him angling in the lakes of Cusworth Hall near Doncaster, and beside the still, cold, umber-coloured water he had been caught by the calmness and the challenge like a perch caught on a hook. The next day he had borrowed tackle from Colin Greengrass and spent eight hours beside the brick-ponds in Bolton-upon-Dearne, and since then school, social obligations and his holiday job delivering milk have been inconveniences to be endured between fishing trips. He works his way around the local waterways, and sometimes catches the early train to Ulleskelf in North Yorkshire where people fish for roach, perch and bream on the banks of the Trent and the Wharfe; in all these places it is not the tranquillity in itself that appeals to him, he explains to his uncomprehending brother, but the combination of quiet concentration and a clearly defined task. He likes the feeling he gets when he blocks out all thoughts except those about fish, and the hum of life grows quieter than the lap of the water in the reeds. Sitting with his gaze on the river, he is incapable of feeling bored. At the end of most days, he wishes that he could travel back in time and do it all over again.

When David reaches his teens he grows his hair down past his collar, and starts going into Goldthorpe to listen to music in Duffield's record shop, and to watch the kids in Ellis's menswear boutique comparing Ben Sherman shirts, Sta Press trousers and jumbo-collar lengths. Sometimes he and Gary buy an LP with pooled pocket money and, if it's by an artist their mam says looks like a druggie, smuggle it into the house together. At other times he listens to records or roams the villages with his school friends Mark Perry and Alan Ogden, but he is equally comfortable fishing or walking the lanes around Thurnscoe on his own, as happy with himself as with anybody else, as his mother puts it.

It is his liking for the outdoors and water that brings David into contact with Marie Poole at school. Opened in the autumn of 1969, Thurnscoe comprehensive is a new building, its straight, clean lines and large windows representing a faith in the power of built environments to foster clearer, fairer minds. In a village where many of the old terraces still have outdoor privies and no bathrooms, and the closeness of the pit means people fight a constant war against dirt, this idea is still radical. Such progressiveness carries through to the school's timetable which has the boys studying cookery and needlework and the girls working with metal and wood. In the fifth year there is an outdoor pursuits option, the first pursuit being the construction of a fibreglass canoe that pupils are taught to use on local lakes. David signs up as soon as the list appears on the noticeboard, and borrows a book about canoeing from the school library.

In the first lesson he is surprised to find that half the group is female. Among them is Marie, one of the good-looking girls frequently discussed by the boys at Ellis's and Duffield's. Marie has long, glossy auburn hair and a way of walking that makes the boys look. In the playground she and the other tonged-haired girls who glue Marc Bolan pictures to their exercise books stand with their arms folded, chewing gum to cover the smell of cigarettes, and scanning the playground as if their maturity means they are intuiting events ahead of anyone else. David Hollingworth likes her because she seems funnier than the other girls in the group, but he has never spoken to her. He permits himself a slight hope that they might discuss a common interest in canoes, but the idea is dashed in the first lesson.

'I didn't have you down as a canoeist, Marie,' says Mr Birchall, their teacher.

'It gets us out of PE, sir,' Marie replies. 'But you never know, do you?'

David sometimes catches her eye over a work bench, but apart from when he passes her a chisel or a carton of glue he does not manage to speak to Marie during the design and building phase. The closest they come to conversation is in the last lesson, when Mr Birchall takes the class to try out the canoes on a lake in a park near Barnsley.

It is a warm Friday afternoon in July. The boys and girls strip down to swimming costumes beneath their uniforms and, at Mr Birchall's orders, carry the canoes from the minibus to the lake and line up along the edge, threatening to push each other in.

Marie, in a purple bikini, says, 'I'm not going in no canoe for anybody, sir! I'm disco-ing tonight and I'm not getting my hair wet and going out looking like a drowned rat. Are you off out, sir?'

David laughs. He has already practised in the canoes in the school baths, so feels confident, and finds Marie's nervousness endearing. When he looks down the line at her, her straight auburn hair looks beautiful against the purple bikini top.

Mr Birchall pushes a canoe into the water and wades in. He is young, bearded and casual and, away from school, speaks to the children as an older brother might. 'Let's have someone in to demonstrate, then,' he says, and before anyone can volunteer he picks out Marie.

'Come on,' he says, looking up at her. 'You start us off.'

'Get lost.'

'Not scared, are you?'

'No, I'm not scared. I don't want to wet my hair.'

'You won't have to.' He makes her get in the boat. Everyone is laughing, and no one is taking canoeing seriously at all. What the boys are taking seriously is Marie Poole.

Mr Birchall holds her upright in the boat and, exaggerating her nervousness, Marie paddles out into the lake. When he tells her to roll the canoe over, she just looks at him, and paddles back. When she gets out she has command of the group, with her friend Tina Cooke playing a supporting role. As the teacher persuades another girl to climb into the canoe, Marie, now feeding off the adulation, stands on the edge of the lake and plays to her audience.

'At least my hair'll look alright tonight,' she says. 'I couldn't have gone out stinking of *pond water*.'

Laughter.

'I couldn't have gone out smelling like a pond, could I, Dave?'

She is talking to him. Why? he wonders. His eyes flick from side to side; everyone is looking.

'What do you reckon, Dave? Smelling of ponds and lakes is no good, is it?'

'I don't mind t' smell of ponds and lakes,' says David, and his friends snigger and groan.

Marie is looking straight at him. 'Don't you?'

'No. Some lakes have got a nice smell.'

'Right,' she says. 'Well now we know.' She looks round at Tina and the other girls. 'Are we going out tonight then, Dave?'

'Don't know,' he says, and feels his eyebrows twitch. Now the girls snigger.

'Don't take any notice of them, Dave. You come out wi' me.'

'We'll see,' he says.

Mr Birchall hears the teasing and laughter, but just grins weakly, as if he is in on Marie's joke, and helps another girl into the canoe.

'Dave's coming out wi' us, in't he, Teen?'

More cackling laughter around the pool. It is not hostile, but it makes David the centre of attention, and he feels his face burning.

When Mr Birchall asks for a new canoeist, David pushes forward and gets in. As he paddles away he hears the laughter fading and, in spite of himself, imagines Marie Poole in her purple bikini behind him on the shore. When they get back to school, however, Marie does not mention going out with him again.

David leaves school with his final report on a summer Friday in 1974. There is no trip to the pit for David's year, but the careers officer encourages him to think about the mines because they're a big employer and the wages have gone up again. Mark Perry and Alan Ogden go to work at the collieries where their fathers are employed, and David goes with half a dozen lads to Greg Brown's paint spraying works, opposite the Albion sewing factory on Lidget Lane, where most of the work is fixing up cars for quick re-sale, or painting old coaches. As he counts the board and lodging from his pay packet into his mam's hand, he knows his childhood is ending there and then. Told what the home's food, rent and heating cost, he suddenly assumes a responsibility to the family; it makes him feel grown up, proud and vulnerable at the same time.

*

The reason David's career officer could urge him to consider the high wages being offered by the pits was that in early 1974 the British miners had gone on strike again, and won another large pay rise. This time, aided by developments in international politics, they had helped to bring down the Conservative government, and fostered a new buoyant and optimistic mood in the coalfields.

The initial problem was that large pay awards in other industries had within months eroded the gains from the 1972 strike. In the summer of 1973 the miners voted for a pay claim of £8–£13 a week in defiance of the Heath government's wage restraint policies, and then in October 1973 a war in the Middle East led to a seventy per cent increase in oil prices. With oil now expensive there was increased demand for coal, which improved the union's bargaining position. Rejecting the Coal Board's offer of less than half the claim, the NUM began an overtime ban in November 1973. Edward Heath declared a state of emergency, with power cuts and a three-day week. In January 1974, the oil price doubled again: wage negotiations failed and the miners voted to strike.

The strike begins at midnight on 9 February. Two days later the Heath government calls a general election for 28 February, asking the public whether the government or the unions is running the country. The public is undecided; a minority Labour government succeeds Heath, and Harold Wilson is returned as Prime Minister. The Pay Board, an agency set up by Heath's government to advise on pay and prices policies, endorses the union's full claim, and the Coal Board awards the largest increase in the history of British mining, raising wages for faceworkers by more than thirty per cent. In October 1974, the Labour Party wins another general election and, with the Coal Board and the NUM, agrees a long-term plan for coal based on national output almost doubling by the end of the century as oil use declines. Some old mines will be closed and some new ones sunk. An important part of the plan is the development of a new 'superpit' in the Vale of York near Selby, thirty miles north of the Dearne Valley. The Selby complex will be the largest pit in Europe and one of the most technologically advanced in the world: 'A New World of Mining', as the Coal Board's promotional leaflets promise.

One big winner in the changes, and now seen as a champion by many Yorkshire miners and an important figure in both the new world of mining and British politics, is Arthur Scargill. Elected president of the Yorkshire Area of the NUM in 1973, he had a high media profile before the 1974 strike, and after it he becomes a national celebrity. Though public opinion about him is divided, even some of his opponents respect the way he has stood up for his members. ('Gordon doesn't like him,' Pauline tells Winnie, 'but he says he wishes Arthur Scargill'd come and run t' National Farmers Union for a bit.') The NUM's Victorian neo-Gothic offices in Barnsley become known as King Arthur's Castle, and *Harpers & Queen* magazine runs a profile of him. One Saturday night he appears on Michael Parkinson's TV chat show. When the host (also the son of a Barnsley coal miner) asks Arthur what, in the event of a communist revolution such as he sought, would happen to the Queen, he replies, 'We'd find her a job in Woolworth's.'

The high wages, and emphasis on skilled work in futuristic mines, kindle the imagination of Gary Hollingworth, now a builder's apprentice with long hair in the style of David Bowie. By 1974, with the novelty of receiving his own wages having worn off, and his dad telling him to get a better job because he could do more than fetch and carry on building sites, he feels restless and ambitious. Regretting the dead squib of his own education, he daydreams about becoming a teacher, the sort of person who would understand boys like him and talk to them decently. He has no idea how a man like him would go about that, though, so for want of any other ideas he tries self-improvement, reading more books and ordering the *Guardian* and *The Times* at the newsagent. One night in the Fairway he meets an intelligent, free-spirited girl called Elaine, and when they start going out Gary finds they understand each other; after a few weeks he decides that he is in love, and suggests they get engaged. Elaine, still in her last year at school, says yes. It is a youthful promise, for Gary the outward sign of an adult relationship, and a clear mark of his ambition.

Next he needs a job suitable for an ambitious husband. In March 1975, to the jeers of his dad who says mining is a dead-end, he applies for a job at Houghton Main, where Kenny works. Besides the good wages and new, lucrative bonus schemes, the Coal Board offers training and education and the chance for a grafter to work his way up to a good job.

At Houghton Main's personnel office Gary does not tell the officer in charge about his tuberculosis, and he is signed up with no questions. After six weeks' surface training at Barnsley Main, he does thirty days in the underground galleries at Grimethorpe colliery. The training officer then pins up a typed list of the newcomers' names and the jobs they have been assigned at their own pits. Gary is to be an air measurer in the Houghton safety team.

When he arrives for his first full day at work, he is directed to the team's brick cabin in the yard. Inside are half a dozen men, some handling air pressure gauges and anemometers on a workbench, others warming themselves on a fat steam pipe on the opposite wall. The cabin smells of oil, cement and tobacco. As he enters, the men look up. He recognises Kenny sitting on the pipe. He and Kenny are the youngest by about ten years.

'Who are thar?' The speaker, a man in his forties, looks at Gary as if he is an inept burglar who has just broken into the cabin by mistake.

'Me?'

'No, him next to thee.' There is no one next to him. 'What's tha want?'

The other men look at him and grin expectantly. It is the miners' hello: the first speaker insults the other and the spoken-to replies with something that must be neither too vicious nor dull. If you are a newcomer, extra care is needed. The easy option of self-deprecation is a bad idea, conveying an untrustworthy need to be liked – unless you are fat, in which case it indicates a sense of humour. The worst thing is to be polite: 'How do?' and a shake of the hand means either that someone will only ever tell you what he thinks you want to hear, or that he privately considers himself superior. You can be bluff and witty, but not a smart-arse.

'I'm working here.'

'Why, does tha need some brass to buy some scissors?' This is a reference to Gary's collar-length hair. The older men, most of whom have served in the armed forces, hate it. In some pit yards there are safety signs saying 'Long Hair? TAKE CARE!' because long-haired young men keep getting their hair caught in machinery. Some of the older men say it serves them right.

Gary says, 'No. They've got up-to-date haircuts in Thurnscoe' – which is a good answer because it moves the subject from himself to the village, and the other Thurnscoe men at the pit.

'They've got lasses' haircuts wi't' look of your two.' He shoots a glance at Kenny. 'Tha wants to watch thysen down there in t' dark . . . What job've they given thee anyroad?'

When the men have established who Gary does and does not know, and where his family is from, the safety engineer instructs Kenny to look after him for his three weeks of close personal supervision. 'He'll show thee where to go,' he says. 'Now bugger off, tha long-haired Thurnscoe bastard.'

The team enforces the colliery's safety measures, and monitors the dust, gas and air in the pit. Pits are ventilated using large fans at the top of air shafts and a series of air doors in the tunnels. The doors stop and direct the air flow so the air is pushed down all the workings and prevented from blowing the quickest route down the main roadways and back to the surface up the upcast shaft. The air measurers check the flow, pressure and composition of the air to ensure that the pit is safe; their jobs carry a lot of responsibility because a single mistake can lead directly to an explosion.

For the first few weeks the long-haired Thurnscoe bastard works as a guffer – a *go for* in the Barnsley twang, meaning a lad who fetches and carries. Kenny teaches him how to take the measurements and how to enter them in the legal records in the safety team offices, and roadway by roadway, seam by seam, Gary learns to navigate the pit. He uses the computers in the offices to find out averages and make projections, and he develops the tact and banter needed to answer back when men complain about safety checks. Checks and enforcement are difficult. The manager, himself under pressure from the area bosses, sets ambitious targets. There is risk-taking out of recklessness, out of wanting to get a job finished, and out of men pushing themselves to ensure enough coal is dug, and the men who intervene are derided. Gary soon realises that if you follow regulations precisely you will not only be disrespected, you will also be measuring your output in spoonfuls. He learns to handle difficult situations by watching and listening to the older members on the team – men who had fought in the Second World War at Alamein, Monte Cassino and Arnhem. They had authority and somehow knew how to order people about, and when to protect them from themselves and their managers.

*

Gary calls Roy from a telephone box in the village once a week, but tries to avoid talking about work because his dad ridicules him.

'You still at t' bloody pit then?'

'Aye, I'm doing alright – '

'Bloody crap job. I don't know where your ambition's gone.'

'I brought nearly £50 home last week.'

'Fifty pound! When I was your age I was driving tanks in t' Army.'

Gary tries to explain that it's different to when Roy was younger, and that the pit pays better than most other jobs. It looks after you: your wages are paid straight into the bank, tax deducted, and the NCB provides you with a house if you need one. When you're on the sick you just put your sick note in and it's all taken care of. Why can't his dad see that?

But Roy can see nothing. He keeps on criticising and by the end of the conversation Gary feels ashamed, and has to walk around the village until the feeling goes off.

His grandad is a little more understanding, but he worries. ('What's tha want to go down t' pit for, lad?' 'Money, Grandad.' 'Well mind tha takes care of it then, and thysen and all!') It is Winnie who most shares his feeling of achievement. Inside, Gary is proud of his job: miners helped to build the nation from iron and coal, and it is still the fuel that powers the country and keeps people warm. Even if the men are cantankerous and cynical about management, he can tell many of them feel the same satisfaction that he does. Some make a point of going home in their pit muck and helmets, as a sort of uniform and statement of pride. Winnie listens to him telling her this with unsentimental approval.

'You say right, Gary,' she says. 'You be proud of yourself, love. You be proud.'

44

The Darkness and the Light

Houghton Main Colliery and Bolton-upon-Dearne, 1975

In the early evening of 12 June 1975, Margaret, Gary and David are watching television at home when the floor, furniture and light fitting tremble faintly for a few seconds. The tremor is not enough to chink the tea mugs on the coffee table, but it does make them look at each other in puzzlement. Three hours later the *News at Ten* has a report from Houghton Main about an explosion 350 yards down in the Melton Field seam. Men are missing underground, feared dead. Margaret and David ask Gary if this was what the tremor was. Maybe not, he says, it might just have been something in Hickleton's workings. None of them wants to think the explosion is what they felt. Some of Houghton's workings are below Thurnscoe village, so the missing men could be 350 yards below their feet.

When Gary arrives at work the next morning the pit yard is in muddy chaos: police cars, television vans and yellow mine-rescue trucks are parked up and ambulances wait near the wooden steps that lead down from the shaft side. Miners stand around in hushed groups. Coming off duty, tired rescue teams in knee pads and breathing apparatus pass fresh ones going underground to take their place. Outside the baths are gathered the families of the trapped and missing, waiting for news; a Salvation Army van serves them drinks and sandwiches. Above everyone's heads the spoked iron winding wheels are still.

Gary goes to the safety team's cabin. All twelve men are quietly waiting to find out if they can help. He hears a scuffle outside and looks out from the open doorway as Arthur Scargill and the government ministers Tony Benn and Eric Varley cross the pit yard to the manager's office. They have been underground; Scargill is wearing an old 1950s metal mining helmet, a type still worn by some men like badges of individuality and long service. Reporters and television cameramen crowd around them, asking questions about the explosion and the casualties.

'Them pillocks want chucking down t' shaft,' says one of the dust control men, meaning the reporters. 'They've been sniffing round t' families like bloody vultures, pretending to be all sad and sorry. They're not so sad and sorry when we're putting a pay claim in.'

Five men have been killed, and one badly injured. The emergency teams are still trying to recover the dead bodies in the dust and the wreckage. Kenny's dad, one of the rescuers, is among them. 'They keep finding pages from a Bible floating about in t' dust,' Kenny says. 'One of t' lads that's been killed always took it down wi' him. Didn't do him much good, did it?'

Gary knows three of the dead men. He feels numbed by the accident and unsure of how to act among the older miners. To him the day feels so abnormal as to be unreal, but in their grim faces he can see the past lives that make it familiar. There are Ukranians and Poles working at Houghton Main, men who have concentration camp tattoos on their wrists and saw family and friends die around them in the war. When these men speak about the accident and the deaths and the families waiting for news, there is disgust in their voices, and also a sort of weariness.

The source of the explosion, everyone knows, will have been ignited gas. An inquiry will conclude that methane was most likely ignited by sparks from one of the fans used to draw air through the mine. With the pit closed and only the senior managers and rescue teams allowed in, the men are sent home, and Gary is not needed for three days. On the fourth day the ventilation officer sends him, Kenny and a deputy down to some disused workings in the Silkstone seam to take measurements and test the system of pipes that drain methane from the air.

Houghton Main works nine seams, and the Silkstone, 940 yards down, is the deepest. As they wait at the shaft side for the cage, Gary is unsettled and fidgety.

'What's up wi' you?' the deputy asks disdainfully.

'What's up wi' me? There's been five men killed down there, and I knew three of 'em. I think it feels a bit macabre.'

The winding wheels above their heads begin to revolve slowly, and the cables tighten as the cage rises up the shaft.

'Does it buggery. They'll not hurt you now, will they?'

Gary looks away. The deputy's scorn is mostly bravado. Pits are superstitious places and according to the men who work there, Houghton has been haunted by miners' ghosts since it was sunk in the 1870s.

'Maybe not, but it's not very pleasant.'

'Get away wi' you. You talk like women.'

The cage comes up in front of them. When its bottom is level with the tub rails, it rattles to a halt, and the banksman yanks back its gates. The men toss their pit checks into a wooden box and step in, bowing to fit their heads under the low roof. When the banksman has secured the gates he presses a button and the cage slides down into the darkness. They drop past the lights of the Melton Field inset, and then the other seams below that: Beamshaw, Barnsley Bed, Dunsil, Fenton, Parkgate, Thorncliffe. At Thorncliffe they get out and take the man-riding conveyor down into the Silkstone.

Near the pit bottom the roadway is as large as an underground railway station and illuminated by electric lights. Further along, the roofs are lower and the floors more uneven, and there are no lights, so the three men have to rely on their cap lamps. They concentrate on finding level footing and do not talk, but Gary can sense a tension in the atmosphere of the whole pit. When they pass other miners in the roadway they hardly acknowledge each other. It is as if everyone is calculating how long it will be until they finish their shift and get back to the surface.

In the disused workings, Gary can see the strain in the others' eyes when he catches their faces in his lampbeam. The air is dank and stale-smelling, the only noises muffled and distant. Gary and Kenny take their tools from their bags as the deputy watches, and collect air samples without speaking.

They have been working for half an hour when the pit's Tannoy communication speakers beep and an operator in the control room up on the surface makes an urgent announcement: '*All men make their way to the pit bottom in orderly fashion. I repeat–*'

They do not wait for a second warning. Gary and Kenny stuff their equipment into the bags and, with the deputy, make their way back towards the main roadway. They break into a jogging run, stepping over stray rocks and girders as nimbly as they can in pit boots. The operator makes more announcements over the Tannoy: '*All men urgently make their way . . .*'

As they draw closer to the drift tunnel that will take them back to the cage, there are men coming into the roadway from other gates and faces: haulage men, button men, face men, deputies, all running, keeping as tight and fast as they can without colliding. The warnings mean that someone has found high gas levels somewhere, possibly in their seam. Another announcement: the pace quickens and the deep, panicky grind of the boots grows louder.

'Tha'd better keep upright, 'Olly,' Gary hears Kenny say behind him when he stumbles. 'If tha goes down I'm off over t' top of thee.'

'Thanks, comrade.'

'Tha's welcome, comrade.'

The men run along the roadway, splash through pooled water, bang through air doors and finally throw themselves onto the conveyor and ride upwards back to where the cage is waiting. At the pit bottom, Gary climbs off the belt. The onsetter is crashing open the cage doors and shouting at them all, come on, hurry up, shift your sorry arses. He is still shouting as Gary piles in and the cage fills up around him.

Usually the men crack jokes as they ride in the cage, but today as it rises through the dark they are silent. At the surface they step out with relief, and jog down the wooden steps into daylight.

'I reckon tha must have a sixth sense,' says Kenny.

'Not really,' says Gary. 'It was just fear.'

'That's same as us all, kid.'

Same as us all. The only difference was how they dealt with it.

There is no explosion. Most men have showers and go home, a few go to a club and get drunk. By the next morning the escape already feels like something that happened a long time ago. It binds the men together with a sort of rough, unspoken intimacy. No one talks about it much.

*

A few months after the accident at Houghton, Gary's fiancée Elaine falls pregnant. Neither she nor Gary feel ready to have children, and Elaine's parents say she doesn't have to marry if she doesn't want to, but for her and Gary there is no question of not marrying. They wed on Boxing Day 1975, a Friday, at the register office in Doncaster. Kenny is Gary's best man, Elaine's friend Sue the maid of honour. Parents and siblings are invited but Roy, away working on the roads and living in caravans with Alwyn and Wendy, neither responds nor attends. After the ceremony Kenny drives them back to Elaine's parents' house in Mexborough for a buffet lunch, and then to a hotel where they have drinks under the Christmas decorations and sing along to 'Bohemian Rhapsody' playing on the sound system.

Gary and Elaine are allocated a pit house on Bolton-upon-Dearne's large, modern NCB estate, known in the Dearne Valley, where people like to reimagine their localities as Wild West outposts, as the Concrete Canyon. The houses are large and square, mostly semi-detached or in short terraces, rendered and painted in greys and browns, and set out on streets whose names recall places in the Empire – Vancouver Drive, Maori Avenue, Caernarvon Crescent. In the evenings and at weekends the streets are busy with young kids re-fighting the Second World War with plastic soldiers, older kids with scabby knees racing on bikes, and lads repairing jacked-up cars with Radio One playing on their stereos. To the north and east the estate joins the village; to the south and west it looks out over farmland and the smoking Manvers complex, its mighty industrial spectacle surrounded by a pastoral landscape of fields, lanes and small stands of trees.

Gary and Elaine's semi looks out over fields. It has a large, unkempt garden and a peeling wooden fence. Inside it is unheated, its windows rattle in their frames, and there is damp on the kitchen walls and ceiling; the floors are bare boards and pock marked lino, and the whole house is infested with mice. Their families give them old furniture: Winnie and Harry bring the vinyl suite from the sitting room, and Pauline and Gordon deliver a fridge and some stair carpet in a livestock trailer. With the £40 savings they have between them, the newlyweds buy a bed in a furniture shop in Mexborough and allow themselves the luxury of a small black-and-white TV rented for 34p a week.

In the spring, Margaret White and Colin Greengrass marry at Barnsley register office. Roy is not mentioned and sends no message. When Elaine and Gary's baby, a ten-pound boy they name Scott, arrives during a summer heatwave that scorches the grass and the fields, there is again no word from Roy.

To work closer to home, Gary transfers temporarily to Manvers Main, where the older men soon realise he is the Juggler's grandson, and look out for him when they work together. He has a feeling of belonging somewhere and for a while, walking home along Coronation Avenue or Commonwealth Drive, he can imagine himself and Elaine being older here, with more children and a colour television and a car. When he transfers back to Houghton Main, the pit-bus ride along the four or five miles of narrow country roads seems long, particularly at dawn at the end of a night shift.

Sometimes on those pale, tired mornings he looks out of the window at the fields and worries that, at just twenty, he is too young to be a father. Afraid of his own inexperience, he would like to be able to ask his own father for advice, but there is scant chance of that. It is strength that he needs, not the Iron Man kind, but the kind that some of the older men at work have. Where did you learn that, though? In a war?

He leans his head against the glass and watches the brightening world pass by, and then he thinks of his son at home, and feels proud and almost tearful. Even if you were twenty and not strong, you could still try to be a decent, loving dad.

45

A Walk Around the Houses

Thurnscoe, 1976

At ten o'clock on a warm Wednesday night in the summer of 1976, eighteen-year-old David Hollingworth and his friend Ian Alder are sitting on the metal-framed chairs around the edge of the Coronation Club function room, drinking lager and watching the dancers. The Coronation Club – or Cora, as everyone calls it – is a modern building the size of a small village primary school. It has an immense main bar, a snooker and billiards room with full-size tables, and dartboards, and a barn-size function room with a stage at one end and a bar at the other. Wednesday night is disco night, a concept introduced by the club's committee for the young people of Thurnscoe who find the more traditional working men's clubs dull and stiff. It has been a much-envied success, and is one of the most popular nights out in the area.

Tonight the dance floor is full as the evening peaks in anticipation of the slow dances that will soon bring the disco to a close. There are a few men dancing, but the floor, lit by flashing red, blue and yellow lights, clearly belongs to the women, in their long skirts, flicked hair and strappy platform sandals. The clothes exaggerate the sways and dips of the women's dancing, and in their presence, the Valley men can only shuffle and look. David is watching so that he can, if necessary, hide from his girlfriend Denise. They have been going out for six weeks, but while their relationship began well, when he asked her if she might like to go fishing with him, she had laughed out loud at him. It was typical:

girls always liked him, but he got bored staying in Thurnscoe, and the girls never wanted to go anywhere else. Tonight he had told Denise he was staying in, then come to the Cora disco to listen out for the heavy rock, which is another thing she dislikes.

'Doesn't look like he's going to play any Deep Purple,' says Ian, leaning in and shouting over the music. Earlier, Ian had requested 'Smoke on the Water'.

'No,' says David. 'It's not been worth coming. Shall we have another drink or go somewhere else?'

'Finish these and try somewhere else I reckon.'

The two boys are about to leave when Ian notices a girl walking over to them. 'Ayup,' he says. 'Who's this?'

The girl had been dancing with a group of friends, and after conferring with one of them while looking over at David and Ian, she is now approaching purposefully, cheesecloth blouse knotted at the waist, maxi-skirt kicking and flouncing around her ankles.

'Ayup, David.' He recognises her as Sue Waine, a girl who was in the year below him at school. She leans near enough for him to smell her perfume, cigarettes and sugary mint chewing gum. 'Will you go wi' our Marie?'

Marie? It takes a couple of seconds to work it out: Sue Waine is a cousin of Marie Poole, the girl from school with the beautiful hair. David can see her in the group that Sue was dancing with. He suspects that Sue is setting up a joke at his expense.

'Umm,' he says, 'maybe not tonight.'

'Why?'

David blushes.

'I'm serious you know! She wants to know if you'll walk her home.'

Marie is sitting down, watching them and smoking a cigarette. When her eyes catch David's, she looks away. He is not, he thinks, going to volunteer himself to be the subject of her banter again.

But Sue is persistent. 'Look,' she says. 'I'll tell her to meet you near t' doors, okay?'

'Okay.'

'Ace! She likes you, you know. Are you coming for a dance?'

'No,' says David, and Sue spins away in a whirl of cotton skirt and cheesecloth to dance to the last of the disco music before the slow songs start.

'You're in there, mate!' says Ian.

'Aye,' says David, 'but for what?'

*

Marie is waiting for him in the foyer near the wooden cabin where the doorman sits checking memberships. To David, who has drunk two pints in quick succession, she seems more self-conscious than he remembers her being at school. They do not speak as they push outside together, but their knuckles brush, and then, somehow, they are holding hands.

The Cora sits at the head of the pit estate, at the pit end of the village. If you live up this end the problem with being walked home from the disco is that the walk is very short, but suggesting that you go the long way round can seem a bit forward. The Pooles live at the other end of the estate, less than five minutes away. David, wishing she lived further away, sets off, but Marie, having got this far, is not going to let social nicety ruin her evening.

'Dave,' she says.

'Aye?' he replies, nervously.

'Let's walk round t' other way, shall we?'

'T' other way?'

'Yes, Dave. The other way.'

'Oh,' he says. 'Right.'

'Just to talk, I don't mean owt like . . . you know.'

The night air is still warm and there is an almost full, white moon above the roofs of the houses. Apart from a few people making their way home, the roads are quiet. The only noise the sound of David and Marie's shoes on the pavement.

'You're quiet, aren't you?' says Marie.

'I suppose so.'

'Would you say you were deep, Dave?'

'I don't think so.'

'I'm not either. But I like you being quiet. I think that's what attracts me to you.'

'Right.'

'But I also think you're lovely looking. I think you look like David Essex wi' your hair like that. I said to Sue when we were sitting outside work watching you all, "David Hollingworth looks like David Essex." She said, "He never does," but I said, "He does, and I think I fancy him!" and so here we are!'

'Here we are,' he says.

She looks at him. 'And then Sue told me to come to t' Cora, she said you'd be in. What do you reckon to that?'

Oh no, thinks David, a question. 'Well, I usually am in,' he says, avoiding it. 'You don't come in much, do you?'

'I never did, because my mam and dad go there and I was underage. How did you come on at school, anyroad?' she asks. 'I got kicked out of Maths and English, I couldn't be doing with them. Do you remember t' canoes?'

They have come to a stop on one of the streets and are just talking. Canoes, the sewing factory where she works, and even David's fishing. 'I'd like to try that,' she says.

She asks if he has a girlfriend.

'No,' he lies. 'Have you got a boyfriend?'

'No. Not apart from you anyroad. Come on, you're supposed to be walking me home not waylaying me.' She pauses, and looks at him. 'Haven't you got lovely ears?'

'Have I?'

'Oh aye,' she says. 'Lovely and little. I hate my ears.'

'I can't see them for your hair.'

'I keep them covered up. Don't ever ask me to show you them.'

They carry on like this for the rest of the walk. David drops her off at the gate and says he'll see her in the Fairway or the Cora at the weekend. He walks back through the estate, then past the old church with the gravestones leaning at drunk, sunk angles. When he gets in, Colin and Margaret have gone to bed but have left him a ham sandwich for his supper. He thinks it is the best-tasting ham sandwich he has ever eaten.

46

Too Late Now, Cocker!

Bolton-upon-Dearne; Highgate; Thurnscoe, 1977

Six months after Lynda and Tony Grainger put their names down on the list for a council house, the council announces plans to demolish their row, and so they are rehoused in a crescent of new semi-detached houses beside the Bolton brickponds. Lynda hopes it will be a fresh start, but the house seems to harden them against each other. She brings home paint and wallpaper, having imagined Tony will want to help, but he sits looking over his newspaper at her toiling, and seems to enjoy it. The sophistication and erudite conversation is gone completely, replaced by talk of work politics and racehorses for his Saturday bets, and she never sees any of the money if he wins.

Lynda finds a crammer course in shorthand and office practice at Barnsley Technical College. She begins in January 1977, dropping Karl off at her mam's at night, taking buses to the college, and then back to her mam's to collect Karl and home. Tony hates the course, or rather the fact of her being enrolled on it. Each time she arrives back home he seems angry to have been left alone. 'It sounds useless to me,' he says, even as she tells him her marks were in the top three again, or shows him certificates for passing her speed-writing module. 'You're wasting your time. You'll do nowt wi' it.'

'Yes I will. I'm going to use it to get a job, aren't I?'

'I doubt it. Who's going to employ *you*?'

He doesn't want me out of the house, she thinks. He doesn't want to be on his own. 'Somebody will. People always want secretaries, why not me?'

'Because you've got a son, stupid. No one's going to employ a woman who's got a kid.'

And because he has said this, she begins to doubt herself.

Tony becomes more miserly with the housekeeping money he gives her, and by the end of the week she is emptying vases for pennies and tuppences to buy a pound of mince for a plate pie. Aside from the family allowance she has no money, and almost no possessions. If she complains, Tony gets angry, and if he feels like it, he'll hit her. One day when she pulls away, he yanks at her hair so hard that she looks up to see a clump of it in his fist.

She reaches her limit one weekend in May. He eats his Sunday dinner in silence, staring straight ahead to show he is fed up with her, and at the end of the meal she snaps inside, the way she did when Margaret Westerman came to see her. After clearing up the kitchen, she takes Karl upstairs, lifts a suitcase down from the wardrobe and calmly packs it with her clothes.

Tony walks in and looks at the case with unthreatened surprise. 'Where are you going?'

'I'm leaving you.' She hears in her own voice the tone of detached conviction that comes from having had enough.

He cocks his head back and smiles. 'You'll be back.'

Ignoring him she puts Karl's clothes and toys into carrier bags, manoeuvres the pushchair, suitcase and Karl out of the house and walks up the street to the bus stop for Highgate Lane.

A few days later, Lynda drives with Tony to the divorce courts in Harry's white Rover. They travel in near silence. On the way back Tony says, 'I wish I'd treated you better, love,' but she knows his pity is really for himself. Men! Even at the very last, their sentimentality and remorse; she has had enough of it to last her the rest of her life.

'Well,' she says, shooting him a sideways look. 'It's too late now, cocker! Shall I drop you off at your house?'

That night, lying in bed at Number 34, she thinks about her mam. How did she manage her marriage? For all that she went through with

Harry, his other women and his staying out, things that a lot of women wouldn't tolerate now, they must have had something. Forty years they'd been together; you couldn't live with someone that long and not have something. Whatever her dad had done or not done, he had always come home in the end, he had always paid her the money and they had stayed together. Lynda had had better chances in life than her mam, yet she always made the wrong choices. And now here she was, twenty-eight, on her own, and living with her parents.

*

Harry has retired from the glass factory, where he spent his last few years driving a forklift in the warehouse. Still in demand as a drummer, he has, to Winnie's vexation, taken over her pristine front room and set up his drum kit permanently so that he can practise during the day. 'It's worse than when we were first married, and he used to play all t' furniture,' Winnie shouts to Lynda, straining to be heard over the din. 'You'd think he'd have had enough of drumming by now.'

Harry has not had enough, not yet, and he spends the afternoons, sometimes with Karl beside him, looking straight ahead through the netted window, beating out memories in quickstep, foxtrot and lingering blues time, as other people might take out old photographs to reminisce over.

As for Winnie, aside from the dispute over the drums, these early years of her husband's retirement continue the more jocund period of her life. She books herself and Harry on holidays to Spain, and in the autumn they stay at Pauline and Gordon's farm, Win looking after the house and Harry driving the tractors during the potato harvest. Her hopes of being rescued by Alf are folded away like old love letters. She has a little boy to love and look after in Karl and, in the Seels's farmhouse, a work world offering variety and friendship. In her nylon pinnies with sweets in their pockets, with her white hair and her scent of Yardley's April Violets, she seems the very essence of the composed and contented English grandmother, and she finds that that role suits her more than any other. 'I don't know why but I find it easier with my grandchildren than I did with you three,' she tells Pauline, the admission part of a new willingness to open up about the past. It is in these years that she will tell her daughters about Walter beating her across her bare back, and the walk with Harry that led to her suspected pregnancy, and marriage.

Her one remaining source of anxiety is Roy. He still turns up at her house sporadically, sometimes alone, sometimes with Alwyn and Wendy, sometimes staying long enough for Wendy to enrol at Dearneside school. During his stays he does not see David, but he does visit Gary, Scott and Elaine, and on family evenings around the fire in Winnie's sitting room he entertains everyone with stories about the interesting people he has met on his travels. To his mam he is caring and flattering, and she will think if only he could settle, if only he could overcome the debt or problem he faces at that particular time, then he would become a good man, and she could put from her mind thoughts of the police and crime. When the moment comes, as it often does, for him to ask her for money, she will collect her wages from Jane Seels, or take cash she has hidden in the sideboard for him. She also passes on gifts that she has received, and even her own ornaments and household goods, all with a hopeful love and the belief that their auras of kindness and domesticity will make them talismans.

He will always leave suddenly, and if he is working on the roads she may not know where he is for months. In the summer of 1977, though, she is pleased to hear that, having completed a motorway spur at Hinckley in the Midlands, he has befriended a local farmer who has allowed him, Alwyn and Wendy to live in one of his fields, in their caravan. It is a permanent arrangement, and Roy is happy. Winnie wishes he would choose a more substantial home but thinks the fixedness will be good for him, and feels optimistic as she crochets winter blankets for them.

*

Equipped with her new course certificates, Lynda applies for office jobs, but the interviewers are prying then dismissive. 'If you've got a kiddy, Mrs Grainger,' they ask, 'how will you go on if you're sick?' She tells them she lives with her mother who looks after him during the day, and they look as if they're listening but the following week a rejection letter arrives in the post. The cost of food and Karl's clothes outstrips her unemployment payments and maintenance money. She forces herself to keep looking at the jobs sections in the papers and writing application letters, but then even when she gets an interview, there are the same jaundiced questions about Karl. Her mind rewinds and replays Tony's prediction – 'Who's going to employ *you*? No one's going to employ a woman who's got a kid' – and flips from self-doubt to determination and back again.

One morning, as if it is feeling Lynda's difficulties and pain itself, Number 34 cracks open – literally. Winnie notices it first, waking up beside Harry one morning with a strong, cold draught on her face and shoulders. The window is closed but the curtains are billowing; coming fully conscious, she lifts her glance up above the window to an eight-inch crack of sky between the wall and the ceiling.

Such ruptures in the fabric of houses and other buildings are not unusual in the Dearne, where subsidence caused by mining means that stretches of yard, road, park and field sag into craters and hollows wide and deep enough to flatten slopes and lower hills in the landscape. Buildings sited on slumping land lurch on their twisted foundations, and their residents awake, or return home, to find roofs askew, chunks of wall fallen to the ground, and windows popped out of their frames. Mining engineers and surveyors design workings to reduce subsidence, but no one is ever shocked to discover a new hole in their garden, say, or a gap between their wall and ceiling.

A council housing officer offers Winnie and Harry a new home at 239 Barnsley Road, in a row of good 1920s houses with views over the main Doncaster–Barnsley road onto open farm fields. The house is at the end of the row, next door but one to a farmyard. The officer shows them a small garden with a brick wall at the front, and at the back a long garden and large shed, all belonging solely to the house. Beyond is a narrow lane with allotment sheds and greenhouses facing onto it, and the allotments themselves. The neighbour on one side, Nancy Woodson, a shy lady who has never married, is an old school friend of Winnie's sister Olive and is already on friendly terms with Winnie herself. So, a better house than Number 34, really; if anything they are grateful for the crack. They accept it, and go home to begin packing.

In a few days' time, after the sideboard has been emptied, the drum kit dismantled and the crockery of ten thousand suppers wrapped and boxed, Harry, Lynda, Karl and neighbours from the yard carry the household tools and treasures through the backings while a lorry-owning mate brings the furniture. And at the end of the afternoon, Winnie and the little gypsy girl walk back to the old, cracked house, say goodbye to its echo-empty and pensive rooms, and finally close the back door of 34 Highgate Lane for the last time.

*

Through the rest of the summer and into the autumn Lynda's job applications follow the same pattern. She is interviewed for a receptionist job at the doctor's surgery, but the doctor asks about Karl and then loses interest in her. The managers at a tennis ball factory in Barnsley seem more positive, but two days later she receives the standard rejection letter. She writes to a Doncaster factory that employs dozens of women in Highgate and Goldthorpe but doesn't even get a reply.

In October she sees in the *South Yorkshire Times* an advert for a job in general services in the offices of Hickleton colliery, and applies for it. She has a good feeling about this one; the NCB is putting money into some pits, and people in Highgate say that Hickleton is being developed and expanded. 'Why not me, eh, cocker?' she says to Karl. 'Why not me?'

Why not her? Because, a friend tells Lynda, her course taught the wrong kind of shorthand for the NCB. The friend has been for an interview at Manvers Main and says the NCB will consider only people with Pitman. Lynda, assured by the college that it has equal weight with employers, has trained in speed-writing.

She has given up on the application when she receives a letter inviting her to an interview. Expecting it to be a waste of time, she doesn't plan an outfit, pulling on a plain beige skirt and blouse from the wardrobe that morning, and not even bothering with make-up. She has a flicker of optimism when the personnel officer says that lacking Pitman shorthand does not rule her out, but it is quickly snuffed out.

'I see you've a little boy, Mrs Grainger?'

'I have, yes.'

'What if he's poorly?'

'I live with my mother, so she looks after him.'

'And are you staying at your mother's?'

'Yes.'

'Hmm.' He says they'll let her know in a week to ten days. Don't call us.

On the following Saturday, Lynda is asleep when Karl comes into her bedroom with something gripped between his hands. 'It's a letter for you, Mam,' he says in his singsong voice.

Lynda, stirring from a deep sleep, sees a brown A4 envelope with 'NCB' on the front. The rejection, she thinks. She digs it open with her thumb and scans the letter, quickly past the Dear Mrs Grainger to the unfamiliar words that she has to read again, and then again, 'I am pleased to inform you . . .'

'Mam!' she shouts downstairs. 'Mam! I've got a job!'

47

You Can't Just Fling a Hook in a River

Thurnscoe and the bank of the River Wharfe at Ulleskelf, North Yorkshire, 1977–80

'Dave!' says Denise. 'Say summat to her!'

'Never mind chuffing "Dave"! Just get lost, before I go and fetch our Sue.'

Marie Poole fixes David's hapless ex-girlfriend with a stare and chews her gum with a slow, steady conviction.

'But Dave . . .'

'I've told you once, shut it. Dave Hollingworth's wi' me. I don't care what he's told you, he's been wi'me for six month. He's a bugger for leading you on, Denise, but I'm not going to let you wreck it for us.'

'You're a flaming liar! How come nobody's ever seen you with him?'

'We don't stay round here like you sad sacks, do we, Dave?'

David, who is watching this argument unfold outside the Cora with horror, says, 'Er, no. No, we don't.'

'Oh aye? Where do you go then?'

'All over,' says Marie. 'We go . . . fishing.'

Denise stops, her glossed lips open. 'Fishing?'

'Yes, Denise. *Fishing*.' Marie makes it sound like a mature, intellectual pursuit beyond Denise's understanding. It is all a lie; so far she and Dave have been no further than the Cora and the edge of Thurnscoe. 'In lakes, and rivers, and all over.'

'You asked me to go fishing with you,' Denise says to David accusingly.

'Aye, but you wouldn't come . . .'

'Yeah, you wouldn't go, would you?' says Marie. 'You wouldn't go because, no offence love, you haven't got what it takes.'

'What does fishing take?'

'If you have to ask, you'll never know.' It is a line that Marie picked up from the pages of a magazine, and it does the job.

Denise makes a final appeal to David. 'Are you just going to stand there?'

'Aye,' he says. 'I'm with Marie.'

*

Marie had volunteered to get rid of Denise when, after their third secret date, David had admitted he had a girlfriend and said he felt guilty about chucking her.

'What will you do?' he asked.

'I dunno, pick a fight then think of summat. I'll tell her we've been going out wi' each other in secret.'

David looked doubtful.

'Gi o'er, she'll be grateful in t' end. Lasses don't mess about. If it were up to lads nowt'd ever get done.'

Denise is done in a confrontation outside the Cora three weeks after David walked Marie home from the disco. Afterwards, for the first few months of their relationship, David and Marie rely on meeting each other when they go out in the village on Wednesday and Saturday nights. He persuades her to come to the Whinwood, which is the only pub in the village to play heavy music. When she says she likes the music and the way it lifts her out of herself, he feels a surge of love and in return makes an effort with David Cassidy. He can talk to Marie more easily than he could his other girlfriends and when he is with her he feels mature and more fully himself. The only problem is that he has competition for her attention.

One Saturday night when they have been going out for three months, they are sitting in their regular seats in the Cora lounge bar. Having regular seats is important; if you sit in someone else's customary place you are not only asked to move ('Them's my seats!'), you have dagger stares directed at you all night. It is like the village church where the families have their own pews, and people guard their spaces almost as doggedly as they do their families' reputations. David and Marie sit on a high-backed padded bench facing Marie's cousin Sue and her boyfriend. Over a table cluttered with pint and shorts glasses and a half-full ashtray, they are talking about a row Marie is having with a manager at work who is trying to ban girls from coming in on Fridays with their rollers in.

'He reckons it's a safety hazard,' says Marie. 'I said, "How is it a hazard? It means my hair's up. It's more of a hazard if your hair's flapping about, like Dave's."'

David swishes his long hair slightly, as a joke.

'What's he going to do?' asks Sue.

'He said it's a disciplinary issue and he's going to give us a warning, but Maureen's got t' union onto him.'

She pulls a cigarette from a packet. 'He's . . . oh, keep talking and look interested. Jed's here.'

Jed Stiles, a pit-top man who works on the screens, is in his late thirties, tall and broad with a quiff atop a receding hairline. He is not unattractive but has never married, though often he has girls around him in bars because the girls know that he will spend on them. His personality is dominated by two conspicuous attributes: first, his all-consuming belief in his own charm, particularly as it affects women, and second, a fixation with Elvis Presley. Elvis's influence on Jed has been such that, since the late 1950s, Jed has tried to deepen his voice and use an accent that blends Memphis and South Yorkshire. 'Hey,' he says, slowly and deeply, as he leans against the bar. With his head at an angle, he runs his comb through the sides of his hair and plumps up the quiff like a potter smoothing out clay.

No one laughs, because he is handy with his fists, big enough to flatten most men in the club and quick to anger if he feels he is being mocked.

'Aww no –' Marie puts her head down so that her hair covers her face, and grimaces at David. 'He's coming over here.'

Jed has tried to woo many of the women in Thurnscoe, and the girls in Marie's family have been among his prime targets. He had once given her sister Carol a wristwatch and then tried all night to chat her up with Elvis-isms, prompting Carol's mother to push him out of the fire-exit door with the advice that an uninterested young woman's mind wasn't going to be changed by a Timex. The next week he had fixed upon Carol's younger sister Joan and presented her with a bag of lettuces from his allotment.

He squeezes himself onto the bench beside Marie. 'How are you, Marie baby?' He emphasises the 'How', and pronounces 'you' as '*ya*', baby as '*baybeh*'.

'I'm all right thanks.'

He takes a sip from his pint. 'I'm well too, honey. Marie, tell me now – do you think I look like Elvis?'

No one around the table dares look at each other, in case they laugh.

'Yeah, Jed. Dead ringer.'

'Thank you, thank you. And are you coming to my wedding?'

This is Jed's chat-up line. The idea is that you say, 'Why, are you getting married?' And he says, 'Of course. To you.' Marie has heard this before so she knows the way to slip out of the conversation is to say, 'Aye, I'll be a bridesmaid.'

'Heh heh,' he replies, slightly on the back foot. 'But I want you to be my bride!'

'I'm taken, Jed. I don't think Dave'd be very pleased with that, do you?'

'Well, if I come up on t' horses –' Jed's use of 't' horses' rather than 'the horses' indicates his cool is slipping – 'I'm a-paying him off and you can move in with me, how about that?'

'Do you want another pint, Jed?' asks Sue's boyfriend, who is quiet but has a good sense of awkward situations.

'Take no notice,' whispers Marie to David. 'I'm with you.'

*

After Christmas, Marie says, 'Well, it's getting on for a year, are you going to make me beg you to take me fishing or what?' And he takes her on the early morning train from Thurnscoe to Ulleskelf, and leads her for miles along the dew-wet tracks to his favourite place on the river bank. It is a steely February morning, and the stillness of the silent, immaculate landscape is broken only by a few restless rooks and scattered pairs of fishermen. On the steep bank, David spreads out a sheet, and pours coffee from his flask.

'I hope it isn't going to be boring for you, Marie.'

She looks around at the river and the fields. 'How can this be boring? It's beautiful.'

'Not everybody sees it like that.'

'Well I do. Now show me how to catch a fish.'

He shows her how to bait the hook and cast the line. The sky clears, and more fishermen walk down the bank. Across the river, cows mosey to the land edge and stare across at them.

'Dave, I've caught one!'

Seeing the silver flash in the water, Marie instinctively pulls up the rod, and steps backwards up the slope. David looks across to see the rod jerk in her hands and her body begin to topple as the line pulls hard.

'Watch, it'll be a pike . . .'

'A what?' She tries to adjust her balance, but overdoes it. Still grasping the rod, she staggers forward down the slope, trips and falls headfirst into the river.

The pike takes both bait and hook. Marie dries herself using the dirty, ragged towel David uses to wipe his hands after a catch. 'I thought at least I'd have caught t' fish, you know,' she says, as they squelch back through the fields towards a pub.

'It's difficult with pike. They're challenging.'

'I never thought it was that hard. You can't just fling a hook in a river, can you?'

'No,' he says. 'No, you can't just do that.'

*

David and one of his friends from work, Houdie, put in application forms for Hickleton Main and Houghton Main collieries, and are offered jobs underground at Hickleton. David had hoped for pit-top employment, but still, even if the work underground is hard, the wages, benefits and training are better than most other jobs and, after the shocks of the first few weeks, he begins to feel a sense of camaraderie with the men and pride in his work.

David and Marie are becoming more serious about their relationship, and when David is not on late shifts they spend the evenings at each other's parents' homes: Mondays and Wednesdays at Colin and Margaret's, Tuesdays and Thursdays at Mrs Poole's, Fridays a quick sandwich anywhere then out to the pub. David's mam likes Marie from the outset, partly because she has a family connection: Margaret's sister Alice now owns a knitting shop in Thurnscoe and had taught Marie to knit. When Marie starts knitting David a cream cable-knit sweater, Mrs Poole recognises the serious intent and allows the pair to use her front room as their own. To David this new domestic element of their courtship is a pleasure in itself.

On summer evenings, freshly showered from the pit baths and wearing wide-flared jeans and a clean band T-shirt, David walks out of the colliery gates and down the road to the Pooles' house where, if he's lucky, Marie will have bribed her dad to go out to the Cora while her mum is at bingo. They eat their tea together in the front room and, with the cutlery chinking on the plates, tell each other about their days at work: rumours of affairs in the offices, new disputes about hair rollers, the tropical butterflies David finds in the pit hatched from chrysalises in the imported pit props. Later, Marie brings her portable record player into the room, and when the last of the LPs has been played, a drowsy calmness fills the room, and David feels as if he has escaped into another life.

'We're like a little old married couple,' says Marie. 'I could live like this, Dave, couldn't you?'

'Aye,' he says.

*

David Hollingworth and Marie Poole marry at St Hilda's Church in Thurnscoe on a summer's day in 1980. Gary is best man, and Roy, with whom David no longer has any contact, is not invited. As David unlocks the front door of their newly rented NCB house, he takes hold of his unsuspecting bride.

'What do you think you're doing?' Marie hisses. 'We're on t' doorstep, everybody can see.'

'Shush a minute –' He slides one arm around her thighs and the other around her shoulders, and hoists her up.

'You'd better not drop me and cause a disaster.'

'I won't.' He carries her through the door and sets her down in the hallway. 'Thank you, Mrs Hollingworth.'

'Thank you, Mr Hollingworth. I never knew you were so old-fashioned.'

A few minutes later they fall into a bickering dispute about honeymoon arrangements that lasts into the next day, and drops only when David fetches a portable black and white television set for them to watch from a neighbour. It's a strange way to find yourselves settling your first argument as a married couple, they agree, but then love and arguments don't always go the ways you expect them to.

48

You Were Always on My Mind

Hickleton Main Colliery and the Coronation Club, Thurnscoe, 1977–78

Lynda's job at Hickleton colliery is that of clerical officer in the General Services Department, which means that she works for every department in the pit. Her desk is among banks of typewriters and banding machines in a Victorian office building with high windows and parquet floors. On her first morning she is given the post to sort into dozens of dark wooden pigeonholes, envelopes and mail for everyone from baths attendants, bricklayers and chemical engineers to facemen, nursing staff and dust control officers. In the afternoon she is asked to minute a meeting. Her speed-writing is accepted (Manvers and Hickleton, it turns out, are in different administrative areas and accept different kinds of shorthand) but when the men begin to talk, she trembles and feels sick because the language is completely incomprehensible to her. In-bye, out-bye, headgear, ripping lips. Longwall shearers. Double-ended ranging drum shearers. She likes the sound of the words but just guesses at the spellings, and when she takes the minutes to Mr Perkins, her manager, he laughs and says, 'Don't worry, we give you a bit of time to get used to it. Let's see how you're going on this time next year.'

In the autumn she organises the laundry of the dirty towels from the pit baths, and answers the calls from underground for ambulances when men are sick or injured. She types letters and rolls copies from the Gestetner machine and indulges her love of filing. She learns that when a deputy sends you to the bakery for some snap you bring back bottles of pop and not cans because cans might make sparks, and that women are not allowed to wear trousers to work, even when it snows. She learns about all the departments and about a lot of the employees, because when the personnel manager, Mr Ashworth, notices the quality of her typing and her bantering conversations with the men, he asks her to help him with the personnel absence reports.

She loves the work, even when Mr Ashworth asks her to type up his private letters to his divorce lawyer. The atmosphere of people working together with a sense of urgency and common underlying purpose suits her. The practical jokes make her weep with laughter and, as she learns the lingo, she comes to love the way it makes a world. She memorises the names of all the collieries in the NCB Doncaster area: Askern, Barnburgh, Bentley, Brodsworth, Cadeby and Denaby, Frickley, Goldthorpe, Highgate, Hatfield, Markham, Rossington, Thorne. At home she recites them to Karl and he memorises them too. She begins to understand what the men are talking about, and work becomes a sort of sanctuary to her.

Using her wages, Lynda takes driving lessons and passes her test. She buys a Vauxhall Viva from the garage across the road, and the next weekend drives herself and Karl into Barnsley to go Christmas shopping. On the way home she glances at him in the rear-view mirror. He is asleep, softly snoring with his head slumped against the seat back, winter pinks streaking the Pennine skies behind him. Just the two of them: her and Karl, partners. She decides that she would rather have money and a car than a man, any day of the week.

'We'll manage, won't we, cocker?' she says to her sleeping son. 'We're going to do alright on our own. Watch this space.'

Her friend Beryl sees the change in her and suggests she start going out again. At first Lynda refuses, but in February, the week before Valentine's Day, Beryl persuades her to go to the disco at the Cora. 'Come on,' she says. 'There'll be plenty of fellas you can talk to now you know about your Longball Shearers. They're all going to love you.'

'Long*wall*,' she corrects. 'But I'm not talking to any men, thank you. I'd rather type up atmospheric pressure figures all night.'

The disco is busy and loud, and its coloured lights give strange casts to people's faces. Lynda clocks men and women she knows from work, and chats briefly with David and Marie, but as she and Beryl stand sipping their sweet Martinis, she feels out of place. How is a person supposed to be when they are in a club or a disco? She feels she has almost forgotten. And her clothes are not quite right: she has chosen a smart pencil skirt, blouse and stilettos, but other people look scruffy. The fashions have moved on: the men peer out from under long shapeless hair, and the women wobble about on platform shoes like something from one of her dad's turns. She looks at a gang of long-haired men near the bar; the kids at Rocky Wall's café in the sixties would have said they looked like tramps.

Beryl goes to the bar leaving Lynda standing against the wall. Out of the crowd appears a wiry, grinning man with a shirt undone to the third button, and a silver necklace around his neck.

'Ayup, Lynda,' he says.

She tenses – and then remembers she is trying to have fun. 'Ayup, Ian.' The man is Ian Davidson, an old acquaintance from Goldthorpe.

'Are y'alright?'

'Yes thank you. Are you?'

'Only down one side, eh?' He flashes her a smile and drinks off some of his pint. Following her vacant gaze he studies the dance floor and comments on some of the dancers. Then, too soon, 'Can I take you home tonight, then?'

Here we go, she thinks. The last of the great romantics.

'No.'

'Why not?'

'It's a long story, Ian. Let's just say I don't want you talking about me with all your mates in t' pit bottom tomorrow morning, and leave it at that.'

'I wouldn't.'

'Yes you would. I work there, remember.'

'Well, if you change your mind – '

'I won't.'

He winks. Lynda looks beyond Ian to the bar, seeking out Beryl. She is talking to one of the men in the long-haired gang. Both have their backs to Lynda, and she wonders if the man is asking if he can walk Beryl home.

Ian persists until Beryl at last comes back with the drinks.

'Getting on wi' Ian, are you?' she asks Lynda, once he has left them.

'No I am flaming not. He was getting on my flaming nerves.'

'I don't think he's so bad.'

Lynda shrugs. She doesn't want to talk about him. 'Who were you talking to anyroad?'

'A pal at t' bar, I've not seen him for a bit. He said he were a friend of yours and he were asking all about you. Have I to bring him over?'

'I don't know, who is he?'

'His name's John Burton,' says Beryl.

Lynda has wondered what she would feel if she saw him out in a pub or met him somewhere unexpectedly. She has imagined herself asking what was wrong with him the day she called to see him with the Elvis record, and he ignored her. It would be like a scene from a film; she would ask him casually and he would explain, and it would all be revealed as a silly misunderstanding between two old mates. As for what happened after that – well, there were several possibilities. But in the event, here in the Coronation Club disco on a February night in 1978, she doesn't feel anything much at all, apart from mild shock, and then amusement at his long hair, moustache and three-quarter-length embroidered Afghan coat.

He keeps shooting looks across to where she and Beryl are standing. She meets his look, but he doesn't respond.

'No, don't worry,' she says. 'I used to go out with him at one time, you know. But I can't be bothered.'

Eventually it is Lynda's turn to go to the bar. Unless she takes a detour around the edge of the room, she will have to walk past John's group. She knows that he has seen her, and that if she does not speak to him it will appear a deliberate snub, so as she passes she touches his arm, and says, 'How's your mother?' She had been on good terms with

Mrs Burton, and asking about his family is the action of a casual old friend rather than a former lover.

'Ayup,' he says, deadpan.

As if you had never ignored me when I tried to give you that record, she thinks. As if you had not gone past my flat on the bus, looking in through the upstairs window.

'She's alright. She were poorly at Christmas but she's all right now. Is tha keeping all right?'

'Yes thanks.'

'I've been going to ring thee.'

I've been going to ring thee? What, since 1967?

'Ring me?' she says. 'What would you be ringing me for?' Previously she was struggling to even hear herself over the music. Now she is barely aware of it, and could hear him if he whispered.

'Work's given me two tickets to Wakefield Theatre Club to go and see Tom O'Connor, free meal and free bar. A load of us have been volunteering for fire duty while t' firemen have been on strike, and they reckon they want to do summat to thank us.'

'Lovely,' she says, unclear as to where this might be going. 'He's good, Tom O'Connor.'

'So will tha come with me?'

Men, she thinks. Bloody, bloody, bloody men. 'Why, who's let you down?'

'Nobody!' He sounds surprised.

'Pull t' other one, kiddo, it's got wedding bells on.'

'I've not asked anybody else if that's what tha means.'

'No, of course not.'

'I've not! I thought of it because of our Glenys. You know, my cousin Glenys? She were at my mam's t' other day and she says, "You'll never guess who's got divorced? Lynda Hollingworth."'

'Great,' says Lynda. 'Thanks.'

'And then I saw it in t' paper!' He wears the expression of a man describing a winning bet on a horse. 'That's why I was going to ring thee, tha sees!'

Lynda has the sensation of looking down on herself while simultaneously taking part in the conversation. She is torn between wanting to talk to John, and not wanting to talk about a date. She very much wants to ask about his moustache.

'So will tha come then?'

'No.'

'Why not?'

'Because . . . I'm not going with you, that's all.'

His tone becomes more earnest. 'Look, don't come to Wakefield if you don't want. But will you come and see me? Come up to my mam's and see us all.'

She feels herself off balance for a moment. She wants to run away. 'I maybe will,' she says. 'See you about, anyroad.'

And as she turns he says, 'Here – ' and in a swift liquid movement he holds her hand, and takes from somewhere a gold ring and puts it on her finger. 'Bring me that back tomorrow, and tell me that you'll come with me.'

She looks at him and thinks she ought to be angry.

'Come up tomorrow afternoon.'

'Alright.'

And then, right there at the bar of the Cora disco, John puts an arm around her shoulders and kisses her. Her reason twists against it, but she feels as if he pulls her blood towards him. It is not a question of deciding.

At the end of the night they walk back to Highgate together, talking. He tells her about Susan. They had moved to Coventry with their baby and had three more children but then Susan had wanted to come home. She moved to Doncaster, and he stayed working in the Midlands, returning home at weekends. When that became strained he moved back to her and the kids in Doncaster, but it didn't work and he left. The time since has been the lowest point in his life. He and Susan are divorcing and he is living at his mam's house in Goldthorpe. He has wanted to visit Lynda, or at least just talk to her on the phone, but hadn't had the courage.

They pass the Halfway Hotel, and walk up to 239 Barnsley Road. Ahead she can see Harry standing on the front doorstep waiting for her. He has done this ever since she started going out on her own in the evening, always watching until she is within about a hundred yards of the house, then slipping back inside to be in bed by the time she arrives, believing that she has not seen him. Tonight, though, he stays on the doorstep, and when Lynda and John reach the gate, he shouts at her, 'Get in that house now, you!'

'Dad? What are you – ' says Lynda.

'And you,' he says to John, 'you can get off home!'

'Mr Hollingworth –'

'I said, get home! She's had enough trouble. You can leave her alone, you bloody reptile.'

Reptile. It is an insult of the old school, and all the worse for it.

John stands for a moment, considering the situation. 'All right.' He pauses, holding up his hands to acknowledge Harry, and says goodnight to them both. Harry tells Lynda to get inside and she reminds him how old she is, and they go inside to argue.

Left alone, John heads back up the road towards Goldthorpe, but had Lynda or Harry stopped arguing and stood on the step to listen for a moment, they might have heard him muttering to himself under his moustache as he walked, 'I'll marry you, Lynda Hollingworth. I'll marry you if it's the only thing I ever do. I don't care what your dad says or your mam says or what anybody says; you are the one love of my life. And this time you're not getting away.'

49

Husbands and Lovers, Fathers and Mothers

Highgate and Thurnscoe, 1978–79

Despite being told to stay away from John, Lynda visits him at his mother's house and they reconvene at the Cora. When John walks her home, Harry enacts a repeat performance on the doorstep; get home you little reptile, get yourself back to your wife and kids. John hesitates to defy him, but Harry knows how to hurt an audience just as he knows how to please it, and he won't stop. 'Harry!' John squeezes his temper in his clenched fists and forces his voice down, because he isn't going to shout in the street. 'Harry. I'm telling thee it's a good job tha's an older man, because if tha weren't, I'd knock thee up and down this street. Now *stop calling me names.*'

All three of them stand dumbstruck.

'No offence meant,' says John. 'Anyway, I'll be off. I'll see thee later, Lynda.'

Harry shouts after him, but he is diminished and he knows it.

When John next meets Lynda, he apologises for the argument. They are both in their late twenties, but of a generation brought up to defer to their elders, and he regrets his language. It is the first time he has called Lynda's father anything other than Mr Hollingworth.

He sends an apology to Harry via Lynda but it makes no difference, and when she sets off to meet him again Winnie upbraids her and demands that she break off the relationship. To make matters worse,

Winnie encourages Tony Grainger to visit the house, welcoming him even when he disregards the timetables agreed in the divorce settlement, or nips at Lynda, picking arguments or blaming her for the breakdown of their marriage. He has been exceeding his allotted times since Lynda walked out. After talking to Karl, he lingers in the kitchen with Winnie while Lynda sits tight-lipped in the sitting room with the television turned up, waiting for him to leave.

'He's got a right to come, Lynda,' Winnie lectures her daughter. 'Tony's our Karl's dad. And children need their dads.'

This is Walter Parkin's daughter talking, Lynda thinks; the girl who loved her dad even as he beat her. She took her punishment in silence, and so must all other women.

'He doesn't have a right to call me names, though, does he?'

'You should ignore him. You should think of our Karl.'

As if she doesn't. As if Karl has not been the only good part of her life for five years, and her only reason for not running away. 'Tell him to keep away, Mother,' she says.

When Tony hears Lynda is seeing John Burton he visits more often, plying Winnie with concocted gossip among the hubbling, bubbling pans and steam-beaded windows of her kitchen. John is trying to lure Lynda away from Winnie; John wants Lynda to stop speaking to her mam altogether; John's been seen looking at houses for him and Lynda to move into. The idea of her daughter being lured into a trap agitates Winnie, and she confronts Lynda with Tony's evidence. ('He's been *seen*, Lynda. Going into that empty house next door to his mam's *with a ladder*.') Lynda corrects her, but Winnie spreads Tony's tales anyway.

'Sorry for my mam, John,' she has to say when she hears her mother has been bad-mouthing him in the Goldthorpe shops again.

'Doesn't matter, love. If she's having a go at me, she's leaving somebody else alone.'

By the autumn they are together more often than they are apart. They go to see rock 'n' roll revival bands, and have parties with their old friends from school and the café. She helps him get a new job in Hickleton pit's lamp room. Some nights they stay in at John's mam's house and play records by the recently deceased Elvis, including the 'Down by the Riverside/When the Saints Go Marching In' EP.

Winnie and Harry remain set against John Burton until two events in the early months of 1979 check the swell of their resentment.

One night not long after New Year, with Harry out and Winnie in bed with a cold, John calls on Lynda at Barnsley Road. Walking home through the backings close to midnight, he notices a man lying face down, smooth leather soles of his brogues facing out, dull against the frosty tarmac.

'Is tha all right, cock?' He sees his face, and realises who it is.

'Where am I?' groans Harry.

'Come on, lad. Let's get thee up . . .' John takes off his coat, and tucks it around Harry's shoulders. He helps him to his feet, and laughs. 'Harry, if tha knew . . .'

'Knew what?'

'Never mind.'

The next morning Harry sees the grazes on his face, and remembers what happened. 'If you see John,' he says to Lynda, 'thank him for me. For helping me last night.'

She is tempted to ask if he would like to add an apology, but she hears the humility in the thanks and lets it pass. 'Alright,' she says. 'I'll tell him.'

After that night, Winnie and Harry do not yet welcome John, but they do afford him a stilted tolerance in their home. One evening he comes back with Lynda after a friend's wedding and he and Winnie find themselves alone in the sitting room. She avoids eye contact and stares at the television.

'Winnie,' he says. 'If you don't want me here, will you just say? Because I'll go if you like, no trouble or hard feelings. Just tell me.'

Her mouth tightens. She still does not meet his gaze. 'We just don't want her to get hurt again, John.'

'She won't. I want to look after her.'

Winnie thinks for a moment, then looks him in the eye. 'Promise me, then.'

'I promise you. I know you're her mam, but you don't understand. Lynda's t' love of my life, I know she is.'

Winnie makes small, slow, chastened nods. These are the sort of words she likes to hear men saying; it is unsettling and inconvenient to hear them from a man she considers unfit for her daughter, but she allows herself to be transported. 'Alright,' she says. 'Well, make sure you do.'

*

In October, John, Lynda and Karl move into a council house ten doors down from Winnie and Harry on the Barnsley Road. Soon afterwards he asks her to marry him. Lynda says she isn't sure, she can't see the need; she's been through it twice now, and in both cases getting married led to nothing but trouble.

'But we should be married!' says John. 'Say no if tha likes, but I'm just going to keep asking.'

And he does. 'Let's get married!' he says, placing drinks on a table in the Cora. 'Come on, marry me, Lynda!' he urges, getting up to change the television channel at home. 'Has tha decided to marry me yet?' he asks, putting down a plate of toast for her breakfast on a Saturday morning. Eventually, fifteen years after she first watched him singing on the steps of the beer-off, she accepts.

Their wedding takes place on a sunny day in May 1980 at St Mark's Methodist chapel in Goldthorpe. Lynda and her mam get up early to prepare the buffet and Lynda ferries carloads of sandwiches and salads for the wedding reception at the Goldthorpe Hotel, a large miners' pub on the Doncaster Road. She washes the crockery and lays out the tables, then goes home and changes into her wedding outfit. One of John's cousins drives Lynda and Harry to the church in his new blue Ford Cortina. Even sitting in the back of the car and walking up the aisle, Lynda can sense her dad's suspicious reluctance; it ought to trouble her, but it doesn't. After a decade and a half – half her lifetime, she thinks – she is, for once, certain.

Winnie and Harry take Karl home in the evening and the party goes on into the small hours. When John and Lynda climb into their bed, they discover that friends and neighbours have tied a bell underneath. John undoes it and jangles it loudly against the wall, and the friends listening behind the wall laugh, and keep laughing until John and Lynda fall asleep and pale daylight edges the curtains of the bedroom.

50

My Arms Won't Go Fast Enough for This Modern Drumming

Goldthorpe and Highgate, 1980–81

The 11 September 1980 edition of the *South Yorkshire Times* carries, on the front page of its Rotherham Extra section, a half-page story illustrated by photographs of an elderly, contented-looking man with a high hairline and a saucy grin that reveals a wide, dark gap where his upper incisors ought to be. In one picture he sits at a drum kit, sticks in one hand, dressed smartly in a wool cardigan, white shirt and striped tie. In another he reclines on a deckchair in a garden, wearing the same cardigan, corduroy trousers and suede boots. His feet are up on a chair and he holds a cigarette between the cocked first two fingers of his right hand in the manner of a jazz-age Noël Coward posing for a portrait. 'It's Umpteen Bars Rest Now For Drummer Harry,' says the headline.

> ***At 70 years old and fifty years of rhythm, he says he's dead beat.***
>
> *THE JUGGLER is hanging up his drumsticks after half a century of rhythm – because he says he's dead beat! Harry Hollingworth, nicknamed after his juggling comedian grandfather, and Dearne's best-known drummer, is retiring at the age of 70.*
>
> ***Too old***
>
> *Said Harry: 'I'm getting too old. My arms won't go fast enough for this modern drumming. I've had enough.'*

Harry first learned to drum when he was about 20. 'He was learning when we were courting,' said his wife Winifred at their home in Barnsley Road, Highgate, Goldthorpe.

During the war Harry entertained the troops with ENSA and toured South Yorkshire with his best-known act, Mother Riley's Roadshow, which featured off-beat percussion instruments. 'I used to wear a woman's dress, stuff pitman's Dudleys and dripping tins underneath it to pad myself out, then play them with drumsticks,' said Harry, an ex-Manvers and Goldthorpe collier.

Farewell

'I'm sorry to have to give up. But when you can't do justice to the artists, that's it,' said Harry.

A testimonial concert for Harry Hollingworth is to be staged at the Unity Club in Goldthorpe.

At the testimonial are neighbours and friends from the collieries, glassworks, pubs, clubs and bands, including Barney from the troupe, and Sonny and May up from the south, children, grandchildren, nieces and nephews, all packed in like a crowd on New Year's Eve. The club is as it was almost a decade ago when Harry told Gary to get out before the kissing started, the bar running down one side and the crucifix still on the wall because no one has yet dared to remove it. The first part of the evening is mid-tempo: Juggler on drums and Albert Blessed from Bolton-upon-Dearne on the organ. During the first break the club steward and committee chairman step onto the stage to present a carriage clock and tankard to Harry, and a bouquet of flowers to Winnie, who stands on stage with her husband for the first time. The chairman gives a speech about Harry's career, recalling venues he has played and some of the acts he performed with. 'Such as Lynne Perrie,' he says, 'better known as Ivy Tilsley from *Coronation Street*. As some of you will know, Lynne was a singer before she broke into acting, and she always said that with Juggler backing her, she sang her very best. There was also Liz Dawn, who of course is the real Vera Duckworth. Juggler backed her many times, and Liz reckoned that he was the best drummer she'd worked with in her whole career!'

There is applause, and they take it, Harry feigning deafness and looking at his watch. When he steps forward to thank the committee, someone calls for the dress and the half-pint, and someone else for the Dudley and the dripping tins, and the noise begins to thicken and rise. The music recommences and the dancing starts. At the end of 'That Old Black Magic', John, to Lynda's alarm, climbs up onto one of the tables.

'John,' says Lynda, snatching up her drink. 'What are you doing?'

'Paying tribute.' He turns to face the stage. 'Albert! Let's have some Elvis!'

Lynda puts her head in her hands, and Albert and Harry peer over the dancers' heads into the audience.

'Come on!' shouts John. '"Don't Be Cruel".'

Harry shakes his head and grins his toothless grin: 'We never used to have this at Carnegie Hall, Albert.' Albert picks out the song's opening chords, and a few bars in Harry finds a beat. Then, in triumphs for both rock 'n' roll and sheer human persistence, John Burton, on his teetering table-stage, sings all four verses of the Elvis classic to his father-in-law's accompaniment. On the final cymbal splash the whole crowd roars out its approval, and Harry salutes John with a friendly and forgiving drumstick.

Now they clamour for more songs. From the bar Sonny Parkin, the former drum-carrier, calls for 'Play a Simple Melody', and Winnie and Pauline recite the ad libs from Harry and Millie's old duet routine. *You're fifty years behind the times, we want something with a kick in it!* To more roars, cheers and whistles, Harry pushes back the stool, stands, and walks to the microphone. He chucks out a few Mother Riley lines, and then counts in Albert to an upbeat 'Dear Hearts and Gentle People'. Sonny cries out, 'Mighty fine!' and the old and young crowd onto the dancefloor.

Harry sings six more songs. He bows, and makes a show of dismissing the pleading and protests from the floor and shoots a look at Albert and begins his encore.

'All of Me'. Winnie sips a port and lemon and joins in with the words. *Why not take all of me? Can't you see . . . I'm no good without you?*

And soon it seems everyone is singing – as if the whole valley is in the club, singing to itself. Lynda watches her mam sing along and wonders what her dad will do instead of this. What will happen to the part of him that comes fully alive only when he steps onstage? Winnie catches her glance, but if she is thinking the same thought she does not show it. They smile at each other, and Harry ends his song to loud, long applause.

'Ladies and gentlemen,' says the Juggler. 'Ladies and gentlemen, it's been a pleasure. Thank you and good night' – and then to the steward behind the bar, 'Right, cock, close all t' doors and don't let anybody out. I'm coming round wi' t' cap.'

*

Four months later, on Saturday 14 February 1981, the family gathers again, this time at Highgate Working Men's Club for Harry and Winnie's golden wedding anniversary party. Everyone meets beforehand at 239 Barnsley Road, filling the kitchen and sitting room. The men, in suits, stand about discussing work, memories and local gossip. The women, smelling of lipstick and hairspray, and wearing new dresses and two-pieces, talk about their families, and tell their kids, running in and out of the rooms and sliding down the chair arms, to calm down. Winnie, immaculate in a cream floral dress, with her thick smoke-white hair freshly permed, sits by the table. When she offers to make tea for each new arrival, Lynda and Pauline tell her to sit down and let them do it, and she flashes a little shrugging, pursed-lip smile at the children.

Roy, who has come with Alwyn and Wendy, is witty and garrulous. He has not seen David for ten years, but when they meet in the room, Roy is casual and seemingly oblivious to his son's awkwardness. He compliments Marie, who is pregnant, and tells them to bring the baby to see him in the caravan.

They wait for Harry, who has been bathing and dressing for more than an hour.

'These young men primping and preening!' says Roy. 'Go and hurry him up, Gary.' But Gary demurs; he understands his grandad's vanity and his nerves, and calmly stands by the sitting-room door to prevent anyone from going up.

At last there are footsteps on the stairs. 'Here he comes,' says Lynda.

'T' Duke of Highgate,' says Winnie.

'I can hear you talking about me.' Gary moves aside to let the door open. Harry, wearing an elegant brown check sports jacket, striped Rocola shirt, and silk tie, enters the room and stiffly thrusts a thick pale-pink envelope at Winnie.

Winnie takes it, and the women smile and ahhh. 'I bet that's t' first card you've ever bought her!' says Lynda.

'Get on wi' you,' he says. 'We never used to send cards like you do. Anyway, we couldn't afford 'em.'

'My mam always sends you one!'

'Aye, because she takes all my brass to buy 'em with.'

'I hope you're going to give her a kiss to go with it anyroad.'

He gives a sigh intended to convey his decades of sufferance with these infinitely demanding women. 'You never mind your kissing.'

Everyone laughs, but Lynda and Pauline can tell he senses a mild reproach in Lynda's words; the disapproval of a younger generation whose lives sometimes seem to consist of nothing but the giving of greetings cards and kisses.

At Highgate Club there is a long table covered with pies, tarts and sandwiches, and tin trayfuls of clinking, slopping glasses of beer and pop ferried from the bar to the tables. Horace Hemsworth makes a speech recalling the day fifty years ago he met Winnie and Harry when they moved into Number 34. ('And now I'm seventy-one,' Winnie says to Pauline. 'It doesn't sound real. I feel more like seventeen.') Horace compares them to Prince Charles and Lady Diana Spencer, engaged eight days ago, and then proposes the toast with a glass of sherry. He nods to the waiting organist and drummer and calls up the golden couple for the first dance.

The floor then fills with dancers and couples swinging young children to the music. Harry strolls to the bar to drink with the men, and Winnie sits down with her daughters, granddaughters and nieces. Around the room distant relatives are reacquainted, old men with leathery hands ruffle kids' hair, and confused teenagers are introduced to second cousins, great aunties, and great aunties of second cousins who last saw them when they were children. Someone pulls together four generations – Harry, Roy, Gary and Scott – for a photo. There are requests for songs or a few jokes from Harry, but he refuses. 'Time for someone else to have a go,' he says. As the hours pass, the dead are remembered. Muv, Walter, Jane, Amy, Clara, Danny and Millie. And Winnie recounts to her granddaughters the story of how she met Harry: 'Miss Marjorie said to me, "You want to get yourself off dancing, Winnie, instead of sitting in reading. You don't know what it might lead to!" And I didn't!'

*

There is also talk that afternoon about the miners taking strike action. That weekend colliers from Wales are in Yorkshire, asking men to strike against the closure of Coegnant pit in Glamorgan. In a separate dispute, the NUM president Joe Gormley is considering a national ballot on strike action against other NCB-proposed closures across the country. This kind of clash has been expected since Margaret Thatcher's Conservative Party won the general election in May 1979. The suspicion that Mrs Thatcher is seeking revenge for the Heath government defeats had been strengthened in 1980, when the government legislated to end the NCB's state subsidies. Since then closure rumours have been blowing about the Dearne like fragments of lit paper in chimney smoke. In January 1981 the Yorkshire miners had voted to strike if the Government tried to close pits, and on the tenth of February, at a bad-tempered meeting between NCB executives and NUM leaders, Derek Ezra, the NCB chairman, let slip that he wanted to close between twenty and fifty collieries in the next five years. In response, Gormley had threatened the ballot, and requested meetings with ministers.

Miners had known there would be some closures and changes to the coal industry, if only because of the Selby superpit coming onstream. They now predict there will be mass redundancies and offensives against the union too, but what they really anticipate is more difficult to define. It is a strategic change; an attack on themselves as a group by people who dislike not only their trade union and industry, but also their ways of thinking, talking and living. 'It'll not be about coal,' says Gary, 'it'll be about putting us back in our place.'

At closing time the guests mill about outside the club, regrouping to go home or on to Barnsley Road to continue the party. There is a smell of earth in the air, and distant sounds of traffic; in the darkness beyond the village, Lucozade-coloured constellations of houses, farms and roads glitter. When a cool night wind whips in over the fields, people set off for Winnie and Harry's, straggling apart and mixing and merging along the narrow paths.

Outside the club, David tells Roy that he and Marie are going home. 'Will you still be at Grandma's tomorrow, so I can come to see you?'

Roy, with his eyes on the crowds heading back to the house, says he doesn't know.

'What about Monday? I could come after work.'

'I just don't know, kid.'

'Or Tuesday?'

Marie, standing to the side of the two men, looks puzzled by this tall, greying father-in-law whom she has met for the first time tonight. He has spent much of his conversation with her explaining that Margaret is a born trouble-causer.

David tries again. 'I just thought it'd be nice to talk while you're here.'

'Don't worry about it, kiddo.'

David gives up. 'See you when I see you then.'

'Aye, okay. See you when I see you.' Roy turns and jogs to catch up the gang walking back. David will not see him for another four years.

Back at the house Winnie ignores her daughters' commands to rest, and constructs foot-high stacks of chicken and tinned-pork sandwiches. Harry goes into the front room to put on some music. Earlier in the week he ran cables from the record player through to extra speakers attached to the sitting-room walls. When a record ends he dashes into the front room to change it and Winnie tells him to let somebody else choose one. 'Somebody else might not know what they're doing,' he says and she tuts and shakes her head and the guests laugh. It is at times like these, hamming up her wisdom and patience in the face of her husband's buffoonery, that Winnie's mastery of the marriage appears almost complete.

It is a joke but in other ways, not a joke, and one that Harry seems to accept.

Later, when some of the guests have left and the house is calmer, Harry goes into the front room to put on a Mario Lanza album, and Lynda sees her mam slip in after him. Through the half-closed door she watches as Winnie and Harry dance sedately in the firelight, their embrace close and their bodies moving in time as Harry leads. Winnie's eyes are closed and Harry is looking down at her white curls. When the song ends she moves back an inch to look up into his face. He meets her look and holds it, and then leans forward to give his wife of fifty years a long and lingering kiss.

*

That summer, Marie Hollingworth gives birth to a baby girl, whom she and David name Lisa. Marie's mam and sisters take it in turns to help her while David is at work, but when he comes home he takes over, cooking, changing the nappies and, when he is on afters, doing the early morning feeds so that Marie can sleep.

It is still the custom that when a new mother first leaves the house she must go directly to a church and have a vicar say a prayer of thanks for the child, and so one afternoon when Lisa is a week old, David and Marie lay her in her pram and walk to St Hilda's in Thurnscoe. The church is cool and dark after the bright sun outside, and as the vicar says the Prayer of Thanksgiving after Childbirth, words weighted and delicate as the young mother and father both feel. *We thank thee and praise thy glorious Name, That thou hast been pleased to bless this thy servant and bestow upon her the gift of a child . . .*

David is not religious, but he does see his child as a blessing and he is a tender and diligent father. Some Saturdays, when the weather is fine, he and Marie rise at four, pack a picnic and take a train to the banks of the River Wharfe where they fish all day, listening to the quiet of the water and the birdsong, watching their little dark-haired daughter as she learns to crawl, and then to walk on the riverside grass. Every

Sunday morning he puts her into the pram and takes her out, past the colliery and up the slope towards Barnburgh, where he calls for a pint of beer and sits watching her sleep, before walking back to the house where Marie is cooking Sunday lunch.

When David thinks of his own dad, it is only with greater incomprehension than he felt before Lisa's birth. Hadn't Roy felt the way David feels? Had he just been too lazy? Best not to wonder, he supposes.

'Does it upset you,' Marie asks him one evening, 'when you think about your dad and when you were little, like our Lisa?'

'To be honest,' David says, 'it doesn't, not really. It just makes me think – ' he picks up Lisa and puts her on his knee. 'It just makes me think that no matter what happens, I'll never let her go through what I went through when I was a kid. That's about all you can do, in't it?'

51

All About a Cabbage

Highgate, 1982

If John Burton's relationship with his father-in-law has been thawed by his rescue in the backings and John's song at the Union Club, it is thoroughly warmed in the early 1980s by the council's installation of a new fireplace in John and Lynda's house. The Rayburn is one of the coke-burning fires that have become popular because, unlike coal, they do not produce polluting smoke. The lit coke can be sealed behind a metal plate for a slow burn, or left open to blaze like a conventional fire. Harry finds it hotter than his and Winnie's Parkray with its closed, glass-windowed door, and that heat now brings him round on autumn and winter evenings to, as he says, 'get a warm'.

'Getting a warm' means first toeing aside Lynda and John's sheepdog Sam, then sliding up the metal plate to increase the airflow to the fire. Once he has admired the look and feel of the glowing coke, he turns to stand in front of the hearth with the heat cooking the backs of his thighs. Soon, other people in the room can smell his trousers heating to the point at which it seems they must be beginning to burn.

'You'll scorch, Dad!' says Lynda.

'I know!' he replies. 'And tha'll not shift me.'

John, Lynda and Karl wait for him to give in. Rocking on his heels on the hearth he ignores their looks, and only at the point when he seems about to burst into flames does he step away. 'It's a right fire, that,' he says.

'Tha's not meant to keep it turned right up tha knows, Harry,' says John.

'Turned up!' says Harry. He is appalled by the idea of controls on a fireplace, but still falls into conversation with his daughter and son-in-law about fires and the best kinds of coal. They move on to gossip from Highgate and Goldthorpe, and in this way their friendship slowly proves like a breadloaf in the warmth.

Harry has slowed slightly, as he acknowledged to the journalist from the *South Yorkshire Times*. He has packed away the drums (Winnie complained they took up too much space, but playing on his own hadn't been the same in any case) and now he spends more time watching television and complaining about the new programmes. 'Them's not comics,' he will say to Karl as they watch a satirist from the sixties, or one of the new 'alternative' comedians. 'They're too daft to laugh at. See what's on t' other side.'

When Harry says he is too tired to manage all of his allotment, John begins helping him. They plan and plant cabbages, carrots, potatoes, cucumbers, chrysanthemums, and as they work through the year's damps and breezes and sun-warmed days, boots sinking in the dark earth, backs dipping and rising together, they become friends in the way that men often do when they grow and make things together. But with the flowering and the harvest comes a family dispute.

One day in May, John notices Harry digging up the last of their spring cabbages. It occurs to John that he has not seen Lynda or Winnie cook any of them. Looking around he notices that far more vegetables of all kinds have been dug up than have been eaten by the family. And then he remembers seeing Tony Grainger leaving Winnie's with heavy, lumpy-looking carrier bags.

It takes only two weeks of watching to spot that Winnie is asking Harry to take the vegetables John has planted so that she can give them to Tony as gifts.

The day John realises he asks Lynda to tell her mam to stop it. He has limits and he isn't going to grow food for Tony.

First she tries her dad. 'Don't tell me,' says Harry. 'Tell your mam.'

When Lynda tells her mam, dropping the request into a casual conversation in Winnie's kitchen one Saturday morning, Winnie snaps, 'That's our Karl's dad.'

'Maybe it is. But I'm with John now, and John doesn't want to grow stuff on that garden for Tony. So forget it.'

'Right then,' says Winnie. Her face is like cold flint. 'If that's it you can get through that door and not come back. Stay away, and don't darken my doorstep again.'

Don't darken my doorstep? The doorstep is only five doors away from mine, thinks Lynda. But she still dare not answer back. 'Fair enough, Mother,' she says, and gets through the door as instructed.

Lynda cannot fully understand Winnie's reasons for wanting to give food to Tony. What she does understand is her mam's desire to maintain control. Winnie believes she has a crude, practical hold over Lynda, because Lynda has no one else with whom she can leave Karl when she works. However, unbeknown to Winnie, this has changed, because John has a new shift pattern that enables him to collect Karl from school.

Lynda does not feel the need to apologise, and so they stop speaking: days, a week, months, though Karl still visits. One day Lynda is walking down Barnsley Road with some shopping when she sees Winnie, red vinyl shopping bag in hand, trudging towards her. Lynda fixes her gaze on her, thinking to speak as they pass, but Winnie keeps her head up and looks straight ahead, ignoring her on the street. The same thing happens when they pass in the backings, and Harry falls in behind her.

Christmas comes and things stay the same. It seems quite possible that they may never speak again.

'She'll come round before I will,' says Winnie on New Year's Eve.

'She'll come round before I will,' says Lynda at roughly the same time.

PART SEVEN

52

The Future is a Foreign Country

Rustenburg, South Africa; Houghton Main Colliery; Grimethorpe Colliery, 1981–82

Although Roy now earns only a modest living as a part-time motor mechanic, he continues to mock Gary for taking a job at the pit. No family visit to Hinckley ever passes without a careers lecture being delivered over the caravan's fold-down table. 'What you *should* be doing,' he usually begins, 'is getting on with computers. That's what it's all going to be about.'

'I'm already on with them, Dad,' says Gary. 'We use computers to monitor all t' ventilation and air pressure at t' pit.'

'*Pit.*' Roy says the word as if it disgusts him. 'T' pit's not computers, it's a bloody dead-end.'

'We do alright. It's not a bad wage, tha knows.'

'You should have a better house and car, then. When I was your age I was earning £30 a week, which was a lot of money. Where's your drive?'

These conversations embarrass Gary and make him feel he is a disappointment to his father. When he was a kid, his dad would talk proudly about what his son was going to achieve; now he berates him for owning a Skoda.

'Get yourself a right job,' says Roy. 'Think about Scott. You're providing for him as well, remember.'

In fact colliery employment is still, in the early eighties, relatively plentiful and among the best-paid work in South Yorkshire.

As steelworks, textile factories and railways had closed down or cut workers, joblessness in the Dearne had been rising through the 1970s, reaching levels described by a phrase brought back from the past: mass unemployment. By 1980 unemployment in the valley stands at 12.6 per cent – more than twenty per cent discounting Youth Opportunity Schemes – and in some places one in four people are out of work. Few teenage lads have jobs, and the older men who are laid off are told not to expect to find work in the immediate future. With employers struggling, the remaining pits become more important to the area's economy; of the jobs that are available in 1980, about thirty per cent are in, or dependent on, coal. And in the main these are good jobs to have. In the schools, the miners' kids are envied for their new trainers and their dads' new cars.

In February 1981, Joe Gormley's request for a meeting with government ministers is at first rejected by Mrs Thatcher, but then she and her Energy Minister David Howell back down, and Howell meets the NCB and NUM leaders. Ezra's figure of fifty closures had been misleading, as many of these had already been discussed and agreed with the union, but Howell says he will look at keeping the threatened pits open, reducing imports and removing the financial constraints the 1980 Act had placed on the NCB. Ezra withdraws the plans, miners who had already come out on strike go back to work, and in the end Gormley wins extra state aid for the industry. Everyone knows it will amount only to a skirmish in a bigger battle yet to come ('Miners v. Tories: the supreme test that faces Mrs Thatcher' runs a *Times* headline the day before the Howell meeting), but it seems grounds for optimism.

Meanwhile, the Selby complex is three-quarters complete and being promoted with images resembling the pictures in sci-fi books Gary and David read as children. The NCB is bullish, talking up the reconstruction of the coal fields as 'one of the most extensive rejuvenation exercises in industrial history'. 'By 1984, when we start to reap the full benefits of our major schemes,' reads the NCB page in *Barnsley, An Industrial Heritage*, a booklet published by the city's Chamber of Commerce in 1981, 'Barnsley will be one of the most productive and profitable areas in the country.'

But Roy's nagging gets to Gary and half-convinces him that if he stays at Houghton Main he could be in a doomed dead-end. A month after Winnie and Harry's golden wedding anniversary, one of Roy's scoldings spurs Gary to reply to an advertisement for mineworkers placed in the *Sun* newspaper by GenCo, a South African mining corporation. He has heard about these jobs at work. Some Canadian and South African companies set up recruitment offices in Barnsley, and offer good terms and grants to young families who want to relocate, and emigration has become a popular subject; Geoff Allan, Lynda's first husband, has not long ago left for Australia. The old men at Houghton tell the young ones to go. 'If I had my time again I'd be off, sirree,' a fitter tells Gary one snap time. 'I had my papers for Australia once, and I wish I'd gone. This country's buggered, and we all know what Maggie'll do to t' pits.'

Gary travels to London for an interview at GenCo's headquarters off Fleet Street, and receives a letter offering him an environmental engineer's post in a mine complex at Bafokeng. He hesitates because of stories on the news about South Africa, because apartheid seems too strange and wrong, and because the NUM is opposed to its members working in South African mines. But then Roy rings and tells him he'd be a bloody fool to pass up the chance, and he wonders what was there to stay for; the coking plant at Manvers had closed, and you could see the same happening all over the county. Most people expected the high unemployment to be permanent. In Sheffield, where foundries and factories are closing down or else making redundancies, someone has spray-painted a bus stop with the words: 'IT IS NOT A GOOD TIME TO BE YOUNG AND SINGLE', and no one seems inclined to clean it off.

Elaine says if Gary wants to go, and if it'll be good for his job, then they should go. What do they have to lose? He writes to accept the job offer, and hands in his notice at Houghton Main.

His dad is delighted, but the adventure goes badly. Three months before they are due to leave, as the newspapers and television news count down to Prince Charles and Lady Diana's wedding, Elaine finds out she is pregnant. She braves it out and decides to have the baby in

South Africa, and they fly out from Heathrow in October, but even at the departure gate Gary realises his notion of their emigration as a singular, distinguished enterprise is false; the cordoned area is full of young men, women and children from Scotland, Wales and the North East, all part of the same exodus. At Jan Smuts International Airport in Johannesburg, a middle-aged sunburned Afrikaner with a clipboard and pistol at his hip directs three planeloads of mining families through the bright, blast-furnace air towards a waiting fleet of minibuses.

*

A South Africa story: one afternoon Gary comes home to his family's apartment in the Bushveld city of Rustenburg and sees a bundle of greasy newspaper on the kitchen worktop beside a handbag. The newspaper contains the remains of the family's fish and chips from the night before; the handbag belongs to Sima, their Zambian maid. Gary is looking at the paper when Sima comes in. She sees him and looks alarmed. When he greets her she mumbles and looks down, so Elaine has to explain that Sima has taken the food from the bin and asked if she can take it for her family. Gary wants to tell her about his grandma, and how she might have done the same thing when she was in service in the 1920s, but realises that even if Sima believed him it would only make her uncomfortable. He goes back out into the garden to spare her any more awkwardness.

For some of the expats, having the maids covet their crumbs feels empowering, because it means you were not on the lower rungs but up high, passing down your scraps. It does not feel like that to Gary and Elaine. What they feel is embarrassment.

They stay for five months, long enough for their baby, a girl they name Claire, to be born, and then decide to come back. The veldt has made them homesick, the terrorist attacks on the mines have unnerved them, and they have struggled to settle socially. The Afrikaners dislike the British, and the segregation seems to put everyone on edge. Gary develops a habit of looking out at the beautiful landscape and daydreaming about wintry weekend afternoons at home in England.

They land at Heathrow in heavy rain and low cloud. In the airport the newspaper headlines are full of the Falklands conflict, and the people in the shops look pale and tired under the over-bright lights. Having given up their house when they left, Gary, Elaine, Scott and Claire move in with Margaret and Colin, and Gary goes out looking for work on an old 100cc East European motorbike he buys from a classified advertisement in a newspaper. Seeing the towns and villages with back-from-abroad eyes, he thinks there has been a deterioration even in the short time he has been away: shops and factories that were open last October have closed, bus shelters have been vandalised, and some of the clubs have new fences, and bars on their windows. There are few job advertisements in any shop windows, and no one he asks has any idea of where he might even begin to look for work. The time of free pork pies and pit-top school trips is long gone. At Houghton Main, Eric the personnel manager blows out through pursed lips and rubs the back of his head. 'No chance here, Gary,' he says. 'I've got a waiting list. Everyone has.'

He takes a job as a painter and decorator, just as he did when he was fifteen. After four months of checking in weekly with Eric, he gets his old job back after some of the ventilation men take redundancy packages. Then, because he has realised that regardless of what his dad says, he likes the Dearne and he enjoys pit work, he does what he should have done in the first place: he enrols at Barnsley Technical College to study for a qualification in air-measurement, ventilation management and environmental engineering. He moves his family into a pit house on Queen Street in Thurnscoe, and at night he sits at the kitchen table studying.

*

One morning in February 1983, as Gary approaches the gates of Houghton Main on his motorbike, he sees ahead through the cold drizzle a cluster of men in anoraks and donkey jackets, standing behind hand-painted wooded signs. They are pickets; it is not uncommon to find a picket line at a pit these days, but usually the men, and the dispute, are local. These men, however, are unknown to him, and their accents are Welsh. They have come to persuade Yorkshire miners to strike with them against the closure of another Welsh pit, Lewis Merthyr in the Rhondda.

A short, dark-haired man about Gary's age, wearing an NCB donkey jacket, says, 'They're starting with us, closing them one by one to see what they can do, mate. Then they'll go after 'em all. You seen Arthur's list, now?'

Arthur Scargill, elected president of the entire NUM at the start of the year, has been campaigning with what he says is a leaked list of fifty pits the NCB wants to close. The Board has been closing the pits that it promised to keep open, and making thousands of men redundant.

'Aye, we've seen t' list,' says Gary. 'I don't know about a strike though. Lads here are scared of losing their jobs.'

'They'll lose 'em anyway if they don't fight.'

'Aye, but . . .'

Aye, but; he means the union leaders seem to talk about strike votes all the time, and a lot of the men have grown sceptical. Besides, this is not 1926 or 1972, when there was little or nothing to lose. Some of them have car and mortgage payments to keep up. They are loyal, but it might take more than a threatened pit in the Welsh valleys to bring them out.

An older man in a nylon rally jacket and a flat cap studded with union and colliery badges joins in. 'Come on, mate. Think about it. This branch has a meeting, you can vote to support us.'

'I'll think about it.'

But in March the NUM members vote against a strike. The Welsh miners go home, and Lewis Merthyr closes down in June. Meanwhile, the Conservative government is reviving its efforts to confront the NUM and shut unprofitable coal mines. In June, boosted by Britain's recapture of the Falkland Islands, Mrs Thatcher's Conservative party is re-elected with a manifesto that contains a coded commitment to reduce the NCB's losses by closing loss-making pits. In September, the Energy Secretary Nigel Lawson announces that from September the NCB will be run by Ian MacGregor, a Scottish industrialist who has fought mining unions in America. In 1980, Sir Keith Joseph, Secretary of State for Industry, had made MacGregor chairman of British Steel, and he had spent his time there reducing losses by closing plants and making redundancies with little apparent sympathy for the unemployed. In the coalfields the significance of the appointment seems clear.

In pit yards in the Dearne, and across all the coalfields, stockpiles of coal rise and rise as the pit managers build up reserves. They tell the men to keep the new layers of coal on the piles thin and even, to reduce the risk of creating air pockets that could cause spontaneous combustion. This is what you do if you're building a large pile that will remain in place for a long time; the sort of pile you might build as a reserve, for example, if you were expecting a long strike.

*

As the rumours spread and thicken across the valley like wet, winter mists, Gary Hollingworth moves to Grimethorpe colliery to become its dust control officer. Grimethorpe is a large village about three miles north-west of Thurnscoe, overlooked by mountainous black and grassy spoil heaps and a hulking church built on a hill. The colliery complex, comprising two pits, a smokeless fuel plant, a power station and the biggest coal preparation plant in Europe, is, like Manvers Main, a small city of girders, chimneys, hoppers, sheds and machinery-strewn yards. To an outsider it looks like a gigantic piece of electronic equipment with its lid taken off. Below the earth its tunnels take up seven square miles, so that when Gary goes down the Number Two Shaft, and travels to the faces, he is half a mile beneath Thurnscoe and miles away from Grimethorpe. He calculates one day that he is working more or less underneath his mam's house.

Gary's responsibilities are to keep the colliery and its six thousand or so men safe; if the dust ignites, the pit goes up. The job does not bring him automatic acceptance, however. All pits, like towns and villages, have their own character, and Grimethorpe is awkward: 'bolshy' in management terms. This is only partly to do with union politics. Despite its scale it is still a village pit in nature, and like all villages, it respects character rather than rank. For men on the lowest levels of management, as Gary now is, this means it can be difficult to give orders – particularly if you are a newcomer and the youngest on the team.

'Get that box of bolts down to t' pit bottom,' the safety engineer tells him in the pit yard on his second day. 'Ask Tommy.' Tommy is the shaft service manager, the man who controls what goes up and down the shaft between pit top and bottom. Gary carries the box across the yard to the shaft top, where a slim man in his forties stands making notes with a pencil stub in a notebook. 'Is thar Tommy?' asks Gary.

'Who wants him?'

'I do, mucker. Will you get us that down to t' shaft side?'

Tommy looks down at the box and back up at Gary. 'Fuck off.'

Gary half-laughs, which he knows immediately is a mistake. 'Go on, mate.'

'No.' Tommy turns to ostentatiously pick at flaking red oxide paint on a girder.

He pauses, which is a better move, because it acknowledges Tommy's unofficial authority. Once this is acknowledged, Tommy can begin to feel some sympathy for him. He stands there, not saying anything.

Tommy cracks first. 'What?'

'It's just that I've got to get this job done, and we're behind.'

'So?'

Gary knows enough not to say, 'because my boss wants me to'. The men run the pit, that's the real rule most of the time; the bosses are merely humoured.

'It needs doing. There's some lads down there can't get on without it.'

Tommy affects boredom. 'Leave it there,' he sighs. 'I'll see what I can do.'

'That's right, lad,' says the safety engineer, when Gary says that Tommy seems an aggressive bugger. 'But Tom's alright. Blokes like that, you just have to learn how to talk to 'em.'

He does learn and he discovers that while some of the aggressive buggers are just bloody-minded, others are the most loyal and cooperative men he has ever met. It is a lesson that he will remember, and apply many years later, in very different circumstances.

*

MacGregor takes over and he and Scargill fall out over a pay claim and alleged pit closures. The mood in the pits grows fractious. NCB chiefs say that, having invested £3 billion to bring new capacity on stream, they need to close old pits that can't be modernised. There are rumours that fifteen pits totalling 15,000 jobs will close by March 1984. The union imposes an overtime ban, but men in some collieries ignore it, and some managers reorganise shifts to fight it. Rag-ups break out at individual pits in South Yorkshire, and some of the men from these disputes picket others.

In January 1984, the NCB announces a new policy for coal, a familiar set of ideas concentrating production on the new, modern superpits, and closing the older, smaller ones, with good redundancy terms. Tensions between managers and men increase. In February miners at Polmaise colliery near Stirling in Scotland go on strike when the NCB says it will close the pit. By March the mood in many coalfields is one of rising chaos. In Yorkshire the teatime local television news carries long round-ups from the local collieries, explaining who is and who is not on strike. In the Dearne Valley, in February, a row over new shift patterns at Manvers Main becomes a rallying point, and when the men walk out, others from Barnburgh, Wath, Kilnhurst, Cadeby and Silverwood walk out in support. In Thurnscoe, word goes around that Arthur Scargill is coming to the Cora to talk to the men, and David Hollingworth and Gary walk down to find the club packed.

Union meetings at the Cora are always well attended, but almost everyone in the village seems to be here, and the mood is urgent and serious. Arthur, in a dark suit, stands in the middle of the stage in front of a poster saying 'NO PIT CLOSURES', and warns them what is to come, telling them Ian MacGregor has been brought in to butcher the industry, and answering questions at the end. The pay claim is more or less forgotten; everyone in Yorkshire knows what it's really about. The mountains of stockpiled coal in Hickleton pit yard are there to remind them.

The atmosphere afterwards in the Cora is opaque with cigarette smoke and rumours. Some of the men are ready to walk out now. David hears one man say he wants to get on with it and get a strike called. He reckons it could all be over in six weeks.

53

An Extra Half-Hour in Bed

Highgate; Thurnscoe; Houghton Main, March–April 1984

At 6.30 on the morning of Monday 12 March, 1984, Lynda Burton is woken by the creak of John's footsteps on the stairs outside the bedroom door. She wonders why he is back at home. He is supposed to be on earlies, and set off for Hickleton pit an hour ago.

'Tha needn't bother getting up for work,' he says, as he comes into the room and tugs off his sweater and T-shirt. 'We're on strike. They've told everybody to go home.'

Lynda sits up and checks the time on the digital radio-alarm clock built into the padded Dralon headboard of their new bed.

'What's gone off?'

'I don't know. Managers are at t' gates turning everybody back, and there's some pickets on.' He shucks off his jeans. 'NUM and COSA's on strike. They said to tell thee not to go in.'

COSA, the Colliery Officials and Staff Association, is John and Lynda's union. Most women in the offices joined COSA or APEX, the Association of Professional, Executive, Clerical and Computer Staff, and most of those in the canteen COSA or the TGWU, the Transport and General Workers' Union. COSA is affiliated to the NUM, and the two unions strike together.

'Bit of extra holiday then.' They came home yesterday after six days in their caravan at Cleethorpes. The lie-in will be a small, unlooked-for luxury.

'Aye, make t' most of it.'

Both assume the strike will be settled in two or three days. Working in the offices, Lynda hears every week about short strikes and rag-ups, sometimes a shift at Hickleton, sometimes a whole pit in the area. In the last year it has been getting worse.

'Is it just Hickleton?'

'No, there's some more, I don't know who though. Shove up.' He yanks back the sheets and blankets, and climbs into bed.

'It'll not last long whatever it is,' she says, and then lies back down for a last twenty minutes before getting up to see Karl off to school.

At noon they listen to the lunchtime news bulletins as reporters explain that miners at collieries across all of Yorkshire are out. The conflict has been developing for several days. Last week, the NCB's South Yorkshire area director had met area union reps in the Manvers Main offices and told them that in five weeks' time he would close the pits at Bulcliffe Wood and Cortonwood. Bulcliffe Wood is a small 'dads-and-lads' pit near Wakefield and its closure is not a great shock to anyone. Cortonwood, which stands in the village of Brampton, four miles west of Bolton-upon-Dearne, is different. Last year the same area director had said it was safe for five years, and the NCB had spent £1 million on improvements. Now he says he has been told to reduce output, and this one closure will achieve more than half his target. All 839 men will get redundancy packages or transfers to other collieries, but the Cortonwood miners object that the decision contravenes the official colliery review process that usually precedes closure. A review would at least give people in the area time to plan and adapt, whereas a sudden shutdown would kill off not only the village's mining jobs but all the other jobs that rely on the pit as well.

After the announcement, the Cortonwood men voted to strike, and 300 of them went to Barnsley to ask the NUM's Yorkshire Area Council to recommend that other pits vote to join them. The council agreed and proposed a strike in Yorkshire to begin after the last shift on 9 March. Delegates took as a mandate the Yorkshire area's 1981 vote for a strike in the event of closures.

The next day, Tuesday 6 March, Ian MacGregor announced his intention to cut 20,000 jobs and close twenty pits. Three pits besides Cortonwood and Bulcliffe Wood – in Scotland, Kent and County Durham – had already been named. He said the jobs would be lost gradually through retirement and redundancy packages, but few miners believed him, and anyway, they asked, what will replace those jobs?

Across the county, miners and their families met in clubs and welfare halls and voted as NUM branches to accept the proposal and strike in support of Cortonwood. Some walked out immediately. By 12 March, all the pits in Yorkshire are still.

Watching the television as they eat their lunch, John and Lynda agree with the line taken by the Hickleton miners and union officials. 'It's Maggie and MacGregor trying it on to see what happens,' says John, feeding scraps of boiled ham to Sam the dog. 'She'll shut half of t' pits in Yorkshire if she can get away with it.'

*

In Thurnscoe, David Hollingworth has also returned home early to tell Marie he is on strike ('We'll have to tighten us belts for a bit, love,' he tells her, worried about mortgage payments as they have just bought their house from the NCB) and taken Lisa and Gemma, the family's Golden Labrador, out for a walk. They stop at the pit gates where a mass picket of about 200 people has gathered, and David talks to some friends; they are cheerful, and full of the usual predictions that it will be settled in a few days or weeks. A mile away to the west, Gary and Kenny have joined the picket at Houghton Main. The Houghton picket is, like Hickleton's, chiefly a show of unity today, as, other than a few officials, there is little traffic in and out. The men are gathered near the manager's office at the bottom of the pit lane, and they boo and jeer when the officials, acting as if they can't see or hear anyone, drive past in their cars. The watching police, who are from Barnsley, laugh.

The preceding Saturday night Gary had attended a meeting at the Cora about Cortonwood and the strike. Hickleton union officials had said that Ian MacGregor had a hit list, and that Thatcher was going to lay waste to their communities. It was the first time Gary had heard ordinary people using the word 'community', and it sounded ominous. People in the crowd had shouted about the need to stand and fight, as if an invading army was about to sail down the River Dearne. Kenny agreed, and had suggested that he and Gary start by joining the picket at Houghton on Monday. It is acceptable to go to your mate's pit, or to the one in your village if you work away, because everyone is standing and fighting for each other.

A member of managerial staff driving a Ford Cortina whizzes past the pickets, and a man standing near Gary shouts, half-joking, 'BACM bastard' at the car (BACM being the British Association of Colliery Management). The driver ignores the low-level heckles and parks up in the yard, and everyone resumes their conversations.

'If nobody's working in Yorkshire we'll all be going somewhere else,' says Kenny.

He means they will be flying pickets at power stations, or at pits where miners are still working. Secondary picketing has been made illegal by the government, but it had been clear at the Cora meeting that people were going to try it anyway.

'Aye, let's hope it's somewhere glamorous. Kent, maybe.'

'Or t' posh pits in Nottinghamshire.' This is only a half joke. Yorkshire miners envy the modern buildings and attractive landscaping of Nottinghamshire's pits, some of which are concealed by tree screens to make their village look prettier. The old colliers in the valley say it has all been a reward for the county's blacklegs who left the Miners' Federation and broke the strike of 1926.

*

The National Union of Mineworkers is a national organisation made up of individual bodies (such as COSA or the Cokemen) and areas such as Yorkshire, South Wales and Nottinghamshire. These bodies and areas are independent unions in their own right, and their members tend to identify as strongly with their own organisation as with the national union as a whole. In 1984 these allegiances partly determine the politics and character of the strike.

It begins with the individual pits in two areas, Cortonwood in Yorkshire and Polmaise in Stirling, voting to walk out and requesting that the NUM's national executive recognise their action as official. This recognition will sanction picketing of other areas as Yorkshire and Scottish miners ask others to strike in support. The executive votes to recognise the action, though some members, knowing that this will lead to a campaign for a national strike, request that the union holds a national ballot as it had in 1972 and 1974. The NUM executive does not hold a ballot, and critics will say this is illegal and undemocratic – indicative of Arthur Scargill and his supporters on the executive wanting a strike regardless of members' wishes. Its defenders will counter that as some areas such as Kent and South Wales immediately and solidly walked out in support of Yorkshire and Scotland, it would be unfeasible to instruct them to return to work, even if a national ballot rejected strike action.

Across the country the strike is therefore uneven from the beginning. At some pits all the men come out, at others none; in some areas most NUM and COSA members stop working, in others the majority carries on. Over the border from South Yorkshire in Nottinghamshire, the area union leaders say they want a ballot before they endorse a strike, and most of the miners in the county continue to work.

To complicate matters further, NACODS (the National Association of Colliery Overmen, Deputies and Shotfirers) votes in favour of a strike, but not with the two-thirds majority required. NACODS members carry out safety checks. If they strike, a lack of maintenance could damage mines, so the NCB has no choice but to negotiate. In March 1984, they refused to cross picket lines except to carry out essential maintenance work, but received full pay, to the annoyance of some striking miners who regarded them as bosses' men. There are arguments and skirmishes in pubs. At Hickleton, a deputy comes out at the end of a shift, flashes his pay packet at the pickets and shouts, 'Keep it up, lads!' When Marie's brother-in-law Maurice, a NACODS member, calls round to visit her and David they all carefully avoid mentioning the strike.

The first day Gary and Kenny go picketing outside South Yorkshire it is to Bilsthorpe, a posh pit in north Nottinghamshire. It is Wednesday 14 March. They drive there with a mate called John and another Hickleton man called Jim, the destination given to them by union men from Hickleton pit. They leave Thurnscoe in the dark at four in the morning in John's Ford Escort and join other cars leaving the Dearne villages and heading for the A1 to take them south. The other miners' cars are identifiable by their snap in bread bags on their rear window shelves.

On some junctions of the A1 there are roadblocks where police officers stop vehicles and turn back cars full of men if they suspect them of being pickets travelling to Nottinghamshire or Derbyshire collieries. John turns off early, and follows narrow back roads and lanes through dark fields until they arrive in Bilsthorpe. The pit stands on the edge of the village, its buildings and towers neatly boxed in corrugated casings and screened by banks of trees. 'Typical,' says Kenny.

Near the pit gates about two hundred men in anoraks, donkey jackets and bobble hats are standing, rubbing their hands against the cold. A line of policemen in black macs and helmets stands opposite and some of the pickets and police swap jokes about who's going to push the hardest. Before the first Bilsthorpe men arrive for the early shift the pickets move to form a barrier, and the police link arms and try to push them out of the way. The struggle looks like a stand-up rugby scrum, the police and pickets' expressions like those of rugby players in a fairly good-natured match. After about ten minutes the police have pushed a way through. The working miners walk, drive or cycle past as the pickets shout 'Scab!' and other insults, and point out they're striking for Nottinghamshire's jobs as well as their own.

'This one's got his mam wi' him, look,' says Gary to Kenny, pointing out a teenage lad accompanied by an older woman. The boy looks at the ground. His mam glares at the pickets, daring them to say something.

'Daren't tha come on thi own?' someone shouts.

'Bugger off back to bloody Yorkshire,' she shouts back.

'Looks like she's doing us out of a job,' a policeman says to Gary.

Gary, Kenny and the others stay all day, trying to stop the other shifts going to work, and to persuade truck drivers not to make their deliveries. Some of the drivers stop and talk or argue with them. No one turns back, although pickets arriving from other places say that at some other pits, whole shifts have been persuaded to go back home. The last snap is eaten, the police shift changes over and the pit night shift goes on at ten o'clock. Some men leave, and other new pickets arrive. The temperature drops. Gary's group are preparing to go home when some new arrivals bring news about big crowds at Ollerton colliery a few miles north. There is a rumour that a picket has been badly hurt and taken to hospital; Arthur Scargill is said to be on his way there. A few carloads head off there themselves. Gary and his mates decide to call it a day and go back to Thurnscoe.

The next morning the local TV news reports that a twenty-four-year-old miner called David Jones from South Kirby, a former employee at Hickleton pit, has died after being injured at Ollerton. The official cause of death given is chest injuries after being struck by a brick, though an inquest will later hear conflicting evidence. Arthur Scargill had arrived at three in the morning and tried to calm the situation by climbing onto the roof of a car and by asking for two minutes' silence from the police and pickets. As news of Jones's death spread, hundreds of pickets had converged on Ollerton, and the pit manager and union men had talked to the crowd to try to contain the growing tension.

In the weeks that follow, Gary hears from other pickets stories about rough handling by the police and about roadblocks leading into coal-fields where miners get themselves or their car windows truncheoned if they refuse to turn back. Yet at most of the pits he goes to in March and April, relations between the managers, police and miners are cordial; managers allow the pickets use of the toilets and telephones, and the police continue to share their snap. In the backs of their police vans they have big cardboard boxes full of provisions: flasks of coffee, soft drinks, sandwiches with fat fillings. When they have breaks to eat it, they bring armfuls across to the pickets. 'Here, lads, get stuck in,' they say. 'We'll never eat all t' lot. T'police force allus thinks we're starving.'

At Cresswell colliery, Derbyshire in April, the pickets are getting ready to leave after the afters shift has gone into work. A policeman, aged about forty with a strong Derbyshire accent, says, 'Right, lads, are we all off home then? Where are you parked?'

Most of them have left their cars about a mile away and have walked over the fields to the pit.

'Up there,' says Gary. 'Bit of a trek.'

'Jump in then.' The policeman opens the back doors of a transit van. 'We'll take you up.'

'You're bloody joking, aren't you?' All of the men look hesitant. Earlier, the policemen have been recounting the story of a colleague who had his hand broken on a picket line.

'It's an honest offer,' says the policeman. 'Up to you.'

The miners pack themselves into several vans. On the way back up the pit lane, Gary's mates and the policeman discuss the strike. The policeman says it's all political and they don't like being dragged into it, although the overtime doesn't go unappreciated.

The police stop and let the miners out as they promised. 'See you later, lads,' says the policeman. 'And good luck.'

54

What Are You Doing for Money?

Goldthorpe, April–May 1984

In theory COSA and the NUM pay their members when they go on strike. In practice their funds are insufficient, and while people can ask for financial help if they face unusual hardship, no one expects support as a matter of course. In the 1970s, the Department of Health and Social Security gave mothers in striking families money for their children's food and clothes, but under new laws DHSS staff must now treat parents on strike as being in receipt of strike pay, regardless of whether they actually receive it or not. When Lynda visits the Goldthorpe DHSS office the woman behind the desk says, 'I'm sorry, love, but we're not allowed to give you anything apart from emergency food vouchers for your lad. They're for £5 a week.' The woman looks sympathetic, but sounds as if she has explained this a hundred times already that morning.

'Even though both me and my husband are on strike?' asks Lynda. 'I know a lot of women have got jobs and can support their husbands, but me and John both work at t' pit.' And, she wants to add, the maintenance from my ex-husband is a rare privilege, and my son will need a uniform for senior school in September. But at the other counters women are saying similar things, and there are still more waiting behind them, and the DHSS woman can't help. 'It makes no difference, I'm afraid. That's t' law, now.'

'Aye, so that women'll nag their husbands to go back to work so they can feed their kids.'

'As I said, Mrs Burton,' says the woman, 'I can give you a voucher.'

Between them, Lynda and John have the £5 voucher each week, vegetables from the allotment, the family allowance, and sometimes maintenance payments from Tony. Some who might have helped Lynda and John either lack the money or the will: John's mam can't help them because all her sons are on strike, while Winnie is still not speaking to them a year on from the argument about Tony and the vegetables. Other friends bring food for them, though: a pound of stewing meat and some potatoes, say, or a packet of mincemeat, or a pork joint from a friend who keeps pigs. For a few weeks they manage, but then the first set of quarterly bills clears most of their savings and they start to feel vulnerable. At the same time, they and everyone else realise the strike might last for far longer than the expected six weeks.

Women from Highgate, Goldthorpe and Bolton-upon-Dearne organise a soup kitchen at the Goldthorpe Miners' Welfare Hall. In the mornings and afternoons they stand outside G. T. Smith's supermarket on Doncaster Road with cardboard boxes, and shoppers throw in tins and packets of food; in the Welfare Hall they cook the food into pies and stews and serve them up as meals for a few pence. Lynda and John go there for dinner. The mood is cheerful, but as she eats her way through a plateful of stew, Lynda looks at all the men and women and kids sat at rows of tables in the hall where Harry used to perform, and feels two competing emotions. The first is admiration of how people are helping each other; the second is sadness that people have to eat in a soup kitchen. It reminds her of her mam's stories about Walter and the distress committees of 1926. We shouldn't be doing this, she thinks, because it's what our grandparents, mams and dads thought they had saved us from. She looks at John, who is not talking much, and guesses that he feels the same; encouraged by the comradeship, but rueful about the circumstances.

Lynda has seen news stories about how women across the mining communities are organising support for the striking miners. Many wives and girlfriends of men on strike have formed their own campaign groups as part of a movement called Women Against Pit Closures. Some say it has changed them; before the strike, they were limited to being mothers and housewives and would never have dared to go on demonstrations, let alone speak publicly at meetings as some of them now do. Some of their mothers dislike it, and tell their daughters they are not being proper wives, but the women say that even when the strike's over they won't revert to the way they lived before. The communities are theirs as much as the men's, aren't they? In Nottinghamshire, the wives of working miners walk with their men to the pit to show support against the pickets, and there and elsewhere the wives of striking miners join the picket lines, hoping that the police won't stop them in their cars.

The press reports do not mention the women from the offices and canteens who are themselves on strike because, she supposes, they don't fit into anyone's stories. But if a reporter had thought to ask Lynda Burton she would have told them that the women who work at the pits are as proud of their industry as the men, and she would have recited for the reporter the name of every pit in the Doncaster area and the names of the seams, and she would have told him which pits are fiery and which are wet, and about when she was a young girl, travelling on the pit bus with her dad driving, and about the miners with their dirty faces getting on the bus and touching the top of her head and putting mint humbugs into her hand. The women had always been involved with coal mining; they might be involved in different ways now, and they were able to talk about it more in public, but the history belonged to them as much as it did the men.

Lynda thinks of her boss and the women at work who are in APEX, and who now sign in every day to be paid for doing nothing. There have been demonstrations at the NCB offices in Doncaster and some young men noticed APEX women going in to work and shouted and spat at them, which had disgusted Lynda and everyone she knew. After all, APEX had not called them out on strike. The division and rancour breaking out between different groups of people shocks her, but the worst thing is that it is hard to resist those feelings entirely. It is not pleasing to think of friends being paid for doing nothing, while you cannot buy your child a school uniform because you are striking to save everyone's jobs.

She walks into Goldthorpe to look for work, past the food collectors, past the Goldthorpe Hotel where the landlady is handing a box of sandwiches to someone to take to the pickets, and past the colliery gates where miners stand guard and police watch them from inside two white vans. Starting at one end of Doncaster Road, she works her way through the pubs, asking and asking, 'Do you need any work doing? . . . Behind t' bar, or anything?' until she finds one that offers her part-time work as a barmaid.

Two days later she is walking home from the pub when she meets Frank Tulley, the manager of Hickleton pit. A dark, pensive man in his fifties, Tulley began as a miner himself and worked his way up, and like many such men, he tacitly supports the men and women on strike. When Lynda tells him she and John are struggling, Tulley tells her to send John to his house so he can pay him to do some painting and repairs. These jobs will help with the next quarter's bills, though not enough for them to live beyond a day-to-day, hand-to-mouth sort of life.

The days lengthen, the weather grows warmer, and there is no sign of the strike ending. Coming out from her shift at the pub one afternoon, Lynda sees hundreds of people and several lines of riot police. There is talk of someone having gone back to work, and the ranks of police having come to push back the pickets so that the man's bus can get through the pit gates. The crowd is angry because no one knows anyone who has gone back to work and it is a colliery where everyone knows everyone else; they think it's a set-up to make it seem that men are going back to work in strikebound pits. In the end, no bus comes. Along the street, kids and women stand watching, waiting for something to happen, and the policemen look as impervious as cats.

55

What I Did in the War, Daddy

Orgreave Coking Works, South Yorkshire, and Hinckley, Leicestershire, June–July 1984

One morning in late April, Gary Hollingworth is on a picket line at Wistow pit sharing sandwiches and coffee handed out by policemen from Whitby when six police vans pull up, discharging dozens of fresh, younger policemen who stand looking about them, grinning and rolling their necks against their shoulders. They have southern accents and their uniforms are unusual, with white shirts rather than the familiar blue. The miners will soon come to recognise the uniform as that of the Metropolitan Police.

One of them, a tall, healthy-looking auburn-whiskered man in his late twenties, walks up to the pickets. He is chewing gum and sticking out his chest like the cocky villain in a Western. 'So this is it, is it?' He scans the lines of men, inspecting them. 'Here they are. *The fucking Yorkshire miners.*'

The pickets look at one another. The young policeman says, 'What's it going to be then, lads? We gonna have a ruck or what?'

'What you on about?' says one of the pickets.

'What-*yooo-on-abaht*,' mimics the policeman.

There follows more bad-tempered, foul-mouthed banter. A Whitby officer tells one of the Met men to calm down. The Met man steps up to him so their faces are only a foot apart. 'We deal with worse shit than this in London, son,' he says, and reels off an itemised list: fucking niggers, fucking queers, the fucking Greenham lezzers. 'And I'll tell you,' he says. 'Greenham was a shithole, but it was fucking paradise compared to this. If we have to live in this fucking shithole, we're going to have a bit of fucking fun.'

'Who do you think you're talking to, pal?' says the Whitby policeman.

'You. And the rest of your fucking Mickey Mouse cops.'

'Watch your bloody mouth.'

Some of the pickets start to laugh.

'You watch it: Fuck. Off.'

This is Gary Hollingworth's first experience of an officer from the Met, one of the forces from non-mining areas which is sending officers to coalfields to police the picket lines as the mass pickets grow, and violence becomes more common. Fights are breaking out of the pushing, and good hidings are dished out by both sides. The police say there are political agitators in the crowds; miners suspect agents provocateurs are being planted. Special magistrates' courts have been set up to deal with the mass arrests. When Gary looks back, this encounter with the London police will mark the point when the conflict became more combative and bitter. As spring turns to summer, talks between the NCB and NUM fail, and some Nottinghamshire miners begin a legal action against the NUM for declaring the strikes official. A friend and colleague of Ian MacGregor, David Hart, sets up an organisation called the National Working Miners' Committee; Bob Copping, a working winder from Houghton Main, goes to one of their meetings.

At the start of June, all striking mine-workers including Gary, David, Lynda and John receive in the post a photocopied letter bearing the Coal Board letterhead and signed by Ian MacGregor.

This is a strike that should never have happened. It is based on a very serious misrepresentation and distortion of the facts. At great financial cost, miners have supported the strike for 14 weeks because your leaders have told you this:

That the Coal Board is out to butcher the coal industry

That we plan to do away with 70,000 jobs

That we plan to close down 86 pits and leave only 100 working collieries.

If these things were true I would not blame miners for getting angry or for being deeply worried. But these things are absolutely untrue. I state that categorically and solemnly. You have been deliberately misled.

Yours sincerely

Ian MacGregor

Chairman, National Coal Board.

For a few days it is the subject of jokes, then it is forgotten.

On 15 June, Joe Green, a picket from Kellingley colliery, a large pit near Pontefract, dies after being hit by a lorry at Ferrybridge Power Station. On the television news, interviewers and newsreaders ask the NUM leaders to condemn the violent pickets. The leaders refuse on the grounds that no one is being asked to condemn violent police officers.

In the Dearne, anger about Joe Green's death is raw as Gary and Kenny organise their transport for a mass picket of the coking plant at Orgreave, a village to the north of Sheffield, on 18 June. Union officials say the plant has been supplying coke to power stations in breach of an agreement with the NUM. There have been large pickets there for the last few weeks, but under Arthur Scargill's direction, union leaders have planned a larger-scale gathering with striking miners and their supporters from across the country. The aim will be to stop the outside contractor lorry drivers getting in or out, but also to make a memorable show of solidarity and support.

Gary, Kenny and John travel down to Orgreave with six other men in a transit van. John's Ford Escort, being lime green, has become known to the police and is guaranteed to be pulled over. Ordinarily a transit would be a target too, but today as they drive south there are no roadblocks and few police patrol cars on the M1. Equally unusual are the policemen stationed along the roads leading towards the coking plant, directing the pickets to a makeshift car park like stewards at a country show. Once they are parked, Gary and the others join crowds ushered to an expanse of brown, scrubby grass in front of the plant's main gates.

As a teenager Gary had thought that coking plants, with their vast orange-glowing ovens and sky-gorging white clouds of steam, looked like scenes from the Apocalypse. Now, as they approach it, Orgreave's looks as if it could open its jaws and swallow them all in a single gulp, should it wish. The squat gas holders and high, smoking chimneys rise over the scrubland like the towers of a black citadel. In front of them is a long line of police about ten men deep. To the side, among some smaller buildings, is an encampment of police vans, horseboxes, ambulances, Portakabins and tents that looks the size of a small housing estate. Thousands more policemen are milling about here, and in some of the tents men are serving food and drinks to officers not deployed on the line. All around the scrubland mounted police wait in wheatfields, and dog handlers stand with their Alsatians on the edges of woodland. One of the men from the van says, 'Are you sure t' signs said "Orgreave"? Cos it looks like we've walked into bloody Agincourt.'

By 7.45 a.m. there are about five or six thousand pickets outside the plant, and Arthur Scargill is giving out instructions using a loudhailer. From the walls of nearby buildings camera crews are filming them. A few men and women are selling political newspapers, and on the ground there are piles of fresh placards stapled to wooden poles for people to take. Some carrying the Socialist Workers Party logo read 'TURN ORGREAVE INTO SALTLEY'.

At 8 a.m., when the lorries are due to collect their loads of coke, the pickets mass in front of the police. Gary and the men from the van are near the front, and watch police wearing visored crash helmets and carrying long Perspex shields move to the front of the police line opposite them, in response, it seems, to people throwing stones and pieces of coke. As the convoy of lorries comes down the road to the plant, Gary joins with the crowd singing 'Here we go, here we go', and surges forward with them against the shields of the police, who block their access to the road. The dark blue line buckles in places, and then pushes back.

This is customary, but this morning, after less than a minute, Gary suddenly feels the crowd behind him falling away and hears men shouting warnings; looking up, he sees the police line open, and mounted officers charge out. He turns and sprints away with the others, the sounds of the hooves on the hard earth loud in his ears. When the horses pull up and trot back behind the lines, the pickets go back to the police angrily asking why the horses were sent in so quickly, and the mounted officers charge again. Some of the police and horses are hit by flying stones.

The police retreat, but now there is movement of officers on foot behind the main line of shields. The officer in charge uses a loudhailer to tell the pickets he will deploy short shield units if they don't move back.

A man next to Gary says, 'A short *what*?' and then the line opens again; this time the horses are followed by policemen wearing blue crash helmets and armed with small shields and drawn truncheons.

'Bloody hell,' says the man.

Assisted by some officers without shields, the policemen in crash helmets chase the pickets as they scatter, randomly grabbing and arresting men and dragging them behind the police line. Some police and pickets throw punches, and some police beat men with their truncheons as they lie on the ground. One of the men from Gary's van, a Grimethorpe miner called Brian, does not turn to run, and is shoved aside by a policeman. Brian, who is known for his truculence and short temper, shoves back, and punches the policeman on his jaw. Seeing this, three other police officers run to Brian, knock him to the ground and half-march, half-drag him back behind their line with his arms up behind his back.

The charge lasts only a few minutes, but to Gary it feels like about half an hour. When the police withdraw the scrubland is hung with clouds of fine dust. Most of the pickets wear T-shirts, jeans, trainers and light jackets, and there are lost shoes, caps and jackets lying about on the ground, as if people have vanished leaving only their clothes behind. On the road, ambulances with flashing lights are already speeding away to take injured men to hospital. Gary finds Kenny and then the others, and they all look for Brian. When they don't find him, they guess that he has been arrested and locked up in a police van.

When the laden lorries emerge at 9.25 a.m., there is more pushing and another charge from the mounted officers and short shield squad.

To cheers from the miners, and with all the cameras turned on him, Arthur Scargill walks along the police line shaking his head in disapproval. After that the police stay in place, and most of the pickets head off to other pits, or into Orgreave village to buy food and drink from an Asda. Those who stay play football, stand about talking, or sunbathe; the strike has given them an unusual opportunity to get a suntan and some are keen to take it even here.

Gary's group eventually finds Brian sitting in the shade of some trees. He has been beaten by policemen: his face is clear but when he lifts his shirt, his torso is livid with cuts and bruising. 'No arrest,' he says. 'They just dumped me here and left me.' The men take him to a waiting ambulance, and one accompanies him to hospital. The others, made freshly determined by Brian's injuries and police tactics, drive in the transit to the picket line at Sutton colliery in Nottinghamshire. As miners arrive at Sutton through the day, they bring news of another big police charge at Orgreave, far more frightening and violent than those that had preceded it.

This charge and its aftermath are given prominence in long TV news reports from Orgreave that evening. Not long after Gary and his group had left, hundreds of police, mounted units, dog handlers and short shield squads charge those pickets remaining on the scrubland. The news reports say this is in response to stone-throwing, but the police will give various reasons and no single cause is ever established. Some police officers are seen beating pickets with their truncheons, and fights break out, but most pickets are chased to the only exit from the scrubland, a narrow footbridge over a steep-sided railway cutting. To escape, men scramble down the cutting sides, then run across the tracks and into Orgreave village. Foot and mounted police pursue them, using their truncheons and swiping down at the people on the ground with long batons. Some of the pickets throw stones, pieces of wood and old car parts from a scrapyard. A scrapped car is dragged across the road as a barricade, and set alight. Others run, or hide behind walls, or try to escape down the snickets between houses. Everywhere among the smoke and rubble there are bleeding men standing dazed or lying in the grass verges. To Gary and Elaine watching the news that evening, it resembles a scene from the troubles in Northern Ireland; it is as if an army has been sent against them. Later, Kenny calls to tell them that Brian is back home but has three broken ribs.

More than ninety men are arrested at Orgreave and put in cells, and seventy-one of them are charged with riot, which carries a maximum term of life imprisonment. A year later all are acquitted when the prosecution withdraws from the trial of the first fifteen men because of unreliable police evidence.

*

On Stuart Street, Thurnscoe, David and Marie watch a TV documentary about the strike featuring a mining village in West Yorkshire. Over opening footage of colliery headgears and terraced houses the narrator solemnly introduces 'a tough and rugged people' and talks about their long history of hardship. He continues in this vein for most of the programme, using the word 'tough' with great frequency.

David, sitting on the settee with Gemma the Labrador at his feet, frowns. 'They always go on like this about people in pit villages being tough, and I never know what they mean. Do you think it means we seem to have no emotion?'

'I don't know,' says Marie. 'I never know either.'

'Maybe it's not emotion. Maybe it's intelligence. Do you think we come over to other people as thick?'

'We might do,' she replies, thinking about it. 'I mean, we probably are thick compared to them on t' telly, aren't we?'

Midsummer is approaching, and the valley now knows that the strike will be long and not withstood by just tightening belts for a few weeks. In the banks and building societies and post offices, tellers pass the last of the savings accounts across the counter; in the back rooms of electrical goods shops, shopkeepers make stacks of washing machines, television sets and video recorders from rental agreements cancelled by mutual consent; along telephone wires, worried voices bargain down bill payments.

David and Marie worry because they have not long ago taken out a mortgage to buy their house from the NCB, and Marie painstakingly budgets, using a calculator borrowed from a neighbour. Fortunate in having an understanding manager at the building society, she works through the mortgage accounts, the gas and the electric, negotiating payments down to £1 weekly. Finally she calls Rediffusion to collect the rented television and video, and British Telecom to cut off the phone. 'It'll be like being back in my mam's front room,' she says to David. 'At least we've still got t' record player. We can sing our way through it.'

On Queen Street, Gary Hollingworth comes home one afternoon to find two bailiffs in his house with a repossession order. It is half expected; the mortgage is unpaid, and while some building-society managers allow striking miners to suspend their payments, his has insisted on a full monthly payment by the start of July. Elaine takes Scott and Claire inside to pack up their belongings, and Gary pleads for time. The bailiffs give them two hours' mercy. Without being asked, their neighbours, who have been watching repossessions on the street for the last two months, file out of their homes for a familiar drill, collecting furniture to store in their houses until the family has somewhere else to live. Gary uses the phone at Kenny's to ring the union offices at Hickleton pit yard, and four hours later someone has found them a pit house in Grimethorpe for a reduced rent for the duration of the strike.

At 229 Barnsley Road, Highgate, Lynda Burton sees through her kitchen window a Yorkshire Electricity Board meter-reader coming down the backings, and wonders momentarily if he is coming to cut them off. The odd-job work for Mr Tulley has been paying for their food, but there is barely enough money for bills, and every morning when she wakes up Lynda thinks first about Karl's new school uniform, and the gym kit and the bag and the books. Sitting at the kitchen table counting pennies and twopences into greasy little stumps, she thinks of her mam. Winnie could afford to lend a little money, but they are still not speaking and Lynda is too angry and proud to ask. When Karl goes to Winnie's house she feeds him, but otherwise, for the first months of the strike, the woman schooled in solidarity by her father saves all her pit-bred obduracy for her daughter ten doors down the street.

Winnie yields on the afternoon that the meter-reader calls. As Lynda walks back into her kitchen after showing him out she sees Karl just returned from Winnie's house and, on the table, a £10 note.

'Grandma sent it round for you. She says it's for t' electric bill.'

Lynda feels shock, and then relief. She is grateful for the money and for the armistice it signifies. At the kitchen window she watches for her mam, and when Winnie comes walking up the backings on her way back from the shops, Lynda steps out to her.

'Ho, Mother!'

She stops, and turns to face her daughter.

'Thank you for that money. And don't worry, I'll make sure you get it back.'

Standing alone on the path with her shopping bag in her hand, Winnie looks subdued, her eyes avoiding Lynda's. It is as if, having gained power, she now doesn't know how to put it to use.

'I don't want it back. I just thought it'd help you out.'

'No,' says Lynda, not knowing what to say. 'I'll pay you back when this strike's over.'

A pause; then her mam simply says 'all right' and turns to walk home with her feelings tucked in tightly about her, soft side in, like a bird's wings, or a cloak that, if she could pull it in tight enough, would make her invisible.

*

At the start of the school summer holidays, Roy sends petrol money so that Gary can drive Scott and Claire down to stay with him at the caravan. They set off one Sunday morning in the Skoda, passing roadblocks and convoys of police vans heading north. When they get to Hinckley, Roy hugs the children, and Gary puts their bags into the caravan, and they all walk down a lane hung with green leaves and laced with cow parsley until they get to Roy's local, where he is taking them for lunch.

Already in the pub are Alwyn, Wendy and her husband Steve. The other people at the bar make a fuss of Scott and Claire, and Alwyn chats with Elaine, Gary with his dad. Roy buys the drinks and everyone seems happy, in a Sunday pub lunch way. They order roast dinners, and go to sit at a large wooden table by a window.

'Where've you been all weekend, anyway?' says Roy, as they start eating. 'We thought you'd be here on Saturday.'

'I've been picketing in Nottinghamshire,' replies Gary, sitting across the table from his dad.

'*Picketing?*' says Roy, making it sound perverse. 'What do you want to go picketing for?'

Gary pauses. Please don't do this now, Dad, he thinks.

'I go because I'm fighting for my job. For t' right to work.'

'Fighting for your job! That's not a job, working in a pit.'

The other adults glance at Gary, and then at Roy. Gary absorbs the insult.

'It's a good job, and I'm providing for my family.'

Roy sneers.

'Dad, if all t' pits get closed all at one go, what do you think'll happen to t' villages?'

'They'll all have to find right jobs, and it'll do 'em good.'

Roy, the former shop steward, believes the unions call too many strikes. He voted for Mrs Thatcher in 1979 and became an enthusiastic supporter during the Falklands War. Last year he had walked into a pub where a man was arguing that the Falkland Islands should be given back to Argentina and ended up punching the man to the ground.

'And this chucking bricks at bobbies,' he says, 'it's a disgrace. They should birch 'em.'

'What about bobbies beating up miners, and riding their horses into us? We get chased for doing absolutely nowt apart from being there.'

'Chased? Who chases you?'

'Coppers. T' other day there were three of us in a car, and they were parked up stopping people. They never flagged us down, so we drove past. Next thing we knew there was a car with a load of them in behind us.'

'Why didn't you just stop?'

'There were four of them. They could've got some reinforcements and given us a good hiding.'

Roy gives a dismissive hiss. 'Give over. I've told you, get yourself a proper job and stay out of trouble.'

Gary feels his skin tingling. It is not just that he disagrees with his dad – he knew he wouldn't approve of the strike – but he wants to try to make him understand why he is taking part in it. He tries again. 'We're fighting for our communities, for them!' He looks at Scott and Claire. 'Can't you see that?'

'*Communities*,' says Roy, as if communities were fairy places. 'All that's long gone, Gary. And you're using them' – he gestures towards the children – 'to justify kow-towing to Scargill.'

Gary looks down at the table. He is aware that some of the people at the bar have gone quiet and are staring. 'I don't want to talk about it any more, Dad.'

'I'm not surprised. Scargill's playing you all for a right bunch of mugs.'

'I think he's doing an all right job. What else can he do?'

'He can stop trying to mine coal where there isn't any. He's like Hitler. He'll not achieve anything when he's done.'

'Dad –' says Wendy.

He acknowledges her and grins, to imply he is joking. 'Maggie ought to get all t' unions together and shoot 'em.'

It sounds to Gary as if his father is talking about him, but at one remove. 'What? Do *I* want shooting then, Dad?' He is hardly listening to Roy now. 'I'm on strike to try to save our jobs and communities. That's all. You can't even understand it. You can't even understand what I mean, because you'd rather listen to stories in t' newspapers and on t' telly from people who don't know what they're talking about, than try to understand me.'

'Don't tell me what I can't understand.'

Gary bolts down the rest of his food, and then goes outside. He does not speak as the party walks back to the caravan, and says only a few words to his dad when he and Elaine leave. As he drives home the angry pulse in his body persists for many miles. And then, as it quietens, he feels the lifting of a hold that Roy had had over him, and his father's power begins to shrink away like the backs of the roadsigns in the wing mirrors of Gary's car.

56

Because You Don't Know My Wife

Highgate; Stainby, North Yorkshire; the Royal Victoria Infirmary, Newcastle-upon-Tyne; Lodge Moor Hospital, Sheffield, August–December 1984

In August, Lynda and John find work at the Blacksmith's Arms, an old run-down pub on the edge of the North York Moors. A Highgate neighbour, Alf Horsman, has retired from the RAF and bought the pub with his wife. For the summer holidays they employ John to rebuild the walls and Lynda to serve at the bar, and put up the family in one of the guest rooms. It is a faultless retreat. Looking from her bedroom window over sunlit moorland seventy miles away from the tensions in the Dearne Valley, Lynda feels as if she has escaped into one long sunlit, heather-scented episode of *All Creatures Great and Small.*

A fortnight after they move there, Alf gives Lynda a lift to the Dearne so that she can collect her wages from the Goldthorpe pub. While Alf does some business in Doncaster, Lynda borrows his car to drive to Highgate to visit her mam and dad. Passing the groups of uniformed police officers, and men in jeans and T-shirts milling about at the end of the pit lanes, she feels thankful to have been away from it all.

Driving back to Doncaster after collecting her money she feels happy, and thinks about John and Karl enjoying themselves up on the moors for the rest of the summer. And then, suddenly, she feels a shock of pain in her spine so intense and severe, with cramps like carving knives stabbing into the root of her back, that she has to pull over to the side of the road. The pain subsides enough for her to drive back to Doncaster, but by the time Alf gets her home, she is writhing in the passenger seat.

It lasts all night. In the morning John calls out a doctor who says yes, backache can be a terrible thing, and prescribes strong painkillers. By the afternoon she is delirious from either the pain, the painkillers or both. When she wakes the next morning she tries to sit up, but she sways and slumps down, too dizzy to move at all. John has to carry her to the toilet, and when he lowers her to the seat her body pitches forward like a sack of water, and he has to catch her. As he carries her downstairs, she loses control of her bladder.

An ambulance takes her to Northallerton Cottage Hospital where a kind nurse fits her with a catheter and a radiographer X-rays her back. A doctor comes and says a disc in her spine has moved and she must go to the Royal Victoria Infirmary in Newcastle-upon-Tyne to be examined further. At the infirmary she is laid on her side so that long needles can be inserted into her spine and more pictures taken; the neurosurgeon, a tall, white-haired gentleman in his sixties called Mr Strong, finds a blood clot on Lynda's spine and tells her he will need to operate right away. She replies that if it means the pain going away, for all she cares he can chop off her legs with an axe.

She signs consent forms, and then she is being wheeled down to theatre. She is tired and delirious again. John is beside her for part of the way and then he is gone, and Lynda hears a nurse saying, in a Geordie lilt, 'Haven't you got lovely eyebrows, do you pluck them yourself?' And it seems very important, this conversation about eyebrows, but she can't keep track of it, and now the nurse is saying, 'Don't worry, you know, Lynda, you'll be alright. Miss Walker is here and she's the anaesthetist and she's very good, and Mr Strong is the surgeon, and Dr Good is helping . . .'

And Lynda says, 'Good . . . Strong . . . Walker.'

'Yes, that's right, pet,' says the nurse. 'Dr Good is helping, Mr Strong is the surgeon . . .'

'No, that's what I'm going to be. A good strong walker. A good strong walker . . .'

And then everything goes dark.

For two days afterwards she sleeps in the deep, dreamy pillows of anaesthesia and morphine, surfacing occasionally in the clean, hushed brightness of Newcastle General Hospital's intensive care unit to see faces she recognises. Sometimes it is the spirits: Clara, Harry's dead sister, comes to her bedside. 'They're coming to take my legs off me, Aunt Clara,' Lynda tells her.

'No, love,' says Clara. 'Nobody's coming. You're all right.'

'*Yes they are!*' insists Lynda, losing patience with the dead woman. 'You're wrong. 'They're coming, and they're going to take my legs away.'

Her mam and dad float into view, Winnie fretful, Harry weeping. They fade, and the next time it is Pauline and Gordon. Sometimes a nurse comes. Always, beside the bed, holding her hand, there is John.

When she regains full consciousness, she is in a corner of a room populated by dark-eyed, nightgowned women, all with closely shaven heads marked by thick scarring and rows of stitches. They look to Lynda as if they have recently risen from the grave. Cheerfully, in tuneful Tyneside accents, they joke about the money they will save on shampoo, and about how the hospital gowns show your bum, like a big white moon. 'Are you with us now, pet?' one of them says to her. 'Back in the land of the living?' She isn't sure until John explains to her that she is on the neurological ward, and most of the women are recovering from brain surgery.

Lynda's own surgery has left a long scar down her spine, but what troubles her, as she becomes more alert, is the numbness of her body. Apart from pins and needles in her legs, now covered in thick, thigh-length surgical stockings, she feels nothing below her chest. She flops when she tries to sit up, and realises it was this numbness that had taken her balance before. John helps her to get her torso at a right angle to the mattress, but she feels as if she is balancing the upper part of her body on an indifferent, wobbly pedestal of flesh.

When Mr Strong comes to see her he is courteous, but reluctant to commit himself. The cause of Lynda's paralysis, he says, is an old blood clot. The clot could be from decades ago, and the cause of its original coagulation is impossible to know. Most likely it was a forgotten wound, or a mole that had erupted unnoticed; an overlooked hurt from the past awaiting its moment. The clot has leaked and poisoned her spinal fluid. He has cut out the clot, but the poison is what is causing the pain and paralysis.

About her legs he says nothing. Perhaps the numbness and the falling over are just side-effects? Could his not mentioning them be a cause for optimism? 'Will the feeling in my legs come back, doctor?'

The kind and understanding white-haired head moves from side to side. 'We can't tell at the moment. We'll have to wait until the swelling and the bruising go down.'

'And what about my balance? Because if I try to sit up, I feel as if I'm falling.'

'The same. We'll have to wait for some time to pass before we know what sort of a recovery you'll make. At this stage, we can't actually tell.' ('*Before we know what sort of recovery you'll make*,' she notes. Not 'when you recover'.)

For two weeks she stays on the ward with the cheerful zombie women. Mr Strong comes to see her each day, and when she asks for a prognosis he says, 'Let's wait and see a little longer.' Each day his voice is less optimistic and a little more procrastinatory, but then again, she reflects, so long as he doesn't rule it out, there is a chance that she will walk again.

'I'm going to get better, you know,' she tells John. 'I'll show these flaming legs.'

'Tell me something I don't know,' he says.

She starts showing the flaming legs who's boss, taking all the exercises and therapies the nurses and physiotherapists offer. When the nurses ask if she'd like to sit in a chair, she sits and holds the arms to stop herself slumping; when the physiotherapist asks if she could manage the tilt table, she says, 'Bring whatever you've got.' When she fancies some chips and a nurse says, 'I'm afraid the café's on the other side of the building, pet,' she says, 'Could I have a go in a wheelchair?'

As John pushes her down the long, straight corridors she feels as though she is flying. 'Steady,' she says to him over her shoulder, 'this feels like I'm going at a hundred miles an hour.'

'We can do better than a hundred,' he says and pushes faster, and faster again, until he is running down the corridor and she is screaming and laughing at the same time.

*

So that she can be nearer to home, Lynda is transferred from Newcastle for Sheffield's Lodge Moor Hospital, a gloomy Victorian pile which sits on the city's western edges looking out over empty Peak District moorland. Built as an isolation hospital in the 1880s, it looks to Lynda, as she is lowered from an ambulance on a quiet September afternoon, like a workhouse. From under its pointy roofs, the narrow windows seem to squint at her with suspicious malice. She sees a similar expression on the first Lodge Moor nurse she meets. 'You'll do it our way here,' snaps the nurse, stripping off Lynda's surgical stockings as if she were skinning an animal. 'Flat on your back for three weeks and no moaning.' Lynda tells her that in Newcastle she exercised on tilt tables and wheelchairs, but the information is taken as an assault on the institution's authority.

'We know what we're doing. You'll be under Dr McCraig.'

'I was under Mr Strong at Newcastle. He was lovely.'

This is another perceived assault, all the more so because of the nurse's obvious admiration of Dr McCraig. 'Dr McCraig is one of the best in the country. You couldn't ask for anybody better,' she says, with a firmness that says: conversation closed.

*

The journey from Highgate to Lodge Moor is fifteen miles, two hours by connecting buses, but the miners' union loans John £60 to tax and repair the family car so that he and Karl can visit Lynda more easily. On Lynda's first day there they go with Harry and Winnie. Karl has just begun the autumn term at Dearneside school, and when he comes into Lynda's two-bed room in the Spinal Injuries Unit, he says, 'Look, Mam,' and takes off his anorak to show off his new school uniform – grey sweater, white shirt, striped tie. The white shirt sets off his honeyed summer skin and blond hair.

She looks at him but cannot speak.

'What's up, Mam?'

She squeezes his hand. 'Take no notice,' she says. 'Tell me how you came on buying your uniform.'

'Me and Grandma bought it all up Goldthorpe last week, didn't we, Grandma?'

'Yes, love,' says Winnie. 'We managed all right, didn't we?'

'Thank you, Mam,' says Lynda, wondering if this is how she will now experience her son's life: horizontal, unmoving, and listening to other people's stories about him.

For ten days she lays and waits for a doctor to tell her about her recovery. Her ward is hot and crowded with flowers. The other bed is taken by a new mother in her twenties called Nelly, who has been paralysed by a bad reaction to an epidural. Nelly lies flat too, and so she and Lynda have to converse while looking up at ceilings, as if seeing each other's meaning in the fans and light fittings.

Nelly has warned that Dr McCraig 'doesn't beat about the bush', and she is right. The man who comes to Lynda's bedside on the eleventh day is a stern, greying Edinburgh martinet who seems bored and somehow disappointed by infirmity. He mutters a greeting and talks to a nurse about Lynda's history. Then, without explanation, he takes from his pocket a slim box containing a set of long, sharp, metal pins. He sticks the pins into various parts of Lynda's body. Back, legs, bottom, feet: each time he sticks, he asks, 'Sharp or blunt?'

'Blunt,' she says the first time.

'Sharp or blunt?'

'Blunt.'

'Sharp or blunt? . . .'

After several minutes he stops, lays the pins back in their box, and returns it to his pocket. 'Well, Mrs Burton,' he says flatly, 'you're never going to walk again, I can tell you that.'

The first clear thought that forms itself concerns housework. How will she bend down to put clothes in the washing machine? How will she reach high enough to peg out clothes on a line? How will she look after Karl? Will John have to do all the cooking and cleaning? She couldn't possibly expect him to do that, but then who else can do it?

Then she thinks of shopping. How will she carry the bags, or push trolleys around supermarkets, or reach up to take packets from high shelves? She comes back to John. Will he have to do that as well? What else will she have to ask of him?

'So,' says Dr McCraig to Lynda, regarding her much as a carpenter might regard a semi-completed cabinet, 'you'll need to tell your husband what has happened. Tell him to come and see me the next time he comes to the hospital, and I'll have a word with him. While you're in here, we'll teach you how to live life in a wheelchair.'

Lynda waits for him to go, the small squeak of his shoes on the lino, the heavy, bass lurch of the doors gradually closing out the noise from the other wards. Then she lies back on the bed, pulls the blankets over her head, and slips through thoughts of John and Karl into tears and, eventually, sleep.

*

'Well,' says John when she tells him what the doctor said, 'they've got that wrong, for a start.'

'I think they know what they're talking about, John.'

He smiles and winks, trying to hide his fear. 'So do I. And I know tha'll walk again, because that's what tha's like, always fighting things. Also, tha's got me. Come here.' He leans in over the bed and hugs her. 'Right. Where's this doctor?'

In his office Dr McCraig invites John to sit down.

'Mr Burton,' he says. 'I'm sorry to tell you that your wife is not going to walk again.' Practised at this, he pauses to allow his words to settle. 'We think –'

'Who says so?'

'I'm sorry?'

'Who says she isn't going to walk again?'

'I do, Mr Burton. I've carried out all the examinations I can, and there's no question of her regaining the use of her legs when the nerves are damaged to that extent. I've seen it before.'

'I know you have,' says John. 'But you haven't seen her, have you? My point is, you don't know her.'

'But we know the results.'

'But things can work different with different people, and you don't know my wife. I reckon you don't know whether she'll walk again or not.'

'Well, I really don't believe there are any possibilities, I'm afraid.'

'We'll see. Anyway, for now you'd better show me how to manage this wheelchair.'

Another doctor comes to Lynda with the results of another test. The news: her blood is clotting in her legs, and the clots could kill her. Nurses move Lynda to a room of her own, and stick in another canula, this one attached to an anti-coagulant drip. The skin on her legs becomes so hot that it feels as if they are logs burning in a fire. Her eyes lose focus. She feels herself float up out of the bed on a tide of painkillers, her mind released from all memories and close once again to the spirits. She listens to far voices, door swings, distant clatterings in the corridors, and she imagines what it will be like to die. The sounds seem to be those of people organising life and death. Is this how it ends, she thinks; are these the last things you hear? As the painkillers wear off the thought lingers and terrifies her. She finds herself feeling overwhelmed by all the flowers people have brought; they fill her room, flowers from the florist, flowers from the garden, flowers from God knows where. She sinks into them and they close around her, and while flowers should represent love and life, their sickly sweet scent makes her think of sickness and mortality. She thinks of Muv smelling flowers when someone she knew had died.

The little room is like a sodding chapel of rest.

'Is there owt I can do for you, love?' asks a nurse.

'Yes, there is as it happens,' says Lynda. 'Get rid of these flaming flowers. All of them. I'm not dying just yet.'

As she floats near the ceiling through the late summer days and nights, she makes plans for her life in a wheelchair. She thinks hard about the practicalities. What kind of a life is John going to have with a wife in that condition? It isn't fair to him, she decides; she will have to let him go. At least they had six happy years.

When John comes next to visit by himself she says, 'I've been thinking about us, John, and I need to tell you that you don't have to stand by me. It's not fair. You're still a young man, and you could find somebody else. I shan't mind.'

John looks at her blankly.

'I mean . . . I won't be any good to you as a wife in t' physical sense, will I? Not like this. I want to set you free. It's not that I don't love you, John. It's because I do.'

'Are you kidding?'

'No.'

His mouth falls slightly open, and he stares down. Lynda's infusion pump beeps, emphasising the quietness of the room.

'But I married you because I love you. Don't send me away, Lynda. Please.'

She feels as if her chest is being wrung of its air and blood. She reaches for his hand.

'It means a lot to me, John. I'll fight it, but Dr McCraig says . . .'

'We'll do more than fight it, cocker. We'll knock it into t' middle of next week. One day you're going to walk back into this hospital, I know you are.'

How does he always make her laugh, even now?

'Is that right?'

'Aye,' he says. 'And back out again.'

*

Three weeks after the clotting is diagnosed the nurses sit her up. They increase the angle by a few degrees each day until her back is straight and she can be lifted from her bed into the grey and chrome wheelchair. She should be all right, says Dr McCraig. They'll have to watch her, but she should be all right.

She is moved to the main ward, back with Nelly and three other pale, paralysed women in casts and braces, and taken to the gym for physiotherapy. Her first exercise is the lassoing of her feet with the waistband of her jogging bottoms so that she can pull them on, a previously thoughtless job now transformed into a humiliating puzzle. The therapy gradually improves her balance, but it also makes her sharply aware of the disconnection between her mind and her unwilling body. It seems to her that this disconnection is the basic problem she must overcome. Her mind is used to commanding a responsive and easily led body; now the body has stopped listening, her mind is next to useless. She decides her best hope is to bypass the thinking, logical brain, and to try to learn to think and feel with her muscles and bones. If she could work her body from her spine, she might be able to move her legs; there were different ways the body and mind could relate to each other, after all.

The gym's Oswestry Standing Frames remind her of stories about her Grandad Parkin, and his convalescence in Oswestry after the war. Walter and Annie had used their minds to heal other people; did that mean you could use your own mind to heal yourself? On the adjoining men's ward is a young amateur motor-racing driver who is partially paralysed having broken his neck in an accident. They discuss Lynda's ideas about healing and he lends her a book about psychosomatic medicine. She reads it, and feels emboldened. At night she lies still and tries to conjure her consciousness down to the base of her spine.

*

Sitting in her chair in a corridor one day, she hears the air ambulance helicopter land in the hospital grounds. Staff hurry in a man on a gurney; his face is dirty, and he is wearing orange NCB overalls. A day later, he is brought to the ward and allocated the bed nearest Lynda's. For twenty-four hours he lies drugged-up and semi-conscious. When he comes round she says hello.

'What's up wi' you, then?'

He sighs and half whispers in a mild Scots accent, 'I've broken my back, among other things. What about yourself?'

'I've lost the use of my legs because of a spinal injury. An old blood clot leaking into my spinal fluid. What have you been doing?'

'I work at Manton pit,' he says.

Manton is in Nottinghamshire. Its 950-foot shafts are known for being among the deepest in Britain. 'I was doing a safety inspection in the shaft. They winched me down, but the cable snapped and I fell.'

'That's awful. How long did it take them to get you out?'

'About half an hour,' he says. 'But I wasn't timing it.'

'Did you say you worked at Manton?'

'Aye, why?'

'I work at Hickleton pit, near Doncaster.'

His face flickers with apprehension.

'We're on strike, though,' she says.

'Oh,' says the man. 'I see.'

The man's name is Murray Clarke. He is an undermanager at Manton and has examined the shafts throughout the strike, maintaining them so the pit would be workable when the men go back. The issue divides miners, even striking ones. Some say if the safety inspections are not carried out there will be no pits to go back to, others that if the undermanagers refuse to do them, it will force the NCB's hand. Murray says the NUM can't win; Lynda replies that if the management supported them they couldn't lose.

'We're not going to fall out about it lying here, are we?' he says.

'Yes, Murray, we are. Lying here or anywhere else.'

'Well, I can't agree with you. And I don't really think you and me'll matter much now we're in here anyway.'

'If I said I was going back to work now, I'd get sick pay and me and my husband wouldn't be struggling while I'm stuck in here, would we? We're making a difference because we're sticking together with other miners. It's unity that makes a difference.'

'So you'll lie there suffering just because you think it means that you're in the right, then.'

'Yes I will. And I'll suffer for as long as it takes.'

The argument becomes heated and ends with Lynda telling Murray not to talk to her. The silence lasts for days, and the two of them lie in their beds, or move around the wards in wheelchairs, ignoring each other. Then one evening Karl and Lynda borrow Murray's wheelchair and return it covered in 'Coal Not Dole' stickers that Karl has brought with him at visiting time.

'We've customised it for you, Murray,' says Lynda.

'That's not right! It's not even mine, or yours.'

'I know! And there's nowt you can do about it, is there? Because you're laid there and you can't shift any faster than me.'

After that they become friends, and do physio together. Murray regains some strength, but Dr McCraig tells him he will never walk again.

Lynda is due to leave for home just before Christmas. She spends the remaining weeks exercising in the gym, with John encouraging her, or trying to get her mind and body into their new alignment. The week before she is discharged, Dr McCraig comes to look at her legs. 'Try to wriggle your toes,' he says, with no real expectation that any wriggling will take place.

Trying her new technique of thinking in her limbs rather than with her brain, she focuses on moving her feet. The doctor looks surprised. 'How long have you been able to do that?'

'What?'

'Wriggle your toes.'

'I didn't know I could.'

'The toes on your left foot are wriggling, which is interesting,' he says. 'We'll look at that when you come back for physio. Happy Christmas.'

57

Riddling Ashes for Coal

Thurnscoe; Goldthorpe; Thurcroft, South Yorkshire; Kiveton Park, South Yorkshire, November 1984

After the battle at Orgreave, relations between striking miners and police in South Yorkshire change. There are more and more police vehicles on the roads, until it seems impossible to travel anywhere without passing convoys of them: Black Marias, minibuses, armoured coaches, sometimes fifty, sixty or seventy at a time. On picket lines police rattle shields, wave pay packets, threaten to call in riot squads. Many of the men being bussed into work wear hoods to obscure their faces, and the men on strike say, Aye, of course they do, because they're not miners. The common belief remains that they are stooges brought in so the Coal Board can say men are working.

In the front room of 239 Barnsley Road, Harry, having abandoned the television, works the dial of his radio, picking up police frequencies and hearing the fuzzy disembodied voices of an invading army. He and Winnie compare it to the strike of 1926, and remark that this 1984 is like the adaptation of George Orwell's *Nineteen Eighty-four* they had watched on the BBC thirty years ago. Both support the striking miners, though Harry is less sure about the cause. When Gary calls in with Scott one Saturday morning, he tries to win his grandad's approval by describing the places he has been on picket duty, and numbering the jobs and pits that the strike will save. 'Well, it's up to you,' says Harry. 'But I've told thee before what I think. If it were up to me I'd shut all t' lot of 'em.'

Talks between the union and the Coal Board are on, then off, then on, then off. Mrs Thatcher makes a speech in which she says that, having defeated the enemy without (Argentina), Britain now has to defeat the enemy within (the striking miners). Some other unions come out on strike in support, but not to the extent that the NUM members had hoped. Pits in some areas are still working, and Coal Board representatives have secret meetings with working miners – as yet a minority of the national membership – to discuss breaking and ending the strike. David Hart coordinates the campaign and organises legal action against the NUM from a suite at Claridge's.

In August, with the TUC's September conference looming, the Coal Board renews its efforts to get striking miners back to work. More men claiming to be from the NCB visit families they know to be in heavy debt and flash wads of £10 notes, offering them as incentives to break the strike. If the men are not in, they work on the wives. 'Tell him to get his sen back to work, love,' they advise, like the husband's best pal trying to make him see sense. 'You tell him. He'll get looked after, and it'll all be over soon anyroad.' At the same time more police flood the Dearne villages. Some of them, mainly officers from distant forces, burn £10 notes in front of miners and say come on, keep it going, you're paying for my kitchen extension, you're paying for our holidays. Some of them work on the women. When Marie's twenty-year-old niece Sandra walks past police officers standing outside the Station Hotel on her way to catch the bus to work, they shout at her, 'Oi slag! You fucking a miner then, love?' and call her a whore. After a week of it Sandra asks her boyfriend Chris, a miner at Hickleton Main, to walk her to the bus stop, but then she worries all the way to work in case they have beaten him up.

The violence gets worse as late summer gives way to autumn. Working and striking miners attack each other. There are stories of catapults and petrol bombs and besieged police stations; the *Barnsley Chronicle* says local police officers have found crates of petrol bombs ready for use. Some police seem to treat their work as a sport now, a private battle between themselves and the pickets. They adopt the tactic of damaging cars so that pickets cannot travel. A story circulates: a car carrying four men, including two brothers, is stopped on its way to Warsop colliery at four in the morning. Instead of it being turned back, police in riot gear pull one of the men out of the car and smash in the car's back window sending glass over the passengers in the back. One of the brothers and his friend get out and the police tell the men to run, and then chase them for more than a mile. When the miners get back to their car, every window is smashed, the side mirror is off, the roof is damaged and the left-hand side kicked in.

One tactic that has been used since the start of the strike, and one that has become more common, is for police to arrive in large numbers and block off streets and wasteland near the collieries so that the police at the colliery gates can use charges to drive the pickets into villages. The retreating men will then find an unexpected bank of uniformed or riot-geared police blocking their way; often they end up in some backings. The police will then charge in, beating men in the street and in gardens. The noise and the speed of it all are awful to see, and people from mining and non-mining families open their house doors to urge men inside, and the police pursue them.

To the families of men on strike, the television coverage of the chasing and the fighting seems to only ever tell one side of the tale. There are pickets who have attacked policemen, but the news rarely shows the truncheon beatings, or the pale faces among the miners whom no one knows, and who are always where the trouble is. On the television news interviewers now ritually ask Arthur Scargill to condemn pickets throwing stones and beating policemen, and Mrs Thatcher compares the miners on picket lines to the IRA. When Scargill says he won't condemn his pickets because the government won't condemn the police, he is criticised in the press, but the striking miners ask what else he can say, when stories and rumours like this are going around?

In all the negotiations and the debates, the argument comes back to the union leadership refusing to accept pit closures on economic grounds, and the NCB saying they are being unrealistic. But while this, and the unemployment that will result from closures, are the political issues that can be articulated simply, there is a belief in the Dearne Valley that the government's chief aim is to weaken the union – and that weakening the union is the decisive step to diminishing the gains that mining people have made through the twentieth century. Closing a colliery could close down a social system, and to Lynda, John, Gary and David Hollingworth at least, it feels as if the government and the police want to attack those systems as much as they want to close coal mines.

*

The TUC promises more support, and there are more court actions against the NUM challenging the union's claim that the strike is official. The government sequestrates funds and assets of the South Wales area over an unpaid fine for disrupting road hauliers' business. As he sits in a debate at the Labour Party conference in Blackpool's Winter Gardens, Arthur Scargill is served with a writ to appear in court. A week later, Lord Justice Nicholls in the High Court fines the NUM £200,000 and Scargill £1,000 for contempt. The fines are ignored, and Nicholls orders the sequestration of the NUM's assets, though the sequestrators have difficulty locating the money, much of which has been moved abroad. By November, the union will have had all its funds sequestrated and become the first trade union to be placed in the hands of a receiver by the High Court.

But there is a boost for the strike from the NACODS men. Hitherto they have not gone on strike, but have continued to refuse to cross picket lines except to do essential maintenance. If they breached the strike it would be impossible to work with the men afterwards, and anyway, many of them object to working when NUM members are out. When the Coal Board sends a letter to NACODS members insisting that they cross NUM picket lines or lose their pay, they respond by voting to strike themselves, demanding assurances about the future of the industry and offering to act as go-betweens in talks between the NCB and the NUM. This worries government ministers because pits cannot operate without NACODS; if they walk out, every pit in the country will come to a halt and the coal supply to the power stations will be cut off. Having previously opposed the involvement of the state arbitration service ACAS, the government now relents and the NUM, NACODS and the Coal Board begin talks.

On Monday 15 October, three days after the IRA bombs the Grand Hotel in Brighton, where the Conservative Party is holding its annual conference, the talks collapse, and the NACODS leaders say they will strike from 25 October. They publicly protest that the government appears to want to see the miners beaten rather than agree a settlement; in turn, the government backs down, denying that there is a list of pits to be closed, and accepting the NACODS suggestion for a fresh closure procedure involving a new independent review body. For a few days it seems as though the NCB will make concessions, the threatened pits will stay open and a compromise will be reached. Then, suddenly, it is all off – the NUM accusing NACODS of reneging on part of their agreement, NACODS seeming to accept assurances rather than choosing to strike and win. The striking miners in the Dearne are disappointed, but unsurprised.

Days later, the BBC correspondent Michael Buerk reports from refugee camps in Ethiopia about the country's 'biblical-scale' famine. The story attracts a wave of public sympathy; pop stars collaborate on a single to raise money for the refugees; the single released the next month stays at number one for five weeks. Meanwhile on 28 October, the *Sunday Times* carries a front-page story about NUM chief executive Roger Windsor meeting Colonel Gaddafi to ask for money on behalf of the union. Many striking miners suspect the story is propaganda, but it will have political repercussions for twenty years. The ACAS talks collapse on 31 October, the news pushed back in the bulletins by coverage of Indian Prime Minister Indira Gandhi's assassination by her bodyguards, and more about the famine in Ethiopia. By November it is clear that the other unions are not, in fact, going to do much striking in support of the NUM. The miners' strike is beginning to feel like old news.

*

The failure of the NACODS deal is disappointing, but to David and Gary Hollingworth's families the summer and autumn's events increase their determination to stay out until they win some concessions from the Coal Board.

David Hollingworth goes on picket duty, first at Hickleton Main and Grimethorpe, and then out to Rossington near Doncaster and down to Nottinghamshire and Derbyshire, believing that if the working men can be persuaded to come out, the strike can still be won and the threatened pits kept open. He gets some work potato-picking with a gang of miners from Bolton-upon-Dearne, and to save money he and Marie pick out winter clothes for Lisa from second-hand stalls on the market, and fill up on pies at the soup kitchen. They add to their food supplies with aid parcels donated by the public and channelled through the Church or the union. Their first one is made up of tinned food from Russia; one tin has a picture of a strange black bird on the front and contains grey meat, which Marie makes into a pie to make it seem less off-putting. The second contains a pair of second-hand Wellington boots from Iceland.

For fuel, David riddles ashes on the rubbish tip across the road from Hickleton pit. Until the mid-sixties the tip had been used for household refuse, but since then it has been fenced off and forgotten about. Patches of weeds and long grass now grow out of it among bits of old furniture and rusting metal, and parents try to warn their children off playing there with stories of rats. Decay and treading down by kids has lowered the tip, but it is still bulked up high, stretching back into the fields and looking almost like something alive in which you can make out the broken forms of things people have used – sofas, motorcycle forks, busted stereo speakers. Below these things, buried deep down, is decades of ash from people's home fires. If you take from these ashes the burned clinkers, and put those clinkers onto a coke-burning inset fire like a Parkray or Rayburn, they will burn again, and this free fuel brings Thurnscoe's striking miners to the tip with sacks, shovels, barrows and homemade wood-and-wire riddles.

Early on autumn mornings in 1984, packs of men in battered coats and jackets clamber over the tip's surface, stopping to dig out old ashes, and sift them through their riddles to leave the clinkers, which they empty into barrows and sacks. Across the road, behind the colliery, others climb the pit spoil heap and riddle for pieces of coal discarded with the waste. Everywhere the men keep a wary lookout for private security guards employed by the Coal Board to patrol the heaps and keep them free of scavengers.

In the between-light of half past seven one morning in November, David is here with a homemade riddle and an old, heavy wooden barrow borrowed from his next-door neighbour. He shovels the ashes from the old fires into the riddle, and then shakes the riddle so that the solid, burnable coals are left. After picking out any stray tin cans, he tips the coals into a wheelbarrow or sack held by a mate. Everyone is trying to fill as many sacks as their trolleys can carry. Because the coke burns faster than new, several sacks are needed if you want to be sure of having enough hot water for two baths.

Earlier, as usual, he and the other Thurnscoe miners had been down to the pit gates to picket the six o'clock shift. Since the summer, four men have gone back to work at Hickleton. One of them lives over the fields in the next village, South Elmsall; the other three had always kept themselves to themselves at work. Last week the union reps had been to see the South Elmsall man and he had told them he would not go in again, but this morning he had been on the bus.

'He'll be sat drinking bloody tea in t' lamp room now,' says Ian Alder, riddling next to David, as sifted grey dust falls onto his boots.

'They'll not be riddling coke,' says David. It is cold, and his fingers on the shovel are white. Scraps of wind blow Ian's ashes about.

'No, same as them buggers,' says another man, looking across to a cluster of policemen standing near a van outside the pit. 'Supping coffee from their flasks on three hundred quid a week overtime.'

Ian notices someone coming up the slope towards them. 'No . . . Ayup, he's here again. What's he want this time?'

Struggling towards them, hands bunched in his anorak pockets and collar turned up against the cold, is a man with his hair loosely combed up into a quiff which the wind tugs down around his ears.

'Hey guys,' he says as he comes within earshot. 'How are you doin' this mornin', huh?'

'Ayup, Jed,' says David.

'Hey, David.' The American accent sounds stronger in this setting. 'You think I'm lookin' like Elvis?'

'Bloody hell, Jed. We're standing on Thurnscoe tip.' Ian edges away, smiling.

'Sure, but in myself?'

David puts down his shovel and leans on it. There is something about the situation that makes him feel the need to be truthful. 'To be honest, Jed,' he says, 'I've always thought you look more like a young Tom Jones.'

*

One morning around the same time, Gary is at Thurcroft, a village just outside Sheffield, waiting with some mates for the other pickets. It is cold and half dark, with sparse birdsong in the damp dawn air. They have parked up at the side of the road, and they stand about, blowing on hands, hunching shoulders and swapping lapel badges.

A police van drives towards them. It stops ten yards back, and a policeman climbs out of the cab. He is Thames Valley Police. His manner is typical of the police now, more authoritarian.

'Move on, please.'

'What for? We're not hurting anybody,' says Gary. It is strange; before the strike, he would never have disagreed with a police officer let alone denied his orders. But no one is awed by the police any more.

The police officer's radio fuzzes loudly. Voices and clicks. It sounds absurd out here in the still village morning, as if an extra-terrestrial had fluffed his arrival by landing in Thurcroft instead of London.

'We've got to keep this road open.'

The men groan. Is this the best he can do?

Gary says, 'What for?'

'For people going to work.'

'For people going to work? This is Thurcroft!' says Gary.

'As I said.'

'It's a pit village! Everybody works at t' pit! Where do you think we are, Surbiton?'

The policeman stares at Gary, and at the rest of the men. It is intended as a show of strength, but it seems ridiculous. Everything about the scene seems ridiculous. The policeman turns and walks back to the van.

More police arrive. Then more pickets, then more police. They are all a long walk from the colliery.

'Jesus,' someone among the pickets calls out. 'How many o' thee does it take?' An officer silently points over their heads, and the lads look around. Behind them, past houses and mist-hung stubble fields, they can see the M18 motorway, which runs along the village's western edge; on a tangle of flyovers and sliproads for the M1 junction more police vans are heading towards the village. The horizon across the fields glows giddy with blue lights. Gary wonders where the vans are going, and then realises the pickets are being set up.

Horse vans park up down the road, and half a dozen mounted officers clop towards the rear of the hundred men on the police line. All for sixty-odd pickets.

They're doing what they like now, he thinks. They've won the PR, they know the television news will cover them. In recent weeks he has felt the atmosphere becoming more brutal. In October some men had gone back to work in Grimethorpe where the strike has to date been solid. Windows were smashed, the word 'SCAB' spray-painted on house doors and people had attacked the police station and thrown stones at the mounted police. It was hard to imagine that happening in any of the villages when he was growing up in the sixties. The whole mood had changed, somehow.

'Come on,' someone in the crowd says. 'We'll not finish this. It's Maggie's militia.' The men walk back to their cars, and drive off in different directions. On the motorway, the vans are still coming. Gary's driver takes them to look for food: roadkill, potatoes taken from field edges, winter vegetables from farms in Lincolnshire.

*

On the damp blue autumn morning of 14 November, the violence comes to Goldthorpe. There has been little trouble here all the way through the strike, even when a man was bussed to work in a blare of police vans that hurtled into the village and past the pickets lined at either side of the road, and through the pit gates. But then, on the fourteenth, a larger detachment of policemen is brought in in a fleet of white vans that parks along Doncaster Road.

At the start of the first shift, the policemen push back the pickets from the pit gates, and a bus carries in a handful of men who are said to be working. There is pushing and jeering, and then the gates close and the pickets ease back, lingering beside the road. As the morning wears on women pass on their way to the shops, ignoring the police still outside the pit, and men and women come to their doors, stand on doorsteps, talk to the pickets. Suddenly, police vans and police in riot clothing are coming down the road towards them all. There is a stand-off, a charge, and then coming up the road in the other direction, more police. The streets are in tumult: men run over the allotments, down the railway bankings, up side streets and down the backs. Police officers follow. Passers-by try to get out of the way. Coming out of the supermarket Jack Gundry, Pam's husband, almost fifty now, sees police officers chasing after men, snatching the older, slower ones from the back and hauling them to the ground as the younger ones escape into the backings and snickets. Winnie is at home. When friends call later on to tell her about it, she and Harry say they cannot believe it; their mums and dads would never have believed it: police chasing people on the streets like they had in flaming 1926.

A few days later two brothers from Goldthorpe, Darren and Paul Holmes, aged fourteen and fifteen, are killed while digging for coal in the railway embankment opposite Bob's Diner, as Rocky Wall's old café is now called. Ten feet below the surface there is a coal seam which had been dug out in the 1920s and 1970s and was now being dug out again. Most of the diggers are children and teenagers looking for coal to give to their parents or to sell. The further anyone digs, the more the holes become tunnels. On Sunday 19 November, Darren and Paul and two other boys are digging into the embankment when the roof caves in. People including the boys' father try to dig them out, but they both die as a result of their injuries. Of the other two boys, one has broken legs and the other, John Farmer, gets out unhurt. It is John that does the interviews on the national news night-time bulletins. Karl Grainger, who has known the two dead boys since they were at junior school together, watches stunned as the reporters try to frame the event with strike angles. Did this say something about the times? Did people blame the strike, or even the government? No, say the people, who are more familiar than the reporters with the random dangers of digging the earth for coal, no, not really. That's not how it works. It was an accident, and it ought to be left at that.

*

Christmas is coming. Understanding that mothers and fathers are trying to work out how they will buy turkeys and a bit o' summat for the kids to open on Christmas morning, the NCB sends letters to miners offering a Christmas bonus and holiday money if miners report back to work by 19 November. 'You can't go back,' says Elaine to Gary, 'but what will we do for t' kids? We need more than you and Kenny can make riddling coal on Grimey stack.' The bonus money is a lot more than you can make riddling coal on the stacks, a lot more; on the TV news on the Monday after the letter is sent, Ian MacGregor says hundreds of miners have gone back that morning, though he doesn't mention the bonus.

At Dearneside school one breaktime, Karl Grainger's best friend accidentally gives away that his dad has gone back to work, and the boys look at each other, frozen. Now Karl understands why his friend has new shoes and smart uniform while the other miners' kids' clothes are make-do. He thinks his friend's dad is wrong, but he sees the sudden fright in his mate's face. Knowing that the other kids whose dads are working have been cut dead by the rest of the school, he changes the subject and says nothing.

Across the coalfields the picket lines are bitter, the threats, beatings and missiles worsen. Norman Willis, the General Secretary of the TUC, addresses miners in the sports centre at Aberavon, South Wales, and men who have climbed into the roof space dangle a rope noose above his head because he is blaming the pickets for the trouble. Two weeks later, also in South Wales, two striking miners in their early twenties drop a concrete block and a concrete post from a bridge onto a taxi taking a working miner, David Williams, to Merthyr Vale colliery. The concrete goes through the taxi windscreen, killing the driver, a thirty-five-year-old man called David Wilkie who has three children and whose fiancée is seven months pregnant.

The police had taken special measures that week to get working miners into collieries, blocking off roads against pickets. Expecting violence, taxi drivers had been accompanied by police cars and motorcycles, and given police riot helmets to wear. On the radio and television news Arthur Scargill says he is deeply shocked by the tragedy. Mrs Thatcher says she is angry at the wrong against the family of a man who 'was only doing his duty and taking someone to work who wanted to go to work'. Kim Howells, a South Wales NUM official, blames the death on the Coal Board's attempts to get miners back to the pits.

In Nottinghamshire, working miners begin assembling their own breakaway organisation, the Union of Democratic Mineworkers. More talks between the NUM and the Coal Board break up with nothing achieved, and the union leaders hold more rallies in the villages. Scargill comes to speak at one at Goldthorpe's Welfare Hall, but when Gary and Elaine walk away at the end, Elaine says, 'Will he be going hungry, though?' and Gary wonders if the women see it all more clearly than the men.

At the end of November, he joins the picket at Kiveton Park, a pit village outside Sheffield near to where Walter Parkin was born. As they stand on the long, straight road leading down to the pit, the police put up lights that shine intense white arcs into the pickets' eyes and turn on a machine that emits a high-pitched noise. Word goes about that somewhere down the road a picket has been trampled by a horse. Using loudhailers the police shout orders: 'Make way! Make way! You are obstructing the path of an ambulance.'

But no one can see an ambulance.

'Where?' The unamplified pickets' voices sound puny.

'We have a casualty. Stop obstructing the ambulance.'

Everyone is looking around. 'You lying bastards, we're not stopping you! You've not even asked for one.'

'Disperse now. We have a casualty.'

Then, without warning, the police lines part to allow through a dozen mounted policemen. The horses gallop into the pickets. In the darkness Gary sees the long truncheons, and the sparks off horseshoes on tarmac.

With the rest of the men he runs for the grass verge. The horses pull up, rein in and go back, and there is a stand-off. Someone says there is a big picket gathering at Harworth, ten miles east. The officers are calling reinforcements in from other collieries. He watches now, but he senses the police will come at them again.

Everyone senses it. In the doorways of houses facing the road, men and women appear and shout to the fleeing miners, come on, get in here quick – and then slam the door shut as the men go inside. But the mounted police charge again, and the foot police follow, smashing the doors open with boots and shoulders. As they enter one garden a woman rushes to the door. 'What are you doing? There's no one in this house!'

The policeman shouts into her face, 'Get out the fucking way, you fucking Yorkshire whore!' She flinches. He kicks the door open and stomps inside, three other policemen following, straight through her house, and out of the back door into the backings.

Soon, it's all the way up the street: police kicking in doors, marching in, dragging men out of houses. Gary sees one mounted policeman ride right up to a house with a broken door, and the horse put its head through the doorway. Women shouting, men shouting, kids crying, dogs barking; and, all along the road, police shouting in their strange accents.

Fucking Yorkshire slags.

Fucking Northern bitches.

Fucking Northern bastards in their fucking Northern slums.

The street lights and the pit lights are still on, but daylight is breaking. Over the rooftops the sunrise looks beautiful.

58

Coming Round the Mountain

Highgate, December 1984

On 21 December, Lynda comes home to Highgate, having told the doctors she wants to be out by Christmas so that she can cook the dinner ('I'm doing it!' she tells John. 'Your mam pokes t' roast taties too much.') John hoiks her up into his arms from the front seat of their Austin Allegro, missing the catheter bag so it swings wildly free, making Lynda shriek with laughter, and carries her into the house at chest-height, like a bride. Finally he lays her on the bed, runs a bath, undresses her, lowers her into the bath so she can wash herself. When she has finished he carries her back to the bed.

'This is the life!' she says.

'Don't get used to it,' says John. 'I'm starting your exercise regime as soon as you've settled in.'

And he does. A friend has lent them an old exercise bike, and John lifts her from her chair into its saddle. She wobbles because of her lost balance, and tumbles sideways.

'I don't know if I can do it, John.'

'You've got to do it. Get on.'

He holds her up with one arm, and with the other hand reaches down to her feet, and puts them on the pedals. The foot that she can wiggle flips, flaps and falls off. He puts it back on. It flaps off again, like a heavy, finless fish. She tries to fix it with her will, but while she can make it move, she cannot control the movements that it makes.

On again. Off again. On. Off.

'Just a minute,' says John. 'Wait there.'

'In case you haven't noticed, I don't have much choice.'

He brings a ball of white string from the kitchen and moves the bike so Lynda can lean against a wall. Then he bends down and ties her feet to the pedals. 'Now pedal.'

'What if I fall off?'

'Don't fall off. And a little less conversation, please. Just *pedal*.'

*

Christmas Day. At half-past two Lynda is in her steam-soaked kitchen with the vegetables boiling on the hob and the turkey in the oven. She wanted to cook on her own, so John is out, and Karl at Winnie and Harry's. So far she has coped in the wheelchair, though it is strange to have her pans and worktops at chest height, unbalancing her if she stretches too far towards them. It is the balance that does for her when she opens the oven door to slide out the turkey for basting. The weight pulls her forward, she jerks back and the roasting tray tips, spilling scalding hot fat over the oven and floor. She twists away. 'Damn you! Bloody damn you!' She shoves the tray back in, slams the door and in anger grabs the nearest object, a full bottle of washing-up liquid, and hurls it across the kitchen towards the door. The bottle thuds against something, and the thing says, 'What the bloody hell's that for? Happy Christmas to thee an' all.'

'Dad?'

He looks at her, and at the fat on the floor.

'What's up wi' you?'

'This bloody thing.' She gestures at her wheelchair, and bursts into tears.

'Ayup,' he says. 'Shut up and come on. Tha'll be all right.'

She would like him to put his arms around her. He has done it before: she thinks of her twenty-first birthday party when he asked the DJ to play 'The Wonder of You' and held her close as they danced around the dancefloor. She knows that would be hard for him in private, though; it is the shyness of the comedian.

It had been clear when they visited her that both Harry and Winnie had been harrowed by Lynda's disability. Beside their daughter's hospital bed, Winnie had cried a little, but had in the main appeared stalwart and encouraging. But with Jane Seels, Winnie had sobbed and confessed to feeling guilty because of her estrangement from Lynda at the time she was admitted to hospital. She had also thanked John for helping Lynda, and then even hugged him, her embrace a sort of apology-gift to them both.

'I know,' Lynda says to her dad, as he puts the washing-up bottle back on the side, 'I will be all right. I'm just feeling sorry for myself.'

'You will be,' he says. 'I know thee.'

Harry is better at doing than talking. In the New Year, he helps Lynda and John to put into action a plan that Lynda made in hospital when she watched a woman walking her dogs on the moor. Together they teach Sam the sheepdog to fetch and retrieve household items in the way that he might have brought sheep for a shepherd. Lynda drills him in bringing her clothes and shoes. John hangs a low clothes line, and she trains Sam to carry the peg basket, and to pick up the pegs that she drops. Harry shows him how to bring sticks from the yard when she is making a fire. It becomes an act at parties: Sam the dog who collects pegs, followed by Karl wheelie-ing the wheelchair around the back garden without touching the front wheels down once.

Lynda attends physio sessions and check-ups at the hospital, and, with John's help, repeats the cycling exercise with the foot she can move. One gloomy morning in February, when the news has been about more miners going back to work, and police vans with keening sirens have been racing up and down Barnsley Road, John helps Lynda into the bath, carrying her from the bedroom over his shoulder like a fireman. He helps her wash herself, and then when she is clean wraps a towel about her and carries her back to the bedroom, dripping over him and the carpet like a bath-warm, Imperial Leather-scented mermaid. He flops her onto a towel laid over the bed. 'Now, you get dried, while I get in t' bath.' Always businesslike and crisp, as if not being able to use your legs is like having a sprained wrist. Lynda, laughing, hauls herself up and sits on the bed edge, and begins drying herself.

From the bathroom comes the sound of her husband splashing and singing 'I'll Remember You'. Through the outside window, beaded with condensation, she sees the squat, strong white-headed shape of Winnie walking slowly down the backings.

Now for her legs. She imagines her mind being in the whole of her body, instead of her brain. She tries to feel her feet without being aware that she is feeling them. Room and house recede. She imagines dancing. She remembers the little girl dancing the part of a bewitched fairy for Mrs Buxton.

'I can't hear you moving! Come on and get those legs going,' calls John. 'We're off jiving tonight!'

When she thinks about something happening, the thinking is what seems to prevent it. It feels more a matter of letting it happen. 'Don't think "connect",' she says, 'just do it.'

Just do it. Suddenly her leg shoots up violently, a damp white, warm limb rearing up before her. It falls back. She thinks it must have been a spasm. She tries to stop thinking and allow the connection, and her leg shoots up again. Then it falls, and rises again.

'John!'

He jumps out of the bath and comes running to the bedroom.

'Look what I can do!'

Her leg is sticking up at ninety degrees to the mattress, and she is keeping it there.

59

Loser's Medals

Grimethorpe colliery, March 1985

In the days leading up to Christmas, the Dearne Valley had been determined to have a good time regardless of money, and it seemed that everyone, miners and non-miners alike, had been generous in trying to help each other. The collection boxes outside G. T. Smith's filled more rapidly, and in Bolton-upon-Dearne, the union men left their homes on Saturday and Sunday mornings to find their front gardens scattered with a silver snow of coins thrown over by villagers walking home from the pubs and clubs. Afterwards there was an unspoken feeling among the striking families that, having coped with Christmas, they should keep going for a full year. Most do, but in the new year the atmosphere in the villages flattens like January light. Christmas had brought people together, but without that to think about the daily challenge of paying for food and bills preoccupies their minds again. The Coal Board offers new incentives for men to go back, and across the country thousands accept them.

New negotiations between the Coal Board and union fail, and the board reneges on the agreement it made with NACODS about reviewing pit closures. The police still seem like an occupying army, and on picket lines the violence continues. One morning Gary and Kenny are at Denby Grange colliery, in the hilly upper reaches of the Dearne Valley, when pickets build a barricade across the road with planks from a timberyard. The police charge them, and Gary and Kenny are chased through woodland by two policemen with dogs, escaping only by clambering over a high wire fence. Revenge and feuding: when the police clatter you with a Perspex shield or push your face into the road they say, 'That's for South Kirkby', 'That's for Goldthorpe', 'That's for Kiveton Park'.

By mid-February, getting on for half of the striking miners across the country have gone back to work. Knowing they have lost, but in many cases thinking they will regroup and strike again later, Yorkshire NUM delegates try to salvage jobs, refusing to return unless the Coal Board declares an amnesty for the striking miners it has sacked for misconduct during the strike. The Coal Board isn't listening, though, and on Sunday 4 March, a national conference of NUM delegates votes to go back with no agreement.

In Grimethorpe, Gary Hollingworth listens to the news on the radio with Elaine, and David and Marie, who have come over for tea. 'I want to say this,' Arthur Scargill tells the miners and journalists gathered in the rain outside the Trades Union Congress headquarters in London. 'We have been involved in the greatest industrial struggle ever seen. I want to say to each and every one of you, I want to thank you from the bottom of my heart.' The two brothers and their wives look at each other, raise their eyebrows and exhale in the way people do when confronted with an event that is somehow both inevitable and unimaginable.

'All for nowt, then,' says Gary, and for several minutes nobody says anything. They feel a loss that is similar to bereavement, but also relief at the prospect of returning to their old lives, although no one will admit that for a while.

*

On the first day back, the families walk to their pits together behind the union banners. In Thurnscoe, under low grey clouds, David Hollingworth pushes Lisa in the buggy, and Marie leads Gemma, their Labrador; in Grimethorpe, Gary and Elaine walk with Claire, Scott being at school; in Goldthorpe, Lynda and John stay at home, worried that they would not cope if fighting broke out between miners and police. At Dearneside school, where the headmaster suspends classes so the pupils can watch the march go past, Karl Grainger pushes his face to the railings and feels a flush of pride. A few older pupils shout at policemen, and some wave to their parents, but mostly the children and their teachers are quiet as the procession passes. Later, the atmosphere in school is uncanny. Teachers and pupils abandon lessons and spend most of the day talking about their families, and the police, and the stories being told in the villages. Karl will remember the day in adulthood, long after the last pits in the Dearne Valley have been closed and their yards demolished and landscaped.

A few days later, on the first pay day after the strike, Elaine Hollingworth accepts Gary's pay packet as he hands it to her in the kitchen, sorts the money, and then pushes a greasy green pound note back across the table. 'Here, take that and have a pint,' she says. 'Bugger t' electric this week.'

'Better not.'

'Take it.' He picks up the note, and looks at it, and is surprised at the thought that comes to him, even as he thinks it. 'A pound to spend. A full pound.'

Ten thousand men across the coalfields have stayed out, and the rest are bearish, their moods gnarled and kinked. Mates sacked because they were convicted of minor, trumped-up offences are banned even from coming into their colliery yards, and those awaiting court hearings cannot go back until they have been tried. Those who worked risk ridicule or worse; managers put them on menial jobs away from the other men or, if they are lucky, transfer them to new pits a distance away.

The moment Gary will remember most often from those first days back comes on a cold drizzly afternoon in the yard. Mick Penny, who works in the headings, comes to work in an anorak decorated with the badges he has collected during the strike. He goes to the ventilation engineers' hut to collect some equipment, and while he waits outside for someone to bring some parts for it, Gary looks at the anorak. Other men from the team come over to look, which makes Mick laugh. A minute later, noticing the little cluster of men gathering, Mr Lumb, one of the managers, detours from a purposeful walk across the pit yard. Mr Lumb is a self-assured man in his early fifties, who makes a show of being straightforward, open and jocose with the men, but takes no sincere interest in anyone below him in rank. When he comes up, the men's laughter dies away. He follows the men's eyes to Mick's jacket.

'I see tha's got thy loser's medals on, then!'

It is the joke of a man who you know wouldn't be able to take one back. The joke of a man who hasn't been without wages for a year. It is all he says. After a moment of silence, he grunts and walks off, making the gravel laugh stiffly under his boots. The men look at each other. Mick raises his eyebrows, another man curses under his breath. Gary feels his heart quicken and his breathing grow fast and shallow. He shakes his head, says, 'I'm off to find them parts for thee,' and heads off across the yard.

He walks anywhere, moving to shake down the adrenaline; past piles of wood, rusting coal hoppers, brick office buildings. The strike had been for Lumb's job, too, hadn't it? The managers didn't want pits to close any more than the other men and women who worked there. The galling thing about men like that was, if you complained about them as a group, they called you a militant or said you have a chip on your shoulder.

He pauses for a moment at the point at which he can see the conveyor belts carrying dirt to the spoil heaps in the distance, the mud and coal and silt gushing off at the ends like a waterfall. He feels the wet spring drizzle lightly whipping his face, and he squints against the wind.

The dirt pours down. Behind him in the yard someone calls his name. He turns and walks back to work.

PART EIGHT

60

Moonlight Promenade

Barnsley Road between Highgate and Darfield, 1985

At the age of seventy-five, Harry Hollingworth still goes to Highgate Club most weekday evenings, sipping at pints of bitter, taking in the news, joining the banter and disputes. Sometimes John is in the club too, and they walk back together. If he isn't there Harry sets his empty glass on the bar at half past ten, and strolls home alone, back to the house where Winnie will have left a slice of bread iced with pale grey dripping and brown-jelly crust for his supper. By the time he arrives she will be in bed, reading a Catherine Cookson novel and listening for the garden gate latch to briefly sound his safe return.

One night in the spring of 1985, when the showery rain has made the streets smell of wet soil, Harry walks home along the Barnsley Road as usual, murmuring an old song over the pavement-click of the segs in his brogues. The Halfway Hotel is still warm and noisy, the farm and the school on the crossroads silent and still. As he passes down the road, cars whizz past carrying shiftworkers and people heading home after nights out, and he glimpses through curtain cracks people eating their suppers and watching TV. This is the road along which he and Millie had cycled on their way to perform in Skegness, and the road edge where he used to stand with his father to watch the motor cars when they were new and rare. It may be because he is lost in such imaginings tonight that he does not notice the pavement beneath his feet turn to grass, and the segs in his shoes falling silent as they move from asphalt to soft, noiseless earth on the edge of the village.

He passes the lowing, muck-musked farmyard that marks the western extent of Highgate and wonders why he hasn't yet come to his own house, but he keeps on walking into the darkness. Open countryside, faster cars; the open fields stretch away into the Pennine landscape and vehicle headlamps make fans of cream light in the blackness. Suddenly he seems to be in a different part of the valley, going downhill, down towards the river. Keep walking. When he was driving lorries, if he got lost in the dark or in fog he used to think, keep on, keep going, keep on the road and you'll always find a place you can navigate from.

'Keep travelling,' he used to say, 'it'll allus bring thee home in t' end.'

Reg Robson, the man who finds Harry and brings him home in his car, is a casual family acquaintance about ten years older than Lynda. As Reg explains to Winnie, Lynda and John in the sitting room of 239 Barnsley Road, he had been out late walking with his dogs when he saw this old lad looking a bit lost. 'He looked like he were heading towards Darfield. And then I looked, and thought, Ayup, in't that t' Juggler? I always remember him because he were a right comic, weren't he?'

After Reg leaves, Harry, who has now understood his lapse of memory, warms his legs in front of the Parkray and explains that he had somehow missed the house. When he noticed, he had become confused and couldn't think where he needed to go. Harry is embarrassed, Winnie half worried and half bemused: she is so used to his kidding and jokes that she finds it difficult to take the incident as seriously as she suspects she ought to. Lynda and John exchange glances, and Lynda tells her dad that he needs to be careful. From now on he must ring John when he wants to come home, so that John can walk over to fetch him.

'Listen to what they're telling you, Harry,' says Winnie.

'Don't start,' says Harry. Winnie glowers, Harry ignores her, and with normal service resumed, Lynda and John go home to bed.

No one will talk about the incident again, but when Win thinks about it the next day, she recalls other times in recent months when his memory has slackened or unknotted itself, moments when he has responded to simple questions with momentary blinking blankness, and it reminds her of her father. She thinks it might not be the drink alone, but another problem. Within a year she will know she was right.

61

Catch Me If I Fall

NCB Yorkshire Area Headquarters, Doncaster; Lodge Moor Hospital; Santa Ponsa, Majorca, 1985

All year Lynda's left leg has continued its unpredictable flipping and twitching. She finds that if she thinks in her new way, with her whole body rather than her brain, she can raise the limb four inches from the ground. It is four inches of hope, and at her weekly Lodge Moor visits she asks the nurses and physiotherapists how she might turn it into a step or two. Their instructions, however, are only to teach her how to cope with her disability, not to indulge her faith that she will walk again. 'That's great,' they say, 'now let's see if we can show you how to be more mobile in your chair.'

John's support and determination bolster her. Lynda is strong, but sometimes someone else's belief in your strength makes you more able to use it. She thinks she is lucky, too; she knows John loves her, but plenty of men love women without loving their steel will.

At the end of the strike Dr McCraig says she is still unfit for work. She doesn't go in, and Frank Tulley, the Hickleton pit manager, calls her at home to ask if she wants to take redundancy. The NCB are offering very good terms to anyone wanting to leave.

'I'll bet they are,' she says. 'But no, I don't want redundancy. It's my legs that don't work, not my brain.'

'Aye. Sorry, Lynda.' Mr Tulley is a compassionate man trying to do right, but he sounds embarrassed. 'I just thought with you being disabled you might not be coming back to work, you know.'

It is the thought of coming back to work that has kept Lynda going. 'I don't think of myself as disabled,' she tells him. 'I can do everything in an office that I used to do, I'll just do it all from a chair that's all – as soon as Lodge Moor'll let me.' She is not as sure of this as she sounds, but she will make herself do anything if it means keeping her job.

'Okay, okay. I'm just asking.'

'And I'm just saying . . .'

'Right,' he says. 'I can tell it's not affected thy tongue.'

That's better, she thinks, back to the sarcasm and cheek. It was when they started cheeking you that you knew you had their respect.

Mr Tulley puts her on sick leave, and she spends the next six months learning to cope at home. John leaves the Hickleton Main lamp room and takes a job at the Sta-Lite battery factory in Highgate, so that he can be closer. While Lynda pumps dumbbells, learns to drive an adapted car, and teaches Sam to fetch the cordless phone handset when it rings, John and Karl install a stairlift, widen the house's doors and build concrete ramps over the outside steps. She bans herself, her family and any visitors to the house from pondering why this should all have happened to her, and, by extension, to them. 'You might as well ask, "Why not me?" All I can do is get on wi' it,' she says. 'Anyway, it's amazing what I find out I can do if I set my mind right.'

Away from public scrutiny, there are moments of solitary, godforsaken despair. She cannot reach to clean the skirting boards. She tries to fill the coal bucket and spills it all down her, until she learns to hold the handle with her teeth as she wheels herself into the house. She worries about who will look after her dad if he gets poorly and her mam can't manage. When John takes her out to clubs she enjoys herself, but finds it hard to watch people dancing because she always wants to get up and dance with them, and she gets in the way as they join or leave the dance floor. 'Just shove me in a corner or a passage somewhere out of t' way, will you?' she says to John one night when they are out watching a Frankie Valli tribute act.

'No,' he says. 'I will not. I'll move thee out of t' way, and I'll stop folks bumping into thee. But so long tha's wi me, tha's going in no passage and no corner. So forget it.'

*

The summer passes. The news is full of talk about Mikhail Gorbachev in the Soviet Union and Live Aid at Wembley Stadium. In South Yorkshire, the NUM campaigns for the reinstatement of miners sacked in the strike, and it seems half the pits in the county are rumoured to be closing in the autumn. At Lodge Moor, Dr McCraig retires and is replaced by Dr Ravichandran, a genial man who is more encouraging to Lynda, without agreeing that she might use her legs again. At their first appointment Lynda tells him that she and her husband have decided that she's going to walk into the hospital one day, and they both laugh.

Lynda returns to work in September. The Victorian offices of Hicklelton colliery cannot be made to accommodate a wheelchair, so the Coal Board transfers her to the statistics department of its Doncaster area headquarters, where the manager has installed ramps, a lavatory, and a locker for her catheters and other medical equipment. Lynda's new workplace is a hushed, windowless computer room where statisticians move between warm, whirring machines, checking printouts and tapping at keyboards. Her job is to record all the accidents from the area's pits, compiling the reports as they come in and storing the information on floppy disks. At first, not having used a computer before, she is tense, afraid that the wrong key might add ten men to a casualty list somewhere or shut down the entire computer system. Her taut nerves are then wound further by Brenda and Henry, two colleagues who are proud members of APEX. Lynda tells them she hasn't worked since the strike started. Brenda gives a tight little smile.

'Oh, well,' she says, 'I didn't have any of that going on. I'm in APEX, same as Henry here.' Henry screws up his face and shakes his head distastefully. Both he and Brenda are about the same age as Lynda.

'Me and my husband were on strike for twelve months.'

'Oh dear,' laughs Brenda. 'We had twelve months of getting paid for doing nowt. We used to sit in here knitting, didn't we, Henry?'

Lynda feels her upper body tingling. 'I don't suppose you felt like you should be supporting t' men who were trying to save your jobs, did you?'

'APEX weren't on strike,' says Henry. 'It didn't have anything to do with us.'

'As it happens I went to a picket line and wished them good luck,' Brenda offers.

'It had plenty to do with all of us. And you could have joined a different union.'

'Now, just a minute.' Brenda taps her desk with an index finger. 'I don't have to apologise for anything. *I* didn't ask them to go out on strike. I don't know where it got you all anyway.'

'No, I don't either sometimes. But I know I can hold my head up and say I supported t' men who support us. I think that's worth summat, even if you don't.' Lynda flings the list of accidents and injuries onto Brenda's desk and wheels herself off, shoving on the handrims harder and faster than ever before.

*

In Yorkshire, the NCB sends its severely injured and disabled employees for therapy at Firbeck Hall, a Miners Welfare Commission rehabilitation centre near Maltby. Firbeck is a huge sixteenth-century house set amid neat lawns and lakes, and populated mainly by miners with amputated limbs, broken backs and damaged skulls. Its young doctors and physiotherapists long ago discovered that their patients respond better to bluntness and black humour than soft-voiced sympathy, and its manners are more pit yard than hospital. Lynda loves it.

'Now then, what's up wi' you?' asks her physio when they first meet. 'Balance? Get away. Your problem is you've forgot how to walk. Let's get that leg shifting.' The physio attaches electrodes to her twitchy leg and applies a strong current. The leg flips up violently, and he guffaws. 'You're jiggling like Elvis! Let's do it again!'

Another physio, who specialises in treating amputees, shows her how to use a walking frame to stand up, and among the limbless and laughing men in the high-ceilinged rooms, she learns to inch her body forward. She still has no balance: if she closes her eyes she isn't even sure which way up she is, and for all she knows could be floating upside down in a pit shaft. But the prickling feelings in her left leg grow sharper, and spread faintly to her right, and about two months after she goes back to work, the feeling is enough for her to stand with a pair of elbow crutches.

One day when she is exercising in the sitting room at home, she feels strong twinges in both legs, and asks John to pass her the two walking sticks that they now keep by the door for Harry. John hands them to her and folds down the wheelchair's foot flaps. Taking one stick in each hand, she leans forward on them, and pushes herself up, knuckles whitening on the handles as she rises out of the chair. For a moment she is standing; then she lets herself fall back into the chair, whumping into the seat lightly panting. And then she does it again.

A few weeks later Dr Ravichandran is in the reception area of Lodge Moor hospital when he catches sight of Lynda Burton approaching the building. Her husband John is wheeling the chair behind her, and she is gripping wooden walking sticks in each hand. Her walk is a slow, careful hobble of small rolls and lurches, but she is nevertheless walking.

Dr Ravichandran pushes through the heavy glass doors to meet her. 'Lynda!' he says. 'How . . . where is your car?'

'Back there.'

'So you have walked . . .' He beams and holds up his arms like a sports coach cheering an athlete. 'I can't believe you are walking! Though you know you shouldn't really be . . .' He moves to her side. 'Here, let me help you.'

'No,' she says, 'don't touch me. I don't want anybody helping me until I'm through those doors.'

'Thad better listen to what she tells thee, cock,' says John, holding the wheelchair fast behind her to catch her in case she falls.

The doctor stands back. 'You are sure you're alright?'

'Aye. Stop worrying, and go and open that door for me.' She walks across the threshold into the hospital, and then half-sits, half-falls back into the wheelchair, sighs a deep sigh, and looks at John.

'We did it!' she says.

Dr Ravichandran has heard stories like this before, but he does not know why Lynda can walk without having any balance. During the physiotherapy session he and his student examine her in a side room. He tells the student her case history and when he has finished the examination, says, 'Can we just demonstrate, Lynda?'

'If you like.'

He stands at the back of her and tells her to shut her eyes. He tells her not to worry as he will catch her if she falls. She falls. He catches her. Setting her upright again, he smiles. Dr Ravichandran turns to the student and says, 'OK, Simon. The thing here is, Lynda can only feel one leg. She has no balance. So how does she walk?'

Simon tries to remember some other element involved in walking but cannot. 'I don't know,' he says.

'No,' says Dr Ravichandran. 'That is the thing. At this moment, neither do I.'

*

Lynda does not fully recover the use of her legs. The blood clot that poisoned her spinal fluid has damaged the nerves, and all her doctors say a repairing operation could make them worse. But she does learn to use sticks to walk short distances and to get around the car so she can heave her wheelchair into the boot then climb in the driver's seat.

She and John make it a rule to try live the way they lived before Lynda's illness. When they have paid off most of their debts from the strike, John and Lynda take Karl for a week's holiday to Santa Ponsa in Majorca. 'Come on, let's go,' says John after checking that the airline takes wheelchairs. 'What's t' worst that can happen?'

At the resort he and Karl push her along the seafront in the hot sunshine, and in and out of the shops and sometimes up the steep hills towards the edges of the town, where the streets are lined by pine trees and they can walk in the cooler air for miles. They stop to look down at the sea beneath them and watch old black-laced Majorcan ladies sitting in the pine-shade, and John complains about how much all his pushing is going to cost him in sandal leather.

One afternoon they set off up one of the long, straight sloping streets when the weather is overcast, seeking clearer air than in the resort which is sultry and quiet under low grey clouds. When they are about halfway up, the sky darkens and Lynda, John and Karl feel spots of rain on their bare sunburned forearms. Ahead of them lies a crossroads and shops, and John, thinking he can shelter Lynda under an awning, pushes harder to reach the crossroads before the rain is heavy. But the rain is heavy at once, and John lowers his body to get more power. Karl helps him to push, but on the wet marble pavement their feet slip and Lynda in the wheelchair rolls backwards, forcing them down the slope. If they scrabble for grip, they tumble to their knees. If they hold still, they slide. Karl grabs the front of the chair, but his feet slither about beneath him.

John glances back; a quarter-mile of empty, steep pavement broken only by a side road. The three of them are sliding. 'Are we all right?' asks Lynda.

'No.'

'I didn't think so.'

He makes a last push, but they slide back and this time he is losing control. 'I'm sorry about this, love,' he says, 'but hold on.'

He squeezes the handles, steps to one side of the chair and, as it slides down past him, pulls up hard on one handle so that one side flies up. The chair overbalances sending Lynda sprawling over the pavement, and then skitters away down the hill.

Lynda is rubbing her arm, but she is unhurt.

'Talk about agile,' says John. 'Tha went down like Gordon Banks there.'

John peers down the slope and looks rueful, almost guilty. 'I was maybe a bit gung-ho coming up there, I never thought about it raining. I'm sorry.'

'We'll know t' next time, won't we?' she says. 'That's t' position we're in from now on. We have to try things to see if we can do them or not. Sometimes they're impossible and sometimes they're not, but I reckon you've got to be a bit gung-ho in this life sometimes, or it's not worth living.'

62

I Think He's Trying to Tell Me That He Loves Me

Highgate and Driffield, East Yorkshire, 1985–86

In June 1985, Harry and Winnie go with Winnie's sister Olive and her husband Frank, to stay in Pauline and Gordon's house on the Yorkshire Wolds to watch over the farm while the family go on holiday. In the evenings Harry drinks in the village pub, where the regulars know him from past visits. 'Got a joke for us, Juggler?' ask the farm workers, mechanics and lorry drivers, their weatherworn faces expectant, and lips already curling into half-smiles. 'Well,' he says, 'I'm not saying my wife's mean, but . . .' The landlord, Norman, a round and jolly man who appreciates Harry's liveliness, occasionally stands him a pint, but at ten o'clock one night he calls the farmhouse and asks for Juggler's missus.

'I think someone'd better come and walk him home,' he says. 'He's alright, aye, nowt wrong really. It's just that he keeps buying people drinks, and it's getting a bit awkward because folks don't want to keep taking off him. To be honest with you, it's like he doesn't know what he's doing.'

Olive walks over to the pub. Harry has a group of men around him, some smiling, others looking concerned. Harry acclaims the arrival of Olive – 'Ayup t' main turn's arrived, what you having to drink, love?' – and weakly protests when she insists he come home with her.

The next morning, Winnie looks in his wallet. She knows how much money he should have, and sees that last night he spent £15 when he would usually have spent about £4. Let's see what happens tonight, she thinks. She makes his bread and dripping as usual and waits up, but there is no call from Norman, and Harry comes back as usual, and she puts the previous evening from her mind.

Back in the Dearne, however, more instances of treating and excessive tap-room generosity demonstrate that Harry Hollingworth's mind is sticking and jamming like an old rusted gearbox. Initially people put this down to his daftness, but such explanations become less and less convincing. The men at Highgate Club realise it is not just his eccentricity the night he pauses, in the middle of ordering a round of drinks, to ask if they can tell him where he is.

Winnie persuades him to see a doctor, the doctor refers him to Barnsley Hospital, and there, in the autumn, he is diagnosed with Parkinson's disease and dementia. He doesn't talk about it, but Winnie becomes the nurse, taking on Harry's portion of the worry as well as her own. 'We'll manage,' she says. 'We always have before.'

At first he mostly stays the same. Whisky in his tea, carping at the telly, performing practical jokes for his grandchildren: when Pauline and Gordon's children come to stay in October, he entertains them with a series of holed and bending joke teaspoons that leak sugar and cause Winnie to slap his arm in reprimand. But as the winter comes on and the nights pull in he forgets where he is again, and leaves strips of whiskers on his chin when he shaves. One teatime, when he can't see his teacup, Winnie tries to show it to him and he flings an angry arm out at her. Two weeks later, when he threatens to punch her, Lynda and Pauline ask the doctors if he can go to a nursing home for a while, to give their mam a rest, but the doctors say the danger is not yet serious enough.

As Christmas comes and goes, he becomes less coherent. He searches for clothes he hasn't had for forty years, waits for Millie to join in when he sings and imagines feeding the pit ponies underground at Manvers Main as he did when he was a boy. 'Where the bloody hell's Winnie?' he asks, searching for her even as she stands in front of him.

John comes round in the evenings to chat with him in the sitting room, or to take him to the club for a slow pint that Harry sometimes loses on the bartop. At weekends, they walk around the village, or down to the allotments. Harry, who cannot bear to have women physically helping him in his frailty, asks for John when he needs assistance, and in the mornings and evenings John helps him dress, guides him as he climbs into the bath, and shaves him with a slow, gentle delicacy, scraping the slackening skin of its white whiskers. John and Lynda worry about Winnie, though, and in the new year Harry justifies their concern. After a spell of lucidity and friendliness, he threatens her with the breadknife and then tries to push her downstairs, his lack of coordination all there is between her and injury.

He begins to weave and wobble climbing the stairs, so John and Karl place a bed in the front room. Some nights, when he has lowered Harry into slumber, or helped him so that he can look out of the window, John stands looking at him, his face a mixture of anger and sad vexation at Harry's weakness.

'John's an angel,' says Winnie, after John has left. 'He's an angel to you, Harry.'

He murmurs in agreement and dozes to the low sound of the television, and the late-night traffic on the Barnsley Road.

*

Sometimes Pauline brings Harry up to the farm to allow Winnie, Lynda and John some respite. She finds old records that he gave her when she was a girl, and asks her children, teenagers now, to record them onto cassettes so that she and her dad can sit at the kitchen table listening to them on a portable cassette player. 'Because', 'Tiger Rag', 'Underneath the Arches', 'Play a Simple Melody'. To some he remembers the words, to others his hands paw and paddle at the table, trying to find the beat on the snare and cymbal. When 'Til We Meet Again' ends, he asks Pauline to rewind the tape and play it again, and when it stops, he asks her again, and again.

'I love that song, Pauline. I used to sing it with your Aunty Millie.'

'I remember,' she says, thinking how small and distant his voice sounds. He stares silently out of the kitchen window to the garden.

'Where are you, Dad?'

He doesn't answer.

One sunny afternoon in July, she takes him with Gordon and the children to the Driffield Agricultural Show. While the rest of the family go to look at livestock, Pauline shuffles with him across the green, tented and marqueed field. Passing the main ring Harry admires a set of dray horses, and tells Pauline about feeding his snap to the pit ponies. They stop and Pauline feeds two green apples to the horse as he watches. As they set off again they hear in the distance the sound of a brass band playing. 'Come on, Dad, let's go and listen to t' band,' says Pauline. He smiles, and their ambling walk becomes a pilgrimage, passing through country crowds and trade stands, drawn by rich, piping music. After fifteen minutes of small, slow steps, they come to a white bandstand gleaming in the sunshine. Inside men and women in neat navy uniforms, their silver buttons winking in the sunshine, are playing popular hymns on brass instruments. Harry, leaning on his dark brown walking stick, gazes at them. When Pauline looks at her dad beside her, there are tears running down his pale cheeks and falling to make small dark spots on his Rocola shirt.

*

He develops pneumonia, and spends three weeks in Barnsley Hospital. Sometimes he is vacant, other times alert, asking questions and trying to work out the controls on the portable cassette player that Pauline has lent him. He says he'll be alright once he gets out of hospital, and repeatedly tells nurses and visitors alike that Roy will soon be coming to see him. Roy tells Winnie he will try to come, but never makes it.

Winnie stays beside him every evening at visiting time, as quiet as she had been sitting on the settee during the parties at 34 Highgate Lane. Under her thick ivory-white hair, behind the pebbly lenses of her gold-framed spectacles, she is moving beyond the sweet contented period of their marriage to the bitter twist at the end; the caring and the fear as he ebbs inexorably away from her. They both seem to cast off old modesty, and touch in public more than they have before. Winnie places her hand in his, tells him that she loves him and squeezes his thumb or fingers. If he is awake he squeezes back, and then she bows to gently kiss his head.

When he comes home, he spends much of the day in his bed in the front room. Although he has lost weight, he is still a large man, and becomes discomforted and sore where his body presses against the mattress. Only John can make him comfortable. 'Tell John to come to me,' Harry says, even when the health visitor is there, and John, being called, lays down his garden tools, or his knife and fork, or his newspaper, and comes. He moves Harry's feet to take the weight off them, lifts his body so that he doesn't hurt his arms, and places pillows and cushions under his ankles, back and shoulders to ease the pain.

'It's wonderful what John has done for you, Harry,' says the health visitor as John stands by the bed watching. 'Not many people would do for you what he's done.'

'Some would,' says John.

'Less and less, though.'

Beneath them Harry's breath labours like the slow, heavy breakers on Bridlington beach.

*

Another winter draws in. On the news, the Stock Exchange is computerised and British Gas shares are floated. The Coal Board announces that Cadeby colliery is to be closed, like Cortonwood and Yorkshire Main last year, and Mrs Thatcher gives Ian MacGregor a knighthood.

In Highgate, Winnie retires from working for Jane Seels. She has less energy, she says, and she is using much of it to care for Harry. When neither Lynda, John nor Karl can be there, she watches over him, leaning against the radiator for warmth, kept company by Sam the dog and the little gypsy girl. The gypsy girl reassures her. Yes, she says, Harry is very poorly, but they are all watching over him – his mam, his dad, old Juggler, Clara and Juggler Jane, watching him and sending him love. And I'm here to watch over you, Winnie.

One day in early December, Lynda comes round to see if her mam wants a hand with the Christmas decorations. She wheels herself through the hall and, hearing her voice in the front room, stops beside the door.

'I always loved you, Harry,' Winnie is saying. 'Whatever happened there was never anybody else I loved like I loved you. I loved you from the day I first set my eyes on you.'

'– Mam?' Lynda knocks gently and pushes open the door. Harry is lying on the bed, awake but unspeaking, eyes yellow with jaundice. Waiting on him, Winnie stands making her final vows from her place by the radiator.

'Are you all right, Mam?'

Winnie nods. 'I was talking to your dad. He was looking at me when I was telling him. I think he was trying to say to me, "And I loved you," but he couldn't get it out.'

*

As Christmas approaches, Harry's illness consumes the household. Olive comes to help with the nursing and John cares for him when he is not working. Every day when Winnie changes the sheets, John comes to lift Harry on to the sofa, laying him there with his thinly haired, weak-necked head resting on the white lace antimacassar. John hates his lightness. A man should weigh something, especially a man like Harry; death ought to make him heavier, not lighter. How could his life seem to weigh so little?

Sometimes when John returns home, he sits in the kitchen, staring, inwardly raging about Harry's condition. 'They say life's cruel,' he says to Lynda one evening. 'I never really knew what they meant until now.'

In the early evening of 28 December, Harry wakes from a long sleep, and shifts uncomfortably in the bed. He looks up at Winnie. 'Will tha get John?' he says. 'Ask him to come and make me comfortable?'

John arranges Harry's bedding, body and sheets to remove the pressure, as he has learned to do for Lynda. 'All right, old lad?' he says when he is finished. 'Can I get thee owt else?'

Harry reaches out a hand to stay him and, wheezing, beckons him closer. John comes close to the bed so that their two heads are almost touching.

'What's up, Harry?'

He looks at him, locks him with his eyes, and says, 'Thank you, John. Thank you for everything.'

Harry dies the following morning. Olive knocks at John and Lynda's back door with the news. The three of them walk along the backings in the cold, winter morning light to find Harry semi-upright in the bed, still and pale in the dimness of the curtained room. His wife is upstairs, sleeping.

After the doctor has briefly attended and Olive has gone upstairs to wake Winnie, and after Lynda has called the undertaker, it is John who lays out the body. In the silence he disconnects the catheter and lays the limbs out, straightening the arms and legs and drawing down the eyelids. Finally, he places a hand beneath the pale, whiskery jaw and gently closes Juggler's gap-toothed grin. 'Goodnight, Harry.'

63

I've Got Somebody Here Who Wants to See You

Highgate, 1987

After the funeral, once the adjustable bed has been removed from the front room, the pale and flowery cards cleared from the sideboard, and Harry's LP records, cufflinks and tiepins distributed among his grandchildren, Winnie is left living alone for the first time in her life. Her aloneness, though, is chiefly a matter of household arrangements and what other people see. What she feels is not solitude but a companionable haunting: she senses Harry's presence in the shifting airs of the house, and hears him in floor creaks, waterpipe judders and latch rattles. Coming home with a quarter of tongue and a bread loaf, she sees him seated in the corner playing a trumpet to a stray Yorkshire terrier. In bed she is woken by him, Danny and Sonny at the back door, singing. From the kitchen window she sees him at the garden gate, joking with men on their way to the allotments. This is not his spirit, the little gypsy girl tells her, just her memories. Harry has passed over now, and if people don't believe in Spirit, they cannot come back to see you. He will come one day, to fetch her. Until then, she must make do with her unspeaking memories.

These memories are now edited and recast by Winnie into scenes of unbroken love and contentment. Old arguments and betrayals become challenges that were overcome by their unchanging mutual devotion, all irritations are forgotten, and Harry's knife-and-fork crockery percussion is recalled with the sighs of a lovelorn nineteen-year-old. It is as if she can now love him with the saved-up love she found unwanted when they first married, half a century of withheld words and tears now released and overwhelming her. Of all Winnie's loves, this widow's reverence may not be the most fierce, but it is the most ardent, impassioned and pure.

Pauline and Lynda are gobsmacked. Was their mam trying to make herself believe she and Harry had always loved each other in spite of their differences, or could it in some way be true? Winnie had once told Pauline that it was hard to change how you felt about things once you were past forty, but she seems to be achieving that now with respect to their dad. Not only that, as Lynda says; her new happy-families version of Hollingworth history wishes away all the hostility that preceded Winnie's conversion to the cause of John.

Sometimes after listening to hours of forlorn and fanciful nostalgia, Lynda has to check an impulse to reprove her mam for her stories.

'I talk to him every night in my mind, you know,' Winnie tells her as they eat their teas with John and Karl.

'I know, Mam. You will do, after all those years.'

'I wish he'd come to fetch me.'

'Don't be daft. Come on, there's no point talking like that . . .'

'I do. There's nowt for me here now.'

'Mam . . .' Lynda manages to damp down the exasperation in her voice and sound sympathetic, and privately she imagines, somewhere out in the spirit circles, Harry rolling his eyes, adjusting his tie in the mirror and going out for a pint to escape his wife's mithering.

*

Although Harry is not ready to come back and take her away, another once-awaited rescuer is. One Saturday afternoon, Lynda is at home tidying away the dinner pots when the phone rings. It is Maureen, one of her cousins on her dad's side of the family.

'Ayup, Lynda,' says Maureen. She sounds hesitant. 'I've got somebody here who wants to see you. Can he come up?'

Maureen's tone gives nothing away, but even so Lynda knows immediately who it is. She feels a light wave of nausea. 'Yes,' she says. 'Yes, alright. Bring him to my mam's.' Just when you're settled, she thinks: just when your mam's improving, your family's alright, and your work's going well. Last weekend they had a little party to cheer themselves up. Karl and his friends had raced up and down the garden paths in her wheelchair, and as she watched them she had felt they were all moving on nicely. And now out of nowhere this; the visitor who wants to see her.

She calls her mam, brushes her hair in the mirror, and wheels herself along the backings to Winnie's back garden gate, where she waits.

When she sees him walking down the backings in his light overcoat and grey suit, her first thought is that he looks younger than she expected. Her second is that he looks a bit like Harry. But then he is a Hollingworth, after all.

'Hello,' she says.

'Hello,' he replies. 'I'm Alf, love. It's good to meet you.'

Over the years since she first told Lynda about Alf, Winnie has loosed enough fragments and details for her to put together the whole story. She knows about his leaving and his promise to return, and all about his character and feelings for her mam. She knows about the features and mannerisms, all fondly described by Winnie, that she has supposedly inherited from him, although on this point, she is unconvinced. Lynda believes that her mam sees similarities in the hairline, or a likeness in the smile, because she wants to see Alf living in her. The idea does not trouble her, it just lives in those seas of her mother's soul that she cannot fathom.

'Are you all right then?' she says, as they wait for Winnie to come downstairs. She is aware of talking as if they were relatives who hadn't seen each other for a few months.

'Yes, thank you, love. Are you?'

'Aye, not so bad.'

'Is your family okay?'

'Aye, they're alright. Our Karl and John have gone to watch Sheffield United this afternoon.'

'Oh.'

The conversation is slow, but then what do you discuss with a man you've never met before but who may be your father? The weather?

'Turned out nice, anyway,' she says.

Winnie comes in with her hair brushed smart, and wearing a cream floral dress. Alf looks across the room with wide eyes and a smile that is half joy and half apprehension.

'Hello, Winnie.'

'Hello.'

To Lynda's surprise, she is curt, almost offhand.

'Are you all right then?'

'Aye, not bad.'

As it turns out the afternoon is not one for revelations or for driving off into the dusk never to return. Lynda makes a pot of tea, and the three of them sit around the table discussing families and the past in Highgate. They do not progress beyond small talk, and at no point go anywhere near the subject of Alf and Winnie's affair, or Lynda's birth. Listening, she feels that she ought to feel upset or enlightened, but more than anything she is indifferent. She feels now as she has always felt: Harry is her dad; behaviour can take precedence over biology. She has chosen her own life, and would never let someone else choose it for her.

Alf is a pleasant man, but she would like to tell him that she is Harry's daughter and that is that. As she cannot, she is obliged to talk to him and her mam about the Hollingworths, and about children and grandchildren, and about Alf's home in the East Riding. Winnie does not ask questions and appears no more interested in Alf than in the mantelpiece clock. Her rescue-ache faded years ago, and even if it hadn't, her attraction to him would have been killed by her renewed and pious posthumous love for Harry.

Lynda wonders briefly if Alf will stay, but at four o'clock, after more tea and slices of cake, he gets up and says he must be making tracks. Had she been younger, she might not have believed that such an infatuation could linger for so long only to end in light chat over tea and fruitcake, but by now she knows that here this is how most things end, give or take the shouting and argument.

She and her mam walk down the path to see him off. He kisses Lynda, and embraces Winnie, and as soon as Alf walks away, Winnie turns and goes back inside.

'Honestly, what did he come for?' she asks, as she tidies away the tea things. 'I'm not starting all that up again!'

'I think he just wanted to see you, Mother.'

'I'm sure I don't know what he wanted.'

'Well I don't think it was . . . you know. You're in your seventies, and he's not so far off.'

'What's that got to do with it? I could tell from t' way he was looking at me he was thinking summat.'

Let her enjoy her outrage, thinks Lynda.

'You can tell him to keep away in future.'

'Alright. I'll tell him.'

But Lynda does not tell him, because Alf has understood. He does not come back. Neither she nor Winnie will see him again.

64

The Indestructible

Highgate, 1988–91

'Mam?' says Lynda. 'Are those stinging nettles?'

'Yes,' replies Winnie. 'What do they look like?'

'Right,' says Lynda. 'And why are you sitting with your tights rolled down?'

It is an autumn Saturday in 1988. Lynda has found her mam seated in a chair with her skirt hitched to her knees, tights rolled down to her ankles, and a bunch of dark green nettles in her right hand. The skin on Winnie's knees is mottled red and puckered with sting-blisters. Winnie explains that Mike down the street, who is a physiotherapist at a non-league football club, has told her that thrashing your joints with nettles holds off arthritis. Muv used to say the same. As her doctor has just diagnosed arthritis in her knees, she is giving it a go.

'But, Mam, even if it works, you don't need to do things like that any more. There are creams you can get that do t' same thing.'

'Get away with you,' says Winnie, who uses Fiery Jack on her back and complains she barely feels it. 'They don't put t' strong stuff in creams you can buy, you have to find other ways.' As if to demonstrate her point, she picks up the nettle stalks, wrapped in a tea towel, and recommences the beating.

This is how Winnie approaches the infirmities of old age, driving them off with punishment as she once drove off the women who interfered with her husband and the schoolteachers who slapped her children. She chases off pain with pain and, so far, it has worked. She might have grown nostalgic and yearn to be fetched by Harry, but outwardly she has aged little since her hair whitened ten years ago. Her house, always an extension of her, retains its sweet tidiness: the various cleaning cloths are wrung and hung about the kitchen, the Hoover lead still immaculately and tightly wound, the rolls of toilet tissue still concealed under the crocheted skirts of a plastic doll.

The nettle treatment seems extreme, but, in being herbal, is typical of Winnie's taste in healthcare – bruises physicked with mustard poultices, barely wrinkled skin preserved with cucumber scraps and homespun face packs of witch hazel and oats. She seems self-sufficient, inventive and durable, and, to her family at least, as invulnerable as she appeared to be at forty.

This is why when Winnie's neighbour Nancy calls Lynda at work and says, 'It's about your mam, love,' Lynda assumes it to be a trivial matter – a request for some groceries to be bought on her drive home from work, perhaps, or a leaking kitchen tap.

'I found her on t' kitchen floor,' says Nancy. 'It looks as if she's had a fall. She isn't really talking.'

What Winnie has had, a doctor tells Lynda at the hospital in Barnsley later that evening in January 1989, is a stroke – probably after falling and hitting her head. Not unusual for a lady of her age, he says.

'No,' says Lynda, 'it's just that my mam, she . . . I suppose no one ever expects it, do they?'

The doctor says they will have to wait and see how she recovers. As it turns out, they do not have to wait long. Watched over by the little gypsy girl, who tells her it isn't her time to go and Harry isn't here yet, Winnie is walking about the ward in a couple of days, and talking about the housework two days after that. She is discharged within the week, showing no apparent ill-effects.

In the early autumn, back in her usual routines, Winnie is in Goldthorpe, crossing the road from the Co-op to the baker's, when an Austin Montego whips around a corner and clips her with its wing. Winnie goes up into the air like a cork, flips over, and lands on her back on the pavement, shaken but fully conscious. She tells the policemen that come running from the station that she was crossing too slowly, but when they come to the house later, they will blame the driver. Apart from the scratches and bruises that she sees off with her poultices, she has no injuries. The only legacy is her veneration of the coat she was wearing at the time of the accident – a fashionable calf-length padded and hooded overcoat that Pauline had bought for her from a street market. Winnie had already been impressed by the warmth of the padding, and she now decides its cushioning, protective qualities have helped to save her. That winter she wears it like armour every time she leaves the house.

'I don't know about her needing a coat,' says John. 'That woman is a Sherman tank.'

*

But while her body forges on like a tank in a pinny, Winnie's short-term memory flickers and fails. Sometimes Lynda sees her pause, floor-cloth in hand, in the kitchen, as if her mind has slipped its moorings and is floating free like a pilotless hot-air balloon in a blank blue sky. 'Are you okay, Mam?' Lynda asks.

'Aye, I just . . . can't think . . . what I was . . . hmm . . .'

At other times she forgets where she was five minutes ago, and on some mornings she will get up at half-past four, ready to make Harry's snap for him.

When Lynda calls one day in the summer of 1990 to find her mam out and the gas burning after being left on all morning, she decides she needs to act. Lynda and John rent their home to one of John's sons, and help Winnie to buy her house from the council, and at the age of eighty she becomes a homeowner. Lynda, John and Karl move in with her, and John makes the alterations to allow her to get around the house, and then redecorates and refurbishes. They install a new kitchen, but leave the sitting room, where she used to sit with Harry, as it was.

A few weeks after they move in, Lynda is cooking the tea when she sees Winnie bringing her best china from the front room to the sitting-room table where they eat. It is the Royal Albert tea service that John

McNeill bought for her when Roy brought him to stay at Highgate Lane in the summer of 1953. Having used the china for perhaps a dozen special birthdays and anniversaries since, Winnie now begins to carefully lay it out on a nondescript weekday evening in September.

She lays five place settings, one of them for Harry. A spoon is placed beside the flowery cup and saucer, as if he might make an encore with the tapped-out tinkling of 'Tiger Rag'.

Lynda comes in and frowns. 'Are you expecting somebody, Mam?'

'You what?' Winnie looks at her as if woken from a dream, struggling to recall where, and possibly who, she is.

'I was wondering what you'd got t' best china out for. You've laid an extra place.'

Winnie absorbs the information, and laughs weakly as if not understanding a joke. She starts to gather up the dishes.

'It's alright,' says Lynda. 'Keep them now you've laid them out, but let's just move these extra ones, eh?'

Winnie nods meekly, but when she sits down to the meal, she says, 'I do miss him, your dad. I do wish he would come for me.'

Winnie restates this almost daily, the sentiment a throwback to the old days of grand funerals, drawn curtains and 'Abide With Me', when death was dramatised. She is uninterested in the modern practices of holding the mystery at bay by celebrating the deceased person's life, and refusing to be sad because that's what they would have wanted; rather than push death aside, she likes to dwell on it. She thinks of it being administrated both by God and the spirits of the once-beloved dead with whom she will be reunited in peace. In a way, it is as if Winnie is now rehearsing for her own death, reordering her feelings and history as it ought to have been, ensuring a dignified, meaningful end to the tale.

But Lynda finds it hard to hear her mam talking of being carried away by Harry. She does not like to think about it, and in any case it seems quite impossible to imagine her mother ever dying.

'Don't be daft, Mam,' says Lynda. 'If my dad was here, he'd tell you to stop talking rubbish.'

'He wouldn't.'

'Mam . . .'

'He wouldn't.'

Lynda relents. In the silence that follows, she reaches across the tablecloth and strokes one of her mother's thin, mottled hands, and its wedding ring catches the light among the tea set's pale lilac roses.

PART NINE

65

Modern History

The Dearne Valley, 1985–89

If you were to peer down like a clairvoyant on South Yorkshire in the late 1980s you would see Lynda and John, Gary and Elaine, and David and Marie all reckoning that the gloomy predictions about mining communities that they hear on TV will not apply to the villages of the Dearne Valley. In frilly-curtained and velour-setteed sitting rooms, on local shopping streets, and at Sheffield's new out-of-town, opulently domed Meadowhall retail centre, they and their friends meet and say, 'Aye, Maggie'll make us suffer, she'll want to finish us off, but she'll not shut all t' pits at once . . . And even if they shut ours I don't think we'd get all t' crime coming in like they do in some places. Folks stick together, don't they? They stuck together in t' strike. They'll not suddenly stop because t' pit's shut.'

From West Yorkshire come stories of closed-down shops, drug dealers on pit estates and break-ins. Well, they say in the Dearne, maybe some of them villages were a bit rough anyway. I can't see that coming here, can you? Their tone is not boastful, naive or complacent, but based on a faith that the majority of people are decent and self-improving, and that, anyway, if someone was dealing drugs, the adults would find them and kick them back to where they came from.

You would also see, in the eighteen months after the strike, three South Yorkshire collieries closing without the immediate aftermath of dead white-eyed shops, empty houses and a rise in crime. In these cases there are other local collieries to take men who want to transfer, and neighbouring villages to supply jobs and customers for the shops and tradesmen. The men who stay in mining can earn good wages and bonuses because South Yorkshire is still a profitable and productive coalfield. At first it is less prone to multiple closures, though if you looked into the NCB's Yorkshire Area offices in Doncaster at this time, you could see Lynda Burton bundling up sheaves of figures for the statisticians, feeding reports down fax lines to headquarters in London, and realising that the bureaucrats are now measuring up the collieries like undertakers measuring up bodies.

If you pan out you can follow those lines down to the NCB head offices near the Department of Energy in Whitehall, and see civil servants and politicians devising a new nameplate: the National Coal Board is renamed the British Coal Corporation and the politicians talk of the rebrand as a step to selling off the pits to private owners. They say the privatisation will accompany that of power generation and supply, and mean that Britain's coal mines will no longer be the preferred suppliers to British electricity-generating power stations, which means that the power generators, whoever they may be, will then be able to import cheaper coal, from countries such as Russia, the United States and Colombia.

And if you move out far enough to take in Colombia's capital city Bogotá, you might see at work a young freelance journalist who had come to England to cover the miners' strike. The journalist had reported on conditions at the Colombian coal mines, where there were few safety standards and children were employed, and wanted to interview British mining families. On the picket line at Houghton Main he had met Gary Hollingworth, and asked him why no one had been at home when he knocked on the doors of the nearby houses. Gary had laughed and explained they were allotment sheds. 'Funny to you, maybe,' said the journalist, 'but in my country the houses of the miners are all like this.'

At Grimethorpe colliery, Gary is made ventilation officer, with twenty-odd men reporting to him and a manager's constant worry as part of the deal. Now, whenever he is outside, even in the garden at home or out with his family, he pays attention to the air; if he feels it dampening or drying he will nip to the pit to check the equipment that depends on atmospheric pressure. As an official he has to leave the National Union of Mineworkers for the Colliery Officials and Staff Association ('COSA bastards' as the men call them). In this position he is ragged and pillocked more than he was before, whether he is instructing people at work, or just getting in rounds in the Grimethorpe pubs, where the pit talk is so thick that the bored shout they can't see for dust.

He has confrontations. If the gas levels are too high he has to have production stopped, and if the men think he is being over-cautious, they rail at him. When redundancies are being made and redundo fever sets in, tempers quicken. Managers push through new shift patterns or scrap old agreements, and there are butts and punches wrapped in the insults. Gary takes it. As he once learned how to talk to the older men to get things done, he now learns to deal with wary, suspicious men who mistrust their employers' new conditions and promises.

Meanwhile, at Hickleton Main, David Hollingworth arrives at the pit for his shift and is then taken by coach with around forty others to Rossington, a big pit near Doncaster. In keeping with plans made at the British Coal head offices in London, and fed down the fax lines to Doncaster and then Thurnscoe, Hickleton has been merged with Goldthorpe and most of its miners transferred or made redundant. When the transfers begin, there are five coaches ferrying out men to their new pits; a year later they will fit into one. Finding it strange to work with men he has never met before, swapping rumours about which of them had scabbed during the strike, and disbelieving most announcements from management and British Coal, David feels a new edginess in the atmosphere, and a change in himself. There is still camaraderie among the men at work, but it becomes gradually less apparent in the village, and he and Marie find they are spending less time than they used to in the Coronation Club.

In March 1988, British Coal closes Hickleton colliery for good. The yard is emptied, the gates locked, and soon the only activity is the work of the trucks and earth movers on the vast black whalebacks of the spoil heap, soon to be grassed down and reclaimed as a public park. At the same time the corporation closes the Manvers complex and impatiently begins razing this old industrial Gormenghast to the ground. In the 1930s the old Manvers Main Colliery Company had owned more than a thousand railway trucks, each emblazoned with the company's name, and recognised on lines across the country. It was so well known that the London Midland South Railway Company used it on its advertising posters. By the start of the 1990s it will be the biggest single area of derelict contaminated land in Europe.

The closure and demolition of South Kirkby colliery follows and after that Barnburgh Main and Royston Drift, near Barnsley. The demolitions leave uncanny spaces in the countryside; the collieries had not been picturesque places, but they had been busy and important and the view had cohered around them. To look at the bare land, with the rubble and raw earth scars underlining the nothingness, is to look at an absence, at missing teeth in a jaw. Passing Manvers, Winnie cannot quite remember where all its buildings had been. Maybe it is that she is just getting old, she thinks. Maybe her memory is growing stiff, like her back and her legs.

Move back now and pause above the Dearne. If you look carefully you will see that the older miners, the war veterans, the men who know all the mines' tales, are melting away. Many of them feel guilty at taking the redundancy packages, because to them it means selling a job that belongs to the next generation, but times are hard and the redundancy packages can go up to £40,000. The deals and conditions seem strange to them. You are entitled to unemployment benefit without needing to look for work; you can draw your pension early, and in some cases you are entitled to free fuel for life. Some men take the 'redundo' and work as contractors at other pits. But as the older men go they take with them their knowledge, steadying influence and authority, there is less mixing between the generations, and managers promote younger men to their jobs.

Across the Yorkshire coalfield there are sporadic attempts to protect jobs for the future. When British Coal introduces a new disciplinary code, there is talk of an all-out strike, but the union goes no further than refusing to cut coal on overtime shifts. The code is dropped, but afterwards it seems more certain that the NUM will not be able to re-stage a campaign like the 1984–85 strike. Three months after Manvers Main and Hickleton pits close, Caphouse colliery near Wakefield reopens as the Yorkshire Mining Museum, employing ex-miners as guides. Lisa Hollingworth, aged nine now, goes there with a friend during the school holidays. As part of the experience the guides take them underground to disused workings, turn on speakers that broadcast the sound of coal-cutting machinery at actual volume, and turn off the lights. Lisa thinks about her dad, working underground at Rossington, and she is horrified. 'How can he do it?' she says to her friend. 'It's *terrifying*.'

The decade is ending. Listen closely and you might hear the Hollingworths saying perhaps Maggie might shut all the pits at once, after all, and that when several pits in neighbouring villages do shut all at once, you do see changes. People move away and are replaced by new families that no one knows. Shops close. You hear stories of drug dealers sending up fireworks over the valley to announce a new drop; of friends and neighbours being burgled, and when some little bugger breaks into a loft to steal copper piping, no one wants to say anything any more, because the old pulling together that was born of common experience has gone. A few years ago you could count on the blokes having a word with their fathers at work, or at the club. A few years ago you knew a lot of the kids would find pit jobs that straightened them out. These were not ideal, failsafe solutions, but they were something. In places where several pits shut at once, though, such self-regulation is becoming rarer. What will they do, they wonder, and what will their villages be like, if the pits close? Would any of their experience, or knowledge, be of use any more?

And in Thurnscoe, Jed Stiles, quiff threaded with grey, gait and grin unaltered, launches a sideline career selling cigarettes from a carrier bag at prices that undercut the shops and machines. He asks all his customers if they think he still looks like Elvis. Some people say that if you say yes, dead ringer, he'll give you a discount.

66

Born Wi't Silver Spoon in Thy Gob

The Selby Complex, Barnsley Main Colliery, Highgate; Doncaster; Hull, 1990–98

In March 1990 news breaks of a scandal involving financial corruption in the NUM. For two weeks it seems that half the pits in South Yorkshire have TV news crews camped at their gates, and journalists pushing microphones at miners for opinions. The accusations, denied by the leaders, are that in the 1984–85 strike the union took large donations of money from Soviet miners and from Colonel Gaddafi and that officials used part of that money to pay off home loans. The NUM members, even the ones disenchanted with Scargill, are sceptical; after the disinformation during the strike, a lot of people suspect that press stories about the NUM are government-generated black propaganda. 'They reckoned he was lying when he said they'd shut pits,' says a ventilation man at Grimethorpe to Gary Hollingworth, as they listen to the news on a battered radio in the safety team's cabin. 'Bollocks to the lot of them.' By 'the lot of them' he means the union as well. There is a lot of this among the men now, grumbling that the NUM won't stand up to the managers or British bloody Coal when they cut corners or put their favourites in the best-paying jobs. Trust is harder to earn than it once was.

A Fraud Squad investigation collapses and the Inland Revenue finds no impropriety. However, Gavin Lightman QC conducts an official inquiry for the union and although he clears Scargill and other officials of using Libyan money to pay their mortgages, he does find there have been 'a number of misapplications of funds and breaches of duty'. To Gary, following the radio news updates, these specific findings are less important than the fact of the story surfacing in the first place. He remembers the skirmish with the Coal Board in 1981, the Welsh miners coming to Yorkshire with their warnings, the coal stockpiles rising before the strike, and wonders if the Scargill story could be a sign. What if someone was raking over the union muck for a reason? The South Yorkshire pits are turning over stories about closures and privatisation like coal on a retreat face, and if the government was going to privatise British Coal, as it was threatening to, it would most likely begin by attacking the NUM.

The uncertainty at work makes Gary feel this may be a good time to move on, and he talks to Elaine about looking for another job. Their standard of living is good: £23,500 a year, a nicely furnished house, a Vauxhall Cavalier SRi outside, Scott training as a civil engineer and Claire at university studying zoology. Even as collieries are closing and an economic recession settles on Britain, some miners are earning good money from new bonus schemes, and from promotions as men leave the industry with their redundancy payments. Like many miners, though, Gary thinks the Conservative government will come for them again; he feels as if he is making the money in the shadows of coming ruination.

What he would secretly like to do is the same as it ever was – teach children, or at least do a job helping other people. Unsure of how to go about it, uncertain about his abilities and nervous of a career change, he distracts himself by enquiring about different engineering jobs. He applies for a couple, and in 1991 is offered a job on the Channel Tunnel project down south, but then as he is considering that he is asked to take the well-paid post of ventilation officer at Whitemoor pit, part of the Selby complex twenty-five miles north of the Dearne.

The Selby complex began producing coal in 1983, its five pitheads living up to their 1970s billing as new-worldly visions. These are posher than Nottinghamshire's very poshest pits, built of buff brick and coordinated chocolate-brown cladding, and screened by rows of fir and laurel trees to blend in with the pretty, non-industrialised North Yorkshire landscape. The headgears are low and encased in rectangular towers so that seen from certain angles across the fields they resemble plain churches rising above the trees and hedges. Underground, Selby is one of the most technologically advanced coal mines in the world, and it is predicted to have a long future. Gary and Elaine plan to move to the area once Gary is settled there, but it soon becomes apparent that even the superpit of the future is insecure, and the mood there is volatile. Managers have been told to be tougher on the men; personnel are going after the ones with records of absenteeism, and area directors' reports assessing the prospects of mines are said to be gloomy. To Gary, it seems that safety measures are being reduced. Soon after he starts work there, the same managers that had been paying generous relocation packages begin offering generous redundancy deals. The basic sell is always the same: thousands of pounds available but for a few days only, take it now or risk losing it for ever. In the spring of 1992, Gary takes it.

As a miner leaving the industry he is entitled to an interview with a Personal Evaluation Consultant, an advisor paid for by the government who is supposed to help redundant miners consider their employment options. Gary is eager for the consultation because it will be a chance to find out how he can retrain to become a teacher. At the meeting, the consultant, a man in his thirties who smiles and admits he doesn't know much about coal mining, refers Gary on to a scheme that helps men to sign up for new jobs and training courses.

At this next interview, conducted in a new, dark-green Portakabin in the pit yard at Barnsley Main, which had closed in 1991, Gary sits across a plain table from a man and woman who are both about his age. The woman wears her hair pulled back from her face, and has on a black cardigan and black trousers. The man wears glasses, and a crew-neck sweater with shirt and tie.

Gary kneads his hands together, and shifts around in his chair. He feels self-conscious, as if he is watching himself in the room.

'Are you working at the moment, Gary?' asks the woman.

'No. I haven't worked since I left Whitemoor.'

'And is there any kind of work you're interested in?'

'Yes. Yes, there is actually . . .' He takes a breath. 'I'd like to try to retrain as a school teacher. And I wondered if you could help me, maybe?'

'Oh!' she says. 'And why do you want to be a teacher?'

'Why?' He hadn't expected that question. 'Well, because . . . because I'd like to work with people, and I've always wanted to teach children. To help them learn, you know. And I think I could do it if I had a chance, so what I'd like is to go to university, and study education.' He hears himself gabbling, and sees confusion on the woman's face. 'I could pay my way through it. I'm not asking to be given owt.'

The confusion changes to a look of regret, and the woman gives Gary an apologetic smile. 'I'm sorry, but we can't help you with that,' she says. 'That's beyond what we would do, you see.'

'What we have,' says the man beside her, 'are things like –' he takes some pamphlets from the desk and passes them to him. 'This . . . or this . . . '

The pamphlets are covered in pictures of men laying bricks and plastering. They are about training courses for builders.

'I don't quite . . . why are you showing me these?'

'Well, because this is what we're set up to do, really,' explains the man.

'But I don't want to be a bricklayer! I've worked in the building trade, and I can go back and do that tomorrow. I thought you were supposed to help us retrain?'

They look at him across the table and the man says, 'I'm sorry, Mr Hollingworth. We do mainly help with building jobs.' The woman suggests that maybe he could drive to a teacher training college and ask there.

'Right. Thank you.'

He takes the pamphlets and walks outside. Alone in the pit yard he imagines arriving at a teacher training college and explaining to the receptionist that a lady on his retraining scheme had advised him to call in. For a moment, he holds to his chest the new ringbinder and A4 notepad he had bought for the meeting, and tries to think of the moment as the start of a journey to a new career. The interview had not been as encouraging as he had hoped, but then perhaps his ambition was greater than he had thought. Perhaps the woman's suggestion was as much as he could have hoped for, and becoming a teacher was going to be a long process that was now beginning.

But he knows he is kidding himself. He doesn't belong in a teacher training college or school, does he? If he did, wouldn't he be there, instead of pretending to himself that the advisors had taken him seriously? All of a sudden the idea of a new career seems a silly fantasy. But then he isn't going back to any building site either.

Having nothing to do for the rest of the day Gary drives to the Dearne to visit Winnie, going the long way round on the country roads. Verges are high with grass and cow parsley, and in the fields the rape is in flower. He passes railway cuttings and low iron bridges, and then the empty ruins of Manvers; littered with bulldozers and diggers, the site reminds him of images of Berlin at the end of the Second World War.

Across the bridge over the Dearne, and up into Highgate. Winnie is in the sitting room, reading a novel as thick as a breadloaf. As he knocks and comes in at the back door she wrestles herself up out of her chair and beams when she sees him.

'Ayup, Grandma. I was just passing. I thought I'd call in and see you.'

'Ayup, love. Have I to make you a sandwich?'

'Go on then.'

Seated with her at the table, he eats the bread and tinned ham and sucks down the strong chestnut-coloured tea. She tells him about her health, and Lynda's work. British Coal is closing the area headquarters at Doncaster and giving staff the option to move to offices near Leeds. Leeds being too far to travel home if Winnie needed her at short notice, Lynda had requested a transfer to a South Yorkshire pit, but as none were suitable for wheelchairs, and British Coal would not adapt them, she is having to take her redundancy. 'She doesn't think she'll get another job, what with being in t' chair,' says Winnie. 'I don't know what she'll do.'

'I don't know what any of us'll do, Grandma.' He tells her about the interview. 'A bit disappointing really. I'd like to do summat . . . useful, if you know what I mean. With people.'

'Aye, love. Like your grandad. He liked people.' She pats his upper arm. 'Sometimes these things find you, you know.'

Winnie has never given Gary actual advice, just made him feel wanted and a part of something. It always works. She clears the crockery, and they sit for a while remembering things that Harry did when Gary was little, and talking about Roy, and recalling the days when Gary used to come and stay. Her memories seem clearer than her understanding of the present, but then, Gary thinks later, you could say the same about most people, in a way.

When he leaves he hugs her, and she is small but solid in his arms. Through her nylon pinnie he can feel the knitted cabling on her sweater, and beneath that the bony knots of her shoulders. He has a strange sense of there being something he would like to say to her, or perhaps ask her, but he doesn't know what it is.

On the way home he stops at Bolton-upon-Dearne cemetery, with its weather-scrubbed, smoke-blackened headstones standing at angles back through centuries: great-uncles, great-grandads, cousins, Hollingworths who may or may not be related, almost all of them coal miners from the early 1800s. Until now.

In Thurnscoe he stops and goes to the Cora for a drink, but the bar is half-empty, and when he tries to read a newspaper, he can't concentrate. He finishes his pint, and buys a bottle of red wine and a four-pack of John Smith's bitter from a shop and takes them home.

Elaine is out, and the house sounds and feels empty and alien. He drinks the beer watching a black-and-white Western on Channel 4, and after draining two cans, he goes up to his and Elaine's bedroom and brings down a small cardboard box containing the keepsakes that his grandad had given him when he was a boy. The brown leather wallet he used when he went out to the club, his old silver wristwatch, the gold-plated tie clip that he wore for best. Gary takes them out and looks at them as he opens the wine. When Elaine comes home he is asleep on the settee, the Western finished, the watch and tie clip in his hand.

*

The story of how Gary Hollingworth eventually finds his new career begins a few weeks after he is asked to paint Highgate Club in the autumn of 1992.

So as not to be unemployed he does some work for a painting and decorating firm in Darfield. The wages are low and the job boring, and he misses the old intimate camaraderie you get working in a group with a single, urgent purpose. Sometimes he even misses the awkward, aggressive blokes who made out they couldn't stand him. He begins drinking more at home in the evenings, bottle of wine, Elaine in bed, him flicking between TV channels on the settee downstairs searching out sitcoms and dramas that he liked when he was young, or those set in the sixties and seventies, like *Heartbeat*. He's in decline, he thinks: he is thirty-four after all. He doesn't understand why he keeps thinking about the past and his childhood, why he feels so out of step with the present.

The boss sends him and two of the other men to paint Highgate Club. The steward, Barry, son of Winnie's neighbour Margaret Westerman, tells them where he wants the creams, whites and dark blue, and gives them a warning: don't get so much as a splash on the mural or he and the committee will bloody well string them up. The mural is above the bar, a large, black and white picture painted by a local man in 1984. Titled *Our Struggle 1984–85*, it is a collage of scenes and public figures from the strike. Gary volunteers to paint the walls around it and he works on the edges with small, slow brushstrokes and daydreams himself into the scenes. Then he imagines he hears an organ and drums, and sees Juggler on the stage. The music stops and Harry looks up at him and says, 'What's tha doing, Gary love? Is tha back painting and decorating?' Before he can answer, the boss comes into view, taking Harry's place.

Gary thinks he is going to moan about him taking too long to paint the edges, but he just stands at the bar contemplating the mural. 'Take your time, mate,' he says. 'Somebody took some time and care over that, once. It doesn't want spoiling.'

Gary begins to look for work at places where he thinks his technical knowledge might be useful, but the interviewers always say he has more experience than they need. At an air-conditioner factory he tries to explain the connection between the products and pit ventilation, but ends up trying to describe colliery airlocks and gas containment systems. He and the two interviewers end up laughing about it, and he apologises.

He takes a temporary job with a team of miners working short-term contracts at Selby. Short-term contractor teams are British Coal's big idea. Managers use them to avoid dealing with the NUM, but lots of the contractors are pro-union, and gung-ho about disputes because they have had their redundancy money and have nothing to fear. British Coal now employs management consultants to sit in pit canteens talking to the men about how everyone could work better together, but Gary doesn't notice relations changing for better or for worse. What he does notice is the worsening quality of work: low air pressures, bad air doors, holes for pipes hacked in the doors. Nobody bothering, nobody checking, because everybody knows they'll be away sooner or later. Some of the pits are friendly, others hard to work in because the full-time men won't cooperate with contractors, and accuse them of having sold their jobs and betrayed the next generation.

He stays on the team for eight months and then, thinking to improve on the skills he already has, he enrols on a part-time course in engineering at a college in Doncaster. Someone he meets on the course mentions that the local further education colleges need more people to teach health and safety regulations to apprentices, and that they like ex-miners because of their attention to detail. He calls some colleges, and two weeks later begins working part-time in the Dearne Valley. He takes a class of sixteen-year-old boys, mostly apprentices employed by local builders working for their City and Guilds. Gary has no idea how to teach a class of boys, so he talks to them as he had talked to the younger lads at Grimethorpe, as an equal. The boys want to learn and they listen and ask questions. By the end of the first lesson they are sharing anecdotes, even cracking jokes. When he walks out of the classroom he briefly closes his eyes and breaks into a smile as wide as the valley itself.

As the weeks pass he notices a boy who is always on his own and not involved in the other boys' banter. Thin, nervy and reluctant to make eye contact, he usually stands or sits towards the back or side of the classroom. His work is fine, a little above the average in fact, but he neither asks questions nor offers answers, and when Gary invites him to talk, he crosses his arms and shrugs.

At home Gary thinks about the kid, and one afternoon at the end of the class he stops him with the excuse of a question about a worksheet.

'And how's t' class going for you, mate?'

'S'alright.'

'Are you getting what you want out of it?'

'Yeah.'

'What are you hoping to do once you've finished?'

A pause: the long, drifting pause of someone who dislikes thinking about themselves or the future. 'Depends if I get a job,' he says, and with his hands tucked inside his sweatshirt cuffs, he crosses his arms across his body and looks away.

It might have been that any teacher in the college would have noticed the boy's behaviour, and intuited that his problems ran deeper than simple shyness. But Gary knows how loneliness and worry sit in a teen-age boy; their troubles might have differed, but feelings of anxiety and unbelonging at home can give someone a certain look. It might also have been that somewhere in Gary's mind, something about the kid connected with the memory of two little boys locked in a caravan in the North East of England, looking out of the window at the other caravans being taken away, and wishing that someone would come.

That night he lies awake thinking about the boy. Should he mind his own business? Is he getting carried away with the teaching?

The next time he is in the college, he plucks up the courage to ask one of the secretaries. 'Excuse me,' he says. 'Could I have a word with you please? It's about one of the students.' The secretary arranges for him to meet the college counsellor, a soft-voiced and purposeful woman who thanks him and promises to talk to the boy.

'We can try, can't we?' she says. He admires how she says 'we'.

Although Gary never knows, nor asks, what the problems are, the counsellor later tells him she has met the boy and his family, and thinks she may have helped them. When Gary asks if the boy is all right, she says she can't discuss it. 'But let's just say it's a good job that you mentioned it,' she adds. 'Thank you.'

The following term a college teacher tells him that as he has worked with children, he can apply to be included on the local Social Services relief register of people who provide emergency help in children's homes when staff levels are low. He applies and, having passed his interviews, starts working night shifts at a home near Doncaster. Most of the children are alienated and angry, but if he tries to guess at their feelings, understand their motivations and talk to them in plain language, he finds he can talk to them. With some it is just a matter of trying to make them feel that they might be wanted somewhere. Some of the staff at the children's home urge him to work there full time but, as they explain, to work for Social Services he would need a diploma, and that would require study at a university. 'Not sure I'd be up to that yet!' he laughs. 'I don't think they'd let me in.' Still, he secretly sends off for a prospectus.

*

'. . . Gary? Gary?' Ten o'clock at night, his dad calling. Drunk. In the last five years Roy has been drinking more heavily, and it is becoming clear that he is suffering from alcoholism. Sometimes when he drinks, he calls late at night, as if he has something important to say. It always turns out to be unimportant, or made up.

'Gary! Do you want to talk to an old soldier?'

'Dad . . .'

'Father to son?'

'Dad. Are you all right?'

'Course I'm bloody all right!' His speech is slurred and irregular. 'Come on, talk to your father.'

'I'm here, what's up?'

'What's up? What's up with you? Have you got a bloody job yet?'

This is how it goes. Twenty years of work, halfway to a new life now, and still this. The conversation will be pointless. 'I've told thee. I'm working at a children's home. They've put me on a temporary contract.'

A confused pause. Roy has forgotten, of course. '*Children's home*? What are you working there for?'

'Because I like it, and I'm good at it. I want to make a career of something like that.'

'Bullshit,' says his dad into the phone. 'You want to get yourself a right job.'

Gary has thought a great deal about his dad since he began work at the home. His thinking leads to questions he cannot quite put into words.

'It's not bullshit. It's helping people.'

Another pause. Then: 'You're an untrustworthy bastard, you. I wouldn't have wanted you behind me in Suez, I'll tell you that.'

'What?'

'In Suez. You'd have stabbed me in the back as soon as look at me.'

'. . . Dad? What are you talking about. It's me, Gary!'

'I know who it is.'

'But what have I . . .?' It is ridiculous. He is a grown man, his father is drunk, and yet Gary's reaction to the insult is to search his memory for an act that might have offended him.

'I was shot at, you know. You couldn't trust any of 'em. You needed a good mate. Not somebody like you.'

'I don't know what you're talking about.'

'You don't know what I'm talking about,' he mimics. 'You'd be a right help in the Army.'

'Dad, leave it . . .'

'You'd run away. I wouldn't trust you as far as I could throw you.'

Snap. With those words, Gary feels something inside him break. 'You wouldn't trust me? Who are you to tell me about trust? Where were you when I needed you?'

'I was there . . .'

'No. No, you were bloody well not there. You weren't there for me or our David, and we've done all right without you. Leave me alone.'

'Don't talk to me like that! Who d'you think you are?'

'Dad . . . Dad, who do you think *you* are?'

'I know who I am. I did my duty . . .'

'Dad . . . I've had enough of this. More than enough. Shut up and goodbye!' says Gary. And seventy miles away, somewhere in the Midlands night, Roy hears the phone crash into its cradle, and he and his eldest son's relationship ends in the sound of a single, high-pitched electronic beep in the darkness.

*

It takes Gary three more years to find the confidence to apply to study for a social work diploma at university, and the process is interwoven with the break-up of his marriage to Elaine.

At home, he begins to feel different. Coming back after the shift at the children's home he wants to talk about the new world he is working in, but it doesn't feel right. A friendship with a woman at work called Heather develops into an affair, and he becomes aggressive with Elaine as a way of concealing and decoying the relationship. One Christmas, Elaine guesses about the affair and in the New Year Gary moves out. Dizzy with a mixture of self-hatred and relief, he crams his clothes into three bin bags and drives away from Grimethorpe with women staring out of their windows along the street. He stays with Margaret and Colin for a few nights, but when he tells his mam the truth she boils up in fury and tells him to leave. For several weeks he rents a mobile home on a caravan park, populated mainly by divorced and unemployed men. Living there, he puts his life in order then, jointly with Heather, buys a semi-detached house on a new development at the edge of Thurnscoe, behind one of the old pit estates.

In 1997 he begins a part-time diploma course at Hull University and gets a daytime field placement as a social worker in another former pit village in the Doncaster hinterlands. In his first week he is awed and nervous, though as there are two ex-miners there already he can hardly use his background to explain that. It is the process that amazes him, all the emails, memos, agendas and bottlecap-twisting meetings that press you under the circuits of talk and the weight of warm printer ink. He wonders what some of the men from Houghton Main and Grimethorpe would have made of it.

Gary keeps quiet, does as he is asked, and tries to mimic the ways staff interact with each other. He shadows case workers and then is assigned his own cases. These are straightforward at first: looking in on lonely old ladies, ensuring that women who have moved away from abusive husbands are being left alone, trying to arrange accommodation for the homeless. It is when he moves to the more difficult cases that he suddenly finds himself accused of being a snooping snob.

One afternoon he visits a man whose arguments with his wife are hardening into thumps on the walls and furniture. The woman is meek and anxious, so Social Services have sent her on an assertiveness course; now she can defy her husband, but he thinks the social workers are using her to hurt him. They live in a semi on an old pit estate. When Gary arrives, a group of shirtless boys is perching on a broken settee on the communal green, smoking and drinking cider, and somewhere a bass-heavy car stereo is shaking the air.

The man opens the front door with no greeting. He is five foot eight, heavy, an ex-miner judging by the black specks and blue scars on his neck. Gary can guess the story: redundancy money spent, no job and no idea what to do, sense of inadequacy taken out on the wife. The man looks hostile, but he defers to Gary. In the chaotic sitting room where two of his children are watching television, he admits to being difficult to live with. 'I suppose now tha's going to tell me how to live my life?'

'No,' says Gary, 'I just wondered if we could have a talk.'

The man answers the first questions comfortably enough, but he knows he is being accused of something. When Gary suggests there may be some problems with the children's school attendance, the man's face reddens and his movements become abrupt. His chest is visibly rising and falling.

'There might be things we could do that would help you get on top of your situation. I can see it's difficult.'

The man gives a dismissive growl. 'You can't see owt. 'As tha got kids?'

'Yeah, I've got two.' You have to be careful with personal details, but Gary wants the man to trust him. From inside the house there is the sound of children running up the stairs. Something heavy falls over. The man shouts at them. Turning back to Gary, he redoubles his attack.

'Aye, and tha were born wi't silver spoon in thy gob. See, when tha goes home, tha'll go in a nice car, to a nice house and a nice view. But when I'm in t' house, I have to sit and look out at that.' He gestures at the net-curtained living-room window and, beyond, to the green and the tired-looking houses.

At the mention of the silver spoon, Gary feels a tingle of indignation. He has a passing urge to dump his bag on the doorstep and go. 'You've got your cushty job,' the man is saying. 'You know nowt about what it's like living here.'

'Oi, mate, I haven't always done this job, have I? I used to do summat totally different, and probably not what tha'd think either. I'm trying to help thee, if tha'll just listen for a minute.'

'Oh aye, I'll bet tha's trying to help me! What did tha do, push a fucking pen?'

'No,' says Gary, and tells him.

They end up sharing old pit stories and later sit down together in the man's front room, and Gary works out a care plan. He encourages the man to make the decisions himself, and to talk about himself and his family. As he talks, the man clasps and squeezes his tea mug, and the mug looks small and delicate in his meaty, tattooed hands. He thinks people look down on him for being unemployed, and he sees schemes for kids and women and everyone else, but nothing for men like him. He had been to the retraining people as well, and had no more luck than Gary. Everybody was moving on, but he was stuck here, trying to get whatever jobs were going in warehouses or supermarkets.

Gary knows that in some ways, seen from the outside, there was no great tragedy to the man's life. The man had lost a job, but he still had a house, a family that loved him and a wife who supported them with her wages. He had friends and he had maintained his interests. What he had lost was evident from the things he didn't mention, at least not in the present tense – work, workmates, social life, politics. With the redundancy he had signed away his idea of his value and his bond to the rest of the world, and for some people those things could be as hard to replace as a home. This didn't excuse anything but, Gary realises, if he is to stop frightening his wife, it would help him if he could start to replace those ideas.

*

As the years pass, Gary settles into the work, both in the field office and at the children's home. The manager at the field office is impressed with his abilities as he deals with problems from domestic abuse and truancy to mental health and homelessness, and he is promoted, and then seconded to cover for the assistant manager of a Wakefield office. At home, he and Heather decorate the house and buy the trappings of modern, comfortable lives. Claire has taken her degree at Nottingham University. Scott marries his girlfriend and in 1998 has a baby son, Reece, making Gary a grandfather.

When he looks back at the changes in his life since leaving Whitemoor, Gary Hollingworth will recall no great epiphanies, nor any determining mentors. He will, however, think back to the pit yards of Houghton Main and Grimethorpe, where stubborn older miners had taught him the need for ingenuity and tact, and, more often, to the parts of his childhood spent at Number 34 Highgate Lane. There, he comes to believe, his grandma and grandad had seeded his desire to help other people by demonstrating how help could be given. Their stories about history had been a part of that, because the stories had connected him to people and ideas that gave him an identity, and that identity had helped him explain himself. Winnie and Harry Hollingworth had shown him how a lonely person could be made to feel wanted, and how that person could change their idea of themselves by being listened to and taken seriously. Those methods could not solve everyone's problems, but they could usually be a start, just as they had once been a start for him.

67

All the Places

Thurnscoe; Rossington Main Colliery; Goldthorpe Colliery; Doncaster College, 1992–95

At five in the afternoon on Tuesday 13 October 1992, David Hollingworth is sleeping in bed before a night shift when he is woken, as usual, by a Michael Jackson song playing in Lisa's bedroom. He sighs, smiles and pads across the landing to the bathroom, squinting against the electric light as he fills the sink with water. 'Sorry if I woke you up, Dad.' Lisa tries to hush her voice as she talks to him through the door; her mam keeps the house quiet when David is on nights, and tells her off if she forgets.

He opens the door. 'You didn't, love, I was getting up anyroad. How've you gone on at school?'

Eleven now, she is in her first term at Dearnside. 'All right,' she says. 'What've you been doi– '

'LISA!' Marie is shouting up the stairs. 'Have you woken your dad up with that music?'

'No, she hasn't,' he shouts back, and Lisa darts back to Michael Jackson singing 'Black or White'. 'I was already up. Can you put t' tea on, and I'll come down and watch t' news?'

The teatime news, watched in the sitting room as the family eats lasagne from plates on their laps, leads with the story that mining families have been half-expecting for years. In the House of Commons, Michael Heseltine, the President of the Board of Trade, announces that

British Coal is to close thirty-one of the last fifty working pits, and make 30,000 miners redundant. The new private power-generating companies, National Power and PowerGen, are, as predicted, reducing the amount of British coal they will use because they can buy cheaper on world markets. This, an economist tells a TV news reporter, will be the largest mass redundancy in British history and another 70,000 jobs will be lost through knock-on effects.

At a press conference Arthur Scargill, sitting in front of a red banner bearing the words 'THE PAST WE INHERIT, THE FUTURE WE BUILD', says he will be urging NUM members to take action. Neil Clarke, the British Coal chairman, says 'the whole situation is a very sad, very damaging, very distressing one, but it is forced on us by the market'. He says the market is 'unfair', which some commentators will take as reference to the government encouraging the new private energy-generating companies to burn gas rather than coal.

A graphic lists the Yorkshire closures one by one, with the number of jobs at each. Maltby, Prince of Wales and Hatfield/Thorne will be mothballed, and eight closed:

Sharlston (750 miners)
Bentley (650)
Frickley (1,000)
Grimethorpe (959)
Houghton Main (440)
Kiveton (775)
Markham Main (734)
Rossington (880) . . .

When Rossington's name appears David grimaces and says he wishes he'd stayed in bed.

'They'll probably close that and all,' says Marie.

*

Later, in the bright, banging locker rooms at Rossington, some of the men are shocked and sad, and some others say, 'Sod it, let me get my figures and get out now.' Pessimism has been thickening since May, when the government formally revealed its plans to privatise coal, but stirred in with it now is confusion. British Coal's recent reports show some of the pits to be productive and profitable: could it really not find other customers? There is talk of strikes and protests, but inside David feels that this time opposition would only put off the inevitable. As he walks to the lamp room in his orange overalls, he notices a Coal Not Dole sticker has been amended with marker pen to 'Dole Not Coal'.

Public opposition is strong though, and most people appear to side with the miners. Perhaps trying to maintain the mass support, Arthur Scargill withdraws calls for a strike. The NUM challenges the legality of the government's announcement in the High Court, and the Labour Party requests that the process be stopped while the Select Committee on Trade and Industry examines the future of coal. Miners' wives revive the Women Against Pit Closures campaign. The police officer who arrested Arthur Scargill at Orgreave, Chief Superintendent John Nesbit, tells the *Daily Mirror* that, in his opinion, Scargill had been right in 1984. The outcry is such that backbench Conservative MPs threaten to vote down Michael Heseltine's bill, and it looks as though John Major, who had replaced Mrs Thatcher as Prime Minister in 1990, will be defeated in the Commons. In response, the Cabinet announces a freeze on the closures pending the outcome of a Department of Trade and Industry investigation of new markets for coal. The report will be published in January 1993, this stalling an old tactic that the miners with their history know from 1925 and 1981.

On Wednesday 21 October 1992, over a hundred thousand miners and supporters march through London with Scargill at their head. Crowds along the route cheer the miners; in Park Lane someone comes out of the crowd and gives Scargill a bouquet of white chrysanthemums. In Kensington and Knightsbridge people lean out of hotel windows and applaud. Four days later, 200,000 people march again. Nevertheless, British Coal stops production at ten of the thirty-one pits listed for closure – Grimethorpe being one of them – and sends the men home on basic pay, no bonuses. They allow men to volunteer for redundancy, hinting that the terms will not be so generous again.

Then, four days before Christmas, the High Court rules that the government has broken the law in announcing the shutdown of such a large portion of the industry without consultation. It also finds invalid Heseltine's offered compromise of closing ten pits after a ninety-day consultation period, and orders a review of the other twenty-one. Government ministers backtrack and John Major declares that he now has an 'open mind' about the industry.

There follow three months of debate, political dealing and protests. At Grimethorpe and the other threatened pits, women set up permanent brazier-lit vigils outside the pit gates. In Westminster, Michael Heseltine solicits the support of MPs. Managers from British Coal propose a compromise plan that would repeal a 1908 Act limiting shifts to seven and a half hours. In March, Heseltine publishes a new White Paper that promises to save thirteen pits, but only for two years while they reduce production costs.

Questioned about this, with the vote on his White Paper approaching and demonstrations outside the House of Commons, Heseltine blames the miners. They may have improved productivity levels but they have not changed quickly enough, he says, and the market has been filled by more competitive fuels. The White Paper passes with a majority of twenty-two, and later the High Court rules that the government has now consulted and is free to make the closures. There are one-day strikes in the NUM pits – members of the Union of Democratic Mineworkers continue to work – and Anne Scargill and three other members of Women Against Pit Closures hold a four-day sit-in at Parkside colliery in Lancashire. ('One hundred thousand people could lose their jobs if these pits go,' Anne tells journalists afterwards, 'yet we mine the cheapest deep-mined coal in the world. We're not dots on a computer screen.')

But British Coal begins the closures immediately. Production stops at Rossington in April, and Grimethorpe, Houghton Main and the other South Yorkshire pits follow. By the end of June even the 'saved' pits are closing. Within a year, thirty-three – two more than had been announced in the first place – have closed, and six of them are sold to private operators.

In the towns and villages and pit yards there is bitter quitting that inverts the optimism of 1947: 'FUCK THE PIT', 'SHUT THE PIT', 'GIVE ME MY MONEY' written on lockers, etched into girders, scrawled over walls in NCB paint. Managers and union men alike are goaded, heads turning away at meetings, voices singing, 'Shut the pit, shut the pit, shut the pit!' to the tune of 'Here we go' when officials come in earshot. As men learn that irreparable large-scale breakdowns can hasten closures, machinery suffers mysterious damage. Those who want to keep the mines open argue and fight with those seeking redundancy. The fever also grips the men who come in trucks and cranes to clear the yards and cap the shafts. Shearers, roadheaders, roof supports, conveyor systems, bucket loaders, machinery worth millions of pounds, is abandoned in tunnels, or tipped down the shafts and sealed under the grey plugs of concrete tipped after it. No one seems responsible. In the Cora, at Highgate Club and in the Unity, people add up the figures: four new locos left down at one pit, barely driven million-pound dumper trucks thrown down the shaft at another; little visible concern for economy there, then, and little sign too of the promised millions of pounds of aid.

*

When British Coal mothballs Rossington in April 1993, David Hollingworth is given compulsory redundancy. He finds the months leading up to that date unpleasant, worse than the strike, because the sour-salted atmosphere corrodes old comradeship. As men leave, the passenger numbers on the bus that still collects them from Hickleton pit dwindle to twenty, then to single figures. Some mornings David walks to work with the streets entirely to himself, as if he were the last man in the village. He meets four or five others on the bus, and they and the driver speed through the valley dawn to Rossington on the near-empty miners' ghost coach. In his second to last week there is just David and one other man. Then the other man leaves and, in his final week, when David walks down the empty road to the deserted pit he sees a single minicab waiting in the darkness. He puts his head to the door and the driver winds down the window.

'Is this for Rosso?' David asks.

'Aye. Is it just thee?'

'Aye.' He gets in, and the driver pulls away. 'Not bad this,' David says. 'My own driver. And they say British Coal are tight.'

David remains unemployed for twelve months. In that time he and Marie notice changes in the valley, though the changes are uneven, some of them hidden. In some places shops and pubs stay open; in others, particularly the larger villages where retailers rely on neighbouring areas for trade, the high street closures are numerous and noticeable. Unemployment rises to fifty per cent in some areas, but the figures are kept down because many of the ex-miners are able to claim long-term disability benefits. There are stories of local crimes which David and Marie find bizarre and incredible. In Highgate, police use the Seels' farm straw stacks to stake out a suspected drug dealer on Highgate Lane and this makes Marie laugh because it sounds like an incident from a TV cop show.

But there are also projects for the future, talk of a new link road, enterprise zones, a university for the valley, a wetland nature reserve at Manvers Main. Spoil heaps are grassed down, and in some places the wild, handsome country is restored to the way it must have looked almost two hundred years ago. Lots of people welcome the promises, because they will bring money, work and choices, but some parts could have done with the regeneration earlier. By the mid-1990s, Grimethorpe is the poorest village in Britain and the Dearne Valley is designated one of the sixty most deprived areas in Europe by an EU study, and one of the four poorest in the UK.

In March 1994, Rossington is leased and reopened by a private owner, RJB Mining – the whole industry is privatised later that year – and the Rossington manager calls to offer David his old job. Within a week, he is back working with Houdie in the headings. The work itself is much as it had been under British Coal, though the union has less influence, and there are fewer men.

In the summer, RJB introduces some new management techniques. 'Everybody reckons they're sending us on a course next,' David tells Marie as they sit in the back garden one afternoon. 'It's to teach us all how to work in a team.'

Marie wrinkles her forehead. 'To teach you *what*?'

'To work as a team. They've got experts that tell you what to do.'

'But how do they teach you that?'

'I don't know. I think they get you to do exercises, and give you tasks to do together, but I haven't a clue.'

'Don't you help each other anyway?'

'Aye,' he says, shrugging. 'I suppose so.'

Marie thinks, staring at the sunlit foxgloves around the garden. 'Do you think it'll be like when we made them canoes, Dave?' They both laugh. 'Or like you learning me to fish when I fell in?'

As it turns out, the managers invite only a few dozen men to go on the courses, those presumably marked out as having the potential to be deputies. Most of the men, including David, are relieved not to be asked.

*

Goldthorpe colliery, the last working pit in the Dearne Valley, closes in spring 1995. On a clear but dullish morning in late March the indifferent cranes come to swing their black iron balls into the buildings, and bulldozers finish off the walls. A small crowd of people stands watching, some of them recording the demolition with cameras and camcorders. Driving past, Lynda Hollingworth slows down to look. She sees the offices go, and then watches as a crane jabs its boom into an iron hopper as high as two houses. The hopper slumps to the ground like a shot cow and black dust hangs over the yard like a veil.

She hadn't known they were knocking it all down today. As she drives away, she thinks of Walter Parkin, Harry and John's family having worked there, and then of all the colliery names she once learned: *Askern, Barnburgh, Bentley, Brodsworth, Cadeby & Denaby, Frickley, Goldthorpe, Highgate, Hatfield, Markham, Rossington* and *Thorne.*

She drives to Doncaster College's arts faculty, where she now works in the admin department, organising, minuting and orchestrating the aesthetes of South Yorkshire in an old redbrick building that had once been Doncaster's Institute of Mechanical Engineering. She likes the work, though most of the academics need all new information to be explained twice, and take days to reply to questions, and use a jargon obscure as pit language. The students are not what she had expected either, all wildly coloured hair, ripped jeans and language that would have made a Hickleton miner blush. Some of their work didn't look much like art to her, but she asks students about their abstract painting and murky, plotless videos and tries to get it, and sometimes she finds their explanations quite interesting. She adapts her mind to them as she has learned to adapt it to the computers and gadgets. If you didn't adapt, you got old.

That morning, as Lynda stops by the pale-blond wood reception desk, she sees Kirsty, a student she knows. Wearing a sack-like dress, with silver rings through her bottom lip and eyebrows, Kirsty is talking to a knot of office staff and students about Goldthorpe pit being knocked down. 'I drove past it this morning,' Lynda says. 'There looked to be enough men there to knock all of Goldthorpe down.'

'I bet there did,' says Kirsty. 'It's sad, don't you think, Lynda?'

'Yes, I do really.' Lynda is mildly surprised. She would not have expected the pierced and artistic Kirsty to have any interest in old collieries at all. 'When I was a bit older than you, I knew t' name of every pit in t' Doncaster area. If you said t' names of all t' pits in South Yorkshire, it used to take you five minutes to get through them all.'

As if, she thinks, that will make any sense to you. As if . . .

'My dad knew all t' Donny ones,' says Kirsty. 'He used to say all t' names for me. "Askern, Bentley, Brodsworth . . ." I could still remember if I tried. He worked at Broddy.'

'Broddy,' says Lynda. 'My dad used to sing at a pub there. They used to call that t' Queen's pit, you know.'

'Yeah, I know. My dad said all t' kings and queens had Brodsworth coal, because it burned t' best.'

'So they did,' says Lynda. 'So they did. I wonder what t' Queen burns now, though?'

68

Where is Everybody?

Highgate and Bolton-upon-Dearne, 1996

A hot, airless Sunday afternoon in August 1996: dogs asleep in the sunshine, children out in the yards, gardens caged by the long shadows of wooden fences. In the garden of 229 Barnsley Road, John is weeding the dry and cracked vegetable beds, and Lynda is reading a Penny Vincenzi novel. Winnie, now eighty-six, has come to the back door of the house and is glowering vengefully at her daughter.

'Lynda,' she snaps. 'What have you done with my fan heater?'

Lynda looks puzzled. 'You haven't got a fan heater,' she says. 'Not unless you count that really old thing.'

'It's not old.'

'It's *quite* old, Mam. You bought it in t' 1960s when Nelly Spencer got hers.'

'Don't you tell me what's old and what isn't. What have you done with it?'

Earlier that afternoon Winnie had called on Nancy, and Nancy had shown off a new fan heater that cooled her house. Heat-flushed and envy-stricken, Winnie came home to root for her heater in the cupboard where it had once been kept. 'I've had every last thing out, and it's not there,' she says. 'Where is it?'

Lynda and John exchange guilty glances. The heater is not there because during a spring clean approximately five years ago they had noticed how rotten and frayed its cables were, and thrown it away. John

stands up, and draws the fire. 'I threw it o
dangerous. It could've caused an accident.'

'You did *what*?'

'I threw it out. I'll go up Goldthorpe tom
one.'

She stares at him. 'You have no bloody bu
stuff out. You're always the bloody same. Y
Swearing; she is spoiling for a fight.

'Don't be so daft, Mam. Me and John'll ge
row. Why don't you go into t' house where
silly?' She forces a matey tone, but it is like t

'You would stick up for him, wouldn't you
both. You're bad 'uns. But if you want me to

She locks herself in her bedroom and ref
rest of the day. The next morning she leave
but Nancy brings her back after seeing her
at the crossroads. The car had almost hit
thankful she is raging against the driver, Na
in Highgate.

'Ring our Pauline, and tell her to fetch me
'I'm going to stay with her, where I'm wante
she visited Pauline Winnie had torn into
rudeness, and after an argument Pauline ha
'Tell her I'm not having her again,' Pauline
time. She can stay where she is.'

And so, as it is harvest time, she stays, but i
forgetfulness and erratic behaviour of recent ye
frequent. She goes to bed at eight in the ev
downstairs five hours later, fully dressed ('Loo
dark outside, can't you see?' 'Where?' she asks
ery she once immaculately washed and wiped
with traces of egg yolk or spots of dried gravy
goes out, she leaves the gas on. She pees on
Lynda, not wanting to ask John, has to climb
scrub it out.

68

Where is Everybody?

Highgate and Bolton-upon-Dearne, 1996

A hot, airless Sunday afternoon in August 1996: dogs asleep in the sunshine, children out in the yards, gardens caged by the long shadows of wooden fences. In the garden of 229 Barnsley Road, John is weeding the dry and cracked vegetable beds, and Lynda is reading a Penny Vincenzi novel. Winnie, now eighty-six, has come to the back door of the house and is glowering vengefully at her daughter.

'Lynda,' she snaps. 'What have you done with my fan heater?'

Lynda looks puzzled. 'You haven't got a fan heater,' she says. 'Not unless you count that really old thing.'

'It's not old.'

'It's *quite* old, Mam. You bought it in t' 1960s when Nelly Spencer got hers.'

'Don't you tell me what's old and what isn't. What have you done with it?'

Earlier that afternoon Winnie had called on Nancy, and Nancy had shown off a new fan heater that cooled her house. Heat-flushed and envy-stricken, Winnie came home to root for her heater in the cupboard where it had once been kept. 'I've had every last thing out, and it's not there,' she says. 'Where is it?'

Lynda and John exchange guilty glances. The heater is not there because during a spring clean approximately five years ago they had noticed how rotten and frayed its cables were, and thrown it away. John stands up, and draws the fire. 'I threw it out, Winnie, because it was dangerous. It could've caused an accident.'

'You did *what*?'

'I threw it out. I'll go up Goldthorpe tomorrow and buy thee a new one.'

She stares at him. 'You have no bloody business throwing any of my stuff out. You're always the bloody same. You do it to cause trouble.' Swearing; she is spoiling for a fight.

'Don't be so daft, Mam. Me and John'll get you a new heater tomorrow. Why don't you go into t' house where it's cooler, and stop being silly?' She forces a matey tone, but it is like throwing sugar on a fire.

'You would stick up for him, wouldn't you? I know you, I know you both. You're bad 'uns. But if you want me to go, I'll go.'

She locks herself in her bedroom and refuses to come out for the rest of the day. The next morning she leaves the house on her own, but Nancy brings her back after seeing her step out in front of a car at the crossroads. The car had almost hit her, but far from being thankful she is raging against the driver, Nancy, Lynda and everyone in Highgate.

'Ring our Pauline, and tell her to fetch me now!' she instructs Lynda. 'I'm going to stay with her, where I'm wanted.' However, the last time she visited Pauline Winnie had torn into Gordon over a perceived rudeness, and after an argument Pauline had driven her home early. 'Tell her I'm not having her again,' Pauline had said. 'Not in harvest time. She can stay where she is.'

And so, as it is harvest time, she stays, but in the days that follow her forgetfulness and erratic behaviour of recent years grow worse and more frequent. She goes to bed at eight in the evening, then comes back downstairs five hours later, fully dressed ('Look, Mam!' says Lynda. 'It's dark outside, can't you see?' 'Where?' she asks plaintively). The crockery she once immaculately washed and wiped is left half clean, marked with traces of egg yolk or spots of dried gravy. Almost every time she goes out, she leaves the gas on. She pees on the bathroom floor and Lynda, not wanting to ask John, has to climb out of her wheelchair to scrub it out.

Sharing recent memories of what they now understand to have been early signs of dementia, Lynda and Pauline also recount past conversations that had made them wonder about their mother's honesty, and in the course of these confessional, venting night-time telephone calls they prick out inconsistencies going back twenty-five years.

For five years Winnie has told Pauline that she, a poor old lady, pays the household bills, while John borrows money from her. No, says Lynda, she pays for the gas and electric and we pay the rest, and John has never taken so much as a promise from her purse.

For twenty years she has told Lynda that Pauline is cold to her when she visits her at the farm, and that she has never helped her with money. 'But I always thought we were good pals!' says Pauline. 'We paid for their holidays, and we bought them no end of bits for the house.' Bits for the house: for twenty-five years both Pauline and Lynda have been buying household ornaments, furnishings and clothes for their mother and, when their mother never displayed or wore them, assumed that she had gifted them to the other sister. From this assumption each has deduced that the other sister was their mother's favourite, despite the relative shortfall in generosity. Only now, with Winnie no longer interposing between them, do they realise that the gifts were not passed on to the other sister at all. Most likely, they guess, all those knick-knacks, all that china and all the woollen blankets and clothes and £5 notes to help with the bills have been offered up to Roy.

At the end of the summer Trisha Brant, a friend of Lynda's who works as a care assistant at a care home in Bolton-upon-Dearne, invites Winnie to spend a week at the home so that Lynda can have a break from worrying during the day and getting up to her in the night. Winnie seems willing – keen even – to go, and so one Saturday morning in September, Lynda helps her to pack her small red suitcase, puts her in the car, and drives her down the hill for her break.

Three days later, Trisha phones to tell Lynda that Winnie is on her way to hospital after suffering a stroke.

*

When Lynda arrives, she finds her mam semi-conscious and paralysed down the right side. Lying in the high hospital bed she looks too small, like a child's doll surrounded by full-size furniture. If I pulled back the sheets, thinks Lynda, a good gust of wind could whisk out of the window and carry her away with the dead leaves to Harry. She holds her left hand and feels its delicate bones and tiny swags of cold thin skin.

'What are we going to do, Mam?' she whispers. 'Tell me what I need to do to make you better.'

*

In fact, Winnie makes a good stab at a recovery. She regains the full use of her body, and at times is as alert as she was before she went to the care home. In rushes of clarity she tells Lynda she will be alright because the gypsy girl is helping, watching over her until it is time to go. Lynda does not dismiss the idea, and she can find it in herself to believe in the little girl guarding her mam, but she knows that spirit guides cannot pick old ladies up from the floor if they fall when their daughters are at work, nor turn off the gas if the ladies shuffle out of the door with the rings still burning. Winnie, it will be found, is in the early stages of leukaemia and Parkinson's disease. Lynda cannot look after her all the time, and the council's social workers cannot provide enough care to make it work; in the end Barnsley council move her from the hospital to a permanent place in the home, the costs to be borne by the council and the DSS.

Bolton Hall was originally a large, stone, gothic-revival house, built in 1830 by a doctor who lived in the village. In the 1980s low-rise, wide-corridored accommodation was added to turn it into a home for elderly people suffering from dementia and physical disability, and now it is a clean, decent place, staffed mainly by women who live in the village, and know the residents' children, if not the residents themselves. At times it can seem like a pastel-painted doll's house version of the old streets; in the reception area on the first day, Winnie and Lynda meet Comfort Eades, wrinkled and bright as a shrunken winter apple. Comfort invites Winnie to come to see her in the West Wing, but Winnie seems unsure of who Comfort might be.

She is happier in her room, with its pale yellow wallpapered walls and the smell of air freshener. Here Lynda decants her clothes from a case into a small pinewood chest of drawers, and arranges framed family photographs on its lace mat-covered top. On the small bedside table, Winnie places a single photograph of Harry.

When Lynda visits her mam in the evenings she finds her sitting in the lounge, a long rubber-tiled room with high-backed chairs around the walls. Seated in the chairs the residents either roost mutely, or chat while their eyes search the room for a younger person who might play the piano for them. In her first weeks Winnie belongs to the former group, keeping herself apart, and twisting her thumbs together as if by concentrating hard enough she could knit the past back out of the air and turn the world inside out, with herself at its centre rather than its edges. 'You'll have plenty of people to talk to, Mam,' enthuses Lynda. Winnie doesn't answer, then asks if Lynda's mam knows that she is here.

Away from her familiar setting, Winnie suffers more memory lapses and her mind seems to deteriorate. Some evenings, Lynda finds little sign of a mind at all. 'Is my dad any better?' she snaps in the middle of a conversation about the home's food.

'You what, Mam?'

'Is he any better? You didn't ought to go out and leave him like that.'

'Is who better?'

'Don't act daft! My *dad*.'

'Who do you think I am, Mam?'

'You're my mother.'

'Mam . . . Mam, I'm Lynda.' Winnie stops and looks down, as if trying to remember where she is. 'Lynda, your daughter.'

'I *know*.'

Lynda asks if she is sleeping well. In response, Winnie looks out of the windows and points. 'That's where our Lynda lives, look. Anyway, where is everybody?'

Still, her decline is not yet relentless. As Christmas passes and the new year greens over, she recoups her strength and the skeins of her composure. Tiny as a pepperpot in her floral chair, pink scalp showing under hair faded to the colour of clear fishing line, she remembers some of her visitors' names, and introduces the staff to the gypsy girl. To exercise her memory, Lynda and Pauline bring from Winnie's sideboard old photographs and newspaper clippings. On the reverse of pictures showing people unrecognisable to the sisters, Winnie writes names and dates in tremulous blue ballpoint pen: Young Juggler Jane is found at a fair in the 1930s, and fourteen-year-old Amy Leather spotted posing in a backyard with her multitudinous family of Welsh Methodists. The man in a black dress and curly wig, playing a washboard and collier's dudley on a stage somewhere in the 1950s, is known to all of them, and it is now that Winnie adds the caption, her copperplate swoops and loops inscribing flights of longing for the daft 'apeth with half a pint of beer up his frock: *Mother Riley. Harry – how I miss him.*

The actual presence of old neighbours and local people of her own age yields little solace or entertainment for her, but she does appoint herself their judge and disciplinarian. 'Look at him, causing trouble!' she will say of a woman several chairs down who is complaining to one of the staff. 'All he ever does is moan, he wants to think himself lucky and shut up.'

This transformation of women into men – usually bad men in want of a good hiding – is her favourite spell, but she will also upbraid female residents guilty of unladylike behaviour. In the spring a pallid, wild-haired woman from Wath comes to live at the home and is seated beside Winnie at meal times. During the meals the woman swears loudly and randomly, bloody this, bugger that, bastard the other, over the mince and mashed potatoes. The cursing awakes in Winnie the bitter censoriousness instilled by her father.

'Shut your filthy mouth,' says Winnie.

'Bugger off, you silly cow,' says the woman.

Smack. Win punches the old lady in the mouth with a bony, loosely bunched fist. Hot tea spills across the table, and when it drips onto the woman's lap she shrieks.

'Don't say I didn't warn you,' says Winnie, and turns back to her food.

'Your mam seems right quiet, but she's feisty when she wants to be, isn't she?' says the home's nursing sister, when she tells Lynda about the punch.

'Yes,' says Lynda. 'I suppose you could say that.'

69

From the Flames to the Winds

The Dearne Valley, 1997–2002

Months and years pass, residents at the hall come and go. Winnie's bouts of delusion lengthen; always she is a young version of herself in her own house, with Walter and Annie and neighbours around her but no husband – or at least not one that she mentions.

'Look who's come to see you, Winnie!' the assistants say when Lynda arrives.

'Yes!' she replies. 'It's my mam!'

When Lynda leaves, Winnie promises to watch out for her getting home. 'I can see your house from my kitchen. I know when you're in, because I can see your light.'

She is too frail to go far, but even if she had been able to travel through it, the surrounding countryside would now have seemed as illusory to her as her visions are to her family. In these years regeneration projects funded by local authorities, the European Union and the New Labour government are changing the look of the valley so rapidly that when Pauline and Gordon drive to see the old Manvers site one day after visiting Winnie, they lose their way and cannot work out where they are. Gigantic windowless warehouses and industrial units seem to be dropped from the sky at night, their fantastical, mystical quality enhanced by their desertedness; no one ever seems to see people either going into or coming out of them. More industrial landscape is reclaimed, and everywhere there are new roads, call centres, golf courses, houses, retail parks, and signs announcing development schemes. Thanks to hoardings erected by firms and agencies working on a re-landscaping project, Grimethorpe acquires what appears to be a corporate branding for a spoil heap. Among these new tidy monuments to shopping, service and leisure, disused industrial buildings, shut-up shops and stretches of closed-up terraced housing loom like elderly relatives at an eighteenth birthday party, hoping to be asked to join in, but suspecting that some of the organisers wish they didn't have to be there in the first place. Leading off from main roads, old pit lanes are blocked off by concrete boulders, their lamp posts broken, railings down, surfaces cracked and whiskered with grass and thistles. Where collieries stood, commemorative winding wheels are planted into the earth like headstones.

In this way the future arrives unevenly, rudely, and, in some places, prettily. As for the past, the authorities seem unsure what to do with it. Where it cannot be hidden under concrete, it is cordoned off and neglected, preserved mainly in the loyalties and stories of the people.

Karl Grainger, Lisa Hollingworth and John Burton move to work at Kostal, a German car components factory on an industrial estate in Highgate. Lynda gets a job at Doncaster College's Faculty of Business and Professional Studies, where she works for the Director of Higher Education, a former mining engineer who keeps his old pit lamp in his office. On her first day with him, he had burst into her office and shouted, 'Where are those bloody minutes from this morning?' and she had replied, 'In your bloody office!' He had done a double-take then said, 'I think you and me are going to get on.'

In Leicestershire, Roy retires and, with his health damaged by barely controlled alcoholism, moves into sheltered housing with Alwyn. On the Yorkshire Wolds, Pauline and Gordon Benson have to sell off their farm when changing economic conditions leave it too small to be viable.

Gary Hollingworth still enjoys his new career in social work, though his caseload and the everyday strains of working in an office can be more challenging than he might have once expected. When he goes to see his GP about a series of throat infections, the doctor tells him he is suffering from stress and needs time off work. Gary is dumbfounded. 'Inside I was seething,' he tells Heather later. 'I wanted to say, "Do you know what I used to be? Do you know what job I used to do? *That* was stressful."'

Sometimes he dreams that he is back working underground at Grimethorpe, waking in the small hours ready to pick up his snap and set off for an early shift. The dreams come when he has new, knotty tasks at work, and in them he has to puzzle out problems in the pit that mutate when he finds a solution. One winter night, having spent much of the day discussing a new flexitime system, he dreams that he has changed his shifts from days to earlies. He rides the conveyors to the coalface and begins taking measurements, but then remembers that he shouldn't be there because the pit is shut. He comes up to the surface, but then realises he has lost his lamp and self-rescue gear; he goes back underground to look for them but they are not there either, and now he panics. If the overman sees Gary's lamp and gear somewhere on the surface, he will assume Gary has come out of the pit, and when the shift ends Gary will be left down there alone. He looks at his watch, but the face is covered in mud. He searches for the pit bottom but he cannot find it anywhere – and then, suddenly he is on the pit top, in sunlight, safe. For a moment he relaxes, but then he realises that everyone else has gone, and there are no gates. He darts around the yard looking for a gate or another person until he wakes up.

It is just past 4 a.m. He gets up, and goes to the window to look out at the snoring and frost-webbed village. No one about on the streets, no lights on in the houses, no late drinking lights burning in the windows of the clubs. The valley keeps the same hours as everywhere else now, he thinks, the old miners labouring away their night shifts in the dream-pit, the grandmas watching from their kitchens for their mams' lights in the darkness.

*

Wednesday 12 December 2001. A cold and dry late afternoon in the valley, shops and houses speckled with Christmas lights, the roads busy with shoppers and people returning home from work. The news is full of talk about economic downturn, the war in Afghanistan, 9/11, and David and Victoria Beckham's social life. Lynda Burton is looking forward to escaping it; as she drives through the dusk towards Bolton Hall, she imagines her and John's coming Christmas holiday in Tenerife, and the thought cheers her. She plans to tell her mam about it later. Even though Winnie will struggle to distinguish the Canary Islands from Skegness, she will at least look and smile at the leaflets about the hotel, looks and smiles now coming to her more easily than actual conversation.

When Lynda finds her mam in the lounge she is seated in a chair by herself. She wears a fine pale sweater and woollen skirt taken by a care assistant from the pool of clothes that morning. Her wedding ring hangs from a chain around her neck, her fingers being too thin to keep it on; denuded and widowed, her hands occupy themselves pleating and rolling the hem of the sweater.

The sister, a stout, jolly local woman who has befriended Lynda, says, 'Look who's here!' but Winnie manages only to glance up, smiling like weak milky tea, and say 'Hello!' Nowadays Winnie doesn't even see her mam, and for the last six months she has not put more than three words together at a time. Always a master of silences and brevity, she now begins her exchanges with properly formed words, but then fades through murmuring 'mmms' to silence. Tonight Lynda thinks she looks more vacant than before, but her alertness fluctuates and it is hard to tell. In full health, a single movement of the eyes could reveal her state of mind, but now she seems a different woman altogether. This is why Lynda feels less distressed than she would have expected to. She feels sympathy for the small, weak woman in the chair, of course, but more than that, she is baffled and sorry at her mam's transformation into this stranger who, but for her appearance, is unrecognisable.

On the seat of an empty chair beside her lie two white rectangular envelopes, slit open along the top.

'Who's been sending you cards then, birthday girl?' says Lynda.

'Yes,' says Winnie, smiling.

'Is one from our Pauline?'

'Mmmm.'

'John and Karl say happy birthday as well. They're both still at work.'

'Mmmm.'

'We're going to have a bit of cake, aren't we?'

'. . .'

Today Winnie is ninety-two years old. Lynda has come early so as to be at the birthday tea.

In the dining room she sits next to her mam among the other residents, and helps her to eat her chicken casserole and mashed potatoes. After the plates are cleared, two carers bring before Winnie a pink-and-white birthday cake decorated with nine candles, and 'Happy Birthday' is sung to her.

'Are you going to blow your candles out, Winnie love?' asks one of the cake-bringers. 'Have you got enough puff?'

Winnie stares into the flames and shakes her puff-less head. The woman herself blows out the candles, making a small cloud of smoke like an extra white head at the table.

Lynda cuts up a slice of the cake for her mam, but she seems wearied by eating, and so they trudge back into the lounge. Lynda talks about Tenerife, and Winnie dozes. Her head ticks forward and then she wakes, startled.

'Are you tired, Mam?' asks Lynda.

'Yes.' Her voice is minute and shy, like a speck of dust confiding in someone.

'Shut your eyes then, and go to sleep. I'm not going anywhere.'

For a moment Winnie's eyelids close and she seems to be sleeping, but then she opens her eyes and looks at Lynda. 'Thank you,' she says, and falls asleep.

In the room, someone clears away teacups. *Who Wants to Be a Millionaire* comes on the television. A carer dims the lights. Lynda eases her mam's right hand into hers, and watches her sleeping.

Thank you, she thinks – strange. Harry had said the same to John just before he died, but Winnie does not appear to be dying. Distant and feeble she may be, but she is still absolutely present. Lynda has many times watched her drift towards the horizon as if to disappear, but she always sails back and re-anchors herself in a way that seems inevitable.

She will not wake again today, though. The sister comes and asks if they should put her to bed, and Lynda agrees. She leans over and kisses the thin white crown of hair. 'Happy birthday, Mam,' she says.

'Thank you' are the last words Winnie Hollingworth says to a member of her family. On 8 January, Lynda receives a phone call in her hotel room in Playa de las Americas. Winnie has been taken to Barnsley hospital because the sister at Bolton Hall saw a lot of blood on her pillow, and guessed that she had had a haemorrhage. In fact she had only cut a gum, the stain's size down to the thinness of Winnie's blood, which is now so short of platelets that a small nick can bleed for hours. 'So it's no problem,' says the nurse. 'She'll just have a transfusion and she'll be fine. No need for you to worry at all.'

The transfusion revives Winnie sufficiently for her to sit up in bed and eat her meals by the evening, and so it comes as a surprise when the following morning – the morning of Lynda's fifty-third birthday – Lynda calls to hear the nurse answer in a tone of professionally restrained urgency. 'Are you the daughter that's in Tenerife? We were just going to call you. Hold on a minute, I've got the doctor here.' There are rasping and knocking sounds in the earpiece as a telephone handset is passed from one reluctant hand to another.

'Mrs Burton?' It is a man, as urgent and concise as the nurse had been. 'Your mother's breathing is very shallow. We're going to put her on different medication. If you ring us back in two hours, we'll let you know how she is.'

Lynda is alone in the room, John out running errands for their return journey tomorrow. The nurses have called Pauline, but there is a dense fog up on the East Yorkshire Wolds and, assuming her mam will recover, she is waiting for it to lift before she leaves for the hospital. Lynda thinks they will not have called Roy.

Before calling the hospital Lynda had begun to pack, and there are two suitcases on the bed looking upwards, open-mouthed, to the ceiling. While she waits she packs again, with that small, calming feeling of executing a single task competently as circumstances develop beyond her control.

She feels guilt at having left her mam, but tries to push the feeling away because she is sure the new medication will work.

Then, only fifteen minutes after she had put down the receiver, the telephone rings again.

*

Winnie's funeral takes place at Barnsley's municipal crematorium on a cold, overcast morning in January 2002. The cortège arrives early, so in the grounds family and friends gather among wintry dregs of ice and dead leaves, their murmured conversations mingling with the caws of rooks and the distant noise of lorries on the main road. All of Winnie's children, grandchildren and great-grandchildren are here, all except Roy; Alwyn, who has come with Wendy and her husband Steve, says he is too unwell to travel, an explanation that causes looks to be exchanged between some of the mourners. Although Lynda and Pauline do not yet notice, friends and neighbours swell the waiting congregation to the same size as the crowd that had gathered for Harry a decade and a half earlier. By the time they have filed into the cream-and-crimson chapel, with its uplighters and light wood and sprays of white flowers, people are standing in rows two and three deep at the back. It is unusual these days, the vicar will tell Lynda later, for someone of ninety-two.

The vicar had not known Winnie – Lynda has had to stress that he should at no point mention the name 'Gertrude' – but he has talked about her with her family and other acquaintances and, he says, in these conversations two qualities always were mentioned: her capacity for hard work, and second, her privacy. He tells the mourners, 'She was a private person, and someone whose home was of the utmost importance to her,' and when they sing the last hymn, 'All Things Bright and Beautiful', it seems to Pauline, seated at the front near the coffin, that even though the hymn is very well known and commonly heard, its lyrics could have been addressed to Winnie because, for better or worse, she had understood the greatness of the small things of home.

For the wake they drive to Highgate Club, back through the cold open countryside along the road that Harry had walked the night he lost himself on his way home. Over the sandwiches, tea and beer the talk is less of Winnie than of the past in general, and of the warm, cheerful, children's-hair-ruffling nights here decades ago. Some people are disappointed to see the miners' strike mural seems to have disappeared, but it turns out to be only hidden by a new ceiling that has been installed to reduce heating bills. Shared memories of the mural leads to a conversation about Muv, Winnie and Walter's working lives, and about Winnie passing on Walter's stories to her children and grandchildren. People reminisce, and laugh, and talk more about the old days and their families, and about who has died and who has got married and who has had kids, and about how tall all these young 'uns are getting. In the early afternoon the gathering thins out, couples and small groups drifting away to resume their daily lives on other stages beyond the club, the remaining mourners hugging them and saying goodbye and knowing that this will be the last time the family assembles like this. Goodbye, Sonny Parkin. See you later, David and Marie. Cheerio Jack and Pam and Brian, ta-ra Alwyn and Wendy, goodbye Gary and Heather. Goodbye everybody, take care and see you later; goodbye, goodbye, goodbye.

At the end, Pauline and Gordon and their children walk back to 239 Barnsley Road with Lynda, John and Karl. Lynda makes cups of tea, and Pauline and Lynda talk about the house. Lynda and John will go back to their old home down the street, Lynda says, so there will be some furniture to move on. They discuss the sideboard, clad in white cards as if in mourning for the old queen, and soon to be moved on with her. Lynda has never liked it much, but had felt compelled to let it stay while ever Winnie was living.

'I don't know why she bought it off Roy in t' first place,' says Pauline, 'except that he needed t' money.'

Lynda looks surprised. 'She always told me that he gave it to her. I remember her saying "Look at this that our Roy's bought for me, Lynda. He buys me some *beautiful* things."'

'I think that's what she wanted to believe. But really she bought it from him because he couldn't keep up his payments, and that way he could pay them all off.'

Over the top of the cards the two sisters catch eyes in the mirror with the pink paper roses around it, looking at each other but also looking into the dark cave of mysteries that was their mother. They purse their lips and raise their eyebrows, then turn back to the room and drink their tea.

Outside in the winter afternoon the street lights are on, and the roads are getting busier. Pauline's family leaves, Karl and his girlfriend Shara walk along the backings to Karl's house, and then just Lynda and John are left, sitting with the memory-ghosts in the room where twenty years ago the family had gathered for the golden wedding party. In this room, and among this furniture at 34 Highgate Lane, Winnie had told Lynda her stories: Walter and Annie, the little gypsy girl, Millie, Sonny and Olive, Clara, Juggler Jane, Pauline and Roy, Alf and Harry. Winnie will be back with them all soon, says Lynda, back helping her dad or dancing with Harry and tightening clothes lines for Comfort and Nellie.

Lynda clears away the crockery and boils the kettle for another pot of tea, and somewhere high above the Dearne Valley the little gypsy girl greets Winnie Hollingworth and tells her to be glad because she is free now, and ready to begin the next, truer part of her life. The girl leads her to where Muv and Walter and Harry are waiting, and Winnie takes her place among the beloved and troublesome dead, ready for the mediums in their churches and assembly rooms, ready with her mother and father to pass down her knowledge to those who know how to ask, ready at last to understand and be understood.

Epilogue

In the years since Winnie's death most members of the Hollingworth family still lived in the same places as they did at the time of the funeral. They are still friends and they still socialise together, although there have been no large-scale family gatherings at Highgate Club since the funeral in 2002. Some have died while others have new children and grandchildren, young people to whom coal is either unknown, or known chiefly as an element in school lessons about global warming.

Roy Hollingworth died in April 2003. When Alwyn told people at the funeral that he was too ill to travel, she was telling the truth. Living in the sheltered accommodation, the two of them had worked part-time at a local pub, but Roy's alcoholism had run unchecked. In February 2003 he began to lose consciousness at unpredictable intervals, and was taken to hospital almost weekly – so often that when Wendy called Gary one night to say Roy was very ill and wanted to talk to him, Gary was not anxious, assuming that he would recover. Gary, who had not spoken to his father since their argument on the telephone, planned to visit him in two days' time, but the following evening Alwyn rang to tell Gary that Roy had died. A blood clot on the lung, she said, although they both knew the real killer, and alcohol poisoning was recorded as the official cause of death.

Gary and Scott, and Lynda and John, attended the funeral, but Pauline and David did not. Waiting in Roy's flat before the service, Gary felt that the rooms looked strange in a way he could not understand, and it was only as people left for the crematorium he realised why; in the entire home there was no object or decoration that was personal to Roy, not even a photograph. It was as if he had succeeded in leaving the minimum trace of himself as he passed through, elusive in death as he had been in life. When Gary looked for a keepsake to have in memory of his father, he couldn't find anything.

Roy was cremated wearing his Royal Tank Regiment uniform, which was decorated with a General Service Medal and Canal Zone clasp. Alwyn died the following year. Wendy lives with her family in Burbage, near Hinckley, and runs a property business.

Margaret and Colin Greengrass lived happily together in Thurnscoe for the rest of their lives, moving to a bungalow in the village in 2000. Colin died in 2011, and Margaret in 2013.

My mother, Pauline Benson, still lives in the village in the East Riding. During the sale of the farm she and Gordon retained a plot of land on which they built a new house. Using an old shed they had kept, they then made a new yard and, with their youngest son Guy, they used the yard to run a straw merchant business. Their daughter Helen is a primary school teacher in Hull. Gordon, my father, died in 2009, while I was writing this book.

Lynda and John oversaw the sale of 239 Barnsley Road, and moved back to their first house down the street. In 2006, Lynda took a new job helping to organise colleges into a network that made it easier for people in Yorkshire to get access to education. The job was partly based at Hull University, and if John had a day off when Lynda was commuting to meetings he would accompany her, eating breakfast among the students in the cafeteria, then walking around the grounds until her meetings were ended. Lynda retired in 2009. Shortly afterwards she became the voluntary secretary for the Dearne Valley Big Local, a group, part of a national scheme, that works to restore the sense of community in the area. John still works at the Kostal components factory in Highgate and until 2008 he also worked as a volunteer at a local home for disabled people. Karl works as a process engineer at the IAC car components factory in Scunthorpe, and lives with his partner Nathalie in the Dearne village of Broomhill.

Dr Ravichandran never explained to Lynda how she had walked when her condition ought to have prevented it. Nor did any doctor comment on her theory that she had a kind of consciousness in her bones and muscles that could move her limbs. However, in 2011 scientists working with a paralysed man at the Frazier Rehab Institute in Louisville, USA, discovered that the human spinal cord could direct leg movement without input from the brain. The scientists and doctors used epidural electrical stimulation of the man's lower spinal cord to mimic signals that his brain should have sent telling the legs to move; having received those signals, the cord's own neural network took sensory input from the legs, and directed the leg movements needed to stand and take steps. With assistance, the man could make walking movements on a treadmill.

Gary Hollingworth became a senior social work practitioner, and moved to a new post in Wakefield in 2004. He is still married to Heather, and he still has dreams about working at the pit. Scott lives in Swinton, just south of the Dearne Valley, and works as a civil engineer. Claire lectures in animal care at Wakefield College, and lives in Grimethorpe.

David was made redundant from Rossington colliery when it closed in 2006, ending the Hollingworth family's last connection to the coal industry. After a period of unemployment and retraining, he took a job at Kostal. He and Marie still live in Thurnscoe, and David still enjoys fishing. Lisa lives with her partner Kevin in Bolton-upon-Dearne, and is a receptionist at Kostal.

Coal production at the Selby complex ended in 2004. At the time of writing, there was one working deep mine in South Yorkshire, at Hatfield. In 1945 there were sixty-seven. Since the decline described in the latter parts of this book, regeneration work and the efforts of local people have restored much of the Dearne Valley's economy, and its natural and built landscapes. It is increasingly popular both as a location for businesses and as a place to live. In July 2006 Goldthorpe's Welfare Hall was refurbished and reopened as the New Dearne Playhouse. The Coronation Club, the Unity Club, the Union Jack Memorial, or 'Comrades' club, and Highgate Working Men's Club all remain open.

Acknowledgements

I was able to write this book only because of my extended family's generosity and willingness to share and record details of their lives, and I am deeply grateful to them for the time they afforded me, and for their patience in helping with my questions, revisions and fact checks. In particular Lynda and John Burton, Gary and Heather Hollingworth, David and Marie Hollingworth, Karl Grainger and Pauline Benson spent what must have seemed to them many long hours remembering and explaining and re-explaining to me. Other family members who helped me with interviews and answers to questions were Anne and Malcolm Askew, my father the late Gordon Benson, Guy Benson, Helen Benson, Claire and Bob Blake, Alan Blow, Amanda Bouskill, Eileen Bullock, Joan Chambers, Kevin Dunkley, Carol Goulding, Tommy Goulding, Jack Graham, Joyce Graham and Janet Graham, the late Margaret Greengrass, the late Pam Gundry and Jack Gundry, Lisa Hollingworth, the late Millie Hollingworth, Scott Hollingworth, Tommy Hollingworth, Wendy Hollingworth, Brian Lunness, the late May Parkin and Heather Wargen. The steward and members of Highgate Working Men's Club, the Unity Club and the Coronation Club, Thurnscoe were helpful, good storytellers, and very good company.

Equally patient and understanding have been the staff at Bloomsbury Publishing. Michael Fishwick and Anna Simpson were incredibly kind, supportive and helpful, and my copyeditor Kate Johnson helped me indescribably, and taught me a great deal about books and writing in the process. Thank you too to Laura Brooke, Katie Bond, Alexa von Hirschberg, Oliver Holden-Rea, Alexandra Pringle and David Ward.

My agent David Godwin and the staff at David Godwin Associates have been sturdy props and good friends.

Dan Johnson helped me with research, and was a great companion and source of insights. Laura Smith also helped to research certain areas. John Threlkeld at the Barnsley Chronicle and author of *Pits: A Pictoral History of Mining* was very generous in helping me with fact-checking. Other people advised me on specific subjects. Jolyon Lawson, proprietor of the coal merchant F. W. Lawson Ltd in Driffield, East Yorkshire, explained the differences between the different forms of coal. Miles Templeton of pre-warboxing.co.uk sourced the historical records of Danny Lunness's boxing bouts. Chris Baker of fourteeneighteen research helped me with Walter Parkin's experience in the First World War, and Jane Hewitt helped with general family history research. Dr Sarah Thornton diagnosed and described medical conditions. Alan Petford, Edward Royle and Sara Crofts of the Chapel Society helped me to visualise the interior of a turn-of-the-century spiritualist church. John 'Jock' Marrs, a veteran of the Korean War and editor of britains-smallwars.com, told me about life as a soldier in the Suez Canal Zone, and this information and the stories on the site were important sources for me when writing about Roy's military experience.

The Shirebrook Local History Group, headed by Ian P. Hill, was welcoming, enthusiastic and learned. I was very lucky to meet the late Mr Harold Daniels, then its oldest member, who recalled attending the spiritualist church with one of Annie Weaver's younger sisters, whom he was courting at the time. He told me that the girls used to trick their boyfriends into going by agreeing to accompany them to the pub on the condition that the young man would later accompany them on an as-yet unspecified date. The boys would always protest, but the girls would reply, 'I've been to your church, now you come to mine.' The story confirmed that Walter's interest would have marked him out as unusual among the men of his age.

Many people helped me to improve my understanding of spiritualism, and to find the building that housed the church in Shirebrook where Walter and Annie's relationship began. Annie Blair of the Spiritualist Association of Great Britain, and the mediums Alan Acton and Richard Neville, described the processes and nature of Spirit when I needed clarification, and Leslie Price and Paul J. Gaunt of the *PsyPioneer Journal* filled in historical sense and detail. The congregation of Mansfield Spiritualist Church, particularly Jean Stevens, welcomed me at their healing services, and John Stanford's memories of spiritualism in Shirebrook were invaluable. Sharon Brailsford of the Shirebrook Local History Group helped to extricate me from an awkward situation when I unintentionally trespassed on a farmyard in my excitement at having discovered the former spiritualist church.

I am especially grateful to Hazel Batley of Barnsley for explaining how nineteenth- and early-twentieth-century spiritualists sought to democratise not only religious faith and epistemology, but also medicine and healing. The more I learned about this as I worked on the book, the more I saw similarities between Lynda's independent thinking about her condition and the spiritualist healers of Walter and Annie's generation, although I fear I have yet to convince Lynda herself of this.

Ex-miner and author David John Douglass was helpful and inspiring, and taught me how to see my grandmother's stories in the context of the miners' sense of history. Coal mining was hard and dangerous work, and pit villages could be harsh places in which to live, but it seems to me that the decent people of Harry and Winnie's generation, and several generations preceding it, had a quiet belief that they were working together to improve themselves, their working conditions and their environments. This lent a sense of purpose, or at least of being headed somewhere; you had made the present more comfortable than the past, and the future would be more comfortable again. From the late twentieth century onwards that sense has ebbed away somewhat, and with it a component of an old sense of identity. One of several ideas that have moved into its old space is nostalgia; a question asked by people trying to revive ex-mining communities is: is it possible to draw lessons and values from the past that can be adapted to the future, and thus used to restore some of that lost identity? David John Douglass considers these questions in his autobiographical trilogy *Coaldust and Stardust*, which is the best account of a modern coal miner's life that I know, and was a source for some of the history in this book. I would also like to thank the writers Barry Hines and Paul Routledge for helping and encouraging me when I talked to them about my family and the Dearne Valley.

Dozens of other people talked to me about family stories or the Dearne Valley in general, including: Albert Blessed; the members of the Bolton-upon-Dearne local history group; Don Booker, former editor of the *Barnsley Chronicle*; Tim Brant of the Merchant Navy Association; Richard Breese, Strategic Director of the South Yorkshire Coalfield Partnership; Marylise Campbell of the Sprotborough Library book group; Ann Carr, church warden at Goldthorpe Parish Church; Betty Cook; Donald Edes; Brian Elliott, historian; Tony Farsides; Dave Feickert, historian; Anne Gray; Richard Gray; Dieter Hopkin, then at the National Mining Museum; Peter Hyman; Margaret Lister, 1972 Yorkshire Coal Queen; Jennifer Kabat; Janet King; Susan Linstead at the Dearne Advanced Learning Centre; Ann Littlewood, author of *Storthes Hall Remembered*; David Lunn, former Bishop of Sheffield; Father Rodney Marshall, former vicar of Goldthorpe; Julie Medlam, Theatre Manager at the Dearne Playhouse; Rick Naylor of the Police Superintendents' Association; Father Peter Needham, the vicar of Grimethorpe; Paul Cornerford and Peter Farnham of WSP Development & Transportation; Anne Scargill; Dirk Sheldon; Inky Thompson, former NUM official and Barnsley councillor; Fred Walker; Barry Westerman, former steward of Highgate Working Men's Club; Geoff Widdop; and Bruce Wilson.

People who helped in other ways include Stephen Armstrong, Kevin and Alan Braddock, the Rev. Marjorie Brown, Richard Budge, the Churchill Centre, Gareth Coombs, Robin Denselow, Allie Dickinson, Andrew Duerden, John Edmondson, Ekow Eshun, Charles Gant, Andrew Harrison, Mark Hodkinson, Anwen Hooson, Graeme Johnson, Ted Kelly, Cllr Graham Kyte, Peter Lyle, Sean Moore, the

National Union of Mineworkers, Stuart Oliver of UK Coal, Julian Rudd, Laura St Quinton, Cllr Ken Sanderson, Rob Sellars, Laura Smith, the Sprotbrough Library book group, Tony Swaby and Kevin and Nicola Welsh. Staff at the following library departments also helped with research: Doncaster Central Library Archives and Local Studies Department, Barnsley Central Library Archives and Local Studies Department, Chesterfield Local Studies Library, Sheffield Archives and Local Studies Library, Shirebrook Library, and the Working Class Movement Library, Salford.

Finally, I would like to thank my wife Laura for her patience, her reading of draft chapters, and for supporting me when other women would have quite rightly chucked me down the nearest coal mine.

A NOTE ON THE TYPE

The text of this book is set in Adobe Garamond. It is one of several versions of Garamond based on the designs of Claude Garamond. It is thought that Garamond based his font on Bembo, cut in 1495 by Francesco Griffo in collaboration with the Italian printer Aldus Manutius. Garamond types were first used in books printed in Paris around 1532. Many of the present-day versions of this type are based on the *Typi Academiae* of Jean Jannon cut in Sedan in 1615.

Claude Garamond was born in Paris in 1480. He learned how to cut type from his father and by the age of fifteen he was able to fashion steel punches the size of a pica with great precision. At the age of sixty he was commissioned by King Francis I to design a Greek alphabet; for this he was given the honourable title of Royal Type Founder. He died in 1561.